This book, based upon a vast range of documentary and secondary sources, shatters the disproven but persistent myth of the closed immobile village in the early modern period. It demonstrates that even in traditionalist Castile, pre-industrial village society was highly dynamic, with continuous inter-village, inter-regional, and rural–urban migration.

The book is rich in human detail, with many vignettes of individuals making decisions in everyday life. Professor Vassberg examines such topics as fairs and markets, the transportation infrastructure, rural artisans and craftsmen, relations with the state, and life-cycle service. The approach is interdisciplinary, and pays special attention to how rural families dealt with economic and social problems. The rural Castile that emerges is a complex society that defies easy generalizations, but one which is unquestionably part of the general European reality.

THE
VILLAGE AND THE
OUTSIDE WORLD IN
GOLDEN AGE
CASTILE

THE
VILLAGE AND THE
OUTSIDE WORLD IN
GOLDEN AGE
CASTILE

Mobility and migration
in everyday rural life

DAVID E. VASSBERG

University of Texas – Pan American

CAMBRIDGE
UNIVERSITY PRESS

Published by the Press Syndicate of the University of Cambridge
The Pitt Building, Trumpington Street, Cambridge CB2 1RP
40 West 20th Street, New York, NY 10011-4211, USA
10 Stamford Road, Oakleigh, Melbourne 3166, Australia

© Cambridge University Press 1996

First published 1996

Printed in Great Britain at the University Press, Cambridge

A catalogue record for this book is available from the British Library

Library of Congress cataloguing in publication data

Vassberg, David E. (David Erland), 1936–
The village and the outside world in Golden Age Castile: mobility
and migration in everyday rural life / David E. Vassberg.
p.   cm.
Includes bibliographical references and index.
ISBN 0 521 56325 9 (hc)
1. Migration, Internal – Spain – Castile – History.   2. Castile
(Spain) – Rural conditions.   3. Villages – Spain – Castile – History.
I. Title.
HB2080.C27V37   1996   95-47247   CIP

ISBN 0 521 56325 9 hardback

CONTENTS

MAPS

FIGURES

TABLES

PREFACE

This is not the book that I had originally intended. After completing my *Land and Society in Golden Age Castile* (Cambridge University Press, 1984), which was a study of early modern Castilian property ownership, I planned a companion volume entitled *Daily Life in a Golden Age Castilian Village*, which would depict the day-to-day activities of the typical rural Castilian. As late as September of 1991 I still thought that my next book would be a general treatment of daily life. But while still in the research stage, I became increasingly intrigued by one aspect of everyday activities: the interrelationship between the village and the wider world. Realizing that this topic deserved book-length treatment, I altered my plans and developed the present volume.

When invited to contribute a paper for the 1992 Meeting of the American Historical Association (Washington, D.C.), I was able to prepare "Mobility and Migration in Sixteenth-Century Spanish Villages" by extracting portions of several chapters in progress. Later, I was invited to present an updated Spanish version of that paper for the Séminaire Histoire et Civilisation de l'Espagne of the Ecole des Hautes Etudes en Sciences Sociales (Paris, 1994). Segments of Chapter 5 went into the paper "Life-Cycle Service as a Form of Age-Specific Migration in the Sixteenth and Seventeenth Centuries: Rural Castile as a Case Study," for the 1st European Conference of the International Commission on Historical Demography: Internal and Medium-Distance Migrations in Europe, 1500–1900 (Santiago de Compostela, 1993). And I used parts of my first chapter for the papers "Sociocentrism and Xenophobia in Golden Age Castilian Villages" for the Meeting of the Society for Spanish and Portuguese Historical Studies (Chicago, 1994); and "Local Loyalties and Inter-Municipal Border Conflicts in Sixteenth-Century Castile" for the Meeting of the Pacific Coast Branch of the American Historical Association (Fullerton, California, 1994). I discovered that the process of developing conference papers from the book in progress was highly beneficial, because the segments involved were invariably improved by the time they returned to their respective chapters. But heretofore, no part of this book has been in print except for the 1993 Santiago paper, which appeared in proceedings (*Actas*) distributed at the Conference, and in a subsequent published version edited by Antonio Eiras Roel and Ofelia Rey Castelao.

I am grateful to my department and to my university for cheerfully allowing me release time for research and writing, even when my absence from the classroom was highly inconvenient. Welcome financial support came from a National Endowment for the Humanities Research Fellowship, and from a Faculty Research Grant and a Title III Program administered by the University of Texas–Pan American. Additional support was provided coincidentally, because of overlapping topics and timetables, by a National Research Service Award for Senior Fellows administered by the National Institutes of Health. I am thankful to the many archivists and librarians who facilitated my research in Spain and in the US. I am grateful to Spain's Ministerio de Cultura and Archivo General de Simancas and Archivo de la Real Chancillería de Valladolid, to the Österreichische Nationalbibliothek, and to the Harry Ransom Humanities Research Center at the University of Texas at Austin for permission to reproduce materials from their collections (specific acknowledgment accompanies the appropriate illustrations). And I am indebted to countless colleagues and friends for their comments and suggestions. The colleague to whom I owe the most is my wife Liliane Mangold Vassberg, who unselfishly put her own career on hold while helping me in Spanish archives, and who supplied the emotional support necessary for the project's completion. And finally, I want to recognize the long-term assistance and loving encouragement of my parents, who were unfailingly supportive, even when neither they nor I knew exactly what direction my life would take. It is appropriate that I dedicate this book to my mother and to the memory of my father, who themselves are exemplars of multigenerational long-range migration in and out of rural communities.

GLOSSARY

Actas: published proceedings of the Castilian Cortes

alcabala: royal sales tax, theoretically 10 percent of the value of all transactions, but in practice usually set at about 3.5 percent

alcaide: governor or warden of a castle or fort

alcalde: municipal official with certain administrative duties, but primarily functioning as a judge with civil and criminal jurisdiction

Alpujarras: mountains in Granada province where Moriscos staged unsuccessful armed rebellions in 1499–1501 and 1568–70

arbitristas: sixteenth- and seventeenth-century reform writers, so called because of their *arbitrios* (reform proposals)

arriero: muleteer

arroba: unit of liquid measure varying by region, but commonly equivalent to about 12.5 liters (3.32 US gallons) of oil, or 16 liters (4.26 US gallons) of wine; as a unit of weight equal to about 11.5 kilograms (25 pounds)

Audiencia: see Chancillería, below

cabrito: suckling kid, or goat, making a tasty meat dish

cañada: especially designated sheep walk or trail for seasonally migratory herds and flocks

cántara: measure of liquid varying by region but commonly equal to about 16 liters (4.25 US gallons)

carga: dry measure equal to 3 or 4 *fanegas*

Chancillería: Supreme Tribunal, or appellate court. After 1505 there were two in Castile: one in Valladolid, and the other in Granada, their jurisdictions separated by the boundary of the Tajo River

complant: medieval contract conferring upon a peasant the ownership of half of a vineyard once he had planted and tended it for the proprietor for a specified number of years

Comuneros (Revolt of): unsuccessful armed rebellion (1521–2) of Castilian cities against the Habsburg emperor Charles V

corregidor: royal official appointed to preside over important towns. Served as president of the municipal council, and had extensive judicial, administrative, and financial authority

Cortes: National Assembly of Castile, composed during Philip II's reign of delegates from eighteen major cities

ducado: unit of account, equal to 375 *maravedís*

escudo: gold coin worth 350 *maravedís* until 1566, and 400 mrs thereafter

fanega: unit of dry measure roughly equivalent to an English bushel, or about 55.5 liters of grain; unit of area varying in size, usually equal to about 0.646 hectares (1.59 acres)

forastero: outsider or outlander, a person from another village or town, or a foreigner

fuero: law code; municipal charter; privilege or exemption granted to a certain province

Guadarrama (Sierra de): mountain range marking the boundary between Old and New Castile

hidalgo: member of the untitled lower nobility, possessing social prestige and certain privileges including tax exemptions

hidalguía: nobility, or the rights and privileges thereof

hospital: charitable institution usually dedicated to the care of the needy; but sometimes a medical facility caring for the sick or injured

jornalero: literally a day laborer, a salaried worker in practice usually contracted for periods longer than a day

juez: judge, or magistrate

labrador: independent peasant-farmer, term often used in contrast to the *jornalero*, who worked for someone else

legua: league, unit of distance of varying length, but in Castile normally about 5.6 kilometers (approximately 3½ miles)

Mancha (La): virtually treeless plain in southern New Castile, mainly in the province of Ciudad Real

maragatos: villagers from the western part of León province, famous throughout Spain as owner-operators of mule trains

maravedí (mr.): unit of account, of depreciating value, used for calculating prices in early modern Castile

Mesta: royally chartered stock owners' association, notorious for the privileges it had gained for its migratory flocks and herds. Mesta power ebbed during the sixteenth and seventeenth centuries

monte: brushland or forest, used for pasture and forest products

Moriscos: Spaniards of Moorish ancestry

mozo (*moza*): an unmarried youth

mozo (or *moza*) *de soldada*: literally a salaried youth, term applied to a life-cycle servant, and often also to adult servants

patria chica: literally "little fatherland," exaggerated loyalty to one's home town

pícaro: clever person able to make a living through various deceitful schemes; a scam artist

pueblo: village, town, or community; or the people thereof *real*: silver coin equal in value to 34 *maravedís*

Reconquest (*Reconquista*): struggle by Christian rulers to regain control over the Iberian peninsula after the Muslim invasion of 711. Concluded with the capture of Granada in 1492

Relaciones [topográficas]: answers to questionnaires sent by the royal government to towns and villages in Castile in the 1570s. A primary source of information about rural society

Rioja (La): district in Logroño province famous for its wines

Santa Hermandad: rural police force, operated by towns and cities under the auspices of the crown

Sierra de Guadarrama: *see* Guadarrama

Sierra Morena: mountain range along the northern boundary of Andalusia

tasa: government ceiling on the price of grain

Tierra de Campos: rich grain-growing area embracing parts of the provinces of León, Palencia, Valladolid, and Zamora

tierras baldías: common lands, or crown lands

vecino: citizen of a village, town, or city; or the citizen head of a household; or (today's usual meaning) a neighbor

villa: municipality possessing juridical independence

villazgo: attainment of *villa* status for a dependent village

ABBREVIATIONS

ACHGR	Archivo de la Chancillería de Granada
ACHVA	Archivo de la Chancillería de Valladolid
AGS	Archivo General de Simancas
BN	Biblioteca Nacional (Madrid)
EH	Expedientes de Hacienda
FA (F)	Fernando Alonso (Fenecidos)
mrs	*maravedís*
PC	Pleitos Civiles

INTRODUCTION

THE MYTH OF THE IMMOBILE VILLAGE

The world has seen so many changes over the past two centuries that many people have come to believe that not only technology, but also family organization, human relationships, and geographical mobility must have been drastically different in pre-industrial times. A tenacious myth of the modern world is that pre-industrial villages were essentially stable communities whose inhabitants rarely ventured beyond their own territory, and that most rural people remained in the village generation after generation.

Historical myths attempt to understand the present by interpreting the past.[1] The immobile village myth, like all successful myths, contains some truth. Most of the world's population before the Industrial Revolution were peasants living in village communities where farming and animal husbandry were the major occupations. Rural families in these villages tried to produce for themselves as much as possible of what they needed, to avoid cash outlays. And villagers used mainly local products, because it was expensive to transport goods from the outside world. Thus the stereotypical pre-industrial village was largely self-sufficient. Historians have reinforced the stereotype, and have nurtured the myth by placing great emphasis on the economic autonomy and isolation of the traditional village community. General texts of Western or World Civilization contain sections describing the "small, narrow, and provincial" world of the European peasant. They explain that in the early medieval period, peasants were "serfs, bound to the land and the village for life."[2] One scholar opens the first chapter of a book about peasants by quoting (without comment) the commonplace that "they are bound to the ground or chained to the soil." Another entitled a section of a book on peasant life "Imprisoned in the Village." Unquestionably villages like that did exist, but it is highly misleading to use them as the basis for generalizations about the entire medieval period. What is worse, even the best texts rarely bother to modify this view of village life, as the narrative moves beyond the Middle Ages. And even historians specializing in the early modern period often

I

perpetuate the notion of the village cut off from the rest of the world: a well-known scholar in a recent book writes that the outside world "did not impinge on the daily life of [typical seventeenth-century] villagers"; a historian of early modern Germany asserts that inter-village movement was not very great;[3] one of the best studies of early modern rural France is entitled *The Immobile Village*;[4] and a respected specialist in rural history concludes that the village was "essentially a self-contained, a self-maintained and a self-reliant entity, remote from the outside world."[5]

Thus, we should not be surprised if our students – or even our colleagues – often visualize the early modern European rural community as a closed, timeless, unchanging institution with an essentially immobile population.[6] It may be argued that the immobile village myth is a discarded cliché that nobody believes any more. After all, the myth undeniably has been thoroughly debunked by recent scholarship documenting the geographical mobility of past populations.[7] But unfortunately, not everyone has assimilated the meaning of this recent scholarship. Consequently, the immobile village myth remains a widespread misconception among the general population, and even within the academic community, as the foregoing examples prove. One reason for this is that historians too often have become glued to an outdated stereotype of the peasantry, and they have been unwilling to give up a distorted idea of the "closed corporate peasant community." Perhaps some of this stereotyping is influenced by Marxist ideology, which regards peasants as hopelessly reactionary, and hostile to the goals of socialist society.[8] Another reason for historians' outdated image of the peasantry is that they have not kept up with developments in the social sciences. Anthropologists and economists a generation ago arrived at a refined definition of the peasantry that has become the social science standard: peasants are rural people who possess (even if they do not own) the means of agricultural production. They are integrated into the structures of the state and surrounding society, and are partially engaged in the marketplace. In this social science categorization, the peasant *by definition* has numerous contacts with the world outside the village. In its relationship with the outside world, the peasantry occupies a position between primitive tribal societies and modern farmers. Whereas tribal societies are far more isolated and autonomous, modern farmers are nearly totally dependent upon the marketplace and the outside world.[9] Perhaps another reason for the widespread acceptance of the immobility myth is that our twentieth-century mentality has difficulty grasping the concept of large-scale population movements before the existence of modern rail, automotive, and air transportation. And finally, it may be that the image of the stable traditional rural community is an illusion created by middle-class city dwellers nostalgic for stability, which they erroneously ascribe to rural communities of a bygone era. The unchanging village is a vision of peace, order, harmony, and security. The idealized traditional village, then, may be regarded as an urban myth.[10] The myth has great symbolic appeal, but the truth is quite different. Far from being static, the early modern village community was surprisingly dynamic, continually in the process of transformation by migration to and from the village, and by changes within the village as well. It turns out that the notion of a stable rural community is seriously flawed. And, in fact, it has been convincingly refuted. But the myth has such emotional power that it must be repeatedly disproven.

VILLAGES IN CASTILE

This book is about villages in early modern Castile. I have to confess that before researching the topic, I had accepted the classic notion that Spain – and Castile in particular – suffered from a tragic curse: it was so traditionalist[11] that it was incapable of responding adequately to the various challenges that it faced. According to this cliché, rural Spain exemplified the very worst tendencies of Iberian society: it was reactionary, unchanging, isolated, and immobile. The image of an unchanging rural Spain has been reinforced by numerous scholarly works,[12] that have encouraged historians to believe in the correctness of the cliché. A reputable history of agricultural technology perfectly reflects the prevailing Black Legend about sixteenth-century rural Spain when it insists that "the only changes since classical times had been introduced by the Moors."[13] A prize-winning work by a respected Spanish scholar describes the "sedentary rural inhabitant," the "peasant-farmer glued to his piece of land," living in a rustic setting characterized by "immobility ... with its unappreciable or nonexistent change." And a beautifully illustrated recent popular work designed to inform the general Spanish readership about daily life in Spain's Golden Age presents a veritable caricature, asserting that the famous conquistadores and adventurers of the day were aberrations, and that for the rural masses "the norm was absolute sedentarism."[14] Whereas I once would have accepted this view, I now know that it is erroneous. Early modern Spanish villages were very much like rural communities in other parts of Western Europe: they were not isolated, but rather were surprisingly integrated economically, socially, and politically into the outside world.[15] And the rural inhabitants of early modern Spain, like their northern European counterparts, showed great ingenuity and flexibility, and they enjoyed a substantial degree of geographical mobility.[16]

The failure of historians to appreciate the full measure of the dynamism of early modern Spanish society is only partly the result of clinging to myths and to the misconceptions of outdated scholarship. It is also the consequence of a void in Spanish historiography. Despite a proliferation during the past twenty-five years of excellent studies dealing with the rural world, existing scholarship has been overwhelmingly concerned with

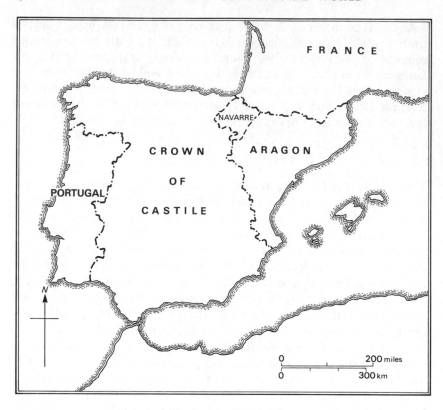

Map 1. Iberian kingdoms in the 1500s and 1600s.

impersonal economic forces, institutions, and social structures. These are crucially important aspects of history, and we are indeed fortunate to have scholars interested in them. But somehow, the *human* element – the lives of ordinary rural people who made up the great bulk of the population of the day – has been largely bypassed by existing scholarship. Perhaps it is normal for historical studies to flesh out the institutional framework before turning to individuals operating within that framework. And, certainly, it is far easier to find and analyze data about institutions than about persons, especially when those persons are illiterate peasants. But for whatever reason, the present stage of early modern Spanish scholarship makes it exceedingly difficult to reconstruct the life story of the average villager four or five centuries ago. We will have to have more family histories, more investigations into life-course transitions, and more studies of family cycles before we can begin to understand how an ordinary villager might have spent his life. Fortunately, there is considerable interest in historical demography in Spain these days, and we can hope that many of our questions will be answered before long. But for now, we have to operate

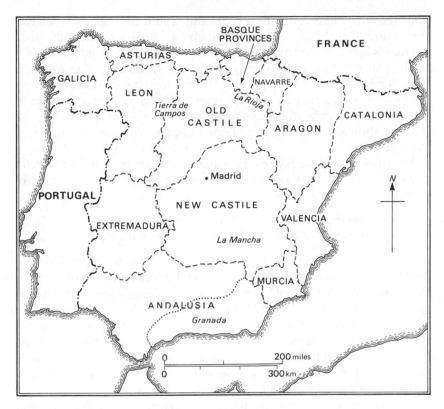

Map 2. Traditional provinces and regions of Spain.

within the existing historiographical setting that lacks both a comprehensive vision, and the necessary local studies to understand fully the kinds of relationships over time that early modern Spanish villagers had with each other, and with the world beyond the village.[17]

In a recent review article James Amelang identified yet another reason for the relative backwardness of early modern Spanish historiography. That is the "pronounced insularity" of Spanish history – an excessive tendency of Spanish historians (and foreign Hispanists, as well) to limit their study to Spain itself, without comparing their findings with developments in other countries.[18] This geographical insularity, along with the disciplinary seclusion that I mentioned previously, has given many otherwise excellent monographs an inordinately restricted perspective. Fortunately, despite the difficulties inherent in widening one's geographical and disciplinary perspectives, the most recent scholarship increasingly brings Spanish history into the mainstream of European historiography.

This book examines the contacts between villagers and the outside world in Castile's Golden Age – a period roughly embracing the sixteenth and the first half of the seventeenth centuries. Spanish villages throughout their history were continually exposed to outside influences. Spaniards had – and maintain to this day – a reputation for intense loyalty to the place of their birth, even calling their home town *"mi patria."*[19] Nevertheless, early modern Spanish villagers were not rooted to the place where they were born, because they responded eagerly to opportunities to migrate to new areas when economic factors, the marriage market, the housing situation, or other conditions indicated that they might better themselves.

The traditional village system of values held stability to be preferable to mobility. A Golden Age Castilian proverb extolled remaining in one's native village:

> *Cada uno donde es nacido*   (Where you are born
> *Bien se está en su nido.*[20]   You have a comfortable nest.)

But the ideals of stability did not correspond to historical reality, and were continually modified through emigration and through other contacts with the outside. We should avoid thinking that rural people were so bound by local conditions that they had no freedom of choice. Early modern villagers were not unthinking robots only responding to the actions of their landlords or rulers, nor did they react brutishly to natural forces. Rather, these rural people were intelligent beings who were fully capable of seizing opportunities when they appeared, even if that meant breaking with customary practices and attitudes.[21]

The outside world was never beyond the reach of early modern rural Spaniards. In the first place, they could usually *see* other villages. An analysis of the *Relaciones topográficas* (answers to questionnaires sent by the royal government to all towns and villages in Castile in the 1570s) shows that another village – or villages – lay only a couple of leagues away from the typical rural settlement. In the province of Madrid over 93 percent of the *Relaciones* villages were situated within two leagues of another town or village. In the province of Cuenca it was more than 76 percent, and in Toledo province over 85 percent.[22]

Moreover, rural society was never hermetically sealed off from the towns and cities. It is tempting to view the city as the antithesis of rural life. But the idea of an urban–rural dichotomy is highly misleading. As Teofilo Ruiz observes in his recent book, "in Castile the boundaries between rural and urban were often vague, at times nonexistent." In fact, rural elements extended even into the largest early modern Spanish cities. Typically, these had gardens, orchards, livestock, and even fields deliberately interwoven within their urbanized area as a safeguard in times of siege or other difficulties. And village life throughout the Mediterranean world – quite in contrast to most other culture areas – possessed a certain "urban" quality. Furthermore, many "cities" and "towns" had large populations of resident peasant farmers and rural laborers who went out to work the surrounding fields. The distinction between urban and rural was so hazy that Braudel characterized the entire Mediterranean world as an "urban" region.[23]

There was considerable interaction between villages and cities, making it all the more difficult to separate the "rural" from the "urban." Large cities and their surrounding villages were profoundly interrelated, socially, economically, and politically. In most cases, the urban oligarchies based their power and prestige upon their rural holdings in surrounding areas. Wealthy city folks often spent part of the year on their rural estates, or even decided to live there; while members of the village elite often moved to the city.[24]

Even in their strictly rural activities, Spanish villagers often became exposed to neighboring areas because of the existence of supra-municipal (or inter-municipal) commons. These lands, usually for pasture, originated during the medieval Reconquest, when certain territories were shared by several settlements under the jurisdiction of a powerful city, bishop, military commander, or noble lord. The towns and villages that participated in these inter-municipal arrangements had their own commons restricted for the exclusive use of the *vecinos* of that particular place. But there were other commons that were shared by the people of two or more places. In some areas of early modern Spain there were veritable federations of municipalities organized to guarantee intercommunal rights. There was one in the province of Avila that embraced over three hundred villages. Rural people of the day were keenly aware of their citizenship rights, locally and in federations. For example, in 1542 a villager testified that he was a native of La Bóveda, but was currently a *vecino* of Villaureña, and of the Tierra of the city of Toro (Zamora), where he had certain rights.[25] It is clear that the existence of such associations encouraged geographical mobility beyond the limits of one's own village, to seek pastures, arable land, firewood, lumber, and other benefits of the system.

ADDITIONAL PRELIMINARY COMMENTS

In this book I use the term "village" for any organized rural community of modest size, regardless of its jurisdictional status.[26] I have concentrated my attention on villages numbering between 50 and 200 households. A few are even smaller, but only a handful exceed 500 households. Geographically, my villages represent all parts of the lands of the crown of Castile (see Map 1), but the great majority are from the traditional regions of Old and New Castile, León, and Extremadura (displayed on Map 2).

Because most of the villages that I cite are small and unfamiliar places, for the convenience of the reader I have placed in parentheses the name of the province (using the modern boundaries shown in Map 3) following my

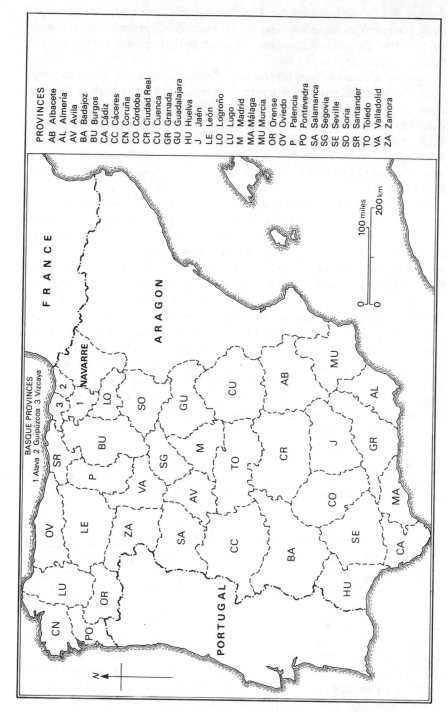

PROVINCES
AB Albacete
AL Almería
AV Avila
BA Badajoz
BU Burgos
CA Cádiz
CC Cáceres
CN Coruña
CO Córdoba
CR Ciudad Real
CU Cuenca
GR Granada
GU Guadalajara
HU Huelva
J Jaén
LE León
LO Logroño
LU Lugo
M Madrid
MA Málaga
MU Murcia
OR Orense
OV Oviedo
P Palencia
PO Pontevedra
SA Salamanca
SG Segovia
SE Seville
SO Soria
SR Santander
TO Toledo
VA Valladolid
ZA Zamora

BASQUE PROVINCES
1 Alava 2 Guipúzcoa 3 Vizcaya

Map 3. Modern provincial subdivisions, for locating villages mentioned in text.

textual references. Similarly, I have identified the province of larger towns and cities mentioned in the text, except when they are provincial capitals (e.g. Burgos), because in those the name of the province is the same.

This book contains numerous maps and tables which provide graphic evidence of the mobility of early modern Castilian villagers. In assembling the data for these, I have tried to be careful not to over-interpret my sources. For example, it is well known that many immigrants to a new place took the name of the village where they were born as a surname. A villager named Marcos de Rejas, naturalized citizen of Meco (Madrid), will serve to illustrate the point: he had been born in the village of Rejas (also in Madrid province), and as a teenager had gone to work as a shepherd in Meco, about 23 kilometers to the northeast. There people called the young outsider "Marcos de Rejas" (Marcos from Rejas) and he simply took that as his name. This practice was so widespread that scholars have used toponymic surnames to estimate the proportion of immigrants in a community.[27] But I have avoided doing that, because once established in the new community, the immigrant and his family tended to retain the new surname generation after generation. The fossilization of the toponymic makes it impossible when we encounter such a name (in the absence of other proof) to know when the immigration occurred. Since I am primarily interested in recent (in the early modern context) population movements, in this book I do not count a person as an immigrant unless the document explicitly states that he or she came from another place. My cautious approach has undoubtedly resulted in my underestimating the amount of migration during the period of my study.[28] Even so, I find an impressive movement of people in and out of sixteenth- and seventeenth-century villages.

A quarter century ago, when I first became interested in studying early modern rural Spain, one of my most formidable problems was the paucity of scholarly work on the topic. But now the problem is quite the opposite: each year there appears an intimidating profusion of theses, dissertations, journal articles, and books dealing with rural Spain. A scholar living in the US has difficulty discovering what is produced, to say nothing of the challenge of gaining access to it. Thanks to the incomparable bibliographical services of Madrid's great bookseller Marcial Pons, academics in North America can conveniently learn of, and purchase, the major publications in the field. Nevertheless, operating from the wrong side of the Atlantic makes it exceedingly difficult to stay abreast of the latest research in the field. So I would be surprised if I had not missed some pieces that would have lent support to my argument. But I trust that the reader will find that my combination of primary and secondary sources makes a convincing case.

The first chapter of this book examines the traditional village community, with its customs of local solidarity and of hostility toward outsiders. A reader who progressed no further might be left with the impression that the early modern Castilian village was indeed reactionary, stable, and isolated. The remaining chapters, however, offer evidence that the village was linked to the outside world by a myriad of significant relationships. Chapter 2 examines market contacts, while Chapter 3 focuses on village manufacturing and artisanal activities. Chapter 4 is dedicated to migrations in and out of the village, and Chapter 5 examines the impact of population mobility on village families. Chapters 6 and 7 are dedicated to relations with the state, and to villagers' contacts with travelers and with "aliens"; and Chapter 8 deals with miscellaneous other exterior contacts that did not seem to belong elsewhere. I am confident that the reader, long before reaching my Conclusion, will have decided that rural Castile in pre-industrial times was a complex and dynamic society with a surprising range of interrelationships with the wider world.

1

THE VILLAGE COMMUNITY

An important characteristic of Hispanic society – both in the Old World and in the Americas – is a profound sense of loyalty to community. This chapter examines community solidarity in fifteenth-, sixteenth-, and seventeenth-century Spanish rural villages, which at the time contained over 80 percent of the country's population. It analyzes the origins and the chief manifestations of local solidarity and of prejudice against outsiders, and how these group sentiments affected community life. The topic has far-reaching implications, because of its importance to questions of group identity, ethnicity, and nationalism.

VILLAGE SOLIDARITY

Throughout Europe in the late medieval and early modern periods, rural people displayed a profound sense of loyalty to their natal village. This feeling of local solidarity, perhaps superseded only by devotion to family, was nowhere more intense than in Spain. Each autonomous village in early modern Spain was almost its own country, essentially self-governing, and with a strong feeling of territoriality. It was normal for Spaniards of the time to refer to their village as "*mi patria.*" It was not the nation but the village that gave rural Spaniards their primary sense of identity and security. Although some sixteenth-century urban intellectuals might have embraced the concept of allegiance to the "nation" or to the sovereign, ordinary rural folks gave their loyalty to that which they knew: their own *pueblo*, because they had only a hazy knowledge of the outside world and its political structure. It made no difference whether the "village" was made up of independent landowners living in dispersed Basque farm-steads, or whether it consisted mainly of landless wage-earners clustered together in an Andalusian agrarian center. It was the village that was the setting for the social, economic, and political life of rural Spaniards.[1] Each village had its own space, precisely defined by periodically renewed stone markers (*mojones*), and the inhabitants were keenly aware of the bound-aries of their territory. The geographical size of this village-world varied according to local conditions: perhaps a mere 10 square kilometers in mountainous zones; but 40 square kilometers or more in the plains.[2]

Community solidarity was intensified by feelings of loyalty to the local parish church, saints, and religious festivals. The village church, its tower dominating the village, provided a physical symbol of local unity. The church bells not only marked the passage of time, but presided over collective life by summoning people to village meetings. Religious ceremonies permeated daily activities to the point where parish and village were almost identical, sharing the same territory and the same people. In the public mind, a good Christian was a good citizen who participated in the activities of the local community.[3] Concerning this matter, anthropologist William Christian concluded that "this collective identification of *pueblo* (people) with *pueblo* (place) ... is at the root of [sixteenth-century rural] religiosity." The obligation to pay the tithe further strengthened the identification of people with the local parish and the village territory.[4] Ties of kinship, of course, were also important in generating a sense of the *patria chica*. And we know that family members often lived next to one another along the same street. But the feeling of neighborhood solidarity may have been even stronger than kinship in fostering local ties.[5]

One reason for the strength of local solidarity was the highly self-sufficient nature of village life. Rural people spent their lives primarily in the village. Although they might produce some goods to sell in nearby urban markets, for most villagers trips to the outside world were infrequent special occasions. It was quite possible to go through life without *ever* leaving the village, because rural communities were not composed exclusively of agriculturalists, but were considerably diversified. Many villagers combined their farming and herding activities with distinctly non-agricultural occupations, providing the community with necessary goods and services. Thus in Spain, as in the rest of Europe, "peasant" villages contained small tradesmen, tavern keepers, and a variety of artisans to meet the needs of the local economy.[6] Furthermore, as we shall see, there were outsiders who came to the village to bring in what was not produced locally.

THE VILLAGE ASSEMBLY

Almost everywhere in Europe since the Middle Ages, rural communities organized themselves politically in village assemblies, which formed the primary territorial units of government. Community cohesiveness was strengthened by these periodic village meetings, at which residents made their own local ordinances, and elected officials from among themselves. Since the High Middle Ages the monarchs of Castile had recognized the right of municipal self-government, and had accepted the principle (although they occasionally violated it) that local offices should be held by

local citizens, with preference to the native-born.[7] The Golden Age poet
Ambrosio de Barros' *Proverbios morales*, first published in 1598, expressed
this principle in the lines:

> *Ni puede en ajena grey*   (Nor in another's community
> *ninguno hacer ordenanzas.*   can anyone make ordinances.)[8]

In Castile – and in the rest of Spain – the inhabitants of every village,
through their elected village council (*concejo*), formed a self-governing
corporation – an administrative/juridical entity whose members had the
right to make and enforce decisions concerning all aspects of their
communal existence. This was true of villages under seignorial as well as
royal jurisdiction. Virtually all Spaniards lived under a similar type of
municipal government, whether they were inhabitants of cities, towns, or
villages, and regardless of the size of the population. The right to local self-
government was regarded as the natural birthright of every Spaniard. We
can see that in the actions of the conquistadores in the New World: one
of the first things that they did everywhere was to set up municipal governments, following the Spanish model familiar to all of them.[9]

SOCIAL SOLIDARITY

The extent of collective discipline in early modern Spanish village communities varied widely in degree, but not in kind: each rural community to
some extent controlled its residents' activities, in the presumed interest of
the group as a whole. And each was involved in some type of collective
economic activity – usually the management and use of communally held
land. Local solidarity was strengthened by the need to protect collective
forest and pasture rights, and to ensure that each villager received a
proportionate share of communal resources. The village governing council
exercised continuous supervision of the daily lives of the people. And the
village government often provided economic assistance to its citizens who
found themselves in hard times.[10]

Social solidarity formed a basic ingredient in these rural communities.
The small size of the typical village engendered a strong feeling of
communal consciousness and unity. Everybody knew everybody else –
their successes and failures, joys and sorrows. As a goatherd from La
Mancha told Don Quixote (I, 12), "In these little villages they talk about
everything and they criticize everything." The villagers worshiped
together, worked together, and rejoiced together in local feasts and cele-
brations. They shared the local common pastures and woodlands, and
they had common friends and adversaries. Although they were divided by
social and economic inequalities, rich and poor felt united by strong bonds
of mutual privilege and responsibility. And although there might be
constant bickering and feuding among villagers, these internal squabbles

occurred within a context of local solidarity. One essential element for a cohesive village community was a feeling of neighborliness. This involved voluntary submission to community rules and traditions regarding political, economic, and social behavior. A good neighbor, for example, was expected to help fellow villagers in need, to attend their weddings and funerals, and to keep a watchful eye over everything that went on in the village. In such a setting, there was powerful social pressure to conform to the community norms.[11]

Each village tried to produce everything that was needed for local consumption. Even predominantly grain-growing areas also raised some animals, and produced wine and other things for local needs. The *Relaciones topográficas* clearly indicate this for villages in New Castile. The difficulty of transportation and communications encouraged people to use local products, rather than things from the outside world. Thus the stereotypical village was largely self-sufficient, with every family trying to produce what it needed, to avoid cash outlays. Rural Basque families were perhaps more successful than any others in Spain in achieving household self-sufficiency. But complete economic autonomy was virtually impossible. The villagers had to purchase salt, iron, and other goods not available locally. They needed money to pay for these outside goods, and also for taxes, rents, and other dues that could not be paid in kind. Consequently, it was practically a matter of survival for villagers to maintain commercial contacts with the outside world.[12]

LOCAL CITIZENSHIP

The inhabitants of rural communities were keenly aware that local solidarity gave them strength in confrontations with external forces. The feeling of local solidarity encouraged an exclusionist attitude toward outsiders.[13] Each village had its own space and its own inhabitants, and each person in the rural world was supposed to belong to some town or village. Outsiders were called *forasteros*, a word with a distinctly pejorative connotation. But other terms were also used: late sixteenth-century censuses from villages in the province of Jaén listed outsiders as *extravagantes*, a word combining the negative implications of *extranjero* (foreigner) and *vagante* (vagrant). And the residents of the village of Rus (Jaén) referred to outsiders as *personas extrañas* (strange persons), even when they came from Baeza, only 3 kilometers away.[14]

Local governments tried to clarify where people belonged by defining and restricting the rights of local citizenship. In order to become a *vecino*, with political, economic, and social rights in the local community, one had to meet a number of conditions. The term *vecino* literally means neighbor. It was derived from the Latin *vicinus* (after *vicus*, meaning farmhouse, village, or neighborhood). But in medieval and early modern Spain the term was applied to a person who had the rights of citizenship (*vecindad*) in the municipality, or federation of municipalities, where he resided. Normally, the *vecino* was an adult family head. As a local citizen, a *vecino* had a series of rights and obligations. Each municipality had its own norms regarding citizenship, but the basic effect of being a *vecino* was to fall under the local juridical system, and to enjoy the protection of the local *fuero* (law code, or set of privileges granted to the people of a certain area). *Vecino* status represented a legal position of personal privilege within a certain community. It was far more than a mere administrative concept: it was a political status more akin to today's concept of nationality than to mere residence.[15]

The *vecino*, or citizen, was expected to participate in the local government. The extent of that participation varied, depending upon the place and the century. There were early Reconquest towns and villages that functioned as direct participatory democracies: all the citizens of a place would meet in open assembly (*concejo general de vecinos*, or *concejo abierto*) to make governmental decisions. But with population growth, and the increasing complexity of municipal life, the open assembly was gradually supplanted by the governing council (*concejo reducido*, or *cabildo*). This council was increasingly dominated by the local socioeconomic elite, especially the hidalgos. The old direct democracies had largely disappeared by the mid-1300s, but they survived much longer in certain small and remote villages where universal poverty encouraged the maintenance of egalitarian customs.[16]

Medieval and early modern censuses recognized several types of citizens. In the first place, they distinguished between resident and absentee citizens (*vecinos presentes* and *vecinos ausentes*). The latter were obliged to pay taxes on property that they owned in the area. And the censuses invariably identified those *vecinos* who were common taxpayers (*pecheros*) as distinguished from those who were hidalgos or clergy, members of privileged estates who claimed tax exemptions. The commoners resented the fact that some individuals were accorded tax-exempt privileges. And some municipalities refused to allow hidalgos or "unneeded" priests to become citizens, only accepting taxpayers who would contribute toward the local fiscal burden. But even in these places, it was normal for some individuals to enjoy tax exemptions by virtue of their position. Certain municipal officials – *jurados* (tax assessors/collectors), for example – were excused from taxes during their tenure. And the indigent poor (*pobres de solemnidad*) were not expected to pay taxes.[17]

But for the overwhelming majority, being a *vecino* was tantamount to being a taxpayer. Many municipalities even obliged their hidalgos, and some even their clergy, to share in the tax burden. In addition to participating in the government and paying taxes, the *vecino* might be called to serve in the municipal militia or in the royal army. In frontier settlements during the Reconquest, military obligations had meant substantial risk, but also an opportunity for profit. But after the conquest of Granada (1492), ordinary soldiers were not likely to profit from military service, unless they struck it rich overseas.[18]

Not all residents of a municipality were *vecinos*. Non-*vecinos* included royal functionaries, travelers, itinerant merchants and other temporary residents, and household servants and other dependents. Normally only adult male family heads were counted as *vecinos*. Widows and orphans who owned property were exceptions in some places, but they usually counted only as half-*vecinos* in fiscal censuses. And normally, a *vecino* had to be a married man living in a home of his own. Because of this, one meaning of *"vecino"* was the head of a household. But in practice, some households contained more than one *vecino*, because of married children living with their parents, or because of other complex household situations.[19]

The son of a citizen automatically acquired citizenship in the place where he lived when he married and left his father's household to establish a household of his own. Such a person was called a *"vecino aumentado"* in Villar de la Yegua (Salamanca), suggesting that before marriage he was considered only as a potential citizen. But taking a wife did not necessarily confer immediate citizenship: in El Vellón (Madrid), newlyweds were not counted as full *vecinos* until they had been married for a year. And the sons of non-*vecinos* did not automatically attain citizenship in this way: they had to apply for it formally, even though they were born in the place.[20]

During the medieval resettlement of frontier lands won from the Muslims, when a new municipality was founded, it was usual for all adult male colonists to be considered *vecinos* of the place when they came to live there with their families. The settlers moving into new areas were typically allotted lands; therefore, the norm in these medieval settlements was for *vecinos* to be adult male *property-owners*. In succeeding centuries, many places retained the idea that property ownership (*tener raíz*) was an essential prerequisite of *vecindad*.[21]

As additional colonists arrived, the municipalities adopted procedures through which the newcomers could become *vecinos* of the locality. These medieval procedures were continued into the early modern period. Official recognition of *vecino* status was conferred by the local government issuing a naturalization certificate (*carta de vecindad*). Most municipalities were eager to attract new residents – to expand the population, to help defend and develop the area, and to broaden the tax base. Consequently, many places provided special incentives to lure prospective citizens. New settlers might be offered tax exemptions for a number of years (typically ten or more), during which they might also be promised that they would be excused from service as tax assessors or collectors, or other responsibilities that might be regarded as onerous.[22]

Many areas proved quite attractive to newcomers, not only because of temporary special incentives, but also because of liberal political, social, and economic advantages embodied in the local *fueros*. This included the right to use the local commons, which in many places included exceedingly valuable pastures, arable land, and forest resources. In fact, the lure of communal benefits and temporary tax exemptions caused a problem of fraudulent applications for *vecino* status by individuals who had no intention of permanently settling in the area. To guard against this abuse, municipal governments required would-be *vecinos* to meet specific requirements. These varied from place to place, but nearly always included a minimum period of residency and house ownership. And some places required a local guarantor (*fiador*) to offer his own property as security to ensure that the new *vecino* would honor his obligations. Many places stipulated that new *vecinos* had to build a certain size and type of house, and to make a minimum monetary investment in real estate. For example, the 1531 Ordinances of Olvera (Cádiz) dictated that to become a *vecino* one had to own a house that measured at least 7 *tixeras* (1 *tixera* = about 1 meter) in width and length, and the house had to have a tile roof. Outsiders who came to live in Olvera were allowed two years to build a house conforming to these standards. Such requirements were calculated to tie newcomers to the area economically, making it difficult for them to leave. Moreover, they forced new residents to acquire taxable property. In theory, if any of these requirements was not met, the newcomer would forfeit his right to citizenship. In practice, however, municipal governments usually seem to have been rather flexible in enforcing these regulations, for they were normally loath to lose taxpaying citizens. But if an individual was elderly, poor, and living in the household of a relative, he might forfeit his *vecino* status. This was true of a certain Juan de Lara, who lived with a son in the village of Viloria de Rioja, in Burgos province. A 1575 census indicated that Lara was "poor and widowed, and has even lost his citizenship" (*hasta desavecinado*).[23]

But not every place was eager to have new citizens. In 1539 the village council of Torbaneja (seemingly in Burgos province) explained that it had always denied *vecino* status to anyone who was unwilling to share in the village tax assessments, and who did not actually live there most of the year. Some people had requested *vecino* status, but Torbaneja had denied their applications unless they agreed to these conditions. And the 1546 Ordinances of the town of Cuéllar (Segovia) tried to make it difficult for outsiders to gain local citizenship by making it unlawful for "outsiders and vagabonds" to stay in anyone's house for more than six days. And the local *vecinos* were forbidden to rent houses to outsiders without securing a license from the town hall. There were Cantabrian villages where one was not accepted as a new *vecino* without first having supplied refreshments (a *refresco*, of bread, cakes, wine, and cheese) for all the existing *vecinos* of the place. And this applied not only to outsiders but also to sons of *vecinos*. But municipal governments were not always even-handed in applying the local requirements for citizenship. Sometimes principle was overcome by pragmatism or by financial need. In some parts of Spain, for instance, the municipal government went so far as to sell *vecino* status to individuals, such as the inhabitants of monasteries, who otherwise might have been ineligible.[24]

PREJUDICE AGAINST OUTSIDERS

The feeling of local solidarity frequently evolved into a distrust, and even dislike, of outsiders, even when they lived in a neighboring village only a short distance down the road. Outsiders were normally assessed stiffer fines than local inhabitants for violating the same local ordinance. Municipal governments viewed homeless vagrants with alarm, for they posed a possible danger to public tranquility. The officials of Paredes de Nava (Palencia) called them *rufianes y vagamundos*. In 1427 they expelled two such undesirable persons, referred to as Baltasar, *el extranjero*, and Catalina, *la sevillana*, both obviously outsiders. The local authorities threatened the pair with arrest and heavy fines if they ever dared return to Paredes. And outsiders, along with their animals who intruded into village territory, were likely to be treated harshly. This unequal treatment and hostility toward outsiders exacerbated inter-village relations, and often led to protracted litigation.[25] In these legal confrontations, the village leaders expected unanimous support from all local residents, and were likely to react unfavorably when they failed to get it. The village of Castrotierra (León) went so far as to adopt an ordinance stipulating monetary fines for any local citizen who testified in favor of an outsider.[26]

Often the anti-outsider feeling reflected a resolve to protect the limited local common pastures and woodlands from damage through overgrazing or excessive cutting, or a desire to reserve for themselves the local arable land.[27] We have a striking example of this in a struggle between the village council of Salvaleón (Badajoz) and the warden (*alcaide*) of the local fortress. In 1584 the governor of the powerful Duchy of Feria, who had installed the warden, ordered the village council to grant the warden a license to build pig pens and to cut firewood and lumber in one of the local commons (a *dehesa*). The council refused, on the grounds that the warden was not a citizen (*vecino*) of the village, and that he owned so many livestock that they would overgraze the said commons, and that the local ordinances forbade the construction of pig pens in the commons. The governor, furious that his orders were not obeyed, threw all the councilmen in jail. But they continued their defiance, and appealed to the Chancillería (Royal Court of Appeals) of Granada, which ordered them released. Eventually, the village was victorious in a lawsuit on the matter, despite the Duke's protest and appeal to the Chancillería.[28]

Fig. 1. View of the countryside between Castroverde de Campos, Vilar de Fallaves (both in Zamora province) and Barcial de la Loma (Valladolid province), drawn between 1509 and 1511 as evidence in a lawsuit over land use.

We have another example of anti-outsider prejudice in the village of Villaconejos (Madrid), which in 1543 confiscated a plot of land owned by Alonso de Tordesillas, a priest from nearby Ciempozuelos. The village council justified the seizure on the grounds that it had never permitted outsiders to use its common lands, and the property in question was used as commons (subject to the *derrota de mieses*, or stubble grazing) during part of the year. The fact that the priest had legally purchased the plot was irrelevant, because he was from a different village 12 kilometers down the road. Similarly, the village government of Rus (Jaén) in 1565 went to court in an effort to prevent residents of Baeza, 3 kilometers away, from owning property within its jusisdiction. The Chancillerías of Granada and Valladolid are full of suits growing out of efforts to restrict territorial rights to local residents. These inter-village squabbles were rarely resolved in a way that was satisfactory to both parties. In fact, in most cases there was no solution at all, and relations between villages simply worsened. Sometimes the dominant city in the region would use its influence to try to settle conflicts through threats, or by sending officials to moderate the dispute. For example, Seville did this on numerous occasions. But it was only rarely that satisfactory settlements were reached, because of the passions involved.[29]

INTER-VILLAGE VIOLENCE

The political/territorial organization of early modern Castile placed neighboring municipalities in an adversarial relationship. Because there was no unincorporated space between municipalities, frequent disagreements arose over boundaries, and over the use of common pastures, woodlands, and arable land. As the population expanded, there was growing competition between municipalities for these scarce resources. In Figure 2 we have an example of the perception that the village was surrounded by competing municipalities.

It is hardly surprising that the sociocentrism and xenophobia of early modern Castilian villages produced occasional acts of violence directed against outsiders. These acts were invariably justified on the grounds that "outlanders" had invaded the local territory or had unfairly taken what should have been reserved for the local people. For example, the young men of one village were likely to resent an outsider courting one of "their" girls, and might riot, extort money, or even resort to violence against him, to show that he had invaded their territory. In Lope de Vega's *La mocedad de Roldán*, there was gang warfare between the youths of the villages of Villarreal and Villaflor. These gang fights involved beatings, vandalizing vineyards and orchards, stealing *cabritos* and lambs, and similar adolescent misdemeanors. But adult rivalry over pasture, arable lands, forest, and other scarce economic resources could lead to far more serious confrontations, often with the destruction of property and the loss of human lives. The great Golden Age writer Cervantes was aware of this. He depicted Don Quixote encountering a boisterous mob of over two hundred rural people on the way to attack a neighboring village. This makeshift peasant army carried lances, pikes, crossbows, and firearms (arquebuses). Sancho Panza, who was obviously familiar with such things, thought it prudent to avoid contact with the group.[30]

Such scenes were not merely the product of a vivid literary imagination: they were all too real. For instance, one day in 1526 an armed band of fifty villagers from El Burgo Ranero (León) invaded and destroyed a wheat field planted on disputed land by the citizens of nearby Villamuñío (both dependent villages [*lugares*] under seignorial jurisdiction). And when the aggrieved farmers appeared with an *alcalde* (judge) to try to stop them, the invading villagers gave them a thrashing and seized their weapons.

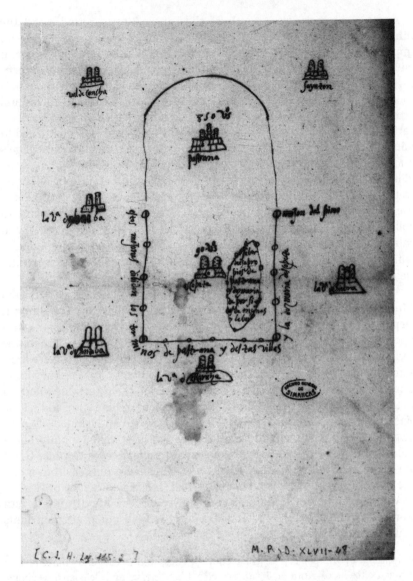

Fig. 2. Map of the territorial boundaries of Pastrana (Guadalajara province) in 1571, showing the placement of neighboring villages.

Spanish villagers of the day were highly defensive of territory that they considered to be theirs, sometimes regardless of legal rulings to the contrary. In fact, in the episode just cited, the farmers from Villamuñío had obtained a court order giving them the right to plant grain on the disputed territory, but the enemy villagers paid it no heed.[31]

Another example, from south of the Duero River: around 1558 the inhabitants of Casaseca de Campeán (Zamora province) made an impromptu raid on the nearby village of El Bahillo, in pursuit of certain citizens of the latter who had denied them grazing rights in disputed territory. A witness testified that the people of Casaseca "rang the church bells to summon everyone in the village, and they rushed out with lances and crossbows and slings, with the intent of wounding and killing their adversaries. And nobody over the age of fourteen – not even women – failed to join in helping the village leaders, armed with roasting spits and cudgels and stones." The angry mob tracked the offending outsiders to the enemy village. Finding their intended victims barricaded in their homes, the frustrated mob went to the house of their adversaries' employer, and vented their fury by throwing heavy rocks on the roof, almost causing it to collapse. And when two officials from the city of Zamora arrived to try to calm things down, the mob nearly killed them. The relation concludes with this marvelous understatement: "From the foregoing, it seems quite clear that these people are overly excited."[32]

A similar episode occurred in the late 1530s in Cumbres de Enmedio (Huelva), which had a dispute with a neighboring village over territory: it seems that the people of Cumbres de Enmedio had impounded some livestock owned by citizens of Cumbres Bajas (probably the present Cumbres de San Bartolomé), on grounds of illegal grazing. One night shortly afterwards, a group of over fifty people from Cumbres Bajas attacked the enemy village, bent on murdering those responsible for the animal seizures. One intended victim testified that the mob smashed open the door of his house, and set the place afire, and that he escaped only by fleeing naked and barefoot over his neighbors' rooftops. At another house, the intended victim stoutly barricaded his door, so the attackers removed tiles from his roof, in order to set the house ablaze. The unlucky fellow was able to save himself from a dire fate by knocking a hole through a back wall (probably of adobe brick).[33]

A final example relates to a dispute between Codesal and Anta de Tera (Zamora), villages about 3 kilometers apart who disputed grazing rights in a certain pasture. One day in 1555 or 1556:

Summoned by the pealing of [their church] bells, and in a riotous manner [the enraged citizens of Anta de Tera], armed with offensive and defensive weapons, rushed to the disputed pastures ... and ... seized and carried off ... more than 50 cows and other livestock, beating them and mistreating them, they brought them to the village of Anta, and ... they thrust their lances against the chests of the shepherds who had been caring for them, and they struck them with lances and clubs, and in many other ways they badly mistreated those animals and shepherds.[34]

Naturally, these violent confrontations further inflamed tensions between rival villages. And they were long remembered, in accounts passed orally from one generation to the next, thus reinforcing and perpetuating inter-municipal hard feelings. Some places even developed folkloric rituals commemorating important battles with enemy villagers. Vinuesa, for example, a hamlet in the pine forests of the province of Soria, in the 1980s continued a centuries-old annual tradition called *La Pinochada*. This was a sort of mock battle celebrating a bloody confrontation with the citizens of nearby Covaleda in the early 1400s. There is scanty documentary evidence concerning the fifteenth-century conflict, and the local legendary versions are contradictory. But it is clear that a violent encounter *did* occur, and that it was merely one episode in a long history of enmity between the two villages.[35]

The passions aroused by these pitched battles did not easily subside, even when there were no major casualties. William Christian found that friction between hostile villages spilled over into local religious observances. The situation became so serious that the bishop of Burgos in 1575 and the bishop of Toledo in 1583 ordered their villages to hold their processions to shrines on separate days, to avoid violent encounters between the faithful from rival villages. Given the strong feelings involved, we should not be surprised that there were skirmishes in various parts of early modern Spain between neighboring villages on religious pilgrimages. Nor should we be surprised to find that inter-village saint's day fighting for centuries remained a part of Castilian rural life, continuing into the second half of the twentieth century.[36]

ECONOMIC PROTECTIONISM

Another manifestation of local solidarity and of hostility toward outsiders was a system of municipal protectionism, or mercantilism. This system, which was the norm in Spanish cities, towns, and villages, was designed to protect both local producers and local consumers from outside competition. Municipal governments established the system through ordinances regulating the movement and sale of goods. For example, Los Santos de Maimona (Badajoz) prohibited its citizens from taking fruit and vegetables from their gardens to sell outside the town, without the permission of local authorities. And the ordinances of Escuredo (León) called for fining any local citizen who sold charcoal to an outsider. The emphasis was upon satisfying local needs before anything could be exported for sale to outsiders. And the policy was to exclude outside products until the supply of local goods had been exhausted. Wine is a good case in point: even if the local wine was almost undrinkable, the local government was likely to force its inhabitants to consume the entire local crop before more palatable outside vintages could be sold.[37]

And in this system of municipal protectionism prices were rigidly controlled – at least in theory. Municipal governments granted monopoly concessions for the sale of meat, wine, fish, oil, and other items. And they imposed countless other regulations. The system was supposed to benefit everyone, but it often caused dissatisfaction. For example, in the late 1500s the government of Yeste (Albacete) imposed price controls on all fruits and vegetables, and also insisted that they be sold solely in its main square. This was not to the liking of producers, whose irrigated and intensively cultivated garden plots were located as much as a half-league from town. The gardeners sued the local government, alleging that they had always been able to sell at free prices in their homes and gardens. They asserted that the fixed prices were unrealistically low, and that the previous unregulated system had been better for the consumer, because it permitted the gardeners' wives to sell their produce from their homes, day and night, for the convenience of buyers.[38]

Ironically, the Castilian village solidarity, prejudice against outsiders, and municipal protectionism outlined in this chapter operated in the context of an open and dynamic society that maintained – and actually encouraged – active contacts with the outside world (as the following chapters will demonstrate). These contacts inevitably brought substantial immigration and emigration to and from the village. The xenophobic tendencies described in the previous pages seem incongruent with the fluid and migratory character of the early modern rural population. Actually, however, the exaggerated "us versus them" mentality may be explained partly by the substantial proportion of immigrants in the typical Castilian village community. The newcomers in the village needed to be hypersensitive to local (as opposed to outside) rights and privileges, lest they be suspected of disloyalty to the community. Hence, they became vigorous defenders of the *patria chica*. The development of local sociocentrism was a complex process, of course, but the attitude of naturalized *vecinos* must have been an important part of it.

2

MARKET CONTACTS WITH THE OUTSIDE WORLD

THE CASTILIAN MARKET SYSTEM

*H*istorians have tended to exaggerate the shortcomings of the market system of early modern Castile. While it is true that geography made transport difficult in the Castilian heartland, and that unreliable harvests hampered the development of market-oriented agriculture, Castile had thriving local and regional markets and financial exchanges during the fifteenth and sixteenth centuries. And these regional markets were integrated into a highly developed peninsular commercial and financial network based in Toledo and Valladolid. Furthermore, the Castilian trade network interacted with markets in Flanders, Italy, and other foreign lands. The impact of incessant warfare and the economic crisis of the early seventeenth century profoundly disturbed these peninsular and international networks, bringing a regression towards regional isolation. But a new peninsular commercial network arose to supplant the old. Controlled by Madrid, it was driven by political as much as economic considerations. The nation-wide cycles of boom and recession, and the structural changes that accompanied them, were felt not only in the major commercial centers but also in rural areas.[1]

The typical early modern Castilian village family placed a high value on economic self-sufficiency. It was the goal of traditional peasant households to minimize their dependence upon the outside world by producing as much as possible of what they needed, especially food. A family could obtain some things that it did not produce by trading with other people in the village. These local transactions were often made through barter, rather than with cash. But there was a need for money, to buy iron, salt, and other items that had to come from outside the village, and to pay taxes. This cash came from selling surplus grain, animals, or other products. But in Spain, as in the rest of Europe at the time, most rural people seem to have maintained a strongly autarkic attitude toward production. They were willing to enter the marketplace when opportunities arose, but they felt that their security depended upon growing subsistence crops. And when they entered the market economy, they preferred to do so as sellers, rather than buyers.[2] The involvement of the typical early modern rural producer in the cash economy may have been slight. But it distinguishes him from his forebears who lived almost completely outside the market system. In fact, for some historians the early modern Spanish agriculturalist was sufficiently involved in the market economy to justify calling him a "farmer," rather than a "peasant."[3]

It is difficult to make generalizations that stand up, because of the widely varying conditions between years, between regions, and even between villages in the same region. But it is clear that Castilian villagers often had surpluses to market, and sometimes these surpluses were quite substantial. It is impossible to be precise about this, because all the production data from the period were provided by the villagers themselves, who regularly understated their income to escape heavy taxation. Mindful of this problem, Bartolomé Yun Casalilla found considerable evidence of crop specialization among sixteenth-century villages in the Tierra de Campos, an agricultural area embracing parts of the provinces of León, Palencia, Valladolid, and Zamora. This specialization is proof of a definite market orientation, but the villages differed widely in what they sold. Some places concentrated on growing wheat, while others focused on wine production. As we would expect, not all villages were equally engaged in the market. Whereas Revellinos marketed only 7.5 percent of the grain that it produced, Villalumbrós sold 22.7 percent. And while Castroponce marketed only 11.5 percent of its wine, Villafáfila sold 70.4 percent. These figures do not include what was sold by the recipients of the tithe, the addition of which would imply an even greater degree of commercialization. Moreover, they do not include everything that the local peasants sold, but only what they declared as their major surpluses.[4]

When villagers had surplus products to sell, they usually offered them in the markets and fairs of their own district. According to a report from Morales de Toro (Zamora) in 1569, "the citizens of this place ... take what they have to sell to the City of Toro, which is nearby, or to other villages within its jurisdiction or even beyond, which is wheat, wine, straw, vine prunings [prized as firewood, because they burned with a minimum of smoke], lambs, draft animals, melons and other similar things." Eighty-three percent of citizens present in the village at the time reported that they had taken things to market. To give a specific example: Miguel de la Torre, who seems to have had a middling standard of living for the village, indicated that he had sold during the previous five years: 20 dozen eggs, 20 chickens, a large load of straw, 20 dozen bundles of vine prunings, 30 measures (millares) of cardón (a plant used in textile manufacturing), and melons from two melon patches. This accounting, like all tax declarations, should be viewed with mistrust, particularly in view of the rounded figures. In any case, de la Torre reported that he sold the straw and vine prunings in Toro, the *cardón* in Valladolid, the melons in Medina de Rioseco and in Villabrágima, and everything else in his own village.[5]

A family's surplus would probably be sold by the man of the house, who would travel by mule or donkey, or on foot, or with his ox-cart to the most convenient market. There were usually several possibilities in neighboring towns and villages. And for the convenience of both buyers and sellers, the local markets were often held on different days of the week. For instance, in the Adelantamiento (administrative district) of León there was a small market every Monday in Santamaría del Rey; on Tuesdays one could go to market in Villafranca del Bierzo or in Mansilla de las Mulas; Wednesday was market day in Mayorga, but it was described as "dismal" (*ruin*); every Thursday there was a market in Benavides (primarily for animals), or you could go to market that day in Valencia de Don Juan and in Venbilas. Apparently there was no market in the area on Fridays.[6] But every Saturday there was a large market in La Bañeza, which specialized in cattle and other animals. In addition to these weekly markets, there were annual fairs in the area. Mansilla de las Mulas held a two-day fair commemorating Saint Martin's Day. In the Bierzo area, Cacabelos sponsored a two-week fair for Saint Mark's Day, but that was the town's only market. There was a tax-free market (*mercado franco*) on Palm Sunday in Cea, which also held a fair and tax-free market on Saint Luke's Day. And Venbilas hosted two annual fairs (on Holy Thursday and on Saint Peter's Day).[7]

The fairs of a major trading city, naturally, dominated commercial exchanges over a large surrounding area. But smaller village fairs coexisted with the big city fairs. Local fairs were more convenient for rural buyers and sellers. Moreover, although ordinary markets were held on a regular basis throughout the year, a fair was an extraordinary event that happened only once a year in most places. And different places tended to have different fair dates, so they did not necessarily compete with one another. Francis Brumont found numerous thriving fairs and markets around the city of Burgos. The agrarian character of these exchanges can be seen in the fact that most of them were held in October and November, after harvest. The *Relaciones topográficas* confirm the importance to Castilian villagers of local and regional markets and fairs.[8]

The fairs, often specializing in certain categories such as animals or grain, were not only occasions for buying and selling. They also offered opportunities for social contacts with people from the extra-village world. And we may suppose that many rural folks attended the fairs even when they had no business to transact. Susan Freeman tells us that the stock fairs of the Cantabrian Pas Valley took on the quality of secular fiestas, where villagers went to eat, drink, and socialize in local taverns. Freeman's observations were in the mid-twentieth century, but we can imagine that the situation was not vastly different for rural folks in the early modern-period.[9]

RURAL MARKETING STRATEGIES

We have an indication of rural marketing strategies in a report submitted to the Royal Treasury by the village of Palomas (Badajoz) in 1575. The inhabitants of Palomas, which at the time had scarcely 200 households, sold their products in the Tuesday market in Mérida, a reported 5 leagues away (1 league = about 5.5 kilometers); the Thursday market in Zafra (6 1/2 leagues), or the Saturday market of Medellín (6 leagues). They marketed most of their grain in Zafra, but took their cattle, hogs, and goats to sell at the annual Saint Mary's fair in August at Mérida, the May Day fair of Medellín, or the fairs of Saint John and Saint Michael (September 24) in Zafra. They also utilized the Saint Matthew's Day (September 21) fairs of Llerena (9 leagues distant), and the May 20 fair in Trujillo (16 leagues from Palomas).[10] Map 4 shows the location of these regional markets, in relation to Palomas.

Villagers learned through experience and from word of mouth where best to market their goods. The most attractive condition was a tax-free market (*mercado franco*), sought out by buyers and sellers alike. Municipal governments tried hard to get royal permission to hold one, knowing that such a privilege was a sure way to spur economic growth. In 1529 Salamanca secured from Charles V the right to have a tax-free market every Thursday. It was specified that villagers within a 12-league radius were exempted from the *alcabala* (sales tax) in Salamanca's market on that day. Thursday seems to have been a favorite day for trade, because Trujillo, Segovia, and Peñafiel also held Thursday markets. There was considerable specialization, and villagers might go to different markets to sell different items. For example, the farmers of Trigueros del Valle (Valladolid) sold their surplus grain either in Valladolid (3 leagues away), or in Dueñas, Palazuelos, or Palencia. But shepherds of the place normally took their sheep to market in Valladolid. If they had wool to sell, however, they brought it to Dueñas or Palencia. We have another report of marketing strategies from Casasola de Arión (Valladolid) in 1569:

This village is 8 leagues from the town of Valladolid, where there is a tax-free fair every year, and 7 leagues from Medina de Rioseco, where there are 2 tax-free fairs each year and several markets, and 13 leagues from the city of Salamanca, and 7 leagues from the city of Zamora, where there are also 2 tax-free fairs, and 3 leagues from the city of Toro, where there are tax-free fairs and markets, and the residents of this village usually sell their wheat, barley, livestock, and almost all of their other goods in the tax-free fairs and markets of those cities and towns.

These reports indicate that villagers were well informed about regional marketing opportunities, and that they took advantage of them.[11]

We may assume that it was primarily a man's job to bring cash crops to market. And the major livestock fairs may have been predominately male affairs. But women also took part in marketing.[12] In fact, early

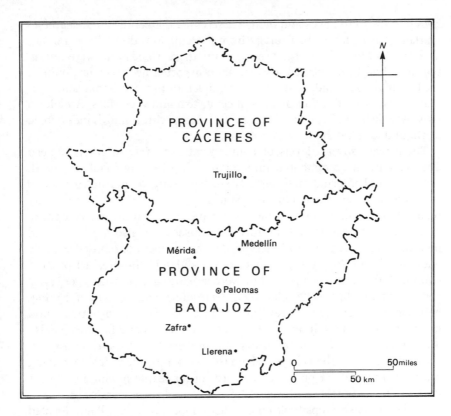

Map 4. Regional markets where villagers of Palomas (Badajoz) sold surpluses in 1575.

modern censuses indicate that recently widowed women often (if not usually) continued to operate the family farm, with the help of their children and/or hired workers. When they had some surplus to sell, the widows undoubtedly often brought it to market themselves. We know from municipal ordinances and from the ordinances of the Cortes of León-Castile that women played an active role in various economic activities, and we have evidence of rural women selling their produce.[13]

In addition to the local fairs where villagers were most likely to offer their cash crops, Castile also had great fairs of regional, and even international, importance. The most famous were the fairs of Medina del Campo (Valladolid), which attracted buyers and sellers from Flanders, France, Italy, and other parts of Europe. These fairs offered opportunities for villagers with agricultural products and handmade goods for sale. And there were numerous lesser fairs: for example, Arévalo (Avila) for wheat, and Badajoz, Mérida (Badajoz), Avila, and Daimiel (Ciudad Real) for livestock – to name a few. It was easier to transport livestock than other merchandise, and flocks and herds crisscrossed the peninsula in search of markets. For instance, hog raisers from Extremadura drove their animals as far as La Mancha, for the livestock fairs there. Goods that were not on the hoof had to be carried, carted, or transported by mules or donkeys. And despite poor roads and high costs, different parts of Spain sold their major cash crops to other areas: Galicia its fish and vegetables; Andalusia its wines, fish, and salt; Old Castile its wheat, wines, and hand-loomed cloth; and La Mancha its wines.[14]

There were several levels of commercial exchange in early modern Castile, with a complicated interrelationship linking local, regional, national, and international fairs. These fairs were of mutual benefit to everyone who participated in them, and had a powerful stimulating effect upon village economies and family incomes. The fairs were centers of exchange not only for agricultural surpluses, but also for household manufactures, such as textiles. Typically, the villagers purchased the raw materials (wool, for example) themselves, and sold the finished product (woven cloth, or whatever else they were making) at fairs whenever it was convenient for them. The fairs, then, were important centers of contact between villagers (who grew or manufactured their products) and merchants (who bought and sold both raw materials and finished goods). But merchants and various agents and brokers (*arrendadores* and *corredores*) also came to the villages, where they became quite visible arranging sales, or contracts for planting vineyards or for textile production – thus uniting the economies and worries of urban and rural worlds.[15]

Marketing cash crops took on a special importance in villages located near large urban centers. Cities like Madrid, Burgos, Granada, Salamanca, Segovia, Toledo, and León contained sizeable populations that needed to be fed. And they gave nearby agricultural producers an opportunity to sell their surpluses at good prices. Accordingly, villages within the orbit of large municipalities tended to become far more market-oriented than others in isolated locations. Everywhere the story was similar: rural people who lived near large urban markets abandoned the idea of a closed, self-sufficient economy to specialize increasingly in the production of grain, wine, olive oil, fruits and vegetables, wool, silk, cloth, and other products that could be sold for cash in the city. In the *Relaciones* the village of Leganés, two leagues from Madrid, reported on the market gardening activities of its inhabitants, saying that they grew onions, eggplants, turnips, and cabbages in gardens irrigated by over a hundred water wheels and other hydraulic devices – all owned by private citizens of the place, and because of the success of this activity, the tithes of the village had grown significantly. And a report from 1575 indicated that the city of Burgos was supplied by carts and mules bringing merchandise from a wide area.[16] Figure 3 depicts the traffic of carts, mounted animals, and pedestrians that one might have seen at the entrance to market towns and cities.

Fig. 3. Detail from Anton Van den Wyngaerde's 1565 drawing of Alcalá de Henares (Madrid), showing approach to town, with loaded carts, mounted travelers, and inn with spacious courtyard in the lower left.

Villagers who took their goods to market in the big city often proved to be surprisingly astute businessmen. And the crafty peasant became a stereotype in Golden Age folklore and literature. For example, the Golden Age writer Carlos García in *La desordenada codicia de los bienes ajenos* (1619) told of a villager who had traveled three leagues to sell some capons and partridges in a city market on Holy Saturday, when there was an especially good demand for meat to serve for dinner on Easter Sunday. The villager in the story bargained for a quarter of an hour with prospective buyers before agreeing on a price. In that literary example, the peasant marketed his produce in person. But that was not always the case. Rural producers living in the vicinity of Málaga were able to market their products indirectly, through a system of consignment (*trecena*) in which they were paid a certain percentage of the sale price. The government of Málaga supervised the system, with the aim of guaranteeing that urban consumers would be satisfied, and that suppliers would be equitably compensated. All goods brought to the city for sale had to be deposited in the municipal warehouse (*alhóndiga*), before they could be taken to the city's network of shops for sale to the public.[17] It would be interesting to know how widespread this system was.

SUPPLYING THE ROYAL COURT

The royal court, with its hordes of officials, nobles, servants, petitioners, and hangers-on, provided a major market for rural products. But land transport was so expensive that producers near the court had a substantial advantage over producers from other regions. For example, the wine growers of Morales de Toro (Zamora province) had enjoyed a lucrative and dependable market in Valladolid while the royal court was there. But when Philip II established Madrid as his capital, the court got its wine primarily from south of the Sierra de Guadarrama, and the producers in Morales suffered sagging demand and lower prices. The white wine of Medina del Campo, similarly, became a favorite of the royal court when Philip III moved the capital to Valladolid in 1601. And Medina's wine producers experienced a boom, but following the court's return to Madrid (1605), Medina's growers were no longer able to compete, because of high cost of transport over the mountains.[18]

The royal court, with all of its entourage, certainly provided market opportunities for nearby villagers. But having the court in the vicinity was a mixed blessing for rural producers, because it was often difficult for local people to supply the court while keeping enough for their own needs. Some rural producers reacted unfavorably when ordered to satisfy the royal demands. For example, when an official from Tocina (Seville) was ordered to turn over his chickens for the use of the court, he replied testily that *he* could eat those chickens just as well as the king and queen.[19]

David Ringrose has given us a penetrating analysis of Madrid's growing influence over Spain. After becoming capital in 1561, Madrid gradually eclipsed all other inland cities to dominate the country economically as well as politically. Spain's capital city treated the rest of the country as merely another part of its colonial empire, to be exploited as necessary for its own well-being. Since Madrid lay in the center of the Iberian peninsula, it could not rely on the inexpensive maritime and river shipping that supplied London, Paris, Amsterdam, and Lisbon. Consequently, the Spanish capital had to depend wholly upon primitive overland transportation in order to grow – a situation made more difficult by the relatively low agricultural productivity of its surrounding countryside. Madrid was forced by geography to regulate the economy of the rest of the country, to guarantee itself a dependable supply of foodstuffs, fuel, and other necessities. In Ringrose's words, "the capital city extracted resources from all over the interior, both by subsidizing its urban market and by administratively re-directing regional commodity flows."[20]

Between 1550 and 1600 Madrid expanded from about 20,000 to 65,000 inhabitants. During that period, the capital remained primarily a political center, while Toledo and Seville continued to dominate the country's economic and social life. But in the first half of the seventeenth century Madrid's population rose to nearly 200,000, sparking a building boom accompanied by a major restructuring of the Castilian economy with the capital in an ever more commanding position. To feed the expanding population of Madrid, the royal government adopted numerous measures, including a price ceiling (*tasa*) on grain, bans on the shipment of grain to destinations other than Madrid, regulating the price of bread, and imposing bread delivery obligations on villages around the capital. Despite this heavy-handed economic interventionism, Madrid was a great consumer market (in fact, it *produced* little but government during this period), providing lucrative incomes for people with things to sell. The seventeenth-century depression brought new changes in the Spanish economy, but Madrid retained its predominant position.[21]

Like most larger towns, Madrid possessed seignorial privileges over the villages in its jurisdiction. These included the right to compel its subject villages to provide bread (*pan de obligación*) for the city at regulated prices. Eventually a complicated system was adopted in which individual villagers as far as 64 kilometers from the capital were assigned quotas of bread to supply for Madrid. But the obligatory bread quotas provided only a tenth of Madrid's annual consumption, leaving a window of opportunity for villagers to sell additional bread in the city (in fact, they were forbidden to ship their surplus bread anywhere else). The government also regulated the price and transfer of wheat. The radius of control grew with the city: Ringrose tells us that in the 1580s it was up to 72 kilometers, and by 1698 it reached as far as 192 kilometers. Moreover, to encourage villagers to sell bread in Madrid, the government set the price of bread in the villages at a lower level than in the capital. The villagers resented Madrid's high-handed control over them, and many communities eventually gained exemptions from the system. But the effects of Madrid's interference with the market were lingering. Moreover, when there were poor crops in the capital's usual supply zones, the city sent purchasing agents as far as Andalusia and Palencia, disrupting the regional market networks of those areas. Madrid similarly regulated the wine market, to guarantee its supply. Thus, outside interference from Madrid became a reality for villagers hundreds of kilometers from the capital, as the central government profoundly disrupted the market for the most basic requirements for life. The city of Madrid had exceptional problems, and possessed extraordinary powers to deal with them. But other cities encountered similar difficulties, and used similar measures to resolve them. Paul Hiltpold and Francis Brumont, for example, found that the city of Burgos sought grain for its bakeries from distances often exceeding 100 kilometers, despite the high costs of carting.[22]

We must view Madrid's overbearing influence over the economy of its hinterland within the context of the general tradition of municipal mercantilism described in Chapter 1. At the time it was usual for municipal governments of all levels – whether cities, towns, or villages – to enact protectionist ordinances regulating the movement and sale of goods.

ITINERANT MERCHANTS

All but the very smallest villages had shops where local inhabitants could purchase items such as fish, salt, and olive oil from the outside world. There were also itinerant vendors who traveled the roads of Spain, periodically visiting all but the most isolated areas, and bringing items of a specialized nature that the villagers were unable to produce themselves, and that might not be available in the local shops. These traveling salesmen (called *trajineros, buhoneros,* or *arrieros*) not only offered goods, but also provided a "window on the wider world" for isolated rural people. The inhabitants of remote mountain villages eagerly looked forward to the visits of these traveling vendors, and to encourage them often renounced the right to charge the normal sales tax (*alcabala*), collected at rates varying from about 3.5 percent to 10 percent. For example, the people of Montenegro de Cameros (Soria), a place with 145 *vecinos* in 1597, assessed only one *maravedí* per *real* (1 to 34), explaining that:

This place is in the mountains, and the terrain is so rugged that not much merchandise reaches it, and if [the vendors] heard that they would have to pay 10 percent, no one would come, because the oil-sellers and other vendors who usually come to the place always try to avoid the 10 percent rate, and if we ever assessed that amount they would never return.[23]

Some villages did not charge a sales tax at all on essential goods from the outside. This was the case of Robledillo (Cáceres), which exempted soap, charcoal, iron and steel, wood for plows, and food, because:

No one in this place makes soap, so many [villagers] get it in Trujillo, and if any outsiders come [to Robledillo] to sell, it is because of the tax exemption. Charcoal has to come 7 or 8 leagues, and if it is ever sold here that is only because of the exemption, and without it there would be a great shortage. And iron and steel and plow-wood come in only once in six years, and are tax exempted to help agriculture, and when we get any wood it is a few plow parts from the town of Garcíaz, which is 6 leagues from here. And we exempt sellers of food items, because if we didn't no one would sell them.[24]

Traveling salesmen often were able to do quite well selling to villagers, even in unfavorable circumstances. For example, in 1504 a cloth merchant visited Mijas (Málaga), a place with less than 50 *vecinos*, including several who were weavers. Nevertheless, he succeeded in selling the villagers 4,118 *maravedís* of material. This was a sizeable sum, and must have represented a considerable quantity of cloth. The vendor must have had a good sales pitch, or else he was offering an attractive price, or goods that the country folks found especially appealing.[25]

These itinerant merchants, especially cloth sellers, found that they could speed up sales by offering their goods on credit against the villagers' coming crop. This type of credit sale, called the *mohatra*, became infamous in 16th-century Spain. Many country folks, beguiled by dazzling merchandise and easy terms, were persuaded to buy more goods than they could really afford. When unable to pay the merchant from that year's crop, they had to carry the debt over to the following year, or years, becoming economic prisoners of the merchant. And what was worse, the merchants often used their share of the crop to speculate in the commodities market, distorting price fluctuations to the disadvantage of the producer.[26]

We know that some itinerant vendors were Portuguese – not only along the border, but far into Spain. And some were Gypsies. A document from 1561 speaks of Gypsies selling and trading goods in Higuera de Martos (apparently the present Higuera de Calatrava, in the province of Jaén). These Gypsies must have come to the town from elsewhere, because they were not listed in the local census. The people of Higuera seemed to have been happy to have the opportunity to trade with the Gypsies.[27] But not all Spaniards were eager to trade with members of this ethnic minority. Chapter 7 deals at greater length with the Gypsies in early modern Spain, and the prejudices against them.

Another minority group who were active as traveling vendors during this period were the Moriscos (Spaniards of Moorish ancestry). In 1570, following a violent insurrection, the Moriscos of the Kingdom of Granada were expelled from their homes and were dispersed in communities throughout Castile. The royal government hoped that this would integrate them into the main fabric of Christian Spanish society. But the results were disappointing; the Moriscos continued to maintain their separate identity. And although it was expected that they would form a sort of rural proletariat, working on lands owned by Old Christian Spaniards, the Moriscos were seldom content in that role. Only a small minority of them remained in the traditional Castilian field activities, and those who did continue in agriculture usually moved to the outskirts of Castile's urban centers, where they became growers/vendors of fruits and vegetables. But the great majority of Moriscos turned to non-agricultural pursuits, because that was where the greatest opportunities lay. By the end of the 1500s there were far more traders than agriculturalists in the Morisco community. And there were almost twice as many artisans as agriculturalists. The Moriscos' economic success, and their continued separate lifestyle, gained them ever-increasing ill will from their Christian neighbors. The *corregidor* of Toro (Zamora) complained that the Moriscos were of no help in the local grape harvest. And the *corregidor* of Medina del Campo (Valladolid) reproached the Moriscos for preferring to be muleteers or itinerant merchants rather than farmers. The mounting Christian resentment against the Moriscos led to their definitive expulsion from Spain in

1609–14.[28] We shall return to the Moriscos in Chapter 7, dealing with them as an "alien" influence.

But the overwhelming majority of traveling vendors were ordinary Spaniards. Many were undoubtedly enterprising city folks with an entrepreneurial spirit. But most were villagers (usually peasant-farmers) who spent the slack months of the year earning cash money by peddling things to villagers down the road, or in other parts of the country. Some peasants from Valdeburón (León), for example, worked winters selling wine and sardines in neighboring areas. And in the Liébana district (Santander), especially in the lower villages of the Valdeprado Valley, many farmers left their fields and flocks in their wives' care after harvest, to sell fruits and vegetables in the markets of Castile. There were certain mountainous parts of Spain that became famous for their traveling vendors. The villages of the mountains of León, for example, produced the highly enterprising *maragatos*, who were astute merchandisers in early modern Spain.[29]

Many – probably most – of these peasant-peddlers sold not only their own products, but also things that they had bought for resale. And they often combined trading with transporting – using their mules, donkeys, or carts to include cargoes for hire alongside their own merchandise. Some of these peasant/peddlers-cum-transporters confined their activities to their own and neighboring villages. Others operated on a much larger scale, traveling wherever there promised to be markets for their wares. Consequently, not only village markets, but also important urban centers like Madrid and Toledo were visited regularly by peasant-vendors and peasant-transporters.[30]

VILLAGERS SHOP IN OUTSIDE MARKETS

Not all villages were visited by traveling salesmen. The residents of Santa María del Monte (León) reported in 1597 that no vendor ever came there to sell anything, because the villagers bought whatever they needed in the city of León, and other places.[31] That was an extreme case, to be sure. But even residents of places frequented by traveling merchants often found it better to make their purchases outside the village. Members of the local elite might go to a nearby city to buy fancy clothing or other luxury items. But even ordinary villagers used outside markets to supply themselves with the things that they needed for everyday life. On one occasion Don Quixote met two peasant-farmers riding donkeys loaded with items that they had undoubtedly bought in some large town, to bring home to their village. We have ample documentary evidence that this was not an unusual sight. According to testimony from the town of Peñafiel (Valladolid), the residents of eighteen or twenty nearby villages came "every day of the week, or on most days, especially Thursdays ... to the markets that are held in the town to buy and take advantage of the provisions and [other] things that they need." This document also mentions that the villagers who came to Peñafiel's market used the occasion to pick up news that would be of concern to them.[32]

Naturally, a given trip to market could be for both selling and buying. For example, we are told that the people of Morales de Toro (Zamora), who sold their grain, grapes, wine, and other products in the fairs and markets of the city of Toro, also took advantage of the opportunity to purchase the things that they needed there. This practice was depicted in the Golden Age tale "El campesino endemoniado," where the villager brought some birds to the city to sell, expecting to use the money to buy shoes, a hat, and various "trifles for himself and his family."[33]

CARTERS AND MULETEERS

During peak seasons the main roads of Castile were choked by caravans of carts and mule trains transporting goods from one part of the country to another. In 1545 the Emperor Charles V remarked to the Cortes representative (*procurador*) from Burgos that there were many places on the road between that city and Medina del Campo where it was impossible to walk, because of the intense traffic of heavily loaded carts. Burgos was the northern hub of Castile's north–south carting network, being the point at which merchandise was transferred between pack mules (used in the mountains farther north) and carts. And transporting was a major occupation for men living in villages around Burgos.[34] The scene that caught the Emperor's attention must have been not only congested but also exceedingly noisy, with creaking cart wheels, sounds of animal hoofbeats and exertion, and the shouted commands, banter, and singing of transporters and travelers. And it was usually dusty, because long-distance transport in early modern Castile was largely a seasonal activity linked to the weather patterns and to the agricultural agenda. The rainy winter months of December and January frequently rendered the country's roads too muddy to use; and the scorching temperatures of August, September, and October made roadside pasture too sparse for convenient travel in an age that depended upon animal power. The agricultural calendar also had a major role in the seasonality of Castilian land transport, because most transporters were part-time farmers. That meant that in January and February they stayed home to plow and sow their fields; in June and July they needed to harvest their grain; and in the fall the Andalusians attended to their olive harvest. During these times the majority of Castile's transporters abandoned the carrying trade to return to the agrarian side of their yearly work cycles. The combination of farm work and transporting made for a far more efficient utilization of mules and oxen than either activity would have permitted by itself. The two activities complemented each other, providing an effective – albeit seasonal – transportation system while producing the basic foodstuffs for the men and beasts who participated in them.[35]

In this way, in Spain as in northern Europe, a substantial number of rural people, especially residents of mountain villages, spent two or three months of the year as muleteers or carters earning extra money to make ends meet. Their absence from home must have produced many awkward situations, not only for their families, but for their entire communities. For example, Pinilla de los Barruecos (Burgos), a village of seventy-one households, reported in 1597 that its tavern keeper, its butcher, and its storekeeper (*arrendador del viento*) had all left the place – along with many other villagers to be sure – to enter the seasonal carting business. The proportion of villagers who did this was probably usually small: Ramón Lanza García has estimated that no more than 10 percent of the peasants of the La Bureba (Burgos) and Liébana (Santander) districts left their villages annually to become carters or muleteers. But their numbers could be impressive in absolute terms: Alain Huetz calculated that over 800 peasant-farmers, from the Reinosa area (Santander) alone, left their villages after harvest with their pack animals and carts to enter the carrying trade in wheat and wine from the Castilian plains. Most of these peasant transporters made three successive trips to the Tierra de Campos and Nava del Rey (Valladolid). Huetz described the situation as it existed in the mid-1700s, but the practice was centuries old.[36]

Most of the peasant-transporters of early modern Castile were basically supported by farming, and considered themselves to be farmers (*labradores*). But their agricultural activities were not sufficient to support their families adequately, or they wanted to earn extra cash during slack farm seasons. Furthermore, agricultural areas that produced surpluses of one commodity often needed to import other products from different regions. Peasants could transport their own surpluses to places where they were needed, and could return transporting the target region's surpluses back home. In that manner, the inter-regional exchanges of forest products, home-manufactured goods, grain, wine, olive oil, and other rural surpluses made it possible for villages to obtain the basic necessities of life.[37] These commercial exchanges with distant areas, often carried out by the producers themselves, were essential for their survival. Thus, regular contacts with the outside world were an indispensable feature of traditional village life.

Although most of Castile's carters and muleteers had some ties to agriculture, some eventually became specialists in the transporting business. The most well-known of these were the *maragatos* from villages in the western part of the province of León. Already by the mid-sixteenth century a number of *maragato* families had established transporting operations on a relatively large scale. *Maragato* mule trains of ten to twenty-five animals brought fish and other goods from the Cantabrian coast to the annual fairs of Medina del Campo and other market centers of Old Castile, where they picked up grain and other surpluses for transport back to coastal and mountain areas. Eventually these enterprising Leonese transporters were seen in the far corners of the peninsula.[38] Figure 4 depicts the type of mule train that was typical of early modern Castilian transport.

The bulk of carting, like pack-transporting, was done by small part-time operators – farmers with a single cart, or with two or three carts. But some parts of Castile, particularly in the Burgos–Soria route, saw a growing professionalization of the carting business. Spain's carting transport industry gained special privileges during the reign of Ferdinand and Isabella, when an unprecedented amount of heavy transport was needed for the war against the Muslim Kingdom of Granada. By that time, artillery had become an effective component of siege warfare. That advancement in military technology enormously enhanced the value of carts, which were the only practical means of transporting bulky and heavy objects over land. In 1489, for example, the siege of Baza (Granada) required thousands of carts, pulled by some 14,000 draft animals. To ensure a dependable supply of carts and skilled drivers, Ferdinand and Isabella accorded the carters a special legal status and a number of privileges, allowing them to use common pastures for their oxen without paying local fees, and exempting them from certain local fees, taxes, and transit duties. Even if there was no nation-wide carting guild, as supposed by some historians, the carters' privileges were consistently recognized by the Castilian courts. In fact, landowners complained that judges' decisions were excessively favorable to carters. Governmental incentives encouraged the expansion of carting. This provided an ample supply of vehicles to rent, or to impress, at times of emergency. In 1636, for instance, the government was able to impress carts from Navarredonda (a carter town in the Sierra de Guadarrama) to transport grain to Madrid during periods of scarcity.[39]

In the sixteenth and seventeenth centuries, carts were the usual means of transport in areas with relatively flat terrain, whereas pack mules were preferable in hilly or mountainous zones. Carts typically traveled in functional caravans (cuadrillas or carreterías) of 20 to 30 vehicles, each caravan operated by a team of 6 or 7 men, with specialized assignments to oversee various aspects of the transport business. Each cart was normally pulled by a yoke of two oxen, making a total of perhaps 60 draft animals working at any given time. And the caravan was followed by an equal number of relief oxen, which alternated in the task of pulling the carts, plus some mules and donkeys for transporting men and supplies to town. Sixteenth-century Spanish carts were usually pulled by oxen. But mules were also used, both to pull carts and as pack animals, and with the passage of time pack-mule trains gradually took the place of carts. By the mid-1700s the

Fig. 4. Mule train and drivers on the road outside Jerez de la Frontera (Cádiz), showing primitive condition of roadbed. Detail from Georg Braun, *Civitatis orbis terrarum*, vol. I, no. 6 (Cologne, 1576–1618).

only parts of Spain where organized commercial carting remained the dominant long-range transport were Soria, Burgos, and Cuenca – all with unusually mountainous roads and a tradition of using oxen in agriculture. But carting as a rural tradition persisted much longer: individual peasants down to the twentieth century continued to use carts to transport their own goods.[40]

Peasant-transporters often followed the same route year after year, or even several times a year. Consequently, they became familiar with the local landscape, and they became acquainted with innkeepers and other local people along the way, looking forward to periodically renewed friendships. A Golden Age Castilian proverb celebrates these repeated human contacts:

> Somos arrieros,   (We are muleteers,
> Y nos encontraremos.[41]   And we shall meet again.)

But peasant-transporters could not always choose where they went with their mules or carts. Villagers, along with their carts and oxen or mules, were subject to being mobilized to serve the royal government in time of war or for other projects. We mentioned above the impressment of carts to transport artillery during the war with Granada and to bring grain to Madrid in the early 1600s. The Crown also ordered peasants to help transport artillery from San Sebastián (Guipúzcoa) to Tordesillas (Valladolid) to put down the Comuneros Revolt (1520–1). And to furnish adequate transport for the mercury mines at Almadén (Ciudad Real), the government recruited carters from as far away as Soria. Since carters by definition were accustomed to road travel, it was not considered an undue hardship to oblige them to work on projects far from their homes. Even so, because of the convenience factor, most transporters were probably from the district or region. For example, the government requisitioned hundreds of oxen and carts from villages around the Escorial building site. But many workers on the monumental construction project were recruited from distant provinces. A case in point is Alvaro Gutiérrez, a peasant-farmer from the village of Garrafe del Torío (León). We do not know how long he had been working in the Escorial building enterprise, but in May of 1581 Gutiérrez returned to spend four or five months in Garrafe, presumably to help with the harvest. Then he went back to the Escorial until June of the following year. At the time, Gutiérrez was no adolescent looking for adventure; he was a mature man of around forty. The document did not say so, but in all probablity, Gutiérrez went to the Escorial with a cart or carts. Although this gave him gainful employment, for which the government was supposed to pay market prices, Gutiérrez was probably a less-than-enthusiastic worker at the Escorial, because the Royal Treasury was notoriously slow to pay its bills.[42]

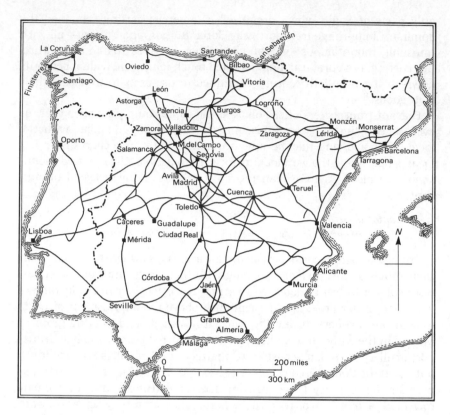

Map 5. Principal roads of Iberian peninsula, according to Juan de Villugas, 1546. Adapted from García Tapia (1989: 49).

MAINTAINING ROADS, STREETS, AND BRIDGES

It was essential to maintain the infrastructure necessary for the movement of goods and people that was so important to early modern Spanish life. The royal government realized this, and took steps to assure that the country's roads, bridges, and streets would be adequate for economic growth. But although the Castilian crown since the days of Ferdinand and Isabella actively sought to improve the kingdom's transportation facilities, it did not dip into the Royal Treasury for that purpose (unlike the French monarchy at the same time). Instead, the Spanish monarchs used royally appointed *corregidores*, judges, and other officials to see that the task was handled by the country's local governments. The transportation infrastructure, then, was the direct responsibility of the cities, towns, and villages with jurisdiction over the territory where the facilities were situated. And the people who were the principal users of the local roads, bridges, and streets, were supposed to build, maintain, and pay for them. The royal government merely exercised oversight authority.[43] Map 5 shows the principal roads of the Iberian peninsula in the mid-sixteenth century. The network was particularly well developed around the leading trading cities of the Castilian heartland: Burgos, Medina del Campo (Valladolid), and Toledo. But many lesser towns and cities were also well connected. The reader should be cautioned that the road system depicted by the map can be misleading: it does not, for example, reveal the transcendent role of Seville in Spanish and world trade; and of course it omits the vast network of local roads linking lesser towns and villages to the major urban centers.

Since medieval times the citizens of Castilian villages had been expected to participate in occasional communal work projects of benefit to the entire community. And it was usual for the local roads and bridges to be periodically maintained using this time-honored system of unpaid citizen labor.[44] But even in those simpler times, major construction projects involved expenses too great for the financial resources of most village governments, making it necessary to seek special revenues. These had to be approved, on a case-by-case basis, by the Royal Council (Consejo Real), the governing body empowered to grant licenses for building, repairing, and financing roads, bridges, and streets. The customary methods for funding such projects were extraordinary tax assessments (*repartimientos*) and special temporary taxes (*sisas*): the first were direct taxes, collected more or less equitably, depending on local practice, while the second were indirect imposts on foodstuffs. But the imposition of new taxes caused dissatisfaction, and even riots. Consequently, many places found it preferable to finance their building projects through bridge tolls or road tolls collected from those who actually used the new or repaired facilities. This might have been preferable to local inhabitants, but the user fees were resisted by outsiders – especially traveling merchants with their caravans of carts or pack animals – from the inhabitants of distant municipalities who thought it unfair that they should pay for someone else's bridge or road. Numerous lawsuits arose over questions of who should pay, and how much, for the use of these facilities.[45]

Maintenance was a never-ending task, and on the roads of a country as large as Spain there was always construction going on somewhere or other. During 1485, for example, at least eight major bridge projects were undertaken in Old Castile alone. But despite the efforts of the Royal Council to see that things were in good repair, many roads and bridges became unusable because of poor construction, inadequate maintenance, or natural disasters. There were frequent complaints, especially from professional transporters and important market centers, about impassable travel routes. For example, in 1593 the city of Valladolid informed the court that several of the roads in the region were in deplorable condition.

When apprised of such problems, the Council would instruct the local *corregidor* to order the appropriate village government to make the necessary repairs – a step often resisted at the local level because of the high costs involved, and because the locals felt that the repairs would benefit outsiders more than themselves. If the road or bridge in question was of obvious benefit to more than one village, the *corregidor* might orchestrate a collaborative effort. For example, in the first decade of the sixteenth century an expensive project to rebuild the road between Laredo and Burgos – about 150 kilometers in length – was financed by no fewer than twenty municipalities along the route.[46]

A far more modest project around 1570 involved a bridge spanning the Duero River. In this case, the village councils of Olivares and Quintanilla (Valladolid), located a quarter league from one another on opposite banks of the Duero, agreed to construct a stone bridge linking them. A bridge of wooden timbers would have been cheaper, but would have been more vulnerable to damage from normal weathering. Moreover, a wooden bridge was more likely to be swept away by periodic floods. The citizens of Leza de Río Leza (Logroño) learned this during a rainy period (1558–60), when their wooden bridges over the Leza River were destroyed twice by floods. After that, the municipal officials decided to rebuild using stone, but the expense was so great that they had to make financial sacrifices to fund the project.[47]

The governments of important market centers knew that it was important to keep their streets and public squares in good condition. That was not easy, because heavily loaded carts and animals were hard on the stone pavement. Testimony from Segovia in 1588 reported that maintaining these facilities was expensive, but essential, because it benefitted, not only the city, but also the villagers in the city's jurisdiction, who came "to sell their merchandise and other things ... particularly on Thursdays, which are market days." But although everyone recognized that it was a good thing to maintain roads and bridges, there were frequent disagreements about who should pay for what. This question led to a suit (1550) between the town of Almazán (Soria) and its surrounding villages. The municipal government of Almazán claimed that the villages should pay three-quarters of the cost of repairing two stone bridges spanning a local arroyo. The villagers refused, on the grounds that those bridges were in Almazán's territory, and should be financed by the taxpayers of Almazán. And the villagers asserted that they were responsible only for the upkeep of roads and bridges in their own territory. It was not that they made no contribution to repairs of mutual benefit, because the town and villages alike cooperated in maintaining the main bridge over the Duero River.[48]

The maintenance of roads and bridges was so important that municipal governments were willing to use force to collect the necessary funds. This often involved overbearing officials from a large town taking advantage of villages in the vicinity. Around 1573, for example, the town of Belorado (Burgos) sent a tax collector to raise funds in the village of Villaescusilla for repairing a bridge that was of benefit to residents of both. Although there was a suit pending on the issue of funding, and Belorado was not supposed to be collecting, a witness from the village testified that the official illegally seized a bushel and a half of wheat and a good cape from one resident, and a load of manure from another.[49] As far as the villagers were concerned, this was no trivial matter.

It should be said that there was no single standard for road and bridge construction. Spain's transportation infrastructure was a hodgepodge dating from Islamic, Visigothic, and even Roman times. Roads and bridges varied in width from one region to the next: the most common being 2.80, 3.50, 3.65, and 4.65 meters. Law II, Title xxxv of the *Novísima recopilación*, decreed by Ferdinand and Isabella in 1497, prescribed vaguely that the roads be "as wide as necessary" (*del anchor que deben*). Although in principle roads were suppposed to be surfaced with paving stones in the Roman fashion, in practice even the country's major thoroughfares were primitive. Seldom paved except when they passed through important towns and cities, in which case they became streets, in many places the so-called "roads" were merely well-trodden trails between towns. These unpaved roadways were arteries of dust when dry, and impassable quagmires when wet. It was not advisable to travel the roads during winter, because mountain passes were likely to be snowbound, and the lower areas frozen and muddy. In any case, the roads tended to have numerous alternative routes, to take when one way became unusable because of weather, or because of damage from traffic (the heavy oxcarts were particularly destructive to road surfaces).[50]

RURAL PEOPLE AND THE HABSBURG DEPRESSION

Traditional histories of Habsburg Spain, based upon writings of the *arbitristas* and other contemporary accounts, described the seventeenth century as a period of financial collapse, scarcity, and unmitigated misery in the rural world. Recent scholarship based upon documentary sources has modified this excessively negative view, without rejecting the concept of a depression. We now know that agrarian production diminished substantially in almost all regions of Spain during the first half of the 1600s, but the various regions did not follow the same timetable, nor were they equally affected. The economic crisis in Castile was especially severe, but even here there were different rhythms of decline and recovery.[51]

During the last two decades of the 1500s, rural folks lost much of their ability to buy manufactured goods in urban markets. Angel García Sanz describes the situation in the province of Segovia, but conditions were similar elsewhere. A growing rural population in the 1500s made it necessary to plant marginal lands, which caused average yields to decline. And as agricultural surpluses diminished, there was a corresponding drop in the standard of living of rural people. This slowly eroded the rural market for manufactured goods, and impacted negatively upon the cities. It was a vicious circle, because with the cities in decline, there was less demand for rural products, and it became more difficult for peasants to market their surpluses.[52]

The Spanish system of municipal protectionism, combined with the national mercantilistic policy, also had a negative impact on the economy. Price regulations, and import and export restrictions on almost everything, were designed to protect Spanish consumers and producers against outside competition. But in practice – despite widespread evasion of regulatory laws – these well-intentioned regulations helped ossify Spain's economic structures, perpetuating obsolete and inefficient technologies, making it difficult for Spanish producers to compete in world markets. Combined with a growing tax burden, exacerbated by chronic budgetary deficits, these governmental market restrictions crippled Spain's once vigorous economy. The result was an enduring economic crisis. By the 1600s, it was clear that Spain – once regarded as the richest and most daring nation in the world – was in serious economic trouble.[53]

The Castilian market network, centered around the fairs, had been a dynamic engine of prosperity during the first half of the sixteenth century, and despite occasional setbacks had continued to function well until the 1570s. But the complex system of exchanges in the Castilian fairs was based largely upon borrowed money. Bartolomé Yun Casalilla tells us that the enormous majority of transactions in the fairs of the Tierra de Campos, for example, were non-cash – that is, they were made on credit. Consequently, the apparently robust system was actually quite vulnerable: it could be severely disturbed by bankruptcies anywhere along the chain of exchange, because when one person was not promptly paid by his debtors, he might be unable to pay his creditors.[54]

During the last two decades of the sixteenth century, the Castilian peasantry began to experience increasing economic difficulties. No single factor was to blame, but rather an unfortunate confluence of negative circumstances: rising land rents; the sale of the *tierras baldías* (see Chapter 6); ever-higher taxes and seignorial duties (also discussed in Chapter 6); government price controls (the *tasa*); and the general price inflation all played their part. It might be noted that all of the aforementioned may be considered as factors coming from outside the village. Moreover, average crop yields dropped because farming had been unwisely expanded into marginal lands, and there was increasing individual indebtedness. All of this made it difficult for young people to get started in agriculture. The 1500s ended with plagues, bankruptcies, and general demographic decline, most acutely visible in the cities of Old Castile. Urban markets shrank, and the peasants reduced production. There seems to have been no Malthusian crisis, however, because the peasants continued to harvest enough food for themselves and the urban populations as well. The agrarian crisis involved structural changes, rather than a food shortage: the economic situation caused small and medium peasant operators to become less engaged than before in the market. There was a growing tendency for property ownership to be concentrated in the hands of rich farmers and urban investors who rented it to people who had to be content with a near-subsistence existence. Rural wages rose, but this brought no improvement in the rural standard of living, because of higher taxes and other unfavorable factors. The villages were faced with the problem of more and more non-taxpaying citizens and vagrants, and with increasing corporate debt.[55]

Recent scholarship tends to stress that the so-called Habsburg depression was really a period of readjustment. Actually, it was both depression and readjustment, as people found it necessary to adapt to new situations. Traditionally, one of the most important responses to economic crisis is population movement. And there is evidence of impoverished rural people deserting their villages during the seventeenth-century depression. But as Juan Gelabert observes, this was countered by a ruralization of Castile: from the late 1500s people left the cities and migrated to smaller centers of population. This migration, however, was not necessarily brought on by the economic crisis. Even in good times there had been substantial permanent migration between Castile's villages and its towns and cities. The state of the economy certainly influenced people's decisions about whether to remain in one place or to migrate, but it would be a mistake to think of migration as a simple reaction to economic conditions.[56] To the best of my understanding, the agricultural depression affected the rural habits of migration primarily by altering the destinations. Whereas during the heyday of the 1500s the cities and towns of Old Castile had attracted rural immigrants, in the early 1600s emigrating villagers went instead to Madrid, Seville, or America. But by the second half of the seventeenth century the Old Castilian economy had recovered enough to be again inviting to immigrants. And during this period there was an influx of villagers from Galicia and Cantabria. In Valladolid, for example, less than 10 percent of marrying couples were immigrants in the 1640s and 1650s, but by the early 1680s the proportion had risen to over 40 percent, of whom over a quarter were from Galicia. And the Galicians were immigrating not only into the cities, but by the end of the century also into the smallest villages.[57] By the end of the 1600s, in other words, the peninsular migratory patterns seem to have returned more or less to normal.

3

MANUFACTURING AND ARTISANAL CONTACTS WITH THE OUTSIDE WORLD

Winter can be quite cold throughout the central Spanish plateau, and it regularly becomes exceedingly cold in mountainous areas. The inhabitants of some mountain villages were effectively isolated from the rest of the world during the winter months because of impassable roads. And for weeks on end they might be unable to work in their fields because of bad weather. Many rural families used these periods of forced immobility to engage in artisanal manufacturing activities. In fact, manufacturing was an ideal solution for families that found themselves with a surplus of labor during slack agricultural seasons. The work kept the entire family busy, and produced goods that could be sold for cash in the spring. Thus manufacturing became a complement of agrarian production, integrated into the domestic economy, and widespread in the villages of Spain. The people of mountain villages were especially interested in this type of activity, because their hillside fields yielded meager crops, and they usually needed some type of part-time work to supplement their farm income.

CARTS, TOOLS, AND OTHER WOODEN ARTICLES

The inhabitants of northern mountain villages came to specialize in the manufacture of wooden articles which could be sold in the markets of the plains of Castile. These mountaineers not only had time on their hands when it was cold, they also lived near the raw material (wood from the local communal forests) for their work. And they already knew how to manufacture wooden items, because they made beds, tables, benches, and various tools and utensils for their own use. Thus, entering the business of producing things for market did not involve a major leap of technology, skills, or experience. One village where this type of manufacturing was practiced was Santa Cruz del Valle, a place of about sixty-seven families in 1567. Santa Cruz lay in the mountains of Burgos province, where snow might cover the ground more than half the year. Four citizens of the village reported that they carved wooden shovels (*palas*) to sell in the fairs of Belorado and Briviesca (respectively about 15 and 33 kilometers to the

48

north). One of these individuals was Juan Garrido del Campo, whose principal occupation was growing grain and raising sheep and other livestock. But Garrido must have spent a lot of his spare time making shovels, because he reported that he usually sold thirty shovels per year, at an average price of ½ real.[1]

The people of the Cantabrian mountains became famous for their production of carts, cartwheels, shovels, and other hand-made wooden articles. The village of Caso (Oviedo), for example, reported in 1586 that "most of its citizens" were in the part-time artisanal business of carving wooden plates and bowls. Since so many families in Caso participated in this activity, there was virtually no local market for these products. Consequently, the plates and bowls had to be sold in "Castile and other parts." Different areas specialized in other things. Valdeburón, for example, was a cart-producing area in the province of León. The typical sixteenth-century Valdeburón family constructed two carts each year to sell in the city of León or in the wheat centers of the Tierra de Campos in the Castilian plains to the south. The proceeds would be used to buy grain and wine, and other items that the family lacked.[2]

The cutting of trees to manufacture wooden items, on top of lumbering and cuttings for firewood, caused worries about the diminishing forest resources. Forest conservation had long been a concern in Spain, and had inspired both national and municipal regulations designed to protect the nation's woodlands. For example, the Cutting Ordinances (Ordenanzas de la Corta) of Puebla de Montalbán (Toledo) permitted citizens of that town to fell ash-trees to construct plows for their own use. But they prohibited the sale of plows to outsiders. Even in the relatively well-forested Cantabrian mountains there was concern about over-cutting. In the 1600s – and possibly even earlier – the municipal governments of the Liébana district (in the province of Santander) fixed a maximum of four pairs of cartwheels that each of its vecinos could make for sale in Castile, and another pair to sell in Liébana, besides an indeterminate number of smaller tools. The justification for restricting production was concern over the diminishing forest resources of the area.[3]

It was not only the villagers of Spain's northern mountains that specialized in the making of such things as carts. The people of Almansa (Albacete province) by the late 1400s had also developed an important industry for cart construction, both for local use and for export to other areas. There seems to have been considerable local specialization in that region, because at the time the neighboring town of Chinchilla had no cartbuilders of its own, and was obliged to purchase carts from Almansa or Villena for the war against the Moorish Kingdom of Granada.[4]

TEXTILES

But for centuries the most important artisanal manufacturing activity by rural Europeans had been the production of textiles. The women of rural families spun, wove, and made clothing from the wool of their own sheep. And under special circumstances – in winter, or when there was no agricultural work – even menfolk became involved in the production of textiles. Villagers also provided ancillary supplies such as dye plants and teasels for wool carding. And many peasants spun thread, or even wove cloth for an external market.[5]

Since medieval times, the textile industry had become quite strong in those parts of Spain specializing in raising sheep. Here many people spent part of the year effectively unemployed, because their herding labor was needed only during certain months. This seasonal labor surplus was employed partly in spinning and weaving. Textile production expanded rapidly in the late 1300s and 1400s, and by the 1500s had become a major national industry. There were numerous centers of rural textile production: around Seville, in the Sierra de Córdoba, in Ubeda-Baeza (Jaén), in La Mancha, in the mountains of Segovia, Avila, and Salamanca, in eastern Castile, and in the Sierra de la Demanda. Increasing numbers of families devoted themselves to textiles in the domestic system of production. For example, 34 of the 74 families of Alameda (Soria) reported that they had sold cloth of their own fabrication in the early 1560s. And Alameda was not a major textile center. Many rural families who worked in the textile industry probably came in contact with the market indirectly, dealing with a merchant-entrepreneur who provided the raw materials for them to finish in their homes. Undoubtedly textiles were produced in a variety of different systems, often coexisting in the same village. We get some evidence of this in a report from Leza de Río Leza (Logroño) in 1561, which said of the local people: "They make coarse cloth, colored and gray, for their own use and to get grocery money ... and some [people] work at carding and spinning wool for wages for citizens of Logroño and Nalda and Viguera, because if they did not do so, they would go hungry."[6]

In some places rural spinners and weavers were able to maintain greater independence by using their own wool, and selling their manufactures on a piece-rate basis. Bartolomé Yun Casalilla found this to be the case in the Tierra de Campos, where he encountered no evidence of anything resembling the *Verlagssystem*. Instead, the villagers of that area acted individually, purchasing wool, weaving it, then taking the cloth to market whenever they found it convenient. Francis Brumont's analysis of the household textile industry, similarly, shows village weavers as independent small-scale entrepreneurs who traveled considerable distances to obtain their raw materials, and to sell their finished products. In any case, the rural artisan usually had to depend upon a cloth merchant to market his products. We should not be surprised if the villagers who carded, spun, and wove were often exploited. Folkloric tales from the sixteenth century depict villagers cheated by unscrupulous wool dealers who used dishonest scales to weigh their production. The system left many peasants deeply in debt, as crop failures placed them at the mercy of merchants who marketed their cloth. The cloth woven in rural Castile was usually of low quality, destined for use by the peasantry and by the lower urban classes. High-quality cloth was usually imported, and unfavorable domestic conditions prevented Castile's rural weavers from adopting new technologies that might have made them competitive.[7]

The *Relaciones topográficas* show that it was quite common for the villagers of New Castile to be involved in textile production. For example, Getafe (Madrid) wrote that "what we make the most of in this village is coarse wool cloth and sacks for pack mules ... and no place in the Kingdom ... makes as much." And the inhabitants of Iniesta (Cuenca) reported that they purchased wool, which they worked to sell in the fairs of Ubeda, Baeza, Alcalá, Tendilla, and other places. There was a degree of specialization, even within textile-exporting towns. For example, the 1580 Tithe Register for Monteagudo (Cuenca) shows that wool producers usually were not weavers. But that should not be taken as typical, because a report of sales made in the early 1560s by the 74 citizens of Alameda (Soria) included 16 who marketed their wool, 18 who sold their woven cloth, and 16 who sold both wool and cloth.[8]

We should not think that these rural textile artisans were involved exclusively in manufacturing. There were some true specialists, to be sure, but the overwhelming majority were also involved in agricultural pursuits: they had grain fields, vineyards, and livestock of their own, or they were laborers on someone else's agro-pastoral operation. So their manufacturing activities were likely to be complementary, rather than primary occupations. For example, the mountain village of Montenegro de Cameros (Soria) specialized in raising sheep, which participated in the annual winter migrations to Extremadura. But many villagers were part-time weavers, and when the shepherds herded their sheep south, they brought some of the village's textile production with them, for sale along the way.[9]

We have another example from Mijas, a village in the province of Málaga: in 1528 Cepedo Benítez, from Mijas, paid another citizen of the village 20 *reales* for a loom. The following year he bought a second loom, for the same price. This enabled Benítez to take in thread from his neighbors, to weave into cloth. But he was not only a weaver, for he also had lands that he cultivated, and a rented olive grove. Thus, we may still consider Benítez to be a peasant-farmer, despite his non-agrarian activities. Even when a person was primarily involved in textiles, he was likely to prefer to think of himself as a farmer first, because farmers enjoyed greater social prestige. Thus, a citizen of Villavaquerín (Valladolid) who testified in a lawsuit in 1549 identified himself as a "farmer and weaver." But for all of that, it might have been *textiles* that gave this witness all of the cash that he had, because he and his family probably had little or no marketable agricultural surpluses.[10]

Most of Spain's textile production was based upon wool, which the country produced in great abundance. But many peasants grew flax, and wove linen cloth from which they made clothing, bedsheets, and other items. Producing linen was labor-intensive, requiring many time-consuming steps. But rural people did not shrink from that kind of work, because it made them more self-sufficient and it produced marketable goods. For example, in the early 1580s most of the forty-one households of Garrafe del Torío (León) spun thread from linen that they harvested from their own fields. One citizen of Garrafe, a certain Felipe García, was identified as a charcoal maker who had no flax field. Nevertheless, García participated in the linen business by purchasing flax from his fellow villagers to spin into linen thread, which he sold in the city of León. García's thread must not have been of the highest quality, because he was paid only 3 *reales* per pound, whereas his neighbors normally received 4 *reales*. Another resident of Garrafe was the widow Francisca Vélez, who died in 1583. The widow used to support herself and her four children with an annual planting of a small field of flax, which yielded a half cart-load of linen. From this she would spin 4 pounds of thread to market in León. She also did "other work" of unspecified character. But she planted no grain, and aside from the flax plantings the widow's only strictly agrarian activities were to keep four cows and an occasional small flock of sheep, which she would sell to get money to feed her cows.[11]

Woolens and linens were commonplace textiles. Silk was something special. The Moors had introduced sericulture into Spain, and under the Islamic government's encouragement and protection it flourished in Muslim Spain. After the Christian Reconquest silk production not only continued, but even spread into new areas. The most important silk centers of sixteenth century Spain were Almería, Barcelona, Córdoba, Jaén, Málaga, Murcia, Toledo, and Valencia. In the seventeenth century Seville also became a major silk producer, while Barcelona, Málaga, and Toledo declined in importance. The Moriscos (Spaniards of Moorish ancestry) dominated silk production until their expulsion, but Christian Spaniards also took up the business, and the late seventeenth-century decline of the silk industry seems to have been caused more by general economic factors and strangulating governmental regulations, than by the loss of skilled sericulturalists.[12]

Peasants – whether Moriscos or not – could readily turn to silk production, because it required a relatively small capital investment, and could easily be integrated into their existing farming routine. Silkworms needed close attention only during about six weeks out of the year, and most of the work could be performed by women and children. The weaving of silk cloth was a jealously guarded and monopolized urban activity, but the production of silk thread was an informal affair in which ordinary rural people played a major role. Many Spanish peasants were already accustomed to arboriculture, and could easily add a few mulberry trees, to feed silkworms. The mulberry is adaptable to a wide variety of conditions, and could be grown around the house, on the borders of fields, or even along the roadside. As a result, areas specializing in silk production became thick with mulberry trees, usually interspersed with other trees.[13]

Silk raising was an activity that involved the entire family. In the spring rural family members gathered mulberry leaves from their own trees, or they purchased leaves, to feed their silkworms. They were able to harvest the cocoons in summer, and normally spent the winter months transforming them into raw silk. This was an ideal activity for the people of the higher villages of the Alpujarras mountains of Granada, because they were often snowbound for several months at a time, and could do no field work. Some silk producers, however, sold their cocoons to professionals for processing in the city. Silk production could be highly profitable, and those who were successful at it could enjoy a relatively high living standard. This, in part, explains why Spain's Old Christians hated the Moriscos. Naturally, not all Moriscos were rich, but many lived well by intensively cultivating small farms, and the Moriscos habitually wore silk undergarments, despite the fact that silk was the most expensive cloth available.[14]

BREADMAKING

Another interesting type of manufacturing, open to inhabitants of villages located not far from large urban markets, was breadmaking (also mentioned in Chapter 2). For example, Tudela de Duero, a place with 479 households in 1553, had about a hundred families who baked bread to sell in the nearby city of Valladolid. Some of these household heads listed breadmaking as their sole trade, but many were peasant-farmers or day laborers, one was a carpenter, another was a miller, and so forth. It was often the wife, however, who actually baked the bread, while the husband was occupied with other work. Documents since medieval times show that breadmaking tended to be a feminine activity, so we should not be surprised to find women active in the trade. In general, however, it was highly unusual for women to be specialists in the artisanal trades. Females normally were relegated to a secondary role.[15]

A similar urban market opportunity transformed the people of Vicálvaro into bakers for the growing city of Madrid. By the mid-1600s Vicálvaro's major industry was breadmaking for the capital. And Pedro de Medina, writing in 1549, told of villages in the vicinity of Málaga that specialized in baking biscuits, presumably for provisioning seagoing vessels. But it was not just urban markets that rural breadmakers could tap. In 1540 a villager from Herguijuela de la Sierra (Salamanca) reported that he earned extra money by selling bread to the residents of outlying mountain areas where he made trips to buy goats. The Cortes (national assembly) recognized the importance of the rural breadmaking industry, and in 1579–82 supported the right of farmers to supplement their income in this way.[16]

WINEMAKING

One of the most widespread agro-artisanal activities was winemaking. Vineyards were almost ubiquitous in early modern Spain, and almost everywhere they were owned by small peasants. The reason for the widespread ownership of vines was that viticulture did not require large plots, and the work schedule of the typical Castilian peasant permitted caring for some vines, in addition to grain, which was almost everywhere the major crop. A small vineyard permitted the peasant to make his own wine, and perhaps even to sell some for pocket money. The great majority of wine producers were small operators primarily interested in self-suffi-ciency, and did not have much surplus to sell.[17] But there was considerable specialization in some parts of Castile.

Francis Brumont has calculated, for example, that in the late 1500s wine production was approximately 69 *cántaras* per household in the Rioja district. If we accept Brumont's estimate of an annual average consump-tion of 25 *cántaras* per household, the typical Rioja peasant had a surplus of 44 *cántaras* that he could market. Marketable surpluses were consider-ably larger in Monzón de Campos (Palencia), with a per-household produc-tion of 98 *cántaras*; in Grajal de Campos (León), with 120; and in Castrojeriz (Burgos), with 125! Since these are *average* figures, certain individual peasants had sizeable surpluses that they could sell. Even the combined village figures are impressive: four-fifths of the total wine production of Castrojeriz could be marketed without cutting into local consumption, and there were many other places in Old Castile with impressive marketable surpluses. Bartolomé Yun Casalilla estimates that around 40 percent of the wine production of Tierra de Campos villages was sent to market. It should be remembered that these were not areas dedicated exclusively to vineyards. Grain, in fact, remained the predomi-nant crop in terms of planted area.[18]

Where did this surplus wine go? In the heyday of the sixteenth century, largely to Castilian cities such as Burgos and Valladolid. If the peasant winemakers lived close enough, they might transport their vintages personally to the target urban markets. Otherwise, they could sell them in regional fairs, from which they would be taken to taverns in towns and cities needing to import wine. Because of the high costs of transport, most wine (like other rural products) went to taverns in the region of production. In the sixteenth century, for example, the primary urban market for New Castile's wine producers was the city of Toledo. When that city's consumption declined with its sharp population loss in the 1600s, Madrid emerged to buy the surpluses formerly drunk in Toledo. But despite the deficiencies of its transportation system, Castile's better wines often traveled considerable distances. For example, Madrid during the sixteenth century drew heavily upon wine centers of Old Castile, especially in the province of Valladolid, as well as La Mancha. In the seventeenth century, however, there was a distinct shift: Old Castilian wines now lost out to cheaper products from areas nearer to the capital. This shift occurred partly because wine producers who had formerly supplied Toledo now sent their stocks to Madrid.[19]

Winemaking was a complicated business requiring numerous skills. A successful producer not only had to care for and harvest grapes, but also to transform the grapes into wine; to store the wine properly (often demanding specialized carpentry and other crafts); and to transport the finished product to market. In other words, the successful peasant wine producer had to be an agriculturalist, a vintner, a craftsman, a transporter, and a merchandiser with entrepreneurial talents. These activities normally required contacts with buyers, transporters, and often also with absentee landowners, who entered into contracts with villagers to plant vines in exchange for a share of the harvest.[20]

CHARCOAL, FIREWOOD, AND LUMBER

Nearly every village in Spain had its communal woodlands or forest (montes) used primarily for pasture, firewood, and hunting. But these woodlands also provided rural people with the raw materials for numerous manufactures. Charcoal making was probably the most widespread. Many people who were involved in the trade were authentic professionals, but charcoal making was also a favorite sideline for peasant-farmers, especially the poorest ones, who needed extra income in order to survive. Lope de Vega in several of his plays depicted charcoal makers (carboneros) selling their products in cities like Seville. We have a factual example in a farmer from Mijas named Alonso Sánchez. In December of 1511 Sánchez sold twelve loads of charcoal to a blacksmith in Málaga. The blacksmith needed the fuel for his trade, and the farmer who supplied it earned cash to complement his agrarian income. In this case, Sánchez had made his charcoal in the nearby mountains, where there was a dense growth of brezo, a shrub whose hard wood and roots produced excellent charcoal. The foregoing examples are from Andalusia, but it should not be thought that charcoal making was an exclusively southern practice, for it existed throughout the peninsula. For example, in the province of Zamora, the residents of La Bóveda made charcoal in the woods along the Duero River, to sell in Medina del Campo. And the poverty-stricken peasants of the Mena Valley (Burgos) used charcoal making as an important sideline. Madrid, of course, drew charcoal from villages in a wide surrounding area, as Jesús Bravo Lozano's recent book on the subject attests.[21]

Perhaps it does not really belong under the category "manufacturing," but for many rural people cutting firewood was another convenient way to earn cash. Virtually all villagers used their local communal woodlands to obtain firewood for their own household use. And while they were at it, they could cut a little extra for sale to others in the village, or in nearby urban centers. The sixteenth century was a period of agricultural expansion, and the continuous clearing of woodland produced a steady supply of firewood for household use and for sale. Woodcutting required scarcely any capital investment beyond the tools that most rural families already owned: an axe, perhaps a pruning hook, and a donkey, mule, or ox-cart to transport the result of their labor. Some people were even able to support themselves exclusively by cutting firewood. In Lope de Vega's *Audiencias del Rey Don Pedro* the old woodcutter (*leñador*) Pedro Rubio says:

> I earn a living,
> Great Lord, for myself and my family,
> For I have a wife and children,
> By selling loads of firewood,
> With a tired old donkey.[22]

Of course, there was nothing to prevent the same person from producing both charcoal and firewood. A 1584 census of Garrafe del Torío (Burgos) included 40-year-old Felipe García, identified as a charcoal maker (*carbonero*) who sold both types of fuel in the city of León. The document indicates that García also farmed enough grain to feed his household for four months, and he grew some flax. But it seems clear that he gained his living primarily from selling fuel.[23]

A large city needed great quantities of firewood, and could provide steady work for many a woodcutter. Burgos, for instance, was supplied by villagers of the nearby Sierra de Juarros, who cut wood from mountain slopes and transported it to the city in ox-carts, even over poorly maintained mountain roads in the rain and snow of winter.[24] This was done voluntarily, by individuals taking advantage of the urban market. But powerful towns and cities could order their subject villages to supply them with firewood. After Madrid became the capital, the government regularly resorted to compulsory firewood exactions to supply the growing city's needs. For instance, in 1591 a royal order came for the village of San Sebastián de los Reyes (Madrid province) to cut and transport 2,000 *arrobas* of firewood to the Royal Palace. The village government protested that the local woodlands were not adequate to supply such a quantity. And the village officials may not have been exaggerating, because deforestation was indeed a problem in a wide radius around virtually all Spanish cities. And the *Relaciones* show that a shortage of firewood was not only an urban problem, but a common complaint of late sixteenth-century Spanish villagers, as well.[25] Despite municipal and national ordinances designed to protect forests and woodlands from overuse, cash-hungry woodsmen found loopholes enabling them to continue to cut trees, and there were widespread illegal cuttings. This led to countless arrests of individuals, and to protracted litigation between towns.[26]

The forests also offered an oportunity for lumber cutting. And many peasant farmers spent their winters working in the lumber business. The tithe records of 1580 show that 17 of the 69 households of Monteagudo (Cuenca) cut and sold cartloads of lumber, and an anonymous writer in 1607 reported that Cuenca's pine lumber was exported as far as Portugal. In some villages in the Liébana district (Santander), over a third of the *vecinos* were lumbermen. And according to the *Relaciones*, the people of Trillo (Guadalajara) specialized in cutting lumber which they floated down the Tajo River to market. There was also an important forest products sector in the area of the old Kingdom of Murcia: Alcaraz, Yeste (both in Albacete province), and Segura de la Sierra (Jaén) were centers which sent lumber down the Segura River and its tributaries, or down the Guadalquivir River system to Andalusia. Soria was also the scene of important lumbering activity. The lumbermen of Soria's villages banded together in a Brotherhood of the Pines (Hermandad de los Pinares), to regulate and coordinate the exploitation of the local timber resources. Already a venerable institution by the 1400s, this Brotherhood used its own carts to market lumber directly in Burgos, Medina del Campo, Valladolid, León, Zamora, and other urban centers.[27]

OTHER MANUFACTURING

The capital requirements of some types of manufacturing made it difficult for ordinary rural people to become independent producers. This difficulty, added to political and economic pressures, enabled wealthy nobles to dominate certain types of manufacturing or processing activities within the area under their jurisdiction. For example, Helen Nader tells us that the Mendoza family maintained on their estates in Guadalajara and Cuenca provinces a near monopoly on the local wine and olive presses, hemp mills, bakeries, forges, tanneries and tallow works, and grain mills. The Mendozas typically owned these facilities, and either rented them out on an annual basis or charged the local residents directly for their use on a piece-rate basis.[28]

The Mendozas were by no means the only Castilian nobles to invest in agro-related manufacturing enterprises. Seignorial lords typically maintained monopoly rights, or at least licensing authority, over many of these activities. Nevertheless, despite the existence of such restrictions, Castilian villagers found abundant opportunities to enter the market for manufactured goods. Inventories of the possessions of rural people show that they owned not only agricultural implements, but also tools related to numerous other trades. And these activities involved a substantial number of rural people. It is impossible to be precise about the proportion of villagers involved in crafts or artisanal activities. Early modern Castilian censuses do not consistently list professions, and even when they do, we cannot be sure that they include the full range of people's economic activities, because someone identified as a "farmer" (*labrador*) often had part-time non-agricultural activities, as we have seen. In the typical small Castilian plains village, perhaps 10 percent of citizens devoted a substantial proportion of their time to working at activities that were not strictly agro-pastoral. But as we have already seen, the proportion was often considerably higher in mountain villages. Even in New Castile, José Gentil da Silva found that about one-third of the active rural population were involved in light industries or service-related professions for urban markets. The larger towns and villages often developed an impressively variegated range of artisanal activities. The 1519 census of Alcalá de Guadaira (Seville), for example, listed no fewer than forty-eight artisan trades, most in traditional areas relating to construction, textiles, and leather. In addition to the items already mentioned, rural people produced many other things for the market: soap, cheese and butter, clay pots and jars, roof tiles and bricks, various articles made of straw and linen, and forged iron – to name just a few.[29] Most of these are things that we would expect to be produced in a pre-industrial rural society. There are some surprises, however: the mountain village of San Andrés de Juarros (Burgos) had a small factory (*molino de papel*) that manufactured paper, which the owners took to market in Burgos and Medina del Campo. There must have been other similar paper manufacturers, in different parts of the country. Perhaps this is the place to mention that sumac (Spanish *zumaque*) was an industrial crop (used in the tanning process) that was a favorite of the poorer inhabitants of villages where leather was an important product.[30] But we must not forget that, despite everything, raising crops and animals was the overwhelmingly predominant economic activity in pre-industrial villages. Figure 5 depicts Basque villagers bringing goods (apparently including some manufactured products) to market.

A widespread artisanal manufacturing activity was soapmaking, which was practiced among rural households both for their own use, and for sale. The manufacturing process was not complicated. It consisted of mixing

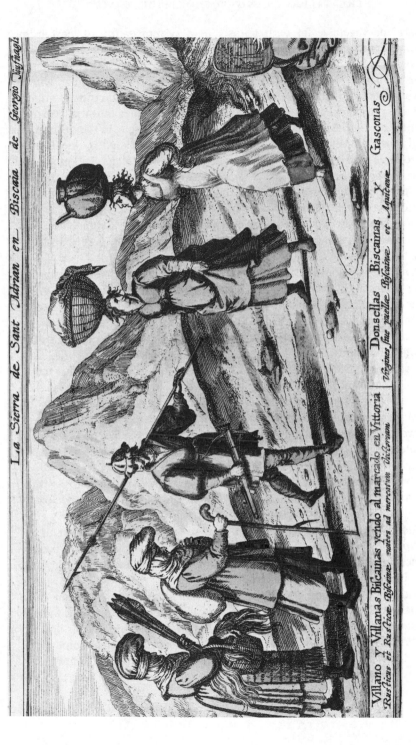

La Sierra de Sant Adrian en Biscaia de Georgio Juffragia

| Villano Y Villanas Biscainas yendo al mercado en Vittoria | Donsellas Biscainas Y Gasconas |
| Rusticus et Rusticæ Biscainæ euntes ad mercatum Victoriam. | Virgines siue puellæ Biscainæ et Aquitenæ |

Fig. 5. Basque villagers carrying goods to market in Vitoria (Alava). Detail from Georg Braun, *Civitatis orbis terrarum*, vol. 3, no. 16 (Cologne, 1576–1618).

animal or vegetable fat with potash, in a system dating at least from Roman times. In early modern Spain the potash was obtained from wood ashes, and the fat from olive oil. Because ashes were essential to the process, it was necessary to make fires in the nearby woodlands, which were protected by local ordinances. The whole process was strictly supervised by municipal governments, often both at the village or town level and at the level of the dominant city in the area. For example, in the 56-household town of Mijas (Málaga), soapmaking was regulated by local ordinances, as well as by the ordinances of the city of Málaga. In Mijas only officially designated soapmakers (*jaboneros*) were allowed to manufacture the product, and even these were forbidden to make fires (for ashes) without a special license. It appears that the soapmaking business was over-regulated in Mijas, because local production did not suffice even for the community's own needs, and it was necessary to import soap from nearby Alhaurín.[31]

A simple way for rural people to obtain cash was to gather, process, and sell resources that were at hand naturally. Wild stands of esparto grass grew in the saline and semi-saline soils of central and southern Spain. Since Roman times this grass had been used in the making of rope, mats, and other items. Peasants (down to the late twentieth century) who had no agricultural work could occupy themselves by gathering and preparing esparto grass. Often they themselves worked it into rope, or woven pieces. In 1504, for example, a citizen of Mijas named Ginés Alonso traded eighty esparto pieces (*enpleitas de esparto*) that he had woven to a straw merchant in Málaga in exchange for a donkey. Alonso was not solely an esparto-weaver, because he also had grain fields and vineyards. But he must have devoted considerable time to esparto, because he made several sizable esparto deals in 1504.[32]

A rather similar activity was the gathering of broom (*retama*). A census of Cazalegas (Toledo), which had 218 households in 1561, included eight individuals identified as broommakers (*retameros*). Unfortunately, the document does not indicate whether these were also involved in agropastoral activities. But it is highly likely that they were, because broom gathering and making would have been an ideal part-time job for peasants who had spare time on their hands.[33]

Some places gained considerable regional prominence for what they manufactured. For example, the *Relaciones* report for Getafe (Madrid) boasted: "what we make in this town better than anywhere else is drilling bits for cartwrights and other woodworkers, because people come forty and fifty leagues for them, made by an artisan named Muñoz, and he is almost as famous for his hoes."[34]

ITINERANT RURAL CRAFTSMEN AND ARTISANS

The artisans and other specialists in small towns and villages often could not find enough business to support themselves and their families where they lived. Consequently, they had to find additional clients by taking to the road, traveling to other places. The villages of Castile were periodically visited by various itinerant specialists.

One of the most important of these was the shoemaker. Not many small villages could provide enough business to support a full-time maker and repairer of footwear. Yet, there was a need for that kind of specialized artisanal work, and this need was often met by itinerant cobblers who traveled from village to village. Hernand Albarez, for example, was a shoemaker who lived in Melgar (seemingly Melgar de Tera, in Zamora province). But he traveled several times a year to Congosto (about four leagues away), and to other villages in the area that needed his services. Shoemakers like Albarez seem to have taken living quarters wherever they happened to be working. We can gather this from a 1630 census of Villanubla (Valladolid), which lists a cobbler named Cristóbal de Arenas among its residents. At the time of the census, Arenas was out of town, but the census takers noted that he kept a house in Villanubla, and that "sometimes" he came to work there.[35] A favorable geographical setting might make it possible for a village of modest size to have several shoemakers. For example, a census of 1577 showed Ampudia, a community of barely 500 households, as the home of *nine* shoemakers. This concentration of footwear specialists was possible because Ampudia lay 20 kilometers from a sizable market town (Palencia) and less than 30 kilometers from a major city (Valladolid). Even so, only three of these shoemakers kept shops in Ampudia – the others were constantly on the road, looking for work in neighboring villages. It is understandable that rural people were eager to obtain the services of a shoemaker. Small and isolated villages might even try to attract one by offering special incentives. Thus Pineda Trasmonte (Burgos), a place with thirty-four households in 1597, reported that it did not require shoemakers who practiced their trade in the village to pay the sales tax (*alcabala*).[36]

Blacksmithing was another trade that was likely to put its rural practitioners on the road. Whereas wood had been the normal material for tools in the Middle Ages, by the sixteenth century improved agricultural technology had made iron a common component of farming implements and tools. We know that some farmers repaired their hoes and other tools themselves, using communal village forges. And they probably even fashioned some of their own tools. But iron toolmaking required practiced skills, and blacksmithing became a specialized trade that was much in demand in the rural world. Censuses made in 1569 of the village of Morales de Toro (Zamora) listed among its inhabitants a blacksmith appropriately named Pablos Herrero (*herrero* means smith, in Spanish). But the documents were careful to stipulate that Herrero did not have citizenship (*vecindad*) in Morales. He had come there only temporarily to earn a living with his forge. He was a citizen of Villavendimio, and intended to return there. One of the censuses noted that Herrero also worked in other villages of the area.[37] In some villages the blacksmith was paid in grain rather than in cash, and was expected not only to work iron, but also to function as a combination farrier and to do basic veterinary tasks as well. The services of smiths and farriers were so essential to the rural world that small villages were willing to guarantee a minimum salary in order to attract one.[38] That being the case, we should not be surprised to find these country artisans taking jobs in villages other than where they were born. That was the case of Pascual Merloque, a farrier (*herrador*) hired by the council of Peñaflor de Hornija (Valladolid). Both Merloque and his wife were natives of Rueda, over 30 kilometers to the south. We can speculate that he may have been a former itinerant artisan, and that he settled down in Peñaflor when offered a full-time job there.[39]

Another activity that was widespread among rural people was carpentry. Farmers regularly kept saws and shaping tools such as chisels and adzes (most likely made by specialists from outside the village), so they could make or repair agricultural implements or furniture, and for general work around the house and farm. Since it was not unusual for farmers to have some experience with carpentry, it is not surprising that many of them became part-time carpenters during their off seasons. This typically required leaving the village, to go wherever there was work. Alonso Hernández del Ladrillar, for example, was a peasant-carpenter from the village of Alberca in the mountains of Salamanca province. In the early 1500s he worked on carpentry projects in various communities of the area, often aided by his son.[40]

What was a sideline for some farmers could become a full-time profession for others. That is what happened to Diego Bayón, a farmer from Garrafe del Torío (León), a village with about forty households. In 1579 Bayón was a typical peasant-farmer, working his fields with two oxen of his own – the average draft team of the day. That year he harvested 8 *cargas* of grain, an amount insufficient for the needs of his household. Bayón also harvested a cartload of flax, from which he (and his wife, presumably) spun 4 pounds of thread that he sold in the city of León. But farming does not seem to have suited Bayón, because he abandoned agriculture the following year and left the village. His wife remained for a time, but soon also departed to take a job as a servant in León. Bayón himself became an itinerant carpenter, working wherever he could find a job. But in the summer of 1585 Bayón and his wife both returned to Garrafe to live. And the census of 1586 reported: "He is a man who lives from carpentry. He owns neither ox nor cow, nor does he harvest any grain." Having tried his hand at farming and

Fig. 6. Country blacksmith at work outside Marchena (Seville province). Detail from Georg Braun, *Civitatis orbis terrarum*, vol. 2, no. 3 (Cologne, 1576–1618).

linen production, Bayón ended up as a full-time professional carpenter who was apparently successful in supporting himself with his trade.[41] Even so, Bayón as a professional carpenter would have had a highly mobile working life, going to wherever there was carpentry to be done. Village censuses often mention such artisans, who lived in the place only until their job was finished. We learn, for example, from a 1586 census of Castrillo de las Piedras (León) that a carpenter named Pedro Juárez spent four months working on the local priest's house. The census does not reveal where Juárez was from, but it was careful to specify that he was *not* a citizen of Castrillo, and that he no longer lived in the village.[42]

Rural people were quite resourceful at supporting themselves and their families, often moving to a different village with better job opportunities, or working at several trades, or even changing trades. But almost everyone retained some involvement in growing crops or animals, and not many people found it possible – or even desirable – to specialize in their artisanal activities. For example, the aforementioned Bayón was not the only carpenter in the village. Seventy-year-old Hernando Gutiérrez was also identified as a carpenter. But Gutiérrez kept three cows, planted some flax, and apparently sometimes harvested some grain. Another peasant-craftsman in Garrafe was Blas García. A census of 1584 describes him as "a blacksmith who lives from his trade. He harvests no grain, because he doesn't plant any, nor does he raise any animals whatever." But García lived with an unmarried sister who helped him with his blacksmithing and who cared for a flax field that yielded half a cart of linen per year, which they spun into 6 pounds of white thread to sell in the city of León.[43]

OTHER SPECIALISTS

Cervantes described two other itinerant rural specialists in *Don Quixote*. One was a swinegelder, who traveled from place to place looking for animal owners with pigs to castrate. In the story, the swinegelder announced his arrival by sounding a reed pipe four or five times as he approached a place where there might be prospective customers. The other Cervantes character was a barber from a village on the slopes of the Sierra Morena. The barber not only served his own village, but also a smaller neighboring settlement that had no resident barber. In the *Quixote* episode the barber traveled on a gray donkey (like Sancho's), carrying a shiny brass basin. He was on his way to the smaller village, to shave one customer and to bleed another. In historical reality, the traveling barber was probably a regular visitor in rural Castile. Francis Brumont found that to be the case in the province of Burgos, where village councils would pay a barber (in grain, rather than in cash) to render services on a specified day of the week. Elsewhere in Castile it seems to have been more common for villages to pay barbers a cash salary, but throughout the rural world it was a widespread practice to share a barber and other skilled professionals.[44]

Castilian villages arranged to share the services of a university-trained physician (*médico*) in much the same way. Anastasio Rojo Vega's recent book about the sixteenth-century Castilian health system tells us how village communities went about contracting the services of a physician. A village that needed a health-care professional, and that possessed the financial resources to hire one, would send a representative to the nearest university city. There the village representative would contact a prominent physician or professor (*catedrático*) at the school of medicine, who would recommend one of his associates or students for the job. A contract would be drawn up, and duly notarized, outlining the newly hired country doctor's responsibilities and salary. The doctor was to be paid out of income from municipal property (*propios*), revenues which could not legally be disbursed without specific royal permission (a requirement fortunate for historians, because it resulted in the preservation of village–doctor contracts among state papers in the archive at Simancas).[45]

The contract between the *licenciado* Juan de Salas and Santo Domingo de Silos (Burgos) in 1555 suggests the type of career that a country doctor could expect. Salas, the son of a peasant family in Gumiel de Hizán (also in Burgos province, 30-some kilometers southwest of Santo Domingo) agreed to serve a three-year term as physician and surgeon for Santo Domingo and also for neighboring Hortezuelos, Hinojar, and Peñacoba. He was expected "to go to those places and see the sick as many times as he was called, and to examine the urine of all of them [an expected medical procedure at the time] without charging a fee." And except for responding to these outlying village calls, Salas was not to leave Santo Domingo for more than a day at a time. In return, he was promised a substantial annual salary (30,000 *maravedís*), the free use of a house, exemption from local taxes, guaranteed salary even in the event of disability, and the right to offer his services (presumably for extra pay) to the monasteries within a three-league radius. Moreover, Salas was also to be provided four ox-carts (with drivers, to be sure) for the purpose of moving his family and furniture to his new place of work.[46]

Poorer villages could not offer such generous terms, and might share a physician with other communities within a day's mule ride. Or, as in the case of Laguna de Duero, a doctor from the city of Valladolid (only 6 kilometers away) was paid to come to the village for consultations every Thursday. It is easy for us to understand why university-educated physicians normally had practices that included patients in more than one place. But in the society of the day, other less-educated health-care specialists also often plied highly mobile careers. Dentists, for example, tended to be as itinerant as barbers. And even folk-healers (*curanderos*), particularly those who attained a measure of notoriety, extended their clientele by traveling from one place to another.[47]

This chapter demonstrates that the inhabitants of Castile's villages had substantial and continual contacts with the outside world through a host of household manufacturing and artisanal and service activities. Ironically, it was often the people of stereotypical "isolated mountain villages" who were the most profoundly engaged through these activities into the economy of the nation at large. Here again, the Castilian historical reality turns out to be quite different from the hypothetical "immobile village."

4

IN-MIGRATION AND OUT-MIGRATION

THE SPANISH TRADITION OF POPULATION MOVEMENTS

By the sixteenth century Spain had a long tradition of population movements. The eight-century-long Christian Reconquest of Muslim territories produced a rural population accustomed to migrating to new areas, and to moving anew, when conditions dictated. Towns and villages established during the Reconquest were founded upon sites chosen for defense. These were not always the most suitable peacetime locations, and after the danger of Muslim attack was gone, many settlements were deserted in favor of new sites that were more convenient to water and other resources. Some of the new locations, in turn, had to be abandoned when it turned out that they were unhealthy (the lower valleys were fertile, but prone to malaria). So there was a continual shifting of the population, not only as the Christian border moved southward, but also within the older Christian-ruled territories. And in the sixteenth century – and even in the seventeenth – some villages were in the process of being deserted, while others were being founded, presumably on better sites.[1]

An example of a village that was losing population, during a period of general demographic expansion in Spain, was La Mina, a settlement in the jurisdiction of Talavera de la Reina (Toledo). It appears to have disappeared in the interim, because I have been unable to locate it on a modern map. The fate of La Mina was already in doubt at the height of Spain's Golden Age. A census of 1575 showed 26 households; but during the next three years 5 men, 1 widow, and 3 propertied orphans (*menores*) died; and in addition, 1 entire family emigrated; and 12 other individuals left the place. The largest group of emigrants were young people who moved to neighboring villages, married, and settled down there.[2] Another example of a village in the process of dissolution was Villalaín, under the jurisdiction of Aguilar de Campos (Valladolid), in the rich grain-producing Tierra de Campos. At the beginning of the sixteenth century Villalaín had been a thriving community of around forty families, but by 1526 most of its adobe-walled houses were crumbling and its population was reduced to a single family. At mid-century Villalaín was only a memory, its former neighbors fighting over its territory. This happened during the boom period of one of the most dynamic parts of Castile. And the fate of Villalaín was by no means unique: Bartolomé Yun Casalilla's map of the Tierra de Campos in 1530 shows over forty ghost villages at a time of full economic expansion. The people of these extinct villages had not died; they had simply moved to better locations. Therefore, we should not bewail their fate, because they participated in a shift to a more rational distribution of population, and in all likelihood they were better off after having moved.[3]

Map 6 offers a graphical depiction of patterns of in- and out-migration from the village of Santa Cruz (Toledo). Though Santa Cruz has now disappeared, in 1579 it was a vibrant community of nearly 200 households. Censuses of 1575 and 1579 show that people were continually moving into and out of Santa Cruz. Most of this migration was to and from other villages within a radius of 30 kilometers, but there was also long-range population movement in both directions. The 1579 census listed 46 outgoing people, and only 29 incoming new residents. The differential may be partly explained by biases in reporting, but it certainly suggests the ultimate disappearance of Santa Cruz. Unfortunately, although the village is mentioned several times in other *Relaciones* accounts, its own report has not survived (if, in fact, it was ever filed).[4]

Ferdinand and Isabella's conquest of the Kingdom of Granada, of course, opened new areas for Christian colonization. And the expulsion in 1571 of Granada's Moriscos (about whom more in Chapter 7) was followed by a repopulation program in which settlers were brought in to occupy the lands and homes confiscated from the Moriscos. Contrary to popular myth, the settlers allotted the ex-Morisco property were not principally from Galicia: they came from all parts of the peninsula, but mainly from the south. Of the 545 families who resettled the Upper Alpujarras: 208 were from Andalusia; 104 from Castile; 34 from Extremadura; and only 135 were Galicians. In the Almanzora Valley over half the settlers were from southeastern Spain, and there were no Galicians at all. And in the Lecrín Valley over 46 percent came from Andalusia, 28 percent from Castile, and only 11 percent from Galicia.[5] Probably it was the fabled Galician mobility that gave rise to the myth of Galician predominance in resettling Morisco lands in Granada.

Because of its proximity, the area supplying the greatest number of settlers for Granada was the Upper Guadalquivir Valley. This part of Spain had a highly unstable demographic history. Social geographer Higueras Arnal concluded that the chief characteristic of the area's population from the thirteenth to the twentieth centuries has been instability, because of endless currents of migration. In the sixteenth century most of this migration was downstream, to cash in on the economic boom in Seville

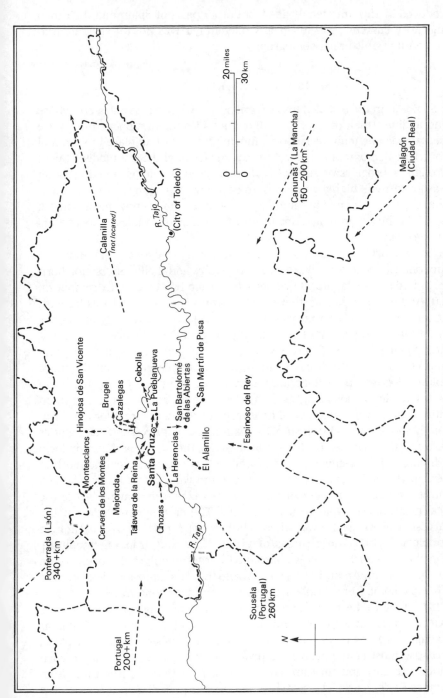

Map 6. In- and out-migration from Santa Cruz (Toledo), 1575–9. According to 1579 census in AGS, EH, 382. • → = out-migration; • ← = in-migration.

produced by the American trade.[6] But other parts of Spain had their own migratory currents, so the Upper Guadalquivir was not an aberration in the country's historical demography.

MIGRATORY FARM WORK

In Spain, as in the rest of Europe, rural people who were landless, or whose landholdings (their own, or rented) did not adequately support them, were likely to become migrant laborers, moving from place to place in search of work. The demographic growth of late medieval and early modern Spain brought a progressive subdivision of property holdings, making small peasant-farmers highly vulnerable to economic hard times. Many found it necessary to become part-time day-laborers to make ends meet. And all too often they eventually ended up in the ranks of landless day-laborers (*jornaleros*).[7]

The proportion of landless laborers varied not only over time, but also from one village to the next. There were also regional differences: northern Spain had proportionately fewer *jornaleros* than La Mancha, Extremadura, and Andalusia. Whereas there were many villages in Old Castile with virtually no *jornaleros*, that was not the case farther south. By the 1570s an estimated 60 percent of rural family heads in New Castile were in that class. Spain's landless laborers were an unstable group: with little or no property to tie them to one location, they were perpetually on the move looking for work. Day-laborers (*jornaleros*), despite the name, were contracted for various lengths of service ranging from a single day to an entire year. But the most usual arrangement was a contract for the duration of some seasonal task such as grain or grape harvest.[8] Their salaries were strictly regulated (in theory, at least) by the Cortes and also by local ordinances. For example, Iznatoraf and Villanueva del Arzobispo (both in Jaén province) not only established maximum wage rates for day-laborers, but also attempted to prevent migratory workers from leaving before the local grain harvest had been completed.[9] The prompt completion of the harvest was a goal everywhere, but it was particularly urgent in Andalusia, with its large areas of grain, olive, and grape monoculture. And the Andalusian harvests attracted hordes of migrant workers from northern Spain. An author in 1631 wrote that "an almost endless number of people come from Castile, La Mancha, and Extremadura."[10]

Extremadura became famous as a source of migrant labor in the sixteenth and seventeenth centuries. A citizen of the village of Palomas (Badajoz) in 1575 reported that it was difficult to collect taxes in the place, "because most of the people are poor, and they go to Andalusia to earn enough to eat, and they are gone most of the year." An account from Zamora in the early 1600s tells a similar story, of poor peasants of the area leaving their homes, wives, and children immediately after planting their fields, to spend the winter working in Andalusian vineyards and olive groves, returning home to harvest their grain. Extremaduran migrant workers came to have an unsavory reputation, notorious for their gambling, thieving, and violent behavior.[11]

But Extremadura was by no means the country's only source of migrant labor. In Spain, as in other parts of Europe, peasants from mountainous areas took to the road to become migrant laborers when winter weather made local agricultural work impossible, or when there was little to do at home. In Santander's Liébana district, for example, small peasant operators left their mountain villages each spring and fall to seek salaried work in the Castilian plain.[12] But not all northern migrants entered the labor markets of Castile. Some went even farther afield to find seasonal jobs. For example, a 1586 census of Hornillos (Logroño) listed several small peasants who left their homes every winter for work in the Kingdom of Valencia. One of these was Sebastián Domínguez, who farmed with a broken-down horse (rocín) and a cow, and ordinarily harvested 25 fanegas of grain on his land. But this was not sufficient to support his wife and three children, so Domínguez spent his winters in Valencia pruning vines, as did many other small peasants in the Rioja district.[13]

In La Mancha grain farmers recruited workers from the north to harvest their crops. But here, as in all places, there were day-laborers from the region who also participated in reaping and other field operations. When seasonal laborers were from nearby villages, they were more likely to include women. The ordinances of the Cortes of Castile-León make numerous references to women field workers working alongside the menfolk. But these local field hands typically had to be supplemented by outside labor because of the need to get the crop in promptly before loss to weather, spoilage, birds, or other factors. In some places the reapers (mesegueros) were paid one-tenth of the harvest, a practice designed to encourage careful and speedy work.[14] Fortunately, differences of geography varied the date of harvest (and other essential operations) from place to place. This facilitated seasonal migratory labor, as it permitted not only landless day-laborers, but also small farmers of one area to become temporary salaried workers in another part of the country. The grain farmers of the La Sagra district of Toledo province, for example, came to expect that harvest time would bring an influx of people from the northern part of Castile, especially Valladolid, Palencia, Soria, and Burgos, and also from Galicia.[15]

Regardless of what part of Spain they were from, migrant laborers far from home tended to be an unruly lot. In 1566 officials of the village of Alpera (Albacete) complained that the migrant reapers who came to the place were mutinous and quarrelsome, often causing disturbances and even knifings, among themselves and with the locals.[16] And it was not only Spain that supplied migrant workers for Spanish agriculture. During the sixteenth and seventeenth centuries there were annual migrations of French rural workers, especially to Catalonia, but also as far afield as La Mancha. And villages in western Spain were likely to include Portuguese – many as *mozos de soldada* (described in Chapter 5), others as seasonal workers.[17] Chapter 7 will devote more space to the presence of foreign workers in Spain.

MIGRATORY HERDING

Transhumant herding is well known, thanks to the prominence of the royal Mesta (association of livestock owners), which receives the attention of virtually all historians dealing with the period.[18] But writings about the Mesta normally concentrate on sheep, wool, governmental policy, taxes, and property rights. The human element in migratory herding is usually given short shrift. That is unfortunate, because long-distance herding had a major impact on the shepherds who were involved, and on their families who remained behind. For example, in the 1590s most of the menfolk of the sheep-raising mountain village of Montenegro de Cameros (Soria) departed each fall to lead the annual sheep migrations to Extremadura. That left the village with no butcher shop from All Saints Day until the end of May, and the villagers who stayed behind were reduced to eating dried meat and salt pork (*zezinas y tozino*) from their own household stocks. The extended annual periods of male absence not only affected the eating habits of mountain villages; they also skewed the chronological distribution of marriages and births.[19] And it was not men alone who followed the itinerant herds, for boys and even girls might accompany their fathers.[20] These mountain villagers who regularly traversed the peninsula, thereby coming in contact with new people, new places, and new ideas, were essential for the continuation of what is called "traditional" and "stable" Spain. The migratory shepherds, of course, led highly *un*stable lives, although their existence did have a certain regularity, and one might even say stability, because of repeated migrations along the same trails.

And it should be said that shepherds led a migratory existence not only when engaged in trans-peninsular transhumance, but also when they practiced a local type of pastoralism within the district where they lived. The very nature of leading animals to pasture is migratory. Furthermore, the shepherds themselves frequently changed their place of residence. This is clearly manifested in censuses from the period: they often list resident shepherds born in other villages, or they comment on the itinerant life style of pastoralists. For example, the 1559 census of Miranda de Duero (Soria) identifies the village cattle herder as one Mateo Sanz, who claimed to be a citizen of the place. According to a witness from Miranda, however, Sanz actually resided a bowshot down the road in Rabanera del Campo, a neighboring village where he and his wife had rented a house. And the

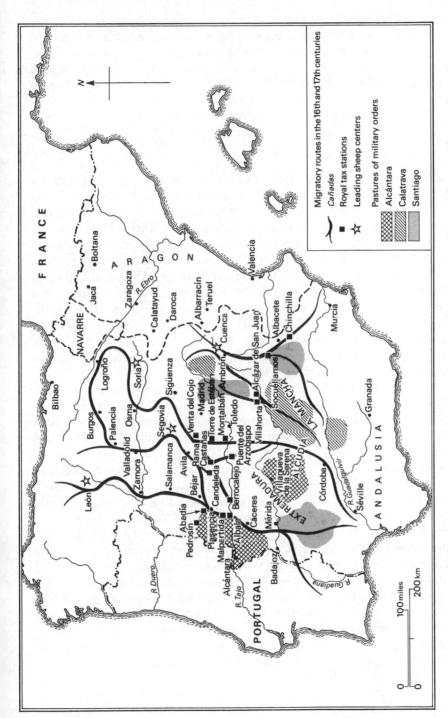

Map 7. Trans-peninsular sheepwalks (*cañadas*), sixteenth–seventeenth centuries. Adapted from Le Flem (1982: 51).

witness depicted Sanz as "a man who comes to live for a while in one place, and then in another, and ... always moving about." Another category of highly mobile rural worker who dealt with animals was the *guarda del campo*, who was hired by the local government to keep grazing livestock out of the village grain fields. In 1575, for example, the *guarda del campo* of Montearagón (Toledo) was one Juan de Rea, a Galician who had arrived only seventeen days before the census was made.[21]

MIGRATION TO AND FROM CASTILIAN TOWNS AND CITIES

Many rural people made their way into towns and cities, not only on temporary marketing outings, but to look for jobs, and to live there. It was a matter of necessity for early modern towns to attract immigrants, because urban birth rates before the nineteenth century seldom exceeded death rates. Thus the towns and cities required a continuous influx of newcomers in order to maintain existing population levels, let alone grow. The immigrants who supplied this need were overwhelmingly villagers from the surrounding rural countryside. In Braudel's words, there was a "standard stable partnership ... between a poor rural region with regular emigration and an active town."[22] Thus Madrid and other urban centers played a prominent part in the life strategies of Castilian villagers. Figure 7 symbolizes the influence of the capital – newly proclaimed, in the year 1566, over the villages of central Spain.

The best study of rural–urban migrations in early modern Spain is David-Sven Reher's recent book on pre-industrial Cuenca, a small urban center similar to dozens of others in Spain. Though most of Reher's data is post-sixteenth century, it is clear that the patterns that he describes had been established long before. In urban Cuenca, over 25 percent of all couples between 1563 and 1700 were non-natives. Most migrants to Cuenca came from surrounding villages, but a substantial minority (25–40 percent) hailed from other provinces. Reher found that opposite ends of the social spectrum were the most likely to migrate. But whereas day-laborers were invariably migrants from nearby villages, people in the professions and in the service sector were likely to come from greater distances – almost half of these were from outside the province. Madrid and other larger urban centers, because they offered greater employment opportunities, were even more likely to attract long-distance migrants. Thus we should not be surprised that Juan Navarro, a tavern keeper (*bodegonero*) from El Puente del Arzobispo, on the western edge of the province of Toledo, by 1561 had emigrated to Córdoba; or that a young man from Ibrillos (Burgos) in 1575 was living in far-flung Jaén.[23]

Leslie Page Moch's recent book demonstrates that pre-industrial European society was highly migratory, and that population mobility was the norm, rather than the exception. Reher in his study of Cuenca agrees

Fig. 7. Detail from 1566 drawing showing Aldea del Fresno, Brunete, Villamanta, and other villages between Madrid and the mountains to the west-southwest. Depicting roads, rivers, mountains and woodlands, with Madrid in the upper-left corner.

that "intense [population] movement was probably the hallmark of pre-industrial urban society in Europe." That was certainly true of Cuenca, where well over 10 percent of the urban population entered the town yearly, in normal times. And the flow of rural people into town was balanced by an equally strong counterstream migration. People circulated between the town and its rural hinterland, highly sensitive to economic and demographic changes, looking for jobs, marriage partners, or better housing arrangements. These circulatory population movements linked urban and rural household economies and families. Over the long haul, when acute subsistence crises made rural life difficult, migrants tended to fill the town; and when urban employment opportunities dried up, they returned to the rural hinterland.[24]

The villagers most likely to emigrate were unmarried young people, especially younger sons who were not designated to inherit the family farm. Because of the economic boom in Seville, Andalusia was a favorite target of migrants, even from as far afield as the Cantabrian region. Many young men from villages in this area migrated to Andalusia to spend three or four years working in urban taverns or shops, before returning home with a bankroll to get established in their native district.[25]

INTER-REGIONAL MIGRATION

But in-migration and out-migration was not only a phenomenon involving cities and villages. Everywhere we look in medieval and early modern Castile, when the documentation exists to permit us to see what was happening in people's lives, we encounter evidence of substantial migration from one part of Spain to another. Not merely from villages to urban centers, as we would expect, but also migration from village to village and from one region to another. We should not find this surprising: when migratory shepherds, seasonal farm workers, peasant-transporters and marketers, and itinerant village craftsmen and artisans traversed the peninsula they became aware of opportunities to relocate in other parts of the country where farmland, pasture, and permanent jobs were easier to find than in their birthplace. Unfortunately, we are unable to know the full extent of this type of migration, because the marriage and funeral registers which would document it are rarely complete before the end of the sixteenth century.[26]

Castilian peasants since the Middle Ages had been alert to differences between villages, and to the fact that some places offered better conditions than others. They were ready to move when they saw that they could improve themselves, and did not hesitate to use the threat of moving to convince overbearing landlords or seignorial masters to lighten their obligations. We can see the importance of inter-village migration in Oña (Burgos), where Francisco Ruiz Gómez estimates that immigrants made up between 15 percent and 20 percent of the population during the 1300s and 1400s. Most of the newcomers were from villages in the same district, but by the end of the 1400s increasing numbers of immigrants came from more distant locations.[27] Although the details are not clear, the situation appears to have been similar in villages around Seville and Talavera de la Reina (Toledo).[28]

Because of the difficulty of sources, few studies exist to document peninsular migratory movements in the 1500s. But Rafael Torres Sánchez finds evidence of substantial sixteenth-century long-distance immigration (mostly from other Castilian provinces) into Cartagena (Murcia); Ofelia Rey Castelao demonstrates that Galician migration to the far parts of the peninsula was a fact of life in the sixteenth and seventeenth centuries alike; Alberto Marcos Martín confirms that there was important migration to Andalusia from northern Spain in the 1500s; and Juan E. Gelabert and Ignacio Atienza Hernández find evidence of peasant migration from royal to seignorial lands in Castile. Jordi Nadal hypothesizes that the late sixteenth-century economic crisis encouraged a current of emigration from Spain's center to its peripheral provinces, and further research may well bear that out, but intra-peninsular migration was clearly a phenomenon of good times as well as bad.[29] We should not regard population movements as evidence of societal dysfunction, because in many respects it gave proof of a society's ability to adapt to changing conditions, and to make better use of its resources.

The existence of in- and out-migration as a normal structural characteristic of Castilian society is enunciated nowhere more clearly than in Reher's book on Cuenca and in the collaborative work by Mercedes Lázaro Ruiz, Pedro A. Gurría García, and Arturo R. Ortega Berruguete for Logroño. Both of these important works prove that our vision of pre-industrial agrarian society has been far too static. They demonstrate that regular emigration of early modern villagers into medium-sized towns such as Cuenca and Logroño was a vital component of the equilibrium between resources and population, and that out-migration from the urban centers was a necessary counterpart maintaining the balance between town and country. Lázaro Ruiz et al. found that rural immigration into Logroño was continuous during the period that they studied (1600–1822), *quite independent of general economic fluctuations*. The impact on the town's population was enormous and ongoing: throughout the period studied about a third of the heads of family living in Logroño were immigrants, and there is every reason to believe that previous centuries were much the same. Immigration into Logroño followed the usual pattern: most newcomers were from surrounding villages or from the same province; but all of northern Spain was represented, especially the Basque country and Old Castile.[30]

MOBILITY AND EDUCATION

Life-cycle service (discussed at length in Chapter 5) was often another form of rural migration – temporary and permanent – to towns and cities. Far less common, but occasionally appearing in village censuses, was rural–urban migration for educational purposes. It was a rare village lad in early modern Spain who was able to pursue higher education. In his study of the educational system of Habsburg Spain, Richard Kagan found that the vast majority of university students were from urban backgrounds. Spain's rural hamlets and villages, although containing over 80 percent of the country's total population, contributed only a tiny proportion of its students. There were numerous reasons for rural Spain's gross under-representation in university halls. A daunting initial handicap for villagers was that training in Latin was a requirement for university entrance, and Castilian villages rarely had a grammar (i.e., Latin) school. A country boy was lucky to have any kind of schooling at all, and if there was a local teacher he was hired to impart literacy in Castilian, rather than Latin. For a young man to go from a village background to a university under those circumstances required extraordinary effort, and probably the financial support and encouragement of some outsider who recognized his scholastic potential.[31] That being the case, perhaps we should be surprised that there were any villagers at all in Spanish universities. Their number certainly was not sufficient to justify the warning of the *arbitrista* Lope de Deza, who wrote in a book published in 1618: "Many robust youths abandon agriculture for university law schools, where they take on effeminate habits, whereas their fathers are rustic farmers, and they ridicule the simple food and dress of their homes, thinking that they have improved themselves by rejecting the virtuous rustic life that provides food for everyone."[32]

It was a far-fetched exaggeration for Deza to suggest that farm boys going to universities was a factor in the decline of Spanish agriculture. But, in fact, local records occasionally mention a village youth who has gone to a university. The 1575 census of Ibrillos (Burgos), for example, lists a widow named Isabel López, whose son Diego was a student at the University of Salamanca. But Diego was no ordinary village lad: he was a brother of the village priest, who must have been quite well-to-do, because his household included five servants. Another widow, in the 1589 census of Puebla del Príncipe (Ciudad Real), also had a son who was a student: he had been in Valencia for the past ten years. In the last case there is no evidence that the household was unusually prosperous, but it must have been expensive to pay for ten years of schooling in another part of Spain. Nevertheless, some village families managed: even in the 1600s, when rural Castile was supposed to be suffering economic recession, we find sons of seemingly ordinary village families who left home for university study.

In Los Balbases (Burgos), for example, in 1612 there was a youth who had left the village to pursue higher studies, and in the 1640s a young man from a rural family in Fuentes de Nava (Palencia) was attending the University of Valladolid. The last was from a *prosperous* family: in rural areas, as in the cities, you were not likely to become a university student unless your family had money.[33] Nevertheless, the idea of a penniless village lad working his way through a program of university studies (as did the protagonist of Cervantes' *El licenciado Vidriera*) was not completely outlandish.

What became of early modern village youths who had the advantage of a university education? – an interesting question that would merit further study. Since I have not seen many documentary references to such people in village documents, I would guess that proportionately few of them returned to their home towns. Instead, they used their education as a springboard for upward socio-economic mobility, which almost inevitably required geographical mobility. There were exceptions, however. Juan de la Herrán, the young man in the previous paragraph from Fuentes de Nava, returned to his village and used his training in law to manage his family's farming business. There must have been many like him, among village elites throughout Spain. Sara Nalle found that the better families of Cuenca's villages often sent their sons to the university, and that many of them eventually returned to their birthplace.[34]

But if a country boy with a university degree settled in a village, rather than in the more exciting environment of a large town or city, it seems likely to have been a village other than his own. We have as an example Juan de Salas, son of a peasant family in Gumiel de Hizán (Burgos). Salas studied medicine at the University of Valladolid, then in 1555 moved to Santo Domingo de Silos (also in Burgos province, some 30 kilometers northeast of Gumiel) to serve as physician for that village and surrounding communities. Perhaps he eventually returned to his home town, but he did not likely do so to practice medicine, because he had an excellent position in Santo Domingo.[35]

Village families with ambitions for social advancement often encouraged a son to enter the clergy. In the first half of the sixteenth century this did not require much formal education, because the lowest order of the priesthood required no more than literacy in Castilian and a knowledge of the church's basic prayers. But even such elementary training was not always available in the village setting. Although the sacristan of every village was supposed to teach basic literacy, as well as prayers, to the local children, this diocesan requirement was usually honored in the breach unless the village government offered to pay a supplementary salary. The small villages that contained the bulk of the rural population could not afford organized schools, and the schools that existed in larger and more prosperous villages were notoriously inept. Consequently, village children who learned to read and write (a minority in early modern Spain) usually picked up these skills from a helpful neighbor or from an itinerant teacher. Because of the meager opportunities for learning in the village, many boys destined for the priesthood traveled to a nearby town or city for their basic schooling, often financed by a benevolent seignorial lord, prosperous local citizen, or bishop. After the reforms of the Council of Trent (1545–63) it was increasingly expected that the clergy should have university-level training, which often involved moving to yet a different town or city.[36] Chapter 8 examines the impact of clergy upon village communities.

As we have indicated above, the inadequate educational opportunities at the village level forced many rural youths to leave home. But some of the larger villages did have schoolteachers. Cervantes knew this: he has Don Quixote advise Sancho Panza (I, 25) to have an important letter recopied in a good hand "at the first village you come to where there is a school-master, or if not, any sacristan will copy it." In historical reality, some sacristans and priests did attempt some basic teaching, but since many priests themselves were barely literate, this was usually on a haphazard basis. To remedy the situation a village of several hundred households might hire a schoolmaster to give lessons to children who wanted to learn. Typically, the village council would enter into a contract with a teacher to come and provide instruction during a specified period (normally a year), in exchange for a modest salary. Since these villages had no such thing as a schoolhouse, the local government would designate for that purpose the local church, the teacher's house, or a building owned by a local religious brotherhood. When the person paid to teach was the local sacristan, as was often the case, the village church became a makeshift schoolroom. A large room was not necessarily required, because few peasants placed a high value on booklearning. They might agree that schooling was a good thing in theory, but in practice they often kept their children away from school. Formal schooling interfered with the rural work requirements, in a society where rural children were expected to participate in the family's productive activities. In such a setting, village schoolteachers had a frustrating life, underpaid and often unappreciated. They tended to move from village to village in search of a place where they could earn a respectable living.[37]

BANISHMENT AND VOLUNTARY EXILE

The use of banishment as punishment for criminal offences produced another type of migrant in early modern Spain. Since the Middle Ages, if not before, Castilian communities had often dealt with adulterous wives, bigamous husbands, and other such violators of societal norms by simply running them out of town. But in sixteenth-century Castile, banishment was even used to punish people guilty of more serious offences such as rape and murder. Michael Weisser found that judges in the villages of the Montes de Toledo *never* applied the harsh sentences prescribed by the national legal codes. Rather than calling for execution, or a term in the galleys, the magistrates dispensing village justice relied upon fines and periods of banishment as the usual penalty for crimes. And these sentencing judges were not villagers displaying leniency toward their neighbors: they were invariably members of the ruling elite of the city of Toledo. This mild treatment of convicted criminals may have been a regional aberration. Although Weisser insists that the harsh penalties of the official law codes were not uniformly enforced *anywhere* in the realm, there is evidence elsewhere in Castile of thieves being flogged and maimed, as well as exiled.[38]

In my examination of village census records I have encountered numerous references to persons serving periods of exile. Although I lack sufficient data for a statistical analysis of banishment, my overall impression is that it was somewhat unusual but by no means rare for a rural community to have one of its own natives living in exile, or to have an outsider residing in the village during a term of banishment. For example, in 1559 the widow Catalina Ximénez was serving a term of exile in the ten-household village of Miranda de Duero (Soria), where she had spent the past three years with three daughters and a son. The widow was a native of the equally small community of Rabanera del Campo, where she was a citizen and property owner. But she had been banished from her home town for a period of six years, for having caused the death (in an unspecified way) of her son-in-law. In this case, the place of exile lay a scant kilometer from the malefactor's home. Nevertheless, banishment obviously made life difficult for Catalina Ximénez, because in Miranda she was living in a hut on land owned by the seignorial lord of the place, while she probably owned a regular house in Rabanera. Moreover, the widow's reputation would have preceded her, and we can be sure that she was not the most respected resident of Miranda.[39] Another village with female exiles was El Puente del Arzobispo (Toledo), where Ysabel and Ana López were living in 1561. These two sisters had been banished from Oropesa, a dozen kilometers to the north. The document does not reveal why the pair were driven from their home town, but it describes them as unmarried and "poor with no property." The two must have had some source of income, however, because at the time of the census they lived in a house in Puente del Arzobispo.[40]

The foregoing examples were of exiled women. But banishment was by no means a punishment reserved for females. For example, in 1631 one of the citizens of Villar de la Yegua (Salamanca) was Francisco García, a household head with a wife and four children. Three years later García's family were still living in his house in the village, but García himself was absent: he had been banished (unfortunately, again for an unstated offence). And banishment was a punishment not only applied to natives; it was also used against outsiders: in 1552 a Portuguese subject living in Olivenza (Badajoz) was banished for two years for illegally plowing lands in the village of Valverde.[41]

Banishment was a type of migration forced upon people who would have preferred to remain at home. There was also a *voluntary* type of exile, of people who left their own communities because they felt that remaining would bring excessive social stress, or problems with creditors or with the law. Some of these were children who had disobeyed their parents; others were people who had fallen hopelessly in debt. Since medieval times a girl who married against the wishes of her parents often left her home town to migrate with her husband to a new community. Similarly, an eloping pair might find it wise to leave town and seek a new place to live, away from parental wrath. And couples who wanted to marry contrary to canon law could migrate to another place, and start a new life where people did not know them. During the medieval Reconquest, Castilian communities were eager to attract colonists, and were willing to accept new citizens without asking too many questions. Background checks would undoubtedly reveal that many of the migrants of Golden Age Castile were also escaping the restrictive norms of their home towns.[42]

The fear of imprisonment for non-payment of debts was also a powerful incentive for people to leave town. We know that in periods of hard times many villagers abandoned their homes and farms and migrated to a city or to another part of the country because they were unable to pay their debts.[43] Consequently, no one will be surprised that village censuses of the early 1600s often list people who fled to avoid debt imprisonment, frequently leaving their families behind. A 1612 census of Los Balbases (Burgos), for example, includes two examples of debt-provoked migration: one man who left the village; and another who sought refuge there. The first was Pedro Díaz Camargo, who abandoned his wife and child in Los Balbases and departed for an unstated destination in the company of his children from a previous marriage. The second was Luis García, who came to Los Balbases because he could not pay his debts in Villamoñico (Santander), where he had a wife and children.[44]

But it would be a mistake to think that fleeing to avoid debts was something that happened only during times of economic crisis, because even in the best of times there were individuals who, through bad luck or poor management, could not make ends meet, and who borrowed more money than they could pay back. In 1586, for example, the Rioja hamlet of Negueruela was fast in the process of disappearing because its menfolk were leaving the place to get away from seemingly unmanageable debts. And even during the mid-sixteenth century Castilian economic boom we find recently abandoned wives and families, many undoubtedly left by husbands who could not meet their financial obligations. We will never be

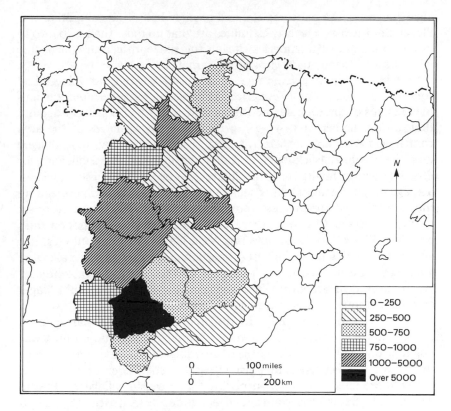

Map 8. Provincial distribution of official emigration to America, 1493–1559.
Adapted from Le Flem (1982: 23).

able to calculate the proportion of migrants motivated by debts, however, because we do not consistently have financial statements for the people involved.[45]

EMIGRATION TO THE INDIES

The lure of America, and the chance to strike it rich, induced thousands of rural Spaniards to leave their villages to seek their fortune across the Atlantic. The demographic impact of this trans-oceanic migration was visible enough to cause concern in the Castilian Cortes and in the writings of *arbitristas*.[46] But migration to America in the sixteenth century was certainly not of mass proportions, because Castile experienced continuous general demographic growth until the plagues of the last decade of the century. And that was even true of Extremadura and Andalusia, the regions most affected by trans-oceanic emigration. We will never know exactly how many Spaniards went to America, because the official lists (of legal emigrants) were incomplete, and possibly half of all emigration was illegal. But the best scholarly estimates are that no more than 250,000 to 300,000 emigrated to America during the sixteenth century, at a time when Castile's population was around 7 million.[47]

Certainly, there were some regions of Castile where most villages had someone who had gone to America. Mercedes Borrero Fernández examined records of the Aljarafe and Ribera districts west of Seville, and found that during the period 1493–1539 each of the 27 villages of the area contributed emigrants for America. The records show that 207 villagers from the two districts left for America (but as indicated above, allowing for illegal crossings might raise the figure to 400). Official lists show an average of 7.67 emigrants per village over the 46-year period, meaning that a person left one of these communities for America about every six years, on average. Of course, there were widely varying emigration rates between villages, no doubt reflecting local conditions and attitudes. But even the villages with the highest proportion of emigration (even allowing for illegals) did not lose enough people to make an irrecoverable impact on the local demography. In fact, the most important emigrant villages enjoyed continued population growth during the period.[48]

We can readily understand why the area around Seville (the center of embarkation for America) was a major source of emigration. But it was not that unusual for northern Castilian villages to have a household or two whose numbers were diminished because the father, or a son, had "gone to the Indies." It is not surprising that a coastal village like Puerto de Santoña (Santander) contributed emigrants to America. In a 1578 census[49] 5 of Santoña's 118 households had someone gone to America, or in the American trade. And 9 additional households had boys or men who were simply "absent" (*ausentes*). Some of these had probably also crossed the Atlantic. And it was not only maritime areas that provided emigrants to the New World; inland villages also contributed to the stream of people (exclusively males, in the censuses that I have seen). About a quarter of the "*ausentes*" in Liébana villages (Santander) had gone to America. And Morales de Toro (Zamora), a place with 250 *vecinos* according to a census of 1569, had 5 men or boys who had gone off to war, 4 who had gone to America, and one "gone off to war or to the Indies ... nobody knows." The language of the census suggests that some of the absent young men had planned a common form of illegal emigration to the New World: would-be emigrants signed up for military service simply to get free passage, planning to go AWOL or to jump ship at the earliest opportunity. In fact, desertion rates for soldiers and seamen sent to America were so high that this form of illegal emigration sometimes exceeded legal emigration.[50]

Whether they went legally or illegally, most villagers who left for America were lost to the home community forever, and the families of many would never learn what became of them – unfortunate, because many emigrants left wives and families behind. A lucky few would return in triumph, enriched with loot from Mexico or Peru. But despite the difficulties of communication, people who remained in the Castilian homeland communities through networks of friendship, kin, and business associates were often able to become surprisingly informed about events in America. Ida Altman found that sixteenth-century Extremadurans eagerly sought out news from the Indies. And they learned about people and events on the other side of the Atlantic through direct contacts with returnees or through letters that they or someone else had received from emigrants. In this way certain individuals who had never left Spain became local experts to whom people would go for information about America. The sense of familiarity with the overseas colonies that Extremadurans gained through such information sources encouraged continued emigration. In Altman's words, many Extremadurans thought of the New World "not as an isolated and remote enclave of the royal domain but ... a significant extension of the arena in which they could function to pursue opportunity and advancement for themselves, their families, and their compatriots."[51]

Not only in Extremadura, but throughout Castile the emergence of America as an opportunity provided an important psychological stimulus for a population that already considered it perfectly normal to leave home to seek one's fortune. The New World expanded the career possibilities that had already existed in Spain, and enormously broadened the geographical parameters of Spanish mobility. The Spanish colonial enterprise did not affect Castile as dramatically as it did Mexico and Peru, but to a large extent the New World and the Iberian motherland functioned for three centuries as parts of an interconnected Hispanic society that changed the lives of everyone, whether they crossed the Atlantic or not.[52]

5

FAMILY RELATIONS WITH THE OUTSIDE WORLD

LIFE-CYCLE SERVICE

Another source of in- and out-migration was life-cycle service, a period of domestic employment for adolescents before they assumed the responsibilities of adulthood. Not only in Spain, but throughout Europe in the early modern period, a substantial proportion of boys and girls went through a period of domestic service as a phase in their lives before coming of age. Usually these adolescent life-cycle servants hired themselves out to rural families in neighboring villages. They performed both household duties and farm labor, primarily the latter.[1] From the standpoint of the employer, it was often better to hire live-in servants than to have to recruit casual labor during planting and harvest time. These child-laborers not only worked for their keep, but also earned a small salary which could be sent home to parents, or accumulated over the years to serve as capital needed for marriage. The wages were exceedingly low for the youngest children, who were scarcely worth their keep, but rose with increasing maturity and usefulness. These young servants were highly mobile, often moving from village to village, and from master to master with each passing year. But for most of them, service was a temporary phase in life. After reaching adulthood they went on to take their places in the community as self-employed farmers or artisans who themselves might hire young life-cycle servants.[2]

In the streets of El Toboso before dawn one morning, Don Quixote and Sancho Panza met a life-cycle servant (*mozo de soldada*) on his way to plow his master's fields. The youth was an outsider (*forastero*) who had arrived only a few days earlier to enter the service of a rich farmer (*labrador*).[3] The scene described by Cervantes is an accurate depiction of the historical reality. Life-cycle service was a normal feature of rural life in Spain, and one of its most salient features was geographical mobility. That is clear in a 1582 census of Espinosa de la Ribera (León), where 12 of 15 live-in servants were from outside the village. And in Villanueva del Camino (Seville) 22 of the 30 life-cycle servants in 1565 were outsiders.[4]

The overwhelming majority of employers of life-cycle servants were relatively prosperous farmers (*labradores*). The situation depicted in a 1587 census of Santa María de Vigo parish of Souto de Vigo (Pontevedra) is fairly typical. Eighteen of the parish's 64 households included live-in servants. Fifteen of the 18 employers were *labradores*; the others were a priest, a shoemaker, and a laborer (*cavador*). A similar situation is portrayed in a 1586 census of Fuentepinilla (Soria), where 36 heads of household had servants. Of these employers 18 were *labradores*, 2 were priests, 6 were merchants, 5 were artisans, 4 were in the service sector, and one was unspecified. Economic data in the Fuentepinilla census clearly indicates that it was the wealthier people – even among *labrador* households – that tended to have servants, and the most prosperous often employed several servants.[5]

If anyone in a village had a servant, it was going to be the priest. It was considered normal for a priest to employ a housekeeper (*ama*). And he often hired other servants (more often female than male), and perhaps had some relatives living with him, as well. The household of Father Domingo de Ybarguena, for example, parish priest of Fuentepinilla (Soria) in 1586, included a male and a female servant in addition to a housekeeper. And in Ibrillos (Burgos), Father García de Carredo had three maidservants (all from outside the village) and three male servants (also all from outside Ibrillos), including a nephew identified as a son of the priest's brother Juan, from Bascuñana. Many priests had young "nephews" or "nieces" living with them, the paternity of these children often uncertain.[6]

It appears that a stint in domestic service was often a necessity for the children of rural families identified on censuses as "poor," especially the children of widows who could barely eke out an existence. Economically straitened parents often pushed their children into domestic service to lighten the drain on the family budget. Not only would this relieve the family of the expense of feeding and clothing the absent child, but the family might also arrange to receive a portion of the child's salary. Some life-cycle servant contracts assigned up to two-thirds of the salary to a parent or grandparent. And the parental share was sometimes even greater. For example, in 1582 a girl working in Abelgas (León) sent her entire salary back home to her mother in Torre de Babia, a practice that she apparently had been following for the previous eight years.[7]

If the family needed hands for its own productive activities, the children would probably remain at home. But if the children were from indigent households, or if they were the children of day-laborers (*jornaleros*), or were otherwise not needed at home, they were likely to enter service. Pascual García, for example, a day-laborer from Castrillo de las Piedras (León), was a widower left with four sons, one of whom – presumably the oldest – he had placed in service in another town. And widows, who tended to be financially disadvantaged, were likely to send their children into service while still minors. María López, for instance, a poor widow who lived in the *hospital* of Viloria de Rioja (Burgos) in 1575, had both of her children in service: a daughter in another town, and a son in Viloria.[8] In Morales de Toro (Zamora) in 1569 there were numerous cases of widows doing this. One widow had three children (two boys and a girl), all in life-cycle service "to earn for her and for themselves." Another widow had two sons, "and she had them with her sometimes, and at other times they were off earning their keep ... [because] they owned no property." It was also quite common (we can see several examples in Morales) for remarried people to send children from previous marriages (often an embarrassment to their new spouses) off to work as life-cycle servants in another village or town. Francisca Morena was such a child. She was born in La Mina (Toledo). But after her mother remarried, Francisca ended up in service in Talavera de la Reina.[9]

Many rural families took in poor relatives, who performed household and agricultural tasks similar to those done by paid servants. The host family may have acted partly out of clan solidarity, but also exploited a convenient and inexpensive labor resource. Widows who remarried often sent children from their first marriage to live with a paternal grandparent, or other kinfolks. Mari Sánchez, for example, from Montearagón (Toledo), did this with a daughter.[10]

In some instances, juveniles joined their own relatives' households as salaried workers. A priest's "nephew" was mentioned earlier, but his status was ambiguous. We can provide many other examples of kin-servants, however. In Estépar (Burgos) in 1553 Juan Delgado's household included a 23-year-old *mozo de soldada* who was identified as Delgado's own brother. In 1559 in Miranda de Duero (Soria) the grass widow Madalena Marco had as a live-in "hired servant" (*criada a soldada*) her young niece Pascuala. And in 1578 a maidservant in Juan del Casuzo's household in Santoña (Santander) was Casuzo's own illegitimate daughter.[11] But even legitimate children might be treated as servants. For example, in Frandovínez (Burgos), when the widow of Alonso de los Moços was asked whether she had any servants, she replied "No, because her two sons and daughter [ages 22 to 14] served her." Spain was certainly not unique in the confusion between kin and servants, because the children of late medieval English families were also often classified as servants within the household.[12]

In some households, a niece or nephew, a grandchild, or some other relative would take the place of a child who had left home, perhaps for life-cycle service in some other location. The replacement kin provided companionship to alleviate the "empty nest" syndrome, to be sure, but they undoubtedly also helped fulfill the household's labor requirements. As a case in point, look at the situation of Pedro de Villadiego, a citizen of Viloria de Rioja (Burgos) in 1575. At the time, Villadiego and his wife had no children of their own at home: a son and a married daughter had moved away, and no longer lived in Viloria; and Villadiego had placed two other daughters in service – one in Belorado, and the other in Burgos. But the Villadiegos had a young grandchild (*un nieto, niño chiquito*) living with them, a son of their married daughter.[13]

It appears that these taken-in relatives were treated neither as children, nor as servants, but sort of in-between. They were fed and clothed, and were expected to work, but were not necessarily paid a salary. For example, a 1580 census of El Cubillo de Uceda (Guadalajara) lists one Alonso de Maricoste, whose household includes the widow of his brother Miguel, with the observation that she had been working for him for many years without a labor contract (*concierto de soldada*). On the other hand, a 1559 census of Miranda de Duero (Soria) lists the previously mentioned grass widow Madalena Marco, who was being helped through an illness by a niece from Borjabad (12 kilometers to the southeast) as a *criada a soldada*.[14] A somewhat similar situation is that of orphans, identified as *menores* in early modern censuses. An orphan who lived in the household of his or her guardian (*curador* or *tutor*) might have been little more than a servant, in practice. This is explicit in some censuses. For instance, in Espinosa de la Ribera (León) in 1582 the widow Leonor Alonso had two young sons living with her. She also had two daughters, but they no longer lived with their mother, for they were "in service with their guardians outside the village."[15]

Life-cycle service could begin at a tender age. In Viloria de Rioja (Burgos) the household of Juan de Zaballos in 1575 included "a little shepherd to care for the lambs." We are not told how old this *pastorcito* was, but the diminutive is revealing. Although life-cycle service typically began at around age twelve, I have documentary evidence of children leaving home to begin work as hired servants as young as seven, and as old as twenty.[16] Unfortunately, censuses rarely give the ages of servants, so obtaining such data is problematical. But censuses from Fernancaballero (Ciudad Real, 1576) and Cordovilla (Salamanca, 1629) suggest that over half of all servants were pre-teens or teenagers.[17] The length of time spent in service varied with the age of initial employment. Some served only a couple of years before marrying and settling down as adult members of the community, whereas others continued in life-cycle service for 15 years or more. A 1582 census of Abelgas (León) listed eight servants: one had already worked for 8 years; two for 5 years; three for 4 years; one for 1½ years; and one for 1 year. And a 1580 census of Jubín (Orense) included eleven servants: one had served for 6 years; two for 2 years; three for 1 year; four for ½ year; and one for an unspecified length of time.[18]

Although life-cycle servants were of both sexes, males almost always outnumbered females. Table 1 shows the gender of servants in half a dozen villages.

Table 1. *Gender of servants*

Place (province)	Year	Males (%)	Females (%)
Bascuñana (Burgos)	1575	10 (59)	7 (41)
Cordovilla (Salamanca)	1629	18 (72)	7 (28)
Espinosa de la Ribera (León)	1582	6 (40)	9 (60)
Jubín (Orense)	1580	7 (64)	4 (36)
Souto de Vigo (Pontevedra)	1575	17 (61)	11 (39)
Villa de Pun (Burgos)	1575	23 (58)	17 (42)
Combined Totals		81 (60)	55 (40)

Source: Censuses in AGS, EH, 268, 368, 273, 299, 99-30, 368.

In the sample, only Espinosa had more female than male servants. The norm was for males to be about half-again as numerous as females.

As early as the mid-1300s the Cortes of Castile made reference to life-cycle servants (*mançebos que ouieren de seruir*) and indicated that it was normal for children of both sexes to enter domestic service. Since life-cycle servants worked in households of families that were wealthier (or at least less poor) than their own, the average size of poor households shrank, while that of richer households grew.[19] Domestic service with wealthier families not only allowed poor children to survive, but even provided a sort of apprenticeship for the most disadvantaged young people. Authentic apprentices appear somewhat rarely in early modern Castilian village censuses, but in 1575 in Escacena del Campo (Huelva) a lad named Benito was listed as "apprentice of Manuel Martín, wineskin maker (*odrero*), in order to learn the trade"; and in 1579 14-year-old Juan Gómez (a native of La Pueblanueva) was apprenticed to the shoemaker Juan García, of Santa Cruz (Toledo).[20] These apprentices were learning a trade, to be sure, but in a certain sense we can think of them as life-cycle servants.

Because of the limited employment opportunities for women in those days, domestic service was a favorite option for rural girls before marriage. In fact, some parents raised their daughters to feel obligated to supplement the family income by migrating to a town or city to spend a few years as servants. It was perfectly understood by employer and employee alike that domestic service for life-cycle girls and boys was a transitory activity serving a specific economic function. And there was normally a rapid turnover in the domestic labor market. In pre-industrial Cuenca, for example, over 35 percent of all servants (who came mostly from outlying villages) entered or left town in a given year, and another 16 to 17 percent changed dwellings every year in town. And service was ordinarily left behind when a girl reached marrying age, or when a young man inherited land or became a day-laborer.[21]

I have not found an explicit documentary reference to a life-cycle servant using accumulated wages as start-up capital for marriage and independent farming. But the practice can be inferred from countless documentary examples of former *mozos de soldada* who married and rapidly attained middling economic stature. Pedro García, for example, in 1586 was a 22-year-old living in Garrafe del Torío (León). Although he had married a mere six months earlier, this young man already had a pair of oxen and three cows, giving him a respectable status as an independent farmer. The document does not divulge how the young García attained such early economic success, but it does mention that he had worked as a servant before he married. And we can guess that his wages helped establish him as a *labrador*. The accumulation of wages for start-up capital is explicit in contracts (*firmas de moças*) in the Archivo Histórico Provincial de Protocolos Notariales de Zaragoza.[22]

TREATMENT OF LIFE-CYCLE SERVANTS

The Augustinian friar Marcos Antonio Camos in *Microcosmia y gobierno universal del hombre cristiano* (1592) prescribed rules of conduct for the good farmer (*labrador*). Camos urged employers to be reasonable with their servants, not requiring them to work excessively. They should be generous, but should maintain a careful watch over their employees' activities.[23] Unfortunately, not all employers followed the friar's admonitions for generosity and moderation. An episode in *Don Quixote* (I, 4) indicates that adolescent servants were sometimes badly mistreated by their employers. In this incident, Quixote encountered a 15-year-old servant (*mozo de soldada*) being brutally thrashed by his rich *labrador* employer for negligence in watching his flock of sheep. Moreover, the employer used the alleged negligence to justify withholding the poor lad's salary. We can hope that this treatment was not the usual thing, but it is clear that unscrupulous employers had almost unlimited opportunities to take advantage of their young servants. Obviously, adolescent servant girls were especially vulnerable to mistreatment. But these abuses must have been quite unusual, because they do not appear to have discouraged the widespread participation of young females in life-cycle service. In fact, working in a strange household was probably generally a positive experience. Social pressures in a small village community might have prevented employers from being excessively abusive or unfair to their charges. And we have evidence that the life-cycle experience could have a happy ending with a romantic twist: the 1578 census of Santoña (Santander) shows the household of a certain Juan Pineda containing a hired girl to whom Pineda was engaged to be married![24]

Life-cycle servants seem to have been contracted by the year, following the local hiring calendar, perhaps beginning on an important saint's day.

In Miranda de Duero (Soria), for example, such contracts began on Saint Michael's Day. In late medieval Spain servants were provided room, board, and clothing, and a salary partly in cash and partly in kind (grain). But by the 1500s the norm seems to have been cash. The obligations and responsibilities of employer and servant were spelled out in the Ordinances of the Cortes, and often in municipal ordinances, as well.[25] In fifteenth-century Zaragoza, life-cycle agreements took the form of written contracts legally executed and entered into the notarial records. But in the overwhelmingly illiterate environment of rural Spain, the agreements may have been oral. In any case, the contracts were flexible enough to permit emergency leave. We can see this in a 1559 census of Miranda de Duero (Soria), which shows the widow Catalina Ximénez being nursed through an illness by her daughter María, who at the time had a job as a *moza de soldada* in the city of Soria. Undoubtedly María expected to return to her job after her mother's recovery.[26]

It is difficult to find sources describing the process through which potential life-cycle servants contacted prospective employers. But ties of kinship and village acquaintance were certainly involved. Reher describes how kinfolk living in town helped their young rural relatives find domestic positions in pre-industrial Cuenca.[27] It seems certain that the same thing was true of other areas, as well.

Although we can imagine that members of the hidalgo class would prefer to avoid domestic service of any type, I found one hidalgo among the ranks of life-cycle servants in Herreruela (Cáceres) in 1586. He is the sole hidalgo life-cycle servant that I have encountered, but Rojo Alboreca found women servants from that class in late medieval Extremadura.[28] In an economic sense, it might have been highly advantageous to become a life-cycle servant, with the lump-sum salary payment that it might bring at the end of the contractual term. Without this advantage, young persons entering adulthood might be forced into the ranks of the landless day-laboring poor, earning wages only on days when they could find work. For a young person using life-cycle service to accumulate start-up capital, the ideal situation was to marry a spouse in the same situation, so they could pool their resources. We know that some did this. And although it was highly unusual, some life-cycle servants married while remaining in service. I have found references to married *mozos de soldada* in Poveda de Obispalía (Cuenca), Palomas (Badajoz), and Villanubla (Valladolid), among others. Unfortunately, the documents give no information about how and when these servants married, or how marriage affected their jobs.[29]

THE INCIDENCE OF LIFE-CYCLE SERVICE

Recent studies indicate that a substantial proportion of early modern European youth entered domestic service. In northwestern Europe up to three-quarters of boys and one-half of girls left home to become life-cycle servants. Thus, domestic service was a normal experience for young people. It encouraged geographical mobility, and it made it easier for young people to delay marriage, if circumstances warranted.[30]

Unfortunately, early modern Spanish censuses do not consistently include life-cycle servants.[31] The reason is that censuses were compiled primarily for fiscal purposes, and juvenile domestic servants rarely owned taxable property. Consequently, many censuses list no servants at all, and this may lead one to the erroneous conclusion that there was no hired help in the place. But the fact is that even when a census is supposed to include servants, it is likely to omit non-property owners. That is implicitly recognized in a 1558 census of Monleón (Salamanca), which reports that a certain citizen "has no servant *who owns any property* [emphasis added]." This language suggests that life-cycle servants who did not own property were considered too unimportant to include in the census.[32] Nevertheless, some censuses do list life-cycle servants, and these give us an approximate idea of the proportion of rural households that included them. But there are many problems in counting life-cycle servants in early modern Spanish documents. For one thing, the terms are vague. In those days (as today), *mozo* does not always mean a young person, nor does *criado* necessarily mean an adult. Words such as *muchacho* or *criado pequeño* are not totally clear, either. When we are not told the age of the servant, we can only guess whether the person in question is a child, an adolescent, or an adult. And unfortunately, some censuses indicate that a household contains *mozos, criados,* or *sirvientes,* without specifying their exact number. Moreover, it is often difficult to ascertain whether servants were members of the employer's household, or whether they lived apart. Some censuses are more clear about this than others.

Table 2 shows the proportion of households with servants in nine villages. It includes all live-in servants, regardless of what they were called (e.g. *mozos,* or *criados*) in the censuses. Hence, an indeterminate number of adults is included. But when the documents did provide age data, it was clear that the overwhelming majority of servants were adolescents or unmarried young adults – i.e., life-cycle servants. The table shows considerable variation in the proportion of households with servants, and we would expect this. But the reader should be aware that the varying proportions may be the result of reporting differences, rather than differences in fact. In any case, the table suggests that at least a quarter of early modern village households had servants at any given time. In many places the proportion was much higher than that. And if all servants had been counted, who knows how high the proportion would have been?

We must acknowledge that the high mobility of life-cycle servants – *all* servants, for that matter – made including them on censuses problematical, as village officials of Zarza de Montánchez (Cáceres) noted in 1597.[33]

Table 2. *Proportion of households with live-in servants*

Place (province)	Year	Total households	With servants	%	Source AGS, EH
Barrios de Villadiego (Burgos)	1597	29	7	24	198
Bascuñana (Burgos)	1575	32	9	28	368–7
Cordovilla (Salamanca)	1629	51	15	29	268
Espinosa de la Ribera (León)	1582	69	12	17	273
Fuentepinilla (Soria)	1586	75	36	48	042
Jubín (Orense)	1580	25	7	28	299
Palomas (Badajoz)	1590	205	25	12	354
Souto de Vigo (Pontevedra)	1587	64	18	28	99–30
Villa de Pun (Burgos)	1575	98	30	31	368
Combined totals		648	159	25	

But adolescent employment was certainly a widespread experience. It seems to have been the norm for girls in fifteenth-century Aragon. And six out of twelve villagers who testified in a lawsuit between Donhierro and Rapariegos (both in Segovia province) reported that in their youth they had been *mozos de soldada*.[34] We should not regard that proportion as the norm; it merely accentuates the fact that life-cycle service was widely practiced in early modern Castile.[35]

Most life-cycle servants – perhaps 60 percent of them – lived in single-servant households. But it was not at all unusual for two or three to be in the same house. And very wealthy people were likely to hire four or five, or even more servants. The highest numbers that I have seen (out of hundreds of censuses with this type of data) were listed in the 1575 census of Escacena del Campo (Huelva), which lists 107 life-cycle servants. Most were in single-servant households. But five households had 2; one had 4; one 6; one 7; one 12; and one 13! Thus, Lope de Vega's stereotypical rich Castilian peasant "Juan Labrador," depicted with 20 plowboys in *El villano en su rincón*, was an exaggeration, but he was by no means beyond the realm of possibilities.[36]

LIFE-CYCLE SERVICE AS GEOGRAPHICAL MOBILITY

Life-cycle service gave rural children an opportunity to broaden their horizons. Their geographical mobility not only affected their own view of the world, but also altered the lives of the communities where they served. Although the norm seems to have been service in a village within one's own district or region, we have already seen evidence of longer-range mobility. This can also be observed in the origin of girls entering domestic service in fifteenth-century Zaragoza: most came from nearby Argonese

Table 3. *Origin of servants in Santa Cruz*

Place	Number (%)
Santa Cruz	1 (5)
Other places in same province (Toledo)	11 (58)
Neighboring provinces (Avila & Cáceres)	2 (11)
Distant provinces (Galicia & Asturias)	2 (11)
Unspecified	1 (5)
Other places not located on map	2 (11)

Source: Census in AGS, EH, 382.

villages, but there were girls from Navarre, Castile, and even Mallorca.[37] A rather typical situation was that in Santa Cruz (Toledo), where the geographical origin of nineteen life-cycle servants in 1575 can be seen in Table 3.

Map 9 provides a graphic display of the same information, showing that even villages in the same province were often a considerable distance from Santa Cruz.

Adolescent servants often did not remain with their initial employers, but switched families, and even moved to different villages several times before adulthood. It appears that many of these young people were on the lookout for potential spouses. And they often married partners far from their natal villages. For example, around 1530 a youth from Mansilla de las Mulas, in the northern Spanish province of León, entered life-cycle service in Rejas, a village near Madrid. He remained there for two years, working for two different masters; then he moved to nearby Alameda (also in the province of Madrid), where he served another three masters. He ended up marrying a girl from Alameda, and settling down there, hundreds of kilometers from his birthplace.[38]

The following example also illustrates the pattern of geographical mobility encouraged by life-cycle service: a lad from Rebolledo (Burgos) at around fifteen went to live in nearby Villamartín de Villadiego, where he was a *mozo de soldada* for around ten years, working for various families. During this period he performed a wide range of agro-pastoral tasks for his masters. Our subject left Villamartín at some point in the 1530s – presumably after having reached twenty-five (the normal age of majority) – and established permanent residency in Puentes (possibly Puentetoma, 12 kilometers to the north, in neighboring Palencia province).[39]

We can get a sense of how the mobility of life-cycle servants could affect rural families by looking at the household of the widower Bartolomé Merinero, a citizen of Bascuñana (Burgos) in 1575. Merinero had three sons: Juan was absent because he was a life-cycle servant in nearby Villa de Pun; Mateo was in Seville (for what purpose we are not told), where he

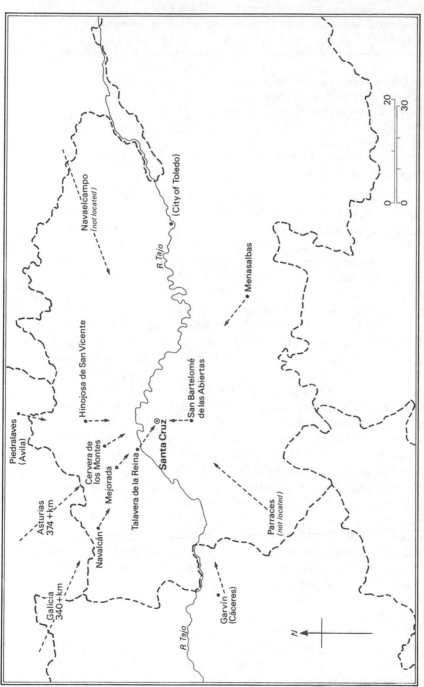

Map 9. Origin of life-cycle servants in Santa Cruz (Toledo), 1575, according to census in AGS, EH, 382. San Bartolomé de las Abiertas supplied three of these servants; Talavera de la Reina and Cervera de los Montes each supplied two; and one life-cycle servant came from an unspecified location.

had been for the past four months; but Bartolomé junior (*el mozo*) lived with his wife and two daughters in his father's household. The younger Bartolomé employed two (life-cycle) servants: a male from Ojacastro (10 kilometers to the southeast, in Logroño province); and a female from Grañón (6 kilometers northeast, also in Logroño). Notice that because of the high mobility of life-cycle servants, this household – in a small and apparently remote village – had contacts with various outside locations.[40]

The evidence that we have about life-cycle servants demonstrates that pre-industrial villages were not static communities whose inhabitants rarely ventured beyond their own territory. On the contrary, the population of early modern village communities was surprisingly dynamic, continually in the process of transformation by migration to and from the village. The life-cycle servants, like other servants in Spain, as in the remainder of Europe, contributed to the process through their high mobility.[41]

MARRIAGE WITH OUTSIDERS

We have seen that life-cycle service offered young people an opportunity to meet potential marriage partners from other places. In fact, the marriage market factor may have been one of the most attractive aspects of life-cycle service. Moreover, the various other types of migration also led to marriage with outsiders. As a result, there was always a proportion of villagers who married spouses from "the outside world," even if that merely meant the next hamlet down the road. But parish records, and other data about marriage patterns, indicate that the overwhelming majority of early modern European villagers took spouses from the same parish, and this was especially true in remote mountain communities.[42]

There were strong social pressures to marry a local spouse. And these social constraints did not stem from mere xenophobia: they had a rational basis. When a local girl married an outsider, she took her dowry with her, causing the village to lose part of its patrimony, which might raise tax rates for those who remained behind. Moreover, when a girl married outside the village, the local marriage pool was depleted, lessening the possibilities for the least desirable local youths to find a bride. Marriage-minded young men realized this, and in some places banded together in bachelor societies which tried to establish a monopoly over the local girls.[43] Furthermore, arranged marriages within the village created a network of alliances that bolstered local solidarity, and that could strengthen the importance of a family over time. Some Spanish village charters tried to discourage outside unions by establishing fines for marrying outsiders. The prejudice against out-marriage is reflected in a proverb from the province of León:

> *Quien va lejos a casar,*   (One who goes afar to marry,
> *Va engañado, o va a engañar.*   Is deceived, or is going to deceive.)

The proverbial warning against outsiders, and the fines for marrying them, were clearly intended to discourage marriage with non-local partners. But the proverb implicitly recognized the attraction of an outside match, and the fines established a procedure for authorizing out-marriage. And there was longstanding precedent for this, because Castile's venerable King Alfonso the Wise (1252–84) had encouraged out-marriage in his famous law code the *Siete Partidas*.[44] Moreover, the church's anti-incest laws encouraged marriage outside the village. A widow was forbidden to marry the brother of her deceased spouse, and had to leave her household if she wished to remarry; a man was not to marry the sister of his deceased wife; and a son could not wed his widowed stepmother to keep her in the household. These church marriage restrictions forced widows to look outside the household where they lived, and often outside the village, to find a new husband. That may explain why a woman who resided in Abelgas (León) had moved so many times: she had lived in Luna with her first husband; when he died she left Luna to marry a citizen of Santamaría del Rey; and after the death of her second spouse she married a husband from Abelgas.[45]

Unfortunately, parish records in Spain were not systematically kept during the sixteenth century. Consequently, socio-demographic studies almost invariably begin in the seventeenth and eighteenth centuries. And these studies indicate a high degree of in-marriage: over two-thirds of brides and grooms in Liébana (Santander) during the period 1600–1850 came from the same parish, and despite the Church's prohibition of consanguineous marriage, the local socio-economic elite frequently married their relatives (especially cousins), as a strategy to accumulate and preserve wealth.[46]

But we should not exaggerate the meaning of in-marriage as the overwhelming norm: if two-thirds of marriages were between people from the same parish, the remaining one-third were mixed marriages involving outsiders. One out of three is a large minority, and would have had a considerable impact on local society. In fact, the data that we have for marriage patterns in seventeenth- and eighteenth-century Castilian villages suggests that the norm may have been for around one-third to involve outsiders. But the proportion varied widely from place to place. Studies of Cantabrian villages (Santander) during this period indicate that from 22 percent to 48 percent of marriages involved outsiders. Marriages with outsiders were somewhat more common in the Estella district (Navarra), ranging between 30 percent and 60 percent in the eighteenth century. And in the La Bañeza district of the province of León around half of eighteenth-century marriages involved spouses who were not from the

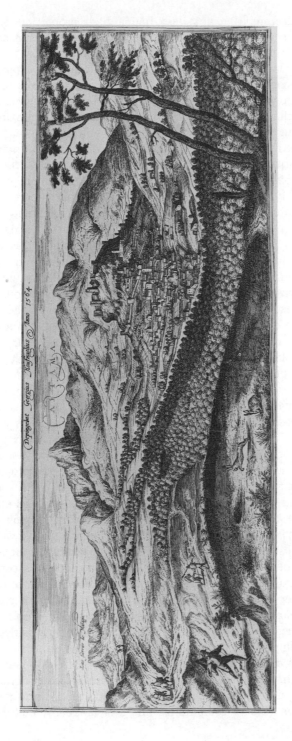

Fig. 8. View of the village of Cartama (Málaga province) in 1564, showing travelers on the road to Málaga, on the left. The people of "secluded" villages like Cartama often married spouses from the outside world. From Georg Braun, *Civitatis orbis terrarum*, vol. 3, no. 11 (Cologne, 1576–1618).

same parish.[47] Llerena (Badajoz) also had a high proportion of out-marriage: in the seventeenth century it was 46.6 percent – considerably higher than the norm for Extremaduran villages (around 35 percent), because Llerena's location along a major road gave it unusual exposure to outsiders. The geographical placement of a community seems to have been a major determining factor. Rute, for example, a relatively inaccessible Cordoban village, maintained an out-marriage rate of approximately 18 percent during the period.[48]

We must be aware, however, that the low proportion of out-marriage suggested by parish records may be misleading, because of the high geographical mobility in rural society. Many immigrants gained local citizenship, married into local families, and were thoroughly integrated into the local community. Thus, an untold number of apparently local marriages may actually have involved outsiders.[49] Of course, the contrary also could be true. In pre-industrial Cuenca, migrants from a given village or district – even when the "migrants" had actually been born in Cuenca of immigrant families – tended to marry spouses from that same rural area. These marriages might appear in parish records as unions with outsiders, whereas they actually were an expression of village solidarity.[50]

Because of the dearth of parish records, few demographic studies go back to the sixteenth century, and those that we have show widely divergent rates. Bartolomé Bennassar calculated that a mere 5 percent of marriages celebrated in Villabáñez (Valladolid) from 1570 to 1600 involved outsiders, while in Geria (also in Valladolid province) it was only 8 percent. Although we have to allow for considerable inter-village variations, those rates seem too low, and we suspect that Bennassar's sources were incomplete. For essentially the same period, Benjamín García Sanz found parish records from the Curiel-Peñafiel area (Valladolid) showing that 35 percent married spouses from a different village. That proportion is consistent with those found by Rodríguez Cancho for sixteenth-century Extremadura, and with others from later centuries, as we have already seen.[51] Since the deficiencies of sixteenth-century record keeping make parish records an unpredictable source for demographic research, we have to look elsewhere. Fortunately, the bureaucratic apparatus of Habsburg Spain comes to our rescue: the General Archive at Simancas contains many fiscal censuses from which we can glean data about marriage patterns and other household information. These data are rarely present, and they are recorded with distressing inconsistency. But despite their shortcomings, the Simancas censuses offer interesting possibilities that would be exceedingly difficult or impossible with other sources. I have found household data for approximately 200 late sixteenth- and early seventeenth-century Castilian villages, and a substantial proportion of my censuses include information about marriage patterns. Unfortunately, I have not yet been able to computerize and systematically analyze this

Table 4. *In-marriage and out-marriage in Bobadilla del Camino (Palencia)*

Category	Number (%)
Outside men who married native brides	24 (33)
Outsiders who married native widows	2 (3)
Native men who married outside brides	15 (21)
Marriages between natives	28 (39)
Marriages between outsiders	3 (4)
Total	72 (100)

Source: Census in AGS, EH, 60-6-iv.

information, and at the moment I can present data about only a few places.[52] It would be foolhardy to generalize from these about the whole of Castile or Spain. But judging from other demographic studies of preindustrial villages in Spain, and elsewhere in Europe, a complete analysis of my data will show a substantial degree of out-marriage, but with wide variations from place to place, and from generation to generation.[53]

A 1550 census of Bobadilla del Camino (Palencia) offers a glimpse at marriage patterns and geographical mobility. The census includes a list of household heads who had married and who had become citizens since the year 1533. There were 72 entries on the list, of a total population of 188 citizens in 1550. The marriages during this 17-year period are categorized in Table 4: This list omits five immigrants from Vizcaya who were married to outsiders (presumably also Basque) before they arrived and established residency in Bobadilla. The data from Bobadilla indicate a surprising degree of out-marriage and of in- and out-migration. But Bobadilla cannot be regarded as typical; it was unusually exposed to outside influences, because like Estella (mentioned three paragraphs above), it lay astride the Pilgrimage Road to Santiago de Compostela.

Table 5 provides another look at marriage patterns, through censuses which identify the residency of married children of local families (I must caution that the list is probably incomplete, because census takers normally did not record this type of information). In the table, the proportion of marriages outside the village ranges from 13 percent in Estépar to 56 percent in Palacios-mil. Although the sample is small, and may not represent all the parties who should have been included, it indicates that out-marriage was not at all unusual in early modern rural Castile. Studies of other parts of Europe, similarly, show that it was perfectly normal for peasant children upon reaching marriage age (if not before) to leave their parents' household to take up residence in a different village. It seems quite clear that children often did this to gain independence from parental control. There are many questions that need to be answered about

Table 5: *Residency of married children of villagers*

Place (province)	AGS EH Leg.	Year of census	Same village (%)	Out- side (%)	Not specified (%)	Totals
Centenera (Guadalajara)	262	1626	21 (40)	15 (28)	17 (32)	53
Estépar (Burgos)	274	1553	7 (88)	1 (13)	0	8
Hérmedes de Cerrato (Burgos)	288	1580	12 (50)	12 (50)	0	24
La Puerta (Guadalajara)	368	1597	22 (51)	20 (47)	1 (2)	43
Palacios-mil (León)	354	1581	3 (33)	5 (56)	1 (11)	9

marriage patterns in early modern Castilian villages: for example, did economic crises increase or decrease the incidence of out-marriage? Additional research may clarify this and other matters.[54]

INTER-FAMILY RELATIONS

Census data indicate that, at any given moment, the overwhelming majority (between 75 percent and 90 percent) of Castilian rural families during this period were of the simple (or nuclear) type. Only about 10 percent corresponded to the extended and multiple family types combined.[55] In other words, village households in Castile resembled those in the rest of Western Europe at the time. But Castilian families, like those in other European areas, were dynamic groups that did not remain frozen in one type of household organization. They evolved over time, and this often brought migration from one village to another. As indicated earlier, life-cycle service modified the composition of households, as adolescents left one family to work in another one – typically in a different village. Thus, both the donor and the recipient households were altered in struc-ture, while ties were established linking the two households and villages. Out-marriage also led to important ties with other rural communities. All of these factors, of course, were linked to the prevailing system of land-holding and other economic considerations, which frequently dictated family size and type, and obliged grown children to strike out on their own rather than remaining at home.[56]

In Castile, as in other parts of Europe, the ideal was for a married couple to live by themselves in their own home. But this ideal was frequently set aside because of pressing economic needs or family responsibilities. Thus, a newly married couple often lived for a while with a parent until they could set up a separate household. And an established family often found it necessary to take in an elderly parent, aunt or uncle, orphaned niece or nephew, or other relative. It is these situations that led to the formation of extended households, or even multiple households in some cases. And these complex households frequently included people from other villages.[57]

Another type of relationship linking households in different villages was that of guardian and charge (*tutor* or *curador* and *menor*). The high mortality rate of those days produced large numbers of orphans (*menores*), with inherited property that had to be managed until the orphans reached legal adulthood. For example, Monteagudo (Cuenca), a village with 116 households in 1575, had 14 *menores*, of whom only 6 were clearly incorporated into the households of guardians in that village. The other 8, presumably, were living with guardians in different villages. The guardians tended to be relatives (usually brothers) of the deceased parents. But they did not necessarily welcome their orphaned nieces and nephews into their households. Many guardians arranged to have their charges work elsewhere as life-cycle servants, perhaps thereby deriving financial benefit out of what otherwise would have been a drain on the family budget. Agustín Díaz, for example, who lived with his wife and small daughter in Santa Cruz de Pinares (Avila), was the guardian of 12-year-old Francisca Pedrera (perhaps a niece). But Francisca did not live in the village, because Díaz for the past eight months had "put her to work in the city of Avila." As indicated earlier in this chapter, the children of widows who remarried were also likely to be sent off as life-cycle servants in a different village or town.[58]

When a son or daughter moved to another village, for whatever reason, the family ties were stretched, but they were seldom completely broken. We have abundant proof that people who were separated by geography from their parents or siblings usually knew where they lived, and presumably kept in touch with them in some way. Through these ties of kinship, extended by a network of friends and acquaintances, villagers gained the information that they needed for intelligent decision making. They knew where the jobs were, for example, and where they could find land to farm.[59] Villagers who emigrated to take advantage of opportunities in a different place often settled down to become citizens of their new homes. But they did not forget their home towns, and some even returned there in old age to die. I have not seen enough examples of this type of return-migration to think that it was very widespread, but it underlines the pervasive mobility of the rural Castilian population.[60]

6

RELATIONS WITH THE STATE

THE IMPACT OF THE MILITARY

In his history of the city of Toledo, published in 1554, Pedro de Alcocer described war, famine, and pestilence as "three rabid wolves," because of their destructive impact upon the Spanish population. Warfare (traditionally bringing famine and pestilence in its wake) was an inescapable element in the history of early modern rural society. In Castile the Revolt of the Comuneros (1520–1) involved many villagers directly as participants in the struggle or as victims of its destructive force.[1] Following the defeat of the Comuneros, Habsburg Castile experienced no further large-scale warfare in its territory. Nevertheless, the monarchy's military campaigns outside of Castile played a significant part in the lives of rural Castilians, both directly and indirectly.

The Spanish armed forces provided numerous avenues of contact between the village and the outside world. And the influence of the various branches of the military was considerable, because Spain had the most powerful war machine in the world at the time.[2] The Spanish army and navy during the sixteenth and seventeenth centuries supported the imperial enterprises of the Habsburgs not only in various parts of Europe, but also in Africa, Asia, and America. The Spanish armed forces, in addition to military hardware, required vast quantities of men, grain, animals, and other supplies from rural Spain. Castile, the most populous, loyal, and docile of the Spanish kingdoms, provided the lion's share of these things. War was practically continuous during the sixteenth and first half of the seventeenth centuries, and the wartime economy profoundly affected rural Castile. Partly, this was because of the men and supplies that rural Castilians had to supply. But perhaps the greatest overall impact of Habsburg imperialism for most Castilian villagers was indirect: through ever-higher taxation for the navies and armies that symbolized and maintained Spanish power. Elsewhere[3] I have described the destructive impact of Habsburg taxation on rural Castile, and later in this chapter I will return to the royal tax system. But first, I want to consider three types of direct contacts between villagers and the military: billeting, provisioning, and troop levies.

THE BILLETING OF TROOPS

According to longstanding custom, when His Majesty's troops were in town, the local people were responsible for feeding and lodging them, and that nearly always meant that the troops would stay in people's homes.[4] The captain of a group of soldiers who were to be quartered in a village, town, or city would prepare a list (*bando*) indicating where he and his men would stay. The soldiers were then given billets (*boletas*) to present to their hosts.[5] These billets were necessary for the host to receive compensation for housing and boarding the troops.

A visit by a military contingent was a form of contact with the outside world that villagers regarded with universal dread, in Spain as in other parts of Europe,[6] because soldiers were notoriously brutal and dishonest. Billeting the king's soldiers was more burdensome than royal taxation, because billeting was a direct interference with daily life. And it made little difference whose army the soldiers belonged to: foreign, or from one's own country. In the first place, the concept of "national" defense was foreign to the early modern Spanish villager. "Spain" was a mere geographical expression in those days, embracing several distinct kingdoms with separate traditions and institutions, although all had been ruled by the same monarchs since the days of Ferdinand and Isabella. The dominant Spanish kingdom was Castile, but the Castilian villagers who comprised the bulk of the population gave their primary political loyalty not to "Castile," a concept that few really understood, but to their local community. Moreover, the sociocentric Golden Age Spanish villager considered soldiers from other regions of Castile – even from other villages in the same region – to be "foreigners" (*forasteros* – literally outsiders, or outlanders). Some of the troops actually were from outside of Spain. This was somewhat rare in the 1500s, but in the first half of the seventeenth century one could frequently see Italian, Portuguese, Flemish, German, and above all Irish units of the Spanish military stationed in Spain. After the mid-1600s, most of the foreign troops were discharged, because Spain's economic crisis made it difficult to pay them. Furthermore, Spain had lost its European hegemony, and had reduced its goals mainly to defense against France.[7]

But in the final analysis, villagers detested *all* soldiers, regardless of nationality. Soldiers – invariably irregularly paid – behaved like an invading army, living off the land they were occupying whether it was friendly or enemy, and brutalizing the local inhabitants. When the soldiers of the famous Spanish Infantry were not ravaging the Netherlands or some other foreign territory, they were abusing their own countrymen at home. Indeed, the contemporary authority Jerónimo Castillo de Bobadilla asserted that the Spanish troops committed "greater atrocities against us than against the enemy."[8] The instructions to an infantry captain from the Council of War (the official body in charge of the military) in 1572 show that the royal government was well aware of the excesses of its soldiers in Spain. But it failed to adopt measures to eliminate those abuses. It is hardly surprising, then, that Spanish villagers treated their own country's soldiers with hostility. In fact, they considered them to be a calamity – a plague to be avoided if at all possible.[9] In the judgment of I.A.A. Thompson, the premier authority on the subject, "The annual movement of [troops] across Castile left in its wake a trail of destruction and rapine ... [and] the coming of a company of soldiers was awaited with the same trepidation as a hurricane."[10]

The *Relaciones* clearly reveal the hostility of Spanish villagers toward the military. Far from feeling protected by soldiers stationed in the vicinity, the villagers regarded soldiers as their natural enemies. It should be understood that the bulk of the obligation to quarter troops fell upon ordinary peasant-farmers (*labradores*), because the local hidalgos and clergy could usually use their privileged legal status to escape this form of servitude.[11] However, there were certain entire villages lucky enough to gain complete exemption from billeting. Fuenlabrada (Madrid) was one of these: it had received that privilege from Ferdinand and Isabella as a reward for its services in the cavalry, and the village council was careful to have the exemption confirmed by Philip II.[12] But Fuenlabrada was a rare exception. All over Spain most villagers were subject to the quartering laws, and they resented this obligation, because it was at best unpleasant to have to host soldiers, and at worst it was equivalent to being sacked and brutalized by an enemy army. The soldiers expected to be well fed, and their hosts had no choice but to feed them. The official instructions to an infantry captain in 1572, urging moderation in the treatment of hosts, suggested no more than one pound of lamb for the captain, and no more than three-quarters of a pound of beef for ordinary soldiers, in addition to a *cuartal* of bread (a quarter of a large 2-pound *hogaza* loaf), and half an *azumbre* of wine (about a liter), per meal![13] The villagers must have been scandalized by the quantity of meat demanded by the soldiers, because the Golden Age peasant's diet did not include much meat, except on feast days. We can understand, then, why the peasants protested when the soldiers not only demanded such meals, but subjected them to personal abuse as well. In 1566 the village of Alpera (Albacete) wrote to the royal government complaining that "many soldiers come through the village ... [and] rob [the local inhabitants], and eat their lambs and chickens, and even attempt – and do – other worse things."[14]

Castillo de Bobadilla had harsh words for Spanish soldiers, calling the bulk of them "ignorant," and the worst "scum." He wrote: "There is no type of wickedness that they do not know and try: each of them seems to be a mutineers' chief and bandit captain. They leave no orchard or garden intact, no foodstuffs untaken, no indecency unattempted, nor insolence uncommitted, and there is no tribunal that punishes them, nor fear or shame to restrain them."[15]

We could fill volumes with the protests and bitter complaints of the victims of billeting, and of military requisitions of grain, draft animals, carts, and other supplies. In theory, the victims – the villagers who supplied these goods and services – were to be given reasonable compensation. But in practice, if they were paid at all – which was not always the case – it was likely to be after months or years of frustrated waiting, and at unsatisfactory rates set by the military procurement officer.[16] That explains why villagers were willing to go to great lengths to avoid billeting soldiers, even bribing the captains to take their troops elsewhere. The council of Illescas (Toledo) did this in 1586, as did that of Villaseca de la Sagra (also in Toledo province) in 1657. Another way to rid oneself of the obligation to billet was to foist the responsibility on one's weaker neighbors: Illescas, for example, in 1604 decided to apportion the troops assigned to stay there, among its subject villages.[17] The presence of soldiers was synonymous with mistreatment and scarcity. This was acknowledged by a royal official (corregidor) in Martos (Jaén), who reported in the late 1500s that the rural inhabitants of his area were in dire straits, as a result of being obliged to quarter troops for three and four months at a time. The presence of the troops not only depleted existing supplies, but led to a drop in future agricultural production, because while the soldiers were there, their peasant hosts were reluctant to leave the house, lest their wives and daughters be molested.[18] Another contemporary source explained:

The company comes to the village and billets a soldier [in the home of a typical peasant]. The soldier eats in a single week what would have fed the peasant and his entire household for a month. The labrador [peasant-farmer], distrustful of his guest, does not leave for work in his fields until daylight, when his family have all gotten up. He hitches his mules at eight, and unhitches them at four in the afternoon, in order to return home while it is still light. He has lost four hours [of his normal workday], which is a third of the day ... because of his guest.[19]

And it was not just machismo-driven paranoidal jealousy that made the labrador reluctant to leave wife and daughter alone with troops in the house. Cervantes – certainly reflecting actual historical events – mentions soldiers carrying off women. Teresa Panza (Sancho's wife) wrote to her husband (Quixote II, 52) that a company of soldiers passing through their village had taken three local girls with them. Teresa remarked: "Perhaps they'll return, and somebody will surely want to marry them despite their blemished honor." In that episode there was no hint that the girls had been forced to accompany the soldiers – in fact, they might have been willingly seduced. But it was all too common for soldiers to rape women and girls from the villages where they were quartered. This type of military misconduct was the subject of several Golden Age Spanish plays, most notably Calderón de la Barca's *El alcalde de Zalamea*, which was inspired by earlier theatrical pieces with the same theme. In this play, Captain Alvaro de Ataide, aided by two of his soldiers, abducted and raped the daughter of the *labrador* in whose house they were quartered.[20]

Captain Ataide may be regarded as the stereotypical bad soldier. But he was no mere literary invention, because there is ample historical evidence that this type of person actually existed, and was not even that unusual. In fact, the soldier-rapist was a constant threat in villages where troops were stationed, and soldiers guilty of sexual assault often went unpunished. For example, when a group of soldiers raped two 14-year-old girls from Puertollano (Ciudad Real), the local *alcalde* blamed the victims rather than the rapists, ignoring evidence that a violent crime had been committed. The *alcalde's* judgment was unquestionably influenced by the presence of a large group of men-at-arms – a clearly intimidating factor. This problem must have occurred with some frequency, because Philip II in 1580 published an edict establishing the death penalty for soldiers guilty of rape or even *attempted* rape.[21] Unfortunately, this failed to solve the problem. The Castilian Cortes with monotonous regularity denounced military abuses against the country's rural inhabitants.[22] But the abuses continued – the system of quartering made them virtually impossible to eliminate. Cervantes in *El coloquio de los perros* (1613) remarked that the royal government's efforts to end the abuses were doomed to failure, "because the necessities of war bring harshness, severity, and inconvenience."[23]

PROVISIONING THE MILITARY

Castilian villages were adversely affected not only by billeting and associated personal abuses, but also by requisitions for provisioning the military. Habsburg Spain was continually at war, and in wartime no one's property was safe from the military procurement officer. The most commonly requisitioned supplies were animals, grain, and carts. These supplies were needed for the war effort, but when they were taken for military purposes, the peasant was deprived of tools essential for his economic survival. Nevertheless, the military was legally empowered to seize whatever it needed by force, if the owner refused to "sell" it voluntarily. Repeatedly, the precarious economic balance of Castilian *labradores* was disturbed – or permanently destroyed – by the loss of seed grain, work animals, and other indispensable supplies. The royal government was not ignorant of the possible damage that this might cause to poor peasants, and ordered carts and animals to be taken only from "powerful and wealthy persons." But these "powerful persons" often controlled the local government, and were able to shift the burden away from themselves toward the common people.[24] Thus, as always in Europe of the Old Regime, it was those least able to bear it who were subjected to these confiscations. And often, although in theory there was just compensation for what was taken, the requisitions amounted to unindemnified confiscation. In 1574 the *labradores* of Briones (Logroño) complained that they had not been paid for their mules and carts. They would be lucky if they were paid promptly, because years of protests and petitions might be required to persuade the Royal Treasury to pay for goods requisitioned by the military. It took the people of Villanueva de Andújar (apparently present-day Villanueva de la Reina, province of Jaén) eleven years to receive compensation for the mules, oxen, carts, boxes, and grain that the military had carried off "for His Majesty's service." And even then they do not appear to have gotten the full value of what they had lost.[25] Unfortunately, that type of experience seems to have been the usual thing, rather than exceptional. For instance, the citizens of Navarre received only about one-thirtieth of the amount they sustained in losses to soldiers in early 1581. The widespread existence of such abuses prompted Lope de Soria to assert, in the mid-1500s, that Spanish soldiers caused "more damage ... to our countrymen than to our enemies."[26]

Nevertheless, it was foolhardy to resist even the most outrageous demand of the procurement officer, because he was supported not only by law, but also by the brute force of his comrades in arms. Under these circumstances, about the best thing that the poor villagers could do was to try to avoid contact with the military as much as possible, but to yield when necessary.[27]

One of the most unfortunate results of quartering was that the military depleted the reserves of local public granaries which had been painstakingly accumulated for emergencies. Thus, quartering not only impoverished individual peasants, but frequently also led to increased indebtedness for the entire corporate village community. We can see this in the example of the town of Bobadilla del Camino (Palencia), which had to mortgage its *propios* (municipal property, which could not legally be mortgaged without specific royal license) in 1567 to help it recover from a sixteen-month stay of a company of soldiers.[28] And El Agineta (apparently La Gineta, province of Albacete) in 1584 obtained a one-year's extension on half of its annual payment to the Royal Treasury, because its inhabitants had become "very impoverished from the previous years, because they contributed to the military campaigns in Granada and Portugal with their carts and mules and men and baggage, and from other demands, and in men of war and soldiers who have passed and pass through [El Agineta] to be quartered there."[29]

Some villages were virtually devastated through excessive exposure to the military (remember, these were peacetime contacts with the country's own military). In the mid-1600s Ardales (Málaga) was practically annihilated in the space of a little over a year, after having been forced to quarter three successive infantry regiments (*tercios*). The village, originally numbering 280 *vecinos*, was reduced to only 30 – the remainder having abandoned their houses and fled the abuses of the soldiers (the last an Irish unit).[30] Various contemporary observers commented that there were noticeably fewer villages along routes frequented by the military, and that existing villages along those routes suffered population losses through emigration to other areas.[31]

It is hardly surprising that soldiers and villagers frequently came to blows, sometimes with tragic consequences. For example, the *Relación* of Getafe (Madrid) describes a violent confrontation between local inhabitants and a group of royal archers stationed there. In this affray, a young villager – apparently an innocent bystander – was killed, and two others were injured.[32] Fortunately, although relations between soldiers and villagers were normally strained, they seldom reached such extremes. But even in Extremadura, the cradle of conquistadores, quartering produced bitter antagonism between soldiers and citizens, physical clashes, and disturbances.[33]

The combination of high taxes, billeting, and military levies – on a rural economy that was often marginally profitable to begin with – encouraged rural Castilians to seek exemptions, or to flee to parts of Spain – for example the Basque provinces, or the Kingdom of Aragon – that enjoyed special fiscal or military privileges limiting such abuses. I know of no statistical study to support the idea, but it is intriguing to hypothesize that there may have been an exodus of rural Castilian villagers to these peripheral areas.[34] That would help explain why the center of Spain suffered such population reversals, at a time when outlying zones were growing.

THE RECRUITMENT AND DRAFTING OF SOLDIERS

Military service took villagers away from home, voluntarily for the most part, but sometimes by force. We have no statistics regarding the proportion of village soldiers who returned home after completing their term in the military, but we can guess that this type of migration was permanent for most of the men involved. During the reign of Philip II, eight or nine thousand men (more during times of crisis) were recruited into the Spanish army annually.[35] And the rank and file of these were ordinary rural men from Castilian villages.[36] Despite the hostility that villagers displayed toward the military, the adventure of the soldier's life was alluring to many a rural youth. This is expressed in Act I of Calderón de la Barca's *El alcalde de Zalamea*. Upon meeting Captain Ataide, the impressionable young Juan Crespo exclaims in an aside: "How gallant and dashing!/I envy the soldier's garb." In Act II, Scene 2, when Juan hears the soldiers' serenade, he remarks that they lead "a great life."[37] And when asked, he replies without hesitation that he would like to join them. That attitude explains why real-life captains like Alonso de Contreras were so successful at recruiting troops in rural Castile. Captain Contreras seems to have had not only a dashing appearance, but also a charismatic personality that appealed to potential volunteers.[38] A literary example of the silver-tongued recruiting captain is don Diego de Valdivia, in Cervantes' exemplary novel *El licenciado Vidriera* (published in 1613).

The experience of actually serving in the military probably cured most recruits of their romantic notions about soldiering. But the Bennassars give the example of a young man from a prosperous La Mancha farm family in Villacañas (Toledo) who volunteered not just once, but twice. This was Juan Rodelgas, a youth of twenty when he first enlisted around the year 1610. He served for a couple of years with the Spanish infantry in Italy, then returned to his natal village for five or six years. But the young Juan found the agrarian village scene boring, so he re-enlisted when he was about twenty-seven. Juan Rodelgas was a farm boy whose curiosity and adventuresome nature found an outlet in the military.[39] There must have been many like him.

And it should be said that young men were not the only villagers seduced by the military. Earlier I mentioned the girls carried off by soldiers passing through Sancho Panza's village – a case where it is unclear whether the girls went willingly or not. But there are numerous examples in Golden Age Spanish literature of a village girl falling in love with the captain billeted in her parents' home. According to the literary formula, the girl then has to disguise herself in men's clothing, to flee from her village to be with her beloved. These literary examples would not have been credible had they not been based upon historical reality.[40]

The monarchy needed fresh soldiers every year for its imperial ventures, and its captains during most of the sixteenth century found it easy to recruit troops in rural Castile. Many village youths were eager for adventure. Furthermore, farm boys made good soldiers: accustomed to hard physical exertions, resourceful, and inured to foul weather and uncomfortable living conditions. The Venetian ambassador wrote during the reign of Philip II that the king of Spain possessed a veritable "nursery for young men, tough both in mind and body." And Gaspar Gutiérrez de los Ríos wrote in 1600 that "in our Spain the best and most valiant soldiers come from where agriculture is practiced."[41]

To ambitious village youths, a military career presented an opportunity not only to see the world, but also for upward social mobility. Early modern Spain had seen numerous examples of village lads who had gone off to war as common soldiers returning as heroes with prestige, wealth, and cushy government jobs. Thus, the dream of fame and fortune was a powerful incentive to enlist. Equally powerful, perhaps, for young men from poor families was the fact that the military offered a convenient alternative to an unpromising future at home. A soldier was paid a salary in addition to lodging, some meals, and an opportunity to visit faraway places.[42] The economic element was depicted by Cervantes in an episode where Don Quixote (II, 24) met a young fellow on the road to Cartagena to enlist in the infantry. The youth was singing the following ditty:

> My poverty leads me to war:
> If I had any money, I really wouldn't go.[43]

An ordinary soldier's salary in the mid- and late 1500s compared unfavorably to what an unskilled laborer could earn, but the soldier received other benefits, in addition to his pay. Moreover, the military salary was exempt from taxes and tithes, and a single man could manage very well on it if he could resist the temptation to squander his pay on gambling, women, and fancy clothes.[44] In fact military salaries, along with the other advantages of the soldierly life, were attractive enough to encourage "bonus jumping" – fraudulent enlistments by men who would desert as soon as they were paid. A document from the Council of War in 1572 indicates that many enlistees disappeared, with their pay, upon reaching the port of embarkment. Some of them developed a regular career (illegal, of course) of jumping from one company to another in this way, all the while enjoying free food, soldierly comradeship, and enlistment bonuses without ever having to go to war.[45]

By the 1590s, however, the Spanish government was faced with severely diminished enlistments. A grave fiscal crisis aggravated by economic recession made it impossible to attract sufficient volunteers by raising military salaries much above civilian pay rates. Furthermore, a string of military defeats took the luster off the soldierly life. Military discipline deteriorated, bringing ever more abuses to the villages where troops were stationed. But although the military life had lost much of its appeal, in a period of economic hard times, hunger remained an inducement for unemployed rural youths to enlist, when they could find no other way to make a living.[46]

In the end, when the number of volunteers proved insufficient for the army's needs, the Crown had to resort to forced troop levies. These were carried out with the assistance of the towns, the local nobles, and even private contractors.[47] The forced levies were highly unpopular, and many men of military age (normally 18–50) left town in order to avoid being drafted. The drafting authorities had to resort to unannounced visits (raids?) to villages, lest they find all eligible men absent.[48] So desperate was the need for troops in the 1640s that the authorities in Cáceres even drafted Portuguese aliens, despite the fact that Portugal and Spain were at war at the time. In 1644 the Council of Castile reported to the king that there was a manpower shortage in some rural areas because of the levies and out of "fear" (read evasion) of the levies. And in 1675 officials of a shelter (*hospital*) in Madrid indicated that many of the capital's homeless young men had recently fled the levies in Galicia. In an effort to compel draft dodgers to serve, municipal governments arrested their families and seized their property. This usually brought in the reluctant draftees, but those tactics were highly unpopular, and the unwilling recruits frequently deserted. Moreover, not only the commoners but even the nobles – who were supposed to be the country's warrior class – had lost their enthusiasm for the military.[49]

The recruitment and drafting of troops had an incalculably great impact on Castilian villages, because most of the men who became soldiers were young – at the beginning of their productive lives, both demographically and economically. Three-quarters of a group of draftees from La Mancha in 1639 were between the ages of twenty and thirty-nine. An additional 20 percent were in their forties, and almost 5 percent were in their fifties or sixties.[50] One wonders how effective some of these older men would have been as soldiers, because they not only lacked the stamina and daring of youth, but also were beginning to lose some of their faculties. For example, a census of the hamlet of Peguerinos (Avila), which had 64 households in 1625, listed two levies – both in their forties. One of these was Juan García, who was described as "shortsighted" (*corto de vista*),[51] and we can be quite sure that the army did not provide him with eyeglasses.

The numbers of men who served in the military could be quite large, even in places with modest populations. For example, a census of Morales de Toro (Zamora), which had a mere 250 *vecinos* in 1569, listed 5 men or boys who had gone off to war, 4 who had gone to America (possibly also in the military), and one "gone off to war or to the Indies ... nobody knows." [52] We have a more striking example in Villarrobledo (Ciudad Real), which estimated in 1642 that over the past six years a total of 400 of its men had been conscripted into the military. That represented an average annual loss of over 65 men, from a place that only had around 3,000 inhabitants. That is, 2.22 percent of the total population was lost annually to the troop levies. Many of these – perhaps most of them – would never return to the village. And that very year (1642) an order was received to raise another 60 troops in Villarrobledo. The municipal government protested that "the farmers and shepherds have abandoned and are abandoning their flocks and fields, and no one is left to care for them, and we fear ruin if things don't change."[53]

We must admit that the foregoing dismal picture was probably deliberately exaggerated by the village leadership, hoping to obtain some relief from royal exactions. But the 2 percent levy may not have been unusual, because the village of Villarejo (Madrid) in the late seventeenth century was also forced to send 2 percent of its population to the army.[54] We must remember that the levies of Habsburg Spain not only removed some of the most productive men from the village, but also brought an additional tax burden for those who remained behind, because the draftees' home town was expected to raise money to pay the soldiers' wages and usually to supply their weapons, as well. If these expenditures could not be met from surplus municipal funds, it would be necessary to borrow money, or to impose new taxes.[55]

THE SOLDIER'S FAMILY

We should not forget that village families with a father, husband, or son in the military often found themselves severely inconvenienced, even if the soldier was not killed or crippled in action. The missing man was unable to contribute to the family's labor requirements, and he did not necessarily help support the family with part of his military pay. At best, the soldier's duties took him away from home for unpredictable periods. We can get an idea of what this meant from the language of a 1575 census of Villa de Pun (not identified on a modern map, but apparently in Burgos province). One of the households of this village of 98 families was headed by Pedro de Vega, a soldier of whom it was said "He is here at times." This soldier was not a native of the place, in fact he was not even a *vecino* (with local citizenship), although he had married a local girl.[56]

A more poignant example is that of Juliana, a resident of Santurdejo (Logroño). During a verification of a local census in 1556, Juliana was asked whether she was actually unmarried (*soltera*), as listed in the census. That was a reasonable question, because at the time Juliana had two young sons. She replied that she "used to be married" to a certain Diego de Treviño, a soldier stationed in Pamplona. Juliana did not reveal how they had met, but we can speculate that it might have been while she was working in Logroño, because that is where she and Treviño were engaged, some eight years earlier. From Logroño they went to Gallinero de Rioja, her home village, where they were married.

Following the wedding they established a household a half league from Gallinero in Santurdejo, where they lived together for "a month or two." Then Juliana's soldier-husband departed, returning to see her "sometimes," but when she gave her testimony, Juliana had not seen her husband for five or six years, nor did she even know his whereabouts. Was Juliana a simple village girl seduced by a gallant soldier who abandoned her after a brief fling? There is some reason to believe so, because Juliana was not even sure where her husband was from. How did Juliana support herself after Diego disappeared? The document is silent about this, but it reports that neither she nor her husband owned any real estate in

Santurdejo, which meant that Juliana surely had to have some kind of job to feed her family. Juliana's eight-year-old was Treviño's son, but she had another son aged "four or five" who "had no father." This younger son was born in Santurdejo, but lived with relatives in the village of Canyelas, in the Val de Comas (apparently on the eastern edge of Spain, near Barcelona!).[57]

Juliana was luckier than María Cides, a woman living in Los Balbases (Burgos) in 1612. María was married to Pedro Abad, a soldier who had been gone for over twenty years.[58] There must have been many Julianas and Marías, in villages all over Spain. In effect, they headed single-parent families, often not knowing whether their spouses were living or dead, and shouldering themselves the responsibilities of child rearing and child support. And that must have often been difficult. Miguel Benito, for example, drafted as a "battalion soldier" from Peguerinos (Avila) in 1625, left a wife and small daughter to fend for themselves. And Juan García, from the same levy in Peguerinos, had to leave behind a wife and four children, the eldest only fourteen. In some cases, the village government took upon itself the responsibility of providing relief for the dependents of soldiers, as did Villaseca de la Sagra (Toledo) in 1640.[59] A study of local records might find that this was common practice. In any case, it was one more burden added to the costs that rural people had to bear for Habsburg imperialism.

The monarchy's military ventures, with the billeting, provisioning, and recruitment and drafting that they required, brought the outside world directly into the daily lives of villagers who otherwise might have had only a passive knowledge of the Habsburg Empire's distant campaigns.

THE ADMINISTRATION OF JUSTICE

Another important way in which the hand of the state reached the village level was through the administration of justice. The legal code of early modern Castile was a bewildering hodgepodge of royal decrees, customary law, local ordinances, and juridical decisions dating from the Visigothic period. By the sixteenth century the law in Castile was so ambiguous and contradictory that almost any issue or case could be interpreted in several ways by clever lawyers and judges. Administering the law was further complicated by the existence of *fueros* (special juridical privileges), which exempted members of specific communities and groups from the ordinary jurisdiction of monarchical law. Among the holders of *fueros* were clergy, soldiers, university students, and members of certain geographical districts within the Kingdom of Castile.[60]

The Castilian court system was as bewilderingly complex as its system of laws. In theory, the king's justice operated on three distinct levels, in a perfectly logical and hierarchical system. At the lowest level the royally appointed *corregidores* supervised the equivalent of today's trial courts. At mid-level were regional appellate tribunals (*audiencias*), which heard appeals against sentences of courts of the *corregidores* and also of municipal and seignorial judges. The highest level was the Royal Council of Castile, which served as the superior court of the land. But in practice each royal tribunal sought to expand its own powers at the expense of the others, leading to many cases being heard in courts where they did not really belong. Moreover, the king's regular magistrates were frequently superseded by special royal investigatory judges (*jueces de comisión* and *jueces pesquisidores*) whose powers cut across the normal judicial hierarchy and procedures.[61]

On the municipal level, the system was similarly muddled. Large cities such as Seville had a variety of courts, with poorly defined and often overlapping jurisdictions. This was a procedural nightmare, but it had the advantage of often enabling people to choose where they wanted their cases heard. In rural areas, for example, the conflicting jurisdictions permitted villagers living under seignorial rule to bypass the local judge (whose sentences almost invariably favored the seignior) for the nearest royal court (which was usually only too happy to intervene).[62]

Villages in Castile either had their own autonomous jurisdiction, or else they were dependent communities under the control of another municipality. Dependent villages (called *aldeas* or *lugares*) did not have full authority over themselves, for they lay within the territory of a town or city (*villa* or *ciudad*), and were subject to its ordinances and judicial control.[63] The subject villages, which had originally been squatter settlements, did not have full legal equality, and their subservient status carried numerous irksome disadvantages. The dependent villages had to obtain the permission of the ruling town, for instance, before they could establish their own separate commons; their judges were limited to hearing petty cases involving local citizens and their property; and the ordinances of the dominant town discriminated in numerous ways against the subject villagers.[64]

In theory the ruling town or city had complete control over its "vassal" villages (although not really appropriate in a land where feudalism was never firmly implanted, the term "vassal" was employed by the dominant municipalities to emphasize their juridical superiority). But in practice, the subject villages enjoyed considerable autonomy. Michael Weisser found that, although the city of Toledo possessed the legal right to choose the councilmen (*regidores*), judges (*alcaldes*), and constables (*alguaciles*) for each of its subject villages in the Montes de Toledo, in practice these officials were nearly always selected by the villagers themselves, with the city merely confirming the appointments. Even so, the villagers increasingly resented the city's authority over them. And eventually they were able to achieve a degree of *de facto* independence by refusing to cooperate fully with intruding city officials who tried to enforce their prerogatives.[65]

THE SALE OF TOWNSHIPS (*VILLAZGOS*)

But dependent villages nevertheless had to contend with discriminatory treatment. For example, Talavera de la Reina (Toledo) forced the villages within its jurisdiction to purchase its own wine, until stocks were exhausted, before they could import wine from other areas. The subject villages complained that Talavera's wine was too expensive and of inferior quality. Elsewhere in Castile, Medina del Campo (Valladolid) tried to compel its villages to purchase poor-quality surplus grain from its warehouses, even when the villages had no need for it.[66] The inhabitants of dependent villages not only had to suffer discriminatory and high-handed treatment from the dominating municipality, they also were obliged to travel there for administrative purposes. And that was often a formidable hardship. For example, the residents of Castilblanco (Badajoz) grumbled understandably that they had to travel 16 leagues (around 90 kilometers) to reach Talavera de la Reina (Toledo), which had jurisdiction over it. What was worse, the villagers explained, the road was in poor condition, and it passed through hazardous mountain passes. Consequently, even in good weather the round trip took at least four days on horseback.[67]

Many villages concluded that their subordinate juridical status was intolerable, and they looked for emancipation. The solution was for village governments to purchase their municipal autonomy from the crown. Helen Nader's recent book on the subject shows how Spain's Habsburg rulers sold charters of municipal autonomy (*villazgos*) to hundreds of villages seeking freedom from oppression by ruling towns and cities. Moreover, the monarchs appropriated into the royal domain, and then sold governing rights to, villages under the jurisdiction of the military orders and of the church. This wholesale conferring of municipal autonomy represented a political decentralization with far-reaching implications. The proportion of autonomous municipalities in Castile nearly doubled: whereas before 1500 only about 40 percent were independent, by the end of Habsburg rule over 75 percent had gained their autonomy.[68]

The royal government gained ready cash from the immediate proceeds of the sales. Furthermore, it benefitted from increased tax-collecting ability through direct negotiations with ever-more-numerous autonomous villages. Politically, the result was an incremental decentralization of power. But the newly autonomous villages turned out to be intensely loyal to the monarchy that had granted their administrative freedom. And they shepherded local resources so efficiently that the Habsburgs were able to extract ever-higher taxes from rural Castile – taxes providing the bulk of the cost of Spain's imperial ventures. Yet despite the disagreeably high taxes, Habsburg Castile after the 1521–2 Comunero Revolt remained surprisingly free of political rebellion. Nader concludes that the reason for this political docility was that personal liberty was not an issue for

Castilians: they had personal freedom, and they felt that they had control of their own affairs through their local councils.[69]

In some cases, the villages gained the rights of municipal autonomy gradually. María Asenjo González found that various villages under the jurisdiction of the powerful city of Segovia were able to win a measure of juridical independence through a royal license of 1505 conferring the authority to resolve some litigation locally, thus reducing the need for trips to Segovia. This increased the village councils' economic power and prestige, and opened the door for them to obtain full municipal autonomy (*villazgos*) later, through direct negotiations with the crown.[70]

The transfer of a village's jurisdictional rights involved not only drafting the proper legal documents and an exchange of money, but also a number of elaborate rituals performed on the spot by representatives of the crown. In the first place, since the price of municipal autonomy was normally based upon the number of citizens in the place, it was necessary to draw up a current census, which had to be witnessed by a royal official.[71] The official transfer of jurisdiction – whether involving a mere conferring of the rights of municipal self-government to a village formerly under a royal town, or whether involving a more complicated multiple-step conversion from ecclesiastical or military order to royal – required crown representatives to visit the village. The ceremonies officially changing a village's jurisdictional status could be performed during a single day in abbreviated form, but usually required a week or more.[72] For example, after Sienes (Guadalajara) purchased its independence from the crown (which had appropriated it from the Bishopric of Sigüenza), the formalities officially conferring municipal autonomy lasted from January 25 until February 13 of 1583. A specially commissioned royal official (in this case, the area's *corregidor*), along with his notary (*escribano*), held meetings with the citizens of Sienes, supervised the election of municipal officers, erected a gallows and stake (*horca* and *picota*), the standard symbols of juridical independence, and made a general inspection tour of the village. The *corregidor* also arranged for Sienes' new officials to meet with their counterparts in neighboring villages, to jointly survey their mutual boundaries.[73] Naturally, that type of prolonged visit by royal officials, wielding their symbols of authority and accompanied by notaries diligently recording every action, must have been witnessed by everyone in the village.

The Habsburg sale of *villazgos* changed the lives of people in rural communities throughout the Kingdom of Castile by giving them greater control over their own affairs through democratic town meetings and elected local officials. But the newly independent villages often were obliged to defend their autonomy through lawsuits against their former masters, who tried to retain their former control over pastures, taxation, and other matters. For instance, Quintanilla (Valladolid) had to go to court in 1551 to force Peñafiel (its former master) to allow its citizens to cut fire-wood in the local common woodlands. Castile's Chancillerías (Appeals Tribunals) heard countless cases of this type, and many of the lawsuits dragged on almost interminably. For example, a suit between the city of Trujillo and its former villages lasted from 1552 until at least 1631. Litigation of that duration was not only irksome but also expensive.[74]

The cost of litigation, added to the initial purchase price of municipal autonomy, often proved a severe drain on the financial resources of the newly independent villages. As the political observer Melchor Soria y Vera wrote in 1633, the villagers purchased their jurisdictional liberty only to fall into an even worse situation. Many had borrowed money to buy their autonomy, and now had to go further into debt, even to meet their normal tax obligations. To cope with the predicament, many village governments authorized the plowing of common pastures, and obtained crown permis-sion to levy special taxes to forestall bankruptcy. The combination of circumstances in many communities had unfavorable consequences, including a substantial loss of population through emigration.[75] Furthermore, in many places a small village elite was able to exploit the situation for its own benefit. In the judgment of the *arbitrista* Miguel Caxa de Leruela (writing in 1631), "The exemption of villages is nothing but a rejection of ancient custom, to abuse the administration of justice, so it can be orchestrated among cronies, and to subject the poor to the rich, dissipate the community's property, and to give free reign to insolence." And indeed, Angel García Sanz found that this happened in Villacastín after it gained its freedom from the jurisdiction of Segovia.[76]

VILLAGERS IN COURT

As we have seen, the issue of municipal autonomy brought many village governments to court, thereby exposing countless ordinary rural folks to the workings of the royal justice system. But since medieval times village governments had grown accustomed to using lawsuits for a variety of purposes. Juan Carlos Martín Cea calls them "almost a daily activity" for late medieval Extremaduran villages. The most numerous suits were between neighboring villages over disputed boundaries. These disagree-ments sprang up constantly, and tended to be unending, at times lasting into several centuries. Extended litigation represented considerable expen-ditures, not only to grease the tracks of the legal system, but also to send representatives with powers of attorney (*procuradores* and *personeros*) to other municipalities, to various tribunals, and even to the court. Local governments often had to finance their expensive litigation through special tax assessments (*repartimientos*), which sometimes precipitated citizen protests and even lawsuits.[77]

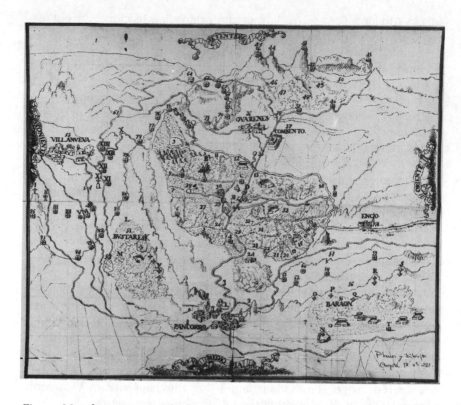

Fig. 9. Map depicting several villages in Burgos province. Submitted as evidence in a lawsuit (1552–1729) over rights to a formerly shared common woodland (*monte*) to which the newly autonomous villages were attempting to establish exclusive jurisdiction. Municipal boundary markers are indicated by capital letters and Roman and Arabic numerals.

Castilian village governments proved adept at using the court system to defend their rights against all threats, whether coming from neighboring municipalities, their own citizens, powerful nobles, or the Mesta. Helen Nader sees in the Castilian litigiousness a sign of confidence in their ability to govern themselves, and an indication of faith in the monarchical system. In any case, suits were plentiful in the sixteenth and early seventeenth centuries.[78] But it was not only through these institutional lawsuits that villagers became involved in court cases. Ordinary individual villagers were also willing to use the courts to obtain satisfaction for perceived injustices. And many of these simple rural people proved remarkably adept at manipulating court procedures to their advantage. Richard Kagan cited the example of a certain Isidro Rapino, resident of the village of Villalobos (León), who successfully employed a variety of disruptive legal tactics to postpone paying for some wheat that he had bought. Kagan found that ordinary peasant-farmers, as well as village artisans, shopkeepers, innkeepers, and itinerant merchants figured prominently in Castile's court cases, because they had property to protect. Many middle-class rural people were literate, they knew how the legal system worked, and they were not afraid to use it. In fact, they found that a lawsuit was (in Kagan's words) "an excellent means of settling scores, exacting revenge, and getting what one hoped to achieve through other, more amicable means." Even paupers were able to use the courts, aided by free legal services provided at each higher tribunal. By the second half of the seventeenth century, however, rising costs and adverse economic circumstances reduced the number of individual peasants using the courts, leaving the expensive appeals process almost exclusively to municipalities and other corporate entities, or to wealthy individuals.[79]

CONTACTS WITH THE SEIGNORIAL LORD

This is not the place to describe the seignorial system as it functioned in early modern Castile. The classic source for the topic is Alfonso María Guilarte's institutional study. It should be supplemented by more recent scholarship by Bartolomé Yun Casalilla, Ignacio Atienza Hernández, and others. Gregorio Colás Latorre supplies an up-to-date historiographical essay on seignorialism from a general Iberian perspective, and Benjamín García Sanz provides an outstanding study of a Castilian district.[80] Previous sections of this chapter have touched upon several aspects of Castilian seignorialism. In the context of this chapter's preceding section about charters of municipal autonomy, we might add that the Habsburg monarchs, at the same time that they were selling *villazgos*, also raised money for the Royal Treasury by selling formerly royal villages (or villages appropriated from the church or military orders) into the seignorial jurisdiction of noblemen. This "refeudalization" of Castile, which assumed major proportions under Charles V and Philip II, brought numerous protests from disgruntled villagers resentful of falling under the control of nobles. The protests frequently were based upon the fact that seignorial lords found it possible to use their power to usurp the local commons and other village property. Cognizant of this problem, the Castilian Cortes repeatedly condemned "the grave damage that the subjects of Your Majesty receive when turned into vassals of private individuals."[81]

A village that strenuously objected to falling under a nobleman's jurisdiction could return to royal status by matching the price that the new lord had paid the Royal Treasury. And many villages did this, while others acquiesced in their new situation. In the end, although there was undeniably an expansion of seignorial power in sixteenth- and seventeenth-century Castile, being under seignorial jurisdiction was not particularly oppressive – no more than being under the jurisdiction of another municipality. Villagers who intensely disliked having a seignorial lord simply emigrated to another place, and there is considerable evidence of this happening. But many Castilian peasants actually preferred to live under the protection of a powerful (and benevolent, of course) lord. And it was in the interest of the lord to treat his peasants well, lest they leave his village, for they were free to do so. In the last quarter of the sixteenth century seignorial jurisdiction became more attractive, as the financially pressed Habsburgs increased fiscal pressure on the royal domain. The existing methods of tax assessment and collection placed an unfair burden on those in the royal domain. Juan E. Gelabert tells us that by the reign of Philip IV, "seignorial territories were seen as taxhavens for the oppressed." And Ignacio Atienza Hernández agrees that the intolerable levels of taxation in royal areas apparently stimulated migration to seignorial enclaves.[82]

Although it was often advantageous to live under seignorial jurisdiction, this was not always so. Undeniably, there were many lords who treated their villagers with arrogance and even cruelty. Villagers who felt abused by their lords frequently took them to court. During the sixteenth century Castile's aristocracy was dragged continuously into court by peasants who used lawsuits to limit seignorial power. The royal appeals courts, perhaps as a way to reduce the pretensions of the nobility, welcomed cases initiated by villages against their lords. Although the peasants did not always win their cases, through litigation they could often postpone unwanted seignorial actions.[83] And we might add that the highly independent Castilian peasantry often simply refused to comply with seignorial obligations that they regarded as unfair or oppressive. In 1527 the lord of Castrillo de Falle (perhaps Castrillo de Haya, in Santander province) had to take the village to court to uphold his traditional feudal right of free room and board when visiting the place.[84]

THE TAX SYSTEM

The backbone of Castile's royal taxation was a sales tax (*alcabala*) of fluctuating rates levied in cash on all market transactions. Village governments could contract to have this and other royal taxes administered by tax farmers, who would pay the Royal Treasury cash in advance, then collect the necessary sum from local inhabitants during the following year. But the tax farmers earned a reputation for unfair and coldhearted methods, leading most villages to opt for direct payment of a fixed annual lump sum through a procedure known as *encabezamiento*. After 1537 the crown offered all autonomous municipalities in Castile the option of paying their royal taxes in this way. Through the *encabezamiento* the municipal council itself was responsible for local tax administration and collection. Each village designed its own system of raising the necessary amount, but typically the operators of the local tavern, inn, butcher shop, and stores would cover part of it, and the remainder would be assessed among the citizenry. The village systems often contained glaring inequities, but they were developed and administered locally, giving the people the feeling that they were in control of their own destiny.[85]

In traditional feudalism, tax collection was a prerogative of the seignorial lord, and this was a considerable source of wealth. In the sixteenth century Castile's royal government in theory discouraged aristocratic tax collection, but in practice many lords by royal concession or long usurpation were able to collect the *alcabala* for themselves, and even to determine the rate. The Castilian lords were able to maintain their revenues, but they lost their direct seignorial control over their peasants, and increasingly the lords negotiated *encabezamientos* for their villages, and turned tax collection over to the village governments. The lords were able to retain a share of the collection for themselves, and this provided a dependable source of revenue, but after the 1540s price inflation caused seignorial income to fall in real terms. By the 1570s the position of the aristocrats had deteriorated so badly that not even the increased royal tax levels and higher land rents were able to compensate for their previous losses. As a consequence, municipal councils were often able to negotiate important benefits from their lords.[86]

Municipalities in Habsburg Castile delivered their royal taxes in several ways, depending upon their jurisdictional status. Villages under royal jurisdiction, or in the military orders, paid their taxes directly to the court, or to the tax officer of the nearest Chancillería. Villages under the jurisdiction of a Cortes town or city delivered their taxes to the governing municipality, which sent them as part of a larger package to Madrid, Granada, or Valladolid. Thus in various ways the process of national tax collection required contacts with the outside world. Furthermore, the collection of the tithe brought outsiders to the village, as did the collection of the crown's share (the *tercias reales*, or royal third) of the tithe. The village council of Garrafe del Torío (León), writing in 1586 of the *tercias* collectors, wrote "they are always people from [the city of] León, and from outside the village." And village people often traveled to towns or cities as representatives of local taxpayers.[87]

It is well known that Castilians paid far more than their fair share of taxes in Habsburg Spain. Exploiting the political docility of the kingdom, the crown drastically increased Castile's tax burden during the course of the sixteenth century. Between 1504 and 1577 the *encabezamientos* rose in value by a factor of 4.89 while the general price level increased only by 2.73. And in 1590 the crown and the Cortes agreed on new tax called the *millones*, introduced as a "temporary" measure, but which became a regular feature of Castilian taxation. After each new tax increase there were anguished protests that excessive taxation was destroying the productive capacity of the country. And it must have been difficult for the country's producers to absorb these tax increases, particularly because several were drastic and sudden. But the tax did not fall equally on all parts of Castile, or on all productive sectors. The system was marred, in fact, by gross inequities.[88]

Along with other historians, I have blamed excessive taxation for bringing an economic crisis to Castilian agriculture. And undoubtedly the high taxes worked a hardship on many rural families. But recent scholarship suggests that the major negative impact of royal taxation on rural Castile was not direct, but indirect. Bartolomé Yun Casalilla remarks that the general level of taxation was not really excessively high. And indeed, Francis Brumont's calculations indicate that the *alcabala* of the 1580s and 90s seldom exceeded 3 percent of the value of rural production in villages of the La Bureba district of Burgos province. Several other scholars have concluded similarly that royal taxation amounted to only a fraction of the tithe during this period. The state, in other words, was hardly imposing a back-breaking tax load. Yun Casalilla suggests that the worst thing about Golden Age taxation was not that it was so high, but that it targeted the wrong people. The sale of *villazgos* left many of Castile's cities and trading towns with unfairly high *encabezamiento* payments, which had been negotiated for years in advance. Needing to raise additional revenues, the trading towns and cities found it convenient to place the bulk of the tax increases on people involved in artisanal and trading activities. This could be justified, because those people were involved in sales, and the basic tax was on sales. But the result was that the urban middle classes with the entrepreneurial vigor that supported the non-subsistence economy were forced to bear a disproportionate share of taxation. That made them particularly vulnerable to economic fluctuations. And when struck by a series of unfavorable factors in the late 1500s, many of these middle-class entrepreneurs were ruined, emigrated, or simply abandoned their activities. That caused Castile's cities to decline, which in turn affected rural areas because of their interconnected economies.[89]

THE SALE OF THE *TIERRAS BALDÍAS*, AND OTHER *ARBITRIOS*

The costs of Habsburg imperialism obliged the Castilian monarchs repeatedly to raise taxes and to borrow vast sums of money. By the time of Philip II, the resources of Castile had been mortgaged for years ahead, and the Royal Treasury was forced to devise new revenue-enhancing schemes called *arbitrios* (expedients). A number of such programs were tried: some were recycled older ideas, while others were totally new. Among the *arbitrios* used by the Habsburg monarchs were sales of: titles of nobility, offices, licenses to mint and export coin, licenses to export grain and mercury, various exemptions, *villazgos*, and *tierras baldías*. The truth is that the Royal Treasury was so strapped for funds that it was willing to sell almost anything to obtain ready cash. And it discovered that it could raise money not only by selling things, but also by selling promises *not* to sell them. Cities with dependent villages, for example, were willing to offer cash in exchange for a crown pledge not to sell *villazgos* in their territory. Moreover, the Treasury was able to sell annulments to sales already made.[90]

Many of the Royal Treasury's *arbitrios* had a direct impact on the lives of Castilian villagers. The sale of *villazgos*, discussed earlier in this chapter, had far-reaching consequences for rural people. The sale of municipal offices and of patents of nobility (*hidalguía*, which conferred tax exemptions) also affected our villagers – in a negative way for those not doing the buying. But arguably the *arbitrio* that had the greatest impact on rural life was the sale of *tierras baldías* undertaken during the reign of Philip II. *Tierras baldías* was a vague term applied to lands of various types, mainly public lands, including village commons used for both pasture and arable. Most villages based their ownership of their commons (or *tierras baldías*) upon longstanding tradition, rather than upon legal titles. This enabled the crown to declare that the lands in question were crown property that had been illegally usurped, and that the occupiers would no longer be permitted to use them *unless* they purchased titles of ownership from the crown.[91]

Many of the *arbitrios* of the period had turned out to be fiscal disappointments, but the sale of the *tierras baldías* was an unequivocal winner for the Royal Treasury, ranking as a major source of crown revenue from the 1560s through the 1590s. The sales began tentatively in the early 1560s, but by the 1570s the Treasury had mounted an extensive campaign, dispatching specially commissioned judges (*jueces*) throughout the kingdom to adjudicate *tierras baldías* to His Majesty, then to sell them to the highest bidder. Since many of these lands were being used by individuals, often through allotments of village common lands, the sales brought a substantial increase in private property ownership. But it was general crown policy to give preference to municipalities over individuals whenever the municipalities could be considered as the landholders. Since the villages controlled not only their commons, but also the other public lands within their jurisdiction, that gave them the option of purchasing their commons, or even *all* the unowned lands (i.e., *tierras baldías*) in their territory. Map 10 shows the provincial distribution of the sale of *tierras baldías* during the reign of Philip II. The greatest revenues came from the wealthiest parts of the kingdom at the time: Andalusia because of the stimulation of the American trade; the central provinces because of Madrid's growing importance as a political and commercial center; and the Tierra de Campos because of its cereal-producing ability and the fairs of Medina del Campo.[92]

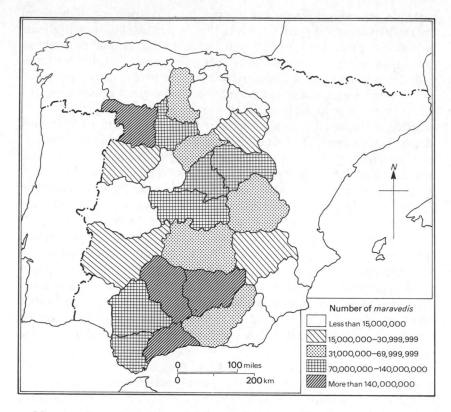

Map 10. Comparative *tierras baldías* sales during reign of Philip II. Adapted from Vassberg (1983: 241).

I first learned of the sale of the *tierras baldías* quite by accident a quarter century ago while engaged in other research. Recognizing the importance of what was a virtually unworked topic, I took it for my doctoral thesis, later published as several articles and a book. It was my hypothesis that the immediate effect of the sales was salutary for rural people because of the advantages of legal ownership, but that the long-range consequences were negative because of increased peasant and village indebtedness at a time of increasing economic problems. Subsequent research by other scholars has vindicated my view. Recent studies of la Mancha by Jerónimo López-Salazar Pérez, and of the province of Madrid by Alfredo Alvar Ezquerra, draw attention to the importance of the sales, without arriving at a clear judgment concerning their long-range consequences.[93] The most thorough analysis of the impact of the sales to date is in Bartolomé Yun Casalilla's study of the Tierra de Campos. Yun Casalilla called the sales "a decisive event in the history of the area ... [because of] the repercussions that they had on municipal finances and on the economic

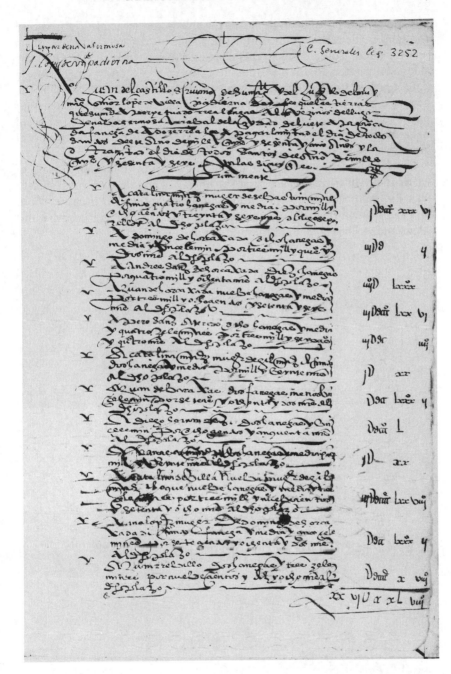

Fig. 10. First page of a roster of villagers from Navahermosa (near Huete, province of Cuenca) who purchased *tierras baldías* from royal *Juez* Lope de Villapadierna in 1565.

situation of local individuals." Yun Casalilla's verdict is clearly negative: the sales made it more difficult for the people of the area to recover from adverse circumstances, often encouraging them to emigrate. In sum, the sales contributed to the seventeenth-century recession.[94] Angel García Sanz reached similar conclusions about the sale of *tierras baldías* in the province of Segovia: by privatizing local common lands, and by extracting payment from poor peasants who were farming them, the sales impacted negatively upon the general peasantry, and favored the concentration of land ownership in the hands of a privileged few.[95]

García Sanz concludes, after examining the Royal Treasury's sale of *villazgos* and of *tierras baldías*, that the impact of the state on rural society was far more consequential than mere fiscal pressure, because those programs unleashed forces that were highly prejudicial to the social and economic wellbeing of the rank and file of villagers.[96]

7

CONTACTS WITH TRAVELERS AND "ALIENS"

INNS

*E*arly modern Spain was a highly mobile society – its people constantly on the move. This brought outsiders through rural areas that lay astride important trade or communications routes. Muleteers and carters, along with other travelers (both Spanish and foreign), thus temporarily entered the village setting, bringing with them new ideas and unfamiliar material possessions that had the potential to disrupt local ways of doing things. Furthermore, although the travelers might not intend to settle in the villages along their travel itineraries, their temporary presence created business opportunities for the local inhabitants. Places along important roads were likely to have inns (*posadas, albergues, mesones, ventas,* or *casas de hospedería*) and taverns (*tabernas*) providing services to travelers. Early modern Castile seems to have had an abundant number of inns. Even small villages, if the location was suitable, might contain several establishments of this type. For example, little Cumbres de Enmedio (Huelva), which had no more than 69 households in 1555, was the site of five inns, because it lay on the road between Seville and Lisbon.[1] Zuñeda (Burgos), with only around 60 households in the 1570s, had four inns because it serviced the Burgos–Vitoria traffic. And there were six inns in Pancorvo (Burgos), a village of some 300 households on the important Burgos-to-Bilbao road.[2]

But places that were bypassed by Spain's network of roads, or that were too close to larger towns or villages, had no such facilities at all. For example, a report from 1579 indicated that in Castrillo de Rucios (Burgos) there was no inn, nor had there *ever* been one, because the village was so out of the way that nobody ever passed through unless he lost his way, and when that happened, a village councilman (*regidor*) would put him up out of charity. Similarly, the remote hamlet of Carril (León) lacked an inn, and required the local tavern keeper to provide a place to sleep for any traveler who needed to pass the night. The *Relaciones* show that inns were lacking in many a village. When there *was* an inn in a remote village it

Fig. 11. Roadside inn and mule train outside Antequera (Málaga province) on the road to Málaga. Detail from Georg Braun, *Civitatis orbis terrarum*, vol. 3, no. 9 (Cologne, 1576–1618).

was likely to be marginally profitable. This was reported by Gonzalo Melia, the innkeeper of Villarrodrigo (Jaén). Melia declared that he could barely support himself and his family, because not many guests stayed there. An inaccessible and unprofitable location posed a difficult problem for places under the jurisdiction of a powerful trade-oriented city that required all of its subject villages to have an inn. That was the situation of little Villalbal, a mountain village with only about a dozen households in the 1580s. Because the city of Burgos compelled them to have an inn, the families of Villalbal took turns as innkeepers, each serving in that capacity for a few months, on a rotating basis.[3]

On the roads of Old Castile, the distance between inns was probably not very great, particularly in the north, where villages were usually not far apart. Furthermore, there was often a need for inns between villages, because many people traveled by foot and could not walk very far in a day. Consequently, some inns – like twentieth-century motels – were situated along major roads rather than in town. For example, some enterprising citizens of the hamlet of Estavillo (Alava) by the late 1400s had gotten into the business of offering rooms to travelers along the Burgos–Vitoria route. This entrepreneurial activity provoked a suit by the innkeepers of the nearby market town Miranda de Ebro, who had lost business as a result of the competition. In fact, there were frequent lawsuits involving inns along this route, which suggests that there were good profits to be made.[4] And here, and elsewhere in Golden Age Spain, many venturesome villagers offered overnight quarters or meals for travelers in their own homes, and it was not unusual for widows to take in travelers as paying guests. In fact, in 1558 the innkeeper of Monleón (Salamanca) was a widow who used her home to put up travelers. Inns like that were similar to twentieth-century bed-and-breakfast establishments. Since most of these inns had not been originally designed to accommodate paying guests, some of them were exceedingly crude. If we can believe the poetry of medieval Castile (fairly realistic, in one scholar's judgment), in isolated areas some shepherds (female shepherds, in fact) made extra money by letting travelers take shelter overnight in their simple dirt-floored huts.[5]

The image of the shepherd-innkeeper is consistent with historical reality, because early modern Spanish village innkeepers rarely were exclusively in the business of running an inn. They normally also had fields and flocks to tend, or some other economic activity, because innkeeping was for most people a sideline, rather than a full-time occupation. For example, Diego Herrero was the innkeeper of Fuentepinilla (Soria) in 1586. But he was also a prosperous farmer who worked his grain fields with two yokes of oxen (a single yoke being the norm). He also owned some other cattle, three donkeys, a few pigs, and a vineyard that yielded 8 *cántaras* (about 128 liters) of wine per year. Clearly, Diego Herrero was a person with standing in his community. Nevertheless, I have not seen enough examples like this to be able to state with certainty that the typical innkeeper ranked among the most prosperous persons in the village, as Huppert found for other parts of Europe. In fact, the two innkeepers of Tórtola (Guadalajara) in 1595 seem to have been among the *least* well-off people in the village. Innkeeping was a sideline for both: one was a farmer, and the other a goat rancher.[6]

Moreover, in the eyes of the Spanish upper classes, innkeeping was a servile occupation. Spain's prestigious Order of Santiago refused membership to innkeepers, along with taverners, painters, and practitioners of other "vile" and "lowly" trades. Perhaps another indication of the profession's low social standing is that many innkeepers were widows or other women who needed the scanty income from an occasional paying guest to keep them from destitution. For example, in 1572 Juana de Castrillo ran an inn in Herrín (apparently Herrín de Campos, province of Valladolid). And in 1561 one of the innkeepers of Puente del Arzobispo (Toledo) was Juana Martínez, a widow with five small children. Juana had no source of income besides her paying guests, and was described as "poor."[7]

But not all inns were marginal operations, nor were all female innkeepers on the edge of poverty. Indeed, another widow-innkeeper of Puente del Arzobispo was Cecilia Hernández, who had an even larger family (six daughters and three sons) to feed. But the widow Hernández was definitely not poor. She owned a house, in addition to her inn, and on top of that she had property worth 1,000 *ducados* – a respectable estate. And Antonia Sánchez, an unmarried innkeeper in Morales de Toro (Zamora) in the 1560s, was one of the most prosperous inhabitants of the village, judging from her sales tax (*alcabala*) assessment. Sánchez was a Basque from Vizcaya, by the way, but unfortunately the document does not divulge how or when she arrived in Morales de Toro.[8]

Contrary to what we might think, the early modern Spanish inn often did not offer its guests much except a bed (frequently no more than a cot or a pile of straw) for themselves, and a stable and fodder for their animals. In fact, according to a tax report of 1558, the *only* supplies used by the inn at Monleón were barley and straw – that is, fodder for the guests' animals.[9] If the traveler himself was hungry at an inn like that, he had to supply his own ingredients for a meal. That meant carrying meat, wine, and other provisions as baggage; otherwise, it was necessary to search out the local butcher shop, tavern, bakery, fish handler, and so forth, because municipal ordinances in many places prohibited innkeepers from selling foodstuffs! That was a privilege reserved for those who held monopoly concessions from the local government. Once the weary guest had located the authorized sellers, and purchased the raw materials for a meal, he could either cook the ingredients himself, or hand them over to the innkeeper to prepare. Obviously, this system made it exceedingly complicated for travelers to stop overnight. To alleviate the situation, in 1560

Philip II authorized innkeepers to sell food and drink to travelers. Nevertheless, many towns and villages retained their monopolistic ordinances, and travelers throughout the seventeenth century continued to complain about the restrictions.[10]

Spanish inns of the period were infamous not only for their failure to provide amenities, but also for their filth, noise, vermin, and their dishonest clientele and owners. Cervantes played to the stereotype of the last in *Don Quixote* (I, 2) where he called an Andalusian innkeeper "as crafty a thief as Cacus" (Vulcan's proverbially thieving son, in Roman mythology). The inns were frequently the scene of violence brought on by wine-provoked arguments between clients. For instance, the people of Cumbres de Enmedio (Huelva) complained that in the local inns there were "many disagreements and fights, and even deaths, between the local citizens and between outsiders, with no law enforcement or punishment."[11] But although Spanish inns were neither clean, comfortable, nor orderly, they were usually inexpensive. Prices were controlled by royal and municipal governments, and innkeepers were required to post their prices (*tener arancel puesto*) prominently for customers to see, to avoid arguments over charges.[12] They were also to display a sign at the door, identifying the place as an inn, and they were to keep on hand accurate dry measures (of one *celemín*, and fractions) for selling fodder. Inns that failed to obey these stipulations were subject to fines.[13]

In fact, as indicated in Chapter 1, Spanish municipalities tried to regulate all sectors of the economy, and the hostelry business was as highly regulated as any. Sometimes there were different levels of municipal regulation. For example, the inns and taverns of Alcalá de Guadaira (Seville) were subject not only to local ordinances, but also to the oversight authority of the nearby city of Seville. Alcalá's inns were obliged to secure a special license from the city every time they wanted to keep a guest overnight. And Alcalá's taverns were forbidden to serve meals to local citizens.[14] These regulations can only be understood in the context of a local economy tightly controlled by municipal governments that were jealous of their own power, and anxious to perpetuate the existing system of municipally established monopolies, because these worked to the fiscal advantage of the local governments. Consistent with the medieval church's condemnation of business for profit, the municipal ordinances of early modern Spain typically expressed an official horror of "profiteering" (*regatonear*). The inns of Antequera, for instance, were not to sell wine, which was supposed to be in the taverns' domain, and the taverns were not to serve meals to their customers. But here, as elsewhere, the local government was flexible in its policy, and when bombarded by protests, the city fathers amended the ordinances to allow taverns to provide meals if they wished, *provided* that they sold bread at the same (municipally regulated) price set for bakers, and that they offered meat at a "just" price.[15]

Although forbidden by municipal law in many places, inns elsewhere *did* have the right to offer food to travelers, and not merely the sardines and caramels sold by an innkeeper of Tórtola.[16] The quality of these roadside meals varied depending upon the establishment, but Spanish inns in general had a reputation for unpalatable cuisine of dubious provenance. According to Spanish Golden Age folklore, if you ordered rabbit at an inn, you risked being served cat, and if you ordered beef, your plate would likely contain horseflesh. Meat pies and meatballs were especial objects of satire, for it was widely thought that these dishes at an inn might contain flies, dog, rat, or even human flesh.[17] The Spanish Captain Alonso de Contreras wrote contemptuously of a supper he had been served at an inn in Hornachos (Badajoz).[18] And Cervantes addressed the topic, where Don Quixote (I, 2) was served at a country inn a barely edible meal consisting of a portion of tough and half-cooked cod, a filthy lump of black bread, and wine. But bad cuisine was not ubiquitous: even discriminating French travelers, such as Barthélemy Joly and François Bertaut, reported that they had found some Spanish inns that served good meals.[19]

But country inns were probably just as important as fuel stations for horses and mules as they were as stopping places for humans. In fact, the inns often serviced the animals while scarcely attending to their owners at all. We can surmise this from the supplies used by the above-mentioned inn in Monleón, and also from an incident where four horsemen rode up to an inn (*venta*) where Don Quixote (I, 43) was staying. They arrived in the early morning hours while the place was still locked up for the night, so they banged noisily on the door for the innkeeper to come out and feed their horses some barley, because they were in a hurry and needed to be on the road again as soon as possible.

Castile's important trading cities had special inns (*casas de carretería*) for carters, who with their vehicles and animals provided essential transport services. These carters' inns were large buildings with courtyards and stables, dining facilities, and sleeping rooms. But undoubtedly the normal thing for carters was simply to camp alongside the road, where their oxen had free pastures, and the carters themselves did not need to pay for a room. The local innkeepers, to be sure, would rather have had the carters as paying customers. And local residents in general were not overjoyed by the presence of camping cart caravans, because the carters' oxen competed with local animals for scarce pasture resources.[20]

TAVERNS

A tavern in early modern Castile was a place licensed by the local government to sell wine. Rather than a special building designed for wine sales, the village tavern was nearly always an ordinary village house that was called a tavern merely because someone living there was an officially designated wine vendor.[21] The tavern keeper in principle held a monopoly concession for local retail wine sales, in exchange for a promise to make wine available at a stipulated price. Taverns – like inns and other business establishments in villages, towns, and cities throughout Spain – were strictly regulated by the municipal government. Prices and profits were fixed, and the tavern keeper was required to keep accurate liquid measures,[22] and to maintain a stock of "good" wine, under penalty of a fine. Since wine was produced almost everywhere in Spain, and the typical villager had a small vineyard, most rural people probably had their own supply of wine. Nevertheless, there were always some rural households that needed to purchase wine, either because they had no grape vines, or because their own production was insufficient for their needs. The tavern was supposed to supply these people with reasonably priced wine.

Municipal regulations were often quite specific about how wine was to be marketed, but these regulations varied enormously from place to place, depending upon local conditions. For example, in Morales de Toro (Zamora) – in an important viticultural zone – the local vineyard owners had the right to sell to the public from their own production, and this normally satisfied local needs most of the year (usually from November through June, if not longer).[23] So in Morales, the task of the tavern keeper mainly was to bring in wine from beyond the village territory after the local supplies had been exhausted. And in villages all over Spain, having a tavern normally meant importing enough wine from the outside world to make up the difference between local production and local consumption. That being the case, it was a distinct advantage for the tavern keeper to have some mules – or at least a donkey – for transporting the wine from its source to his tavern. In some places, the agreement between the municipal government and the taverner stipulated where the imported wines would come from. For instance, in the late 1500s the tavern keeper of Montenegro de Cameros (Soria) was expected to get his stocks from Nájera (7 leagues away), Navarrete (8 leagues), and Logroño (9 leagues).[24] These areas were conveniently located, holding the cost of transportation to a minimum; moreover, they lay within the Rioja zone, the origin of some of Spain's finest vintages.

Just as some villages had more than one inn, some had more than one tavern. For example, in the mid-1560s Morales de Toro had two taverners, although the place was in wine country, and had only 250 households.[25] But that should not be taken as evidence that running a tavern was a lucrative business, because there is ample proof that it was only marginally profitable in the typical village. In fact, operating a tavern – like having an inn – was usually a part-time activity, rather than a full-time occupation. For example, the tavern keeper of Barrios de Villadiego (Burgos) in 1597 was Juan de García, a day-laborer (jornalero). García worked in the fields of others, because he had none of his own, but he had two burros to use in his wine business, and he was also half-owner of a flock of ten sheep.[26] The part-time nature of wine selling was stressed by the tavern keeper of Montenegro de Cameros (Soria) in 1587. A 54-year-old who had operated the local tavern for the past two years, the taverner complained that he really didn't make enough profit on wine to make it economically interesting. In fact, he declared that he would not have been able to continue the tavern if he had not also held the village bread concession (*panadería*), and if he had not earned additional money by transporting textiles with his mules.[27]

The truth is that small villages found it difficult to find anyone willing to serve as a tavern keeper. A report in 1586 from Garrafe del Torío (León), a place with barely forty families, indicated that the village government was seldom able to persuade anyone to take the responsibility, and had even considered *paying* somebody to run the local tavern. And in Castellanos (León), and in Castrillo de Rucios (Burgos) the village government actually *did* pay someone to be their tavern keepers, because they had found that otherwise no one would accept the position. How else could a village with only fifteen families (Castrillo de Rucios) expect to have a tavern?[28] In small places like that it appears that running the tavern was more of a service activity than a moneymaking enterprise.[29] The language of the above-mentioned Garrafe report suggests as much. Furthermore, that might explain why there was often such a rapid turnover of tavern keepers. For example, in the six-year period 1552–7 four different people held the position in Monleón (Salamanca).[30] That would also explain why the tavern keeper was frequently a non-native of the village, and was often a woman. Catalina de Anbrona, for instance, ran the tavern of Sienes (Guadalajara) in 1583; and Mari González was the taverner for the villages of the Hermandad de Barrundia (Alava) in 1581–2. Female tavern keepers were not a Golden Age innovation, for we know that women since medieval times had done that type of work. Thus, the female taverner in the story "Un vino barato," from Carlos García's *La desordenada codicia de los bienes ajenos* (1619), is a totally credible character, from a historical standpoint.[31]

That does not mean that taverns were never profitable. A tavern keeper in a populous village that needed to buy a large quantity of wine might have done quite well economically, and might even have been able to devote him/herself exclusively to wine selling. That appears to have been the case of Domingo Bravo, who operated the tavern of Aravaca (Madrid) in 1627. Aravaca had fewer than a hundred *vecinos* at the time, but its proximity to Madrid seems to have made the wine business unusually profitable. A village along a major thoroughfare, similarly, might have a tavern that sold a large quantity of wine. Surely that explains why the tavern of Calera (Toledo), a place with only 230 *vecinos*, was able to sell 4,000 *arrobas* of wine in 1590 – far more (around 74 gallons/*vecino*) than we would expect for a village of that size.[32]

Although serving as a tavern keeper might not have brought much profit, that did not keep an hidalgo from accepting the job in Abelgas (León), according to a 1582 census.[33] But Abelgas lay in Spain's mountainous north, where a large proportion of ordinary working people claimed hidalgo status. And on the whole, tavern keeping was regarded as a menial occupation near the bottom of the socioeconomic scale. As mentioned above, taverners and innkeepers were denied membership in the prestigious order of Santiago.[34]

Municipal regulations were designed to guarantee not only the price, but also the quality of the wines sold in the local taverns. But despite prohibitions against selling adulterated products, the temptation must have been great to increase profits by surreptitiously adding a bit of water to the stocks. Spanish folklore from the period displays the unshakable conviction that tavern keepers regularly "baptized" their wine. The famous Golden Age writer Quevedo (d. 1645) echoed this sentiment by calling tavern keepers "waterers" (aguadores).[35] But although this stereotyping certainly reflected historical reality, it is somewhat misleading. City dwellers might have accepted watered wine, but rural people accustomed to drinking their own unadulterated vintages would more likely have demanded the real thing. Moreover, in the village setting the threat of social ostracism might have deterred tavern keepers from defrauding their customers – unless, of course, they were travelers passing through.[36]

In any case, taverns and inns provided the infrastructure for encouraging a stream of outsiders to pass through the territory of early modern Spanish villages, and perhaps even to tarry a while. Regardless of the social-juridical category of the travelers, and regardless of their reason for being on the road, their temporary presence left a mark on everyone in the local community.

MORISCOS

The subject of the Moriscos (nominally Christian Spaniards of Moorish ancestry) has fascinated generations of historians. Consequently, the Moriscos' tragic history is quite well known, and here I will merely summarize the overall story, before looking at how the Moriscos influenced village life. After the conquest (1492) of the Islamic Kingdom of Granada, despite a promise to respect Islamic traditions, Ferdinand and Isabella permitted fanatical priests forcibly to baptize the defeated Moors. This provoked a serious rebellion in 1499, which had to be militarily suppressed. Two years later, all Muslims throughout the Kingdom of Castile were ordered to convert or leave. That made the entire country officially a homogeneous nation of Christians, the Jews having been expelled in 1492. After that, the forcibly converted Moors (now called Moriscos) lived an uneasy existence under Christian rule, trying to preserve their ancestral culture in the face of Christian hostility. Relations between the rulers and the Morisco minority grew increasingly tense, reaching breaking point in 1567, with the publication of a royal decree designed forcibly to assimilate the Moriscos into the dominant culture. The decree forbade the continued use of the Morisco language (Arabic), cuisine, dress, and other ancestral traditions. Furthermore, it ordered Morisco children to be taken from their parents to be brought up in a Christian environment. The result was the Second Rebellion (the First having occurred in 1499–1501) of the Alpujarras (1568–70), which was suppressed after savage fighting and bloody massacres by both sides. After that, the royal government ordered the surviving Moriscos of the Kingdom of Granada to be dispersed in small numbers throughout Castile, Extremadura, and western Andalusia. At least 80,000 Moriscos were forcibly resettled in this fashion, with great cruelty and needless suffering and death.[37] Figure 12 depicts Moriscos in the Kingdom of Granada, prior to their expulsion.

The resettlement of the Granadan Moriscos was supposed to destroy their traditional societal bonds, thereby hastening their assimilation into mainstream Christian society. But the policy failed. For one thing, the communities that received the Moriscos viewed the new residents as aliens, and typically received them with suspicion and hostility. The Inquisition exacerbated matters by persecuting the Moriscos, and a disproportionate number of Moriscos were sent to the galleys. The ill will of the Christian host communities interfered with the process of assimilation.[38] Furthermore, most of the Moriscos from Granada had been small farmers, who the royal officials hoped would become agricultural laborers (jornaleros) in the Christian communities where they were resettled. But things did not work out that way. The Moriscos were unaccustomed to the Castilian type of agriculture, which was extensive rather than the intensive irrigated farming of the Islamic tradition. Moreover, the uprooted Granadans resisted the idea of being transformed into a rural proletariat to be exploited by Castilian landowners.[39] Consequently, most Moriscos eventually abandoned the villages, to become independent horticulturalists supplying urban markets with fruits and vegetables, as they did around Segovia and Palencia,[40] or they turned to peddling, mule-driving, or other service trades. In the late 1500s the corregidores of León, Medina del Campo, Cuenca, Huete, Avila, and Ciudad Real complained that altogether too many Moriscos had become traveling merchants, or were involved in the carrying trades.[41] Such highly mobile occupations enabled the dispersed Morisco communities to maintain contact with each other and to retain their sense of cultural unity despite their geographical separation. Moreover, over time the Moriscos in Castile tended to abandon the rural areas where they had been placed, and to gravitate toward towns and cities. There they could more easily ply their trades, and they could strengthen their in-group ties. By 1595 most of the Moriscos of north-

Fig. 12. Moriscos (with women in traditional dress) on the road outside Granada. Detail from Georg Braun, *Civitatis orbis terrarum*, vol. 3, no. 14 (Cologne, 1576–1618).

western Spain lived in cities. In fact, three-quarters of them lived in eight urban centers: Valladolid, Avila, Salamanca, Segovia, Medina del Campo, Burgos, Palencia, and Arévalo. The growing urbanization of the Castilian Moriscos tended to ghettoize them, although the royal government had wished precisely to *de*segregate the minority group. To a large extent, the

Moriscos re-established their own separate communities in a normal sociological response of a marginated group surrounded by a hostile population.[42]

Thus the Moriscos remained an unassimilated minority, and Spain's Christian leadership grew increasingly apprehensive about the presence of this alien group. Despite being native-born Spaniards with ancestral roots eight centuries old in Spain, the Moriscos were a distinctly foreign group, in the eyes of other Spaniards. The foreignness was not in physiognomy, for the average Morisco did not differ appreciably from his average Old Christian neighbor. The difference was cultural: in language, dress, cuisine, values, manners, and other habits. These differences triggered the xenophobic tendencies of Old Christian Spaniards. Many resented the frugality and economic success of the Moriscos despite their mistreatment and pariah status. Others were indignant at the failure of the Moriscos to become fervent Roman Catholics, although the Christian leadership had not provided adequate doctrinal instruction for them. But most worrisome to the royal government was the fear that the Moriscos might assist the Ottoman Turks in an attack on Spain. This threat was largely fanciful, for the Turks had no real plans to invade Spain at that time. Nevertheless, in the troubled international climate of the late sixteenth and early seventeenth centuries it seemed plausible, and the menace of a Turco-Morisco alliance gained credence as the Inquisition uncovered a number of conspiracies involving the Moriscos and their trans-Mediterranean Islamic cousins. The fear of Morisco collaboration with Spain's foreign enemies was reinforced with the discovery of secret negotiations between Moriscos and agents of France's King Henry IV (an enemy of Spain).[43]

In the end, although there appears to have been no clear national consensus demanding the measure, the royal government decided to expel the entire Spanish Morisco community. The expulsion was carried out mainly from 1609 to 1611, with some additional deportations as late as 1614. All told, approximately 300,000 Moriscos were forcibly expelled from Spain during this period. An untold number of these were truly Christian, or were peaceful citizens with no subversive thoughts, but they were expelled as dangerous aliens nevertheless. The Moriscos had represented only about 4 percent of Spain's total population, but they were unequally distributed, and some regions were greatly affected by the expulsion. In Valencia, nearly a third of the population had been Moriscos, and they had been the most productive agriculturalists of the area. Several parts of Aragon and Murcia were also hard-hit, for the same reason. Old and New Castile were the least affected regions of Spain, because they had only around 45,000 Moriscos between them, and these lived in small groups scattered throughout their territory. However, the Moriscos had been prominent as carters and muleteers in Castile, and there is some evidence that their expulsion brought a shortage of transport. In fact, the

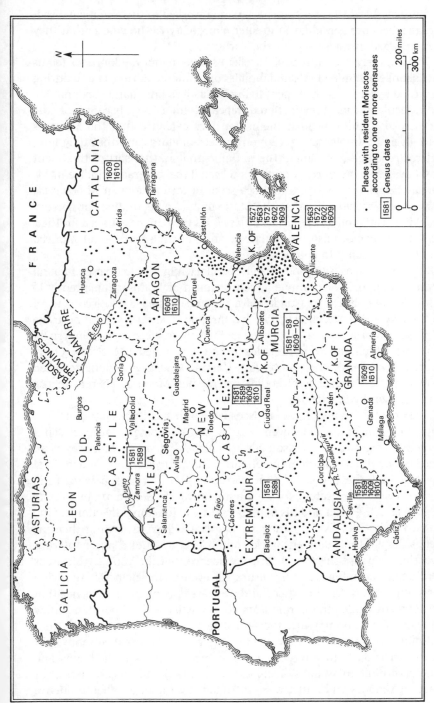

Map 11. Geographical distribution of Moriscos before their expulsion. Adapted from Le Flem (1982: 95).

mobility of these Morisco transporters had worked to their political disadvantage, because it had given greater plausibility to the charge that they were engaged in espionage for the Turks.[44]

Unfortunately, the numerous excellent studies about the Moriscos tell us little about how individuals and families of Granada Moriscos fared during the 30-odd years that they spent living in Castile's Christian heartland. We can speculate that they suffered repeated injustices, because of the widespread hostility against them. We have evidence that the Moriscos were given an unpleasant reception in Extremadura, and that they later suffered repeated harassment there. Unfortunately, that sort of treatment may have been the norm. Cervantes reflected the general prejudice in his *Novelas ejemplares* (1613): a Morisca seller of love-potions in *El licenciado Vidriera* was credible because the Moriscos had a reputation for sorcery and witchcraft; and in *El coloquio de los perros* they are denounced for their avarice, rapacious business practices, and concupiscence – all Morisco qualities, according to popular stereotype.[45]

But the Moriscos' situation in a given village might not correspond at all to the stereotype. For example, a census taken of El Casar (apparently El Casar de Talamanca, in Guadalajara province) listed 8 Moriscos out of 413 *vecinos*, with the observation "all [are] poor, and they have no trade or business other than their work."[46] And a census of Herreruela (Cáceres), which had 80 households in 1586, identified 4 Moriscos: 3 daylaborers (*jornaleros*), and one servant (*[mozo] de soldada*) – none reported as owning any property, although several non-Morisco laborers in the town *did* own livestock.[47]

We know that many of the Moriscos were well acculturated to Christian ways, and that many had even become sincere Roman Catholics. That being the case, we can reasonably speculate that many Moriscos were accepted by their Castilian neighbors. The *corregidor* of Ciudad Real reported that the people of that city gave the Moriscos a warm and generous welcome, grateful for their agricultural skills. And in *Don Quixote* (II, 54) Sancho Panza and his neighbors display touching affection for the Moriscos who had lived in their La Mancha village, accepting them as friends despite their different background. This was not a purely literary invention, because there is historical evidence that the younger Moriscos were often becoming quite acculturated, even to the point of marrying Christian spouses. On the other hand, we have documentary evidence that the Moriscos tended to migrate from rural Castile to the cities. Since they abandoned the countryside, they must not have found village life very appealing. There is a need for additional local studies to shed more light on the question.[48] In any case, the presence of Moriscos in towns and villages throughout Spain's Castilian heartland – whether as settlers or as itinerant vendors and muleteers – introduced yet another alien influence into supposedly isolated rural areas.

GYPSIES

The Gypsies were another ethnic minority with a culture distinct in many ways from that of the Spanish mainstream. And like the Moriscos, although their ancestors might have lived in Spain for generations, the Gypsies were obviously different, and lived on the margins of Spanish society.[49] The exact origin of the Spanish Gypsies is uncertain, but they appear to have descended from groups who migrated from India toward Europe in the tenth century. It is not certain when the first Gypsies arrived in Spain, but by the mid-1400s their presence was well known, and they stood out as a distinctly alien group. A royal decree of 1499 aimed at assimilation: the Gypsies were to abandon their migratory existence, to obtain local citizenship, to take up a trade, to cease the use of their distinctive language and dress, and to become integrated into the larger community. But this decree seems to have had little impact, for the Gypsies continued their marginated existence. And the Gypsies remained clearly different from other Spaniards. Although intermarriage with Europeans and others (northern Africans and Moriscos, for example) had modified their original physiognomy, Gypsies tended to have darker skin and features that suggested a foreign background. Far more importantly, however, was the fact that they *acted* like outsiders: the Gypsies spoke an alien tongue (Romany) among themselves; they wore bizarre clothing; they belonged to tribe-like groups; they maintained a migratory life style; and they seemed to function within a completely different moral system. Although officially Roman Catholic Christians (like everyone else in Spain by 1502), the Gypsies' religious practices were so divergent from the Spanish norm that they were branded scandalous, impious, blasphemous, or even downright satanic. Like the Moriscos, Gypsies in the public mind were often associated with witchcraft and sorcery. And the Gypsies were not averse to exploiting this reputation, as fortune tellers and hawkers of magic spells and paraphernalia.[50]

The predominant Romany economic activities were animal trading, sheep-shearing, metal working, and musical performance and dance – the last gaining lasting prominence as *flamenco*. Although "Flamenco" was a misnomer (Spanish for "Flemish"), the term served to accentuate the alien and exotic character of this art form. The Gypsies, in addition to their legal occupations, were infamous thieves and scam artists. Mainstream Spaniards were distrustful and contemptuous of the Gypsies, although they found them fascinating in many ways. Cervantes reflected the popular feeling of the day in his exemplary novel *La gitanilla* (1613): "It seems that the Gypsies came into this world to be thieves; they are born to thieving parents, they grow up with thieves, they study to be thieves, and in the end, they turn out to be nothing but thieves; and their desire to steal and stealing are inseparable qualities that only disappear with death."[51]

The Cortes of Castile repeatedly complained about the Gypsies' conduct. In some parts of Spain Gypsy bandits made raids on undefended isolated settlements, in 1630 a Gypsy group was accused of murdering a royal post carrier in Sepúlveda, and in 1638 a band of Gypsies was blamed for an attack on a merchant convoy. It is hardly surprising that there were calls for harsh measures against them. Beginning with a decision of Charles V in 1539, the preferred sentence for Gypsy lawbreakers was a term in the galleys. And after the battle of Lepanto (1571), when the Spanish navy needed increasing numbers of oarsmen, the government decided simply to impress members of the despised alien minority. In 1575 *all* able-bodied Gypsy men were ordered to the galleys – not as punishment for theft or some other crime, but as a suitable penalty for the mere fact of being a Gypsy. An erratically enforced nation-wide Gypsy hunt ensued, in the interest of supplying the galleys. In Cuenca, for example, 19 Gypsy men were arrested, of whom 15 were deemed suitable as oarsmen. Most were between seventeen and twenty-five years of age. And these included not only itinerant vagabonds, but also Gypsies with sedentary occupations. The latter were paid a small salary, whereas their migratory brothers were forced to row without pay. The seventeenth century brought an even greater effort to impress Gypsies into galley service: in 1609 the Council of Castile ordered six years of unpaid galley service for all adult male Gypsies not engaged in agriculture; in 1635 a royal decree ordered all unemployed Gypsy men between 20 and 50 to the galleys; and in 1639 an order went out for *all* Gypsy men to be sent to the galleys, because "the galleys need oarsmen, at a time when that infamous race are too numerous."[52] In this way, many unfortunate Gypsies ended up on the galleys, but it is clear that the orders for mass sentencing were not rigorously executed. And since there seemed to be just as many Gypsies as ever, eventually there were calls for totally expelling them from Spain. The *arbitrista* Juan de Quiñones proposed this in 1630, as did his contemporary Father Pedro de Figueroa, who wrote of the Gypsies:

Their actions place the Faith in grave danger, because they live an impious life, they intend nothing but wickedness, and their life goal is the greater neglect of their soul. Their deceits are either pacts with the demon, or lies in order to steal ... I was correct to call them vassals of the demon because a band of Gypsies is nothing but an army of Satan.

And in the eighth discourse of his *Restauración política de España* (1619) Sancho de Moncada argued that the job begun with the expulsion of the Moriscos would be incomplete until the Gypsies were similarly driven from Spain.[53]

If this was the general Spanish view, why were the Romany spared the fate of the Moriscos? Possibly the answer lies in the fact that the Gypsies were such a small minority that they provoked more loathing than fear.

And the Gypsies never posed the foreign policy threat attributed to the Moriscos. Furthermore, by the 1630s many thoughtful Spaniards had realized that the expulsions of the past had done far more harm than good. And in 1633 Philip IV decreed that it would be unwise to expel the Gypsies, since that would further depopulate his kingdom.[54] So the Gypsies remained in Spain, although a despised and alien caste living on the margins of society. They maintained their separate identity, partly because that is how the Gypsies wanted it. And therein lies one explanation for the fact that Gypsies do not seem to have had a major direct impact on the life of Spanish villages. The Romany life style and economic enterprises demanded the proximity of large non-Gypsy populations. Therefore, the Gypsies either inhabited their own districts in towns or cities, or they lived in camps within easy commuting distance of towns or cities.

How large a presence did Gypsies have in the early modern Castilian village setting? The question is not easy to answer. Spain's Romany population was small and tended to concentrate in or near urban areas, but the Gypsies were highly migratory, and bands of them traversed the country-side as they wandered from place to place. Consequently, they inevitably came into contact with villages, particularly along major roads. The records of the Spanish Inquisition (which persecuted the Gypsies for their unorthodox religious practices) document the presence of Gypsies in villages along important trade routes.[55] But the Gypsies also found their way to relatively inaccessible villages. They seldom show up in local censuses, because they were transients, rather than permanent residents. Nevertheless, the Gypsy presence was documented from time to time. The parish records of Rute, for example, a village in the rugged south of Córdoba province, indicate that fourteen Gypsy children were baptized there between 1570 and 1620. Since there were no official Gypsy residents of the place, we may suppose that those children were brought in for baptism while their parents happened to be passing through.[56] In the end, because of the Gypsies' migratory life style and legendary shiftiness, the average Castilian villager probably knew about Gypsies, even if he had never had direct contact with one. And despite the distinctly unsavory reputation of Gypsy traders, they were often welcomed by villagers eager to buy their wares.[57] Bernard Leblon, in his study of Spanish Gypsies, found that early modern villagers were often favorably disposed toward the minority group, even when they were engaged in illicit activities (such as banned horse trading), because they expanded the range of local economic choices. In fact, Leblon provides numerous examples of village officials protecting Gypsies from prosecution by the Santa Hermandad and other outside authorities – even when the Council of Castile appointed special judges to punish Gypsy lawbreakers. In these instances the villagers felt more solidarity with the Gypsies, who were viewed as providers of useful goods and services, than with the intruding royal officials and Hermandad officers, who were perceived as outsiders with an even worse reputation for corruption, greed, and untrustworthiness.[58]

On the other hand, Castilian villagers were capable of intense anti-Gypsy prejudice. I found proof of this in a document from Casasola (Zamora), which tells of a certain Alonso Maldonado, a reputed Gypsy who ran the local store (*habacería y tienda*). Maldonado in 1568 had been awarded a one-year concession to operate the store, but he was forced out after only ten months, accused of adulterating his merchandise, and of using dishonest weights. According to one witness (the most obviously prejudiced and hostile of a group of four who testified):

Not long after [Maldonado] began to serve in that business, the people began to develop hatred and enmity towards him, and to avoid the fish and oil of his store; because it was notorious that he added horse urine to the fish [to increase the weight], and that he mixed lamp fuel with the cooking oil, and that he did other bad things ... and even the day laborers said that they would buy nothing but bread from his store, and not fish; and because [Maldonado] refused to sell merchandise to any citizen of the village on credit; and that he was considered to be a bad Christian because of the above and because he always went to church late, and only on Sundays; and because of the reprimand that the village priest made because of it; and because [Maldonado] was deceitful ... and because of all of that and because of many other things, the people of the village abhorred him, and they decided that he should not finish out his term of supplying [the local store]; and [Maldonado] left ... so he couldn't be arrested and punished; and it is rumored in this village ... that [Maldonado] was from a band of Gypsies, and they nick-named him Alonso Maldonado Gypsy.[59]

The testimony from Casasola does not prove conclusively that Maldonado was a Gypsy, but it reveals a rural mentality so biased against the Gypsies that a person accused of nonconformism or dishonest practices was likely to be considered a member of that despised group on the flimsiest evidence. Some rural Spaniards were so convinced of the malignant nature of the Gypsies that they even blamed them for natural catastrophes that ruined their crops. Since urban Spaniards were similarly prejudiced, it is a marvel that the Romanies did not fall under the exclusionist policy that resulted in the expulsion of the country's Jews and Muslims.[60]

SLAVES AND EX-SLAVES

Slaves occupied a special legal category. The institution of slavery, widespread in Roman times, had greatly diminished in Europe during the Middle Ages, but had never completely disappeared. Under the influence of Christianity, however, refined by ethnocentric sentiments, the people of Europe gradually decided that it was morally repugnant to enslave their fellow Europeans. Consequently, they reserved chattel slavery for those outside the European community, chiefly Muslims, black Africans, and Native Americans.[61]

However, although early modern European society generally rejected the idea of subjecting its own kind to slavery, it did not shrink from the notion of forced labor for prisoners. And the various European countries regularly compelled political and criminal prisoners to man their galleys, to perform plantation labor, and to supply the human labor for other forced work projects.[62] The prisoners who were assigned to work gangs or galley service were marched under guard across the countryside to the work site or to the port of embarkation. Don Quixote (I, 22) on the road near the Sierra Morena met a gang of about a dozen criminals who had been sentenced to the galleys. They were on foot, strung together by chains linking their necks, with manacles on their hands. This was a type of mobility that the participants did not relish, for galley service was exceedingly rigorous. In any case, the proportion of rural Spaniards who were sent to the galleys seems to have been relatively low. A study by I.A.A. Thompson indicates that only between one-third and two-fifths of forced galley workers had been directly employed in agriculture (i.e., were from villages), at a time when close to 90 percent of the population was involved in rural pursuits.[63]

Human slavery had been an accepted practice in Islamic Spain, and the Muslims introduced slaves from throughout the known world, including sub-Saharan Africa. In medieval and early modern Christian Spain, incessant conflicts with the Islamic world produced a steady supply of human chattels, because prisoners of war could be enslaved. Ferdinand and Isabella's conquest of the Muslim Kingdom of Granada (1482–92), the rebellions of the conquered people of that area (1499–1500 and 1568–70), the naval victory of Lepanto (1571), and assorted raids into North Africa resulted in the enslavement of veritable droves of Islamic peoples. For example, when the city of Málaga fell to the Christian army in 1487 the entire surviving population was enslaved, of whom around 2,300 persons reached Seville alone.[64] Moreover, at least as early as the 1300s Spanish merchants plying the trans-Saharan trade had brought black slaves to Seville. And in the mid-1400s, Spanish sea captains exploring the coast of West Africa returned with black slaves, along with large numbers of enslaved *guanches*, tawny-skinned natives of the Canary Islands. But the major suppliers of black slaves for Spain were the Portuguese, who in 1479 secured from the Castilian monarchy a monopoly on the introduction of sub-Saharan African slaves. When Portugal came under Spanish domination in 1580, Portuguese slave traders found it even easier to import African blacks into Spain. And until 1640, when Portugal regained its independence and Portuguese slavers were excluded from the Spanish market, there developed a lively trade in African slaves. Owing to the Portuguese connection, towns along the overland routes from Lisbon and the Algarve were well supplied with black slaves.[65]

Despite its importance to the history of the country, slavery in early modern Spain has not yet received the attention that it deserves. We now have a number of excellent local studies, however, and a general synthesis is forthcoming.[66] Certainly there is no lack of evidence about Iberian slavery, because local and central archives are rich in this type of documentation. There are lacunae, however, in the data about slaves. For example, because of inconsistent reporting and missing records, we will never know how many Africans were forcibly brought into Spain during this period. Antonio Domínguez Ortiz, who has demonstrated an uncanny knack for reaching correct conclusions despite faulty sources, has calculated that by the end of the sixteenth century there were no more than 100,000 slaves in Spain, of whom roughly half were white (Berbers, Turks, and Levantines) and the rest black. But recent research has caused Bernard Vincent to conclude that this figure is too low.[67] In any case, all authorities agree that the overwhelming majority of slaves ended up in large Spanish cities, especially Seville, Madrid, Valencia, and Málaga. There they were employed chiefly as domestic servants – often as articles of luxury to flaunt the owners' wealth. Cervantes memorialized Seville's black household slaves, and the prevailing prejudices against them, in his *Coloquio de los perros*, published in 1613. Blacks in Spain stood out because of their physical characteristics, and this caused many observers to exaggerate their numbers. For instance, the Spanish Jesuit Baltasar Gracián (1584–1658) wrote that the inhabitants of Seville were "neither completely white nor completely black," while another writer of the day likened that metropolis to a gigantic chessboard, asserting with unabashed hyperbole that it contained as many blacks as whites.[68] This, of course, referred to the city of Seville, and not to Spain as a whole. As the country's slave capital, Seville had an unusually heterogeneous ethnic composition. But so did the whole of southern Spain: in fact, Alessandro Stella concluded in a recent article that the population of Golden Age Andalusia was probably duskier and blacker than that of Paris in the 1990s, where non-whites are highly visible.[69]

We may be tempted to think that slaves, being forced to live with their masters, would not have had much mobility. But the evidence that we have about slaves indicates that they often crisscrossed the Iberian peninsula and the western Mediterranean. Henry Kamen found an astonishing degree of geographical mobility for eight Moorish slaves captured in Valencia in the late 1600s, much of which was the result of the slaves' own spirit of vagabondage.[70]

As Bernard Vincent has noted, many of Spain's so-called "domestic" slaves spent part of their time tending their owners' crops or animals. Hence "urban" slaves often were involved in agricultural activities. For example, Vincent found a 1581 census of the city of Málaga listing 534 slaves, of whom 118 were used primarily for agricultural work, and an additional 51 partly in agriculture. But for Castile in general, it appears that only a small proportion of slaves were used exclusively in rural productive activities, and these were concentrated in Lower Andalusia, especially around Seville and Málaga. Even here, however, there were few villages where slaves constituted an appreciable proportion of the population. There was no plantation slavery in early modern Spain, except in the Canary Islands, nor was rural slave labor an activity involving large groups working together. Instead, slaves in Castilian villages tended to appear singly, or as a few isolated individuals in an economy overwhelmingly dominated by free labor.[71] The documentary references to rural slaves that I have seen have involved isolated individuals, rather than groups representing a numerous servile underclass. For example, a prosperous citizen of the village of Canillas de Aceituno (Málaga) owned a black slave who served him as a goatherd. In that case, the slave's race and status apparently were mentioned in the document precisely because they were out of the ordinary. An example from central Castile: in Caballar (a 68-household village in Segovia province), a census included one Bartolomé de la Torre, identified as a slave without naming his owner. Though his origin is unstated, de la Torre was probably a Morisco expelled from the Kingdom of Granada. In any case, despite his "slave" status, he was described as an independent horticulturalist who made a living by growing fruit to sell in the city of Segovia and surrounding towns.[72]

Although there were few slaves in Spain employed strictly in agriculture, there were enough urban slaves around the country – even in medium-sized cities – to make rural Spaniards aware of their existence even if they had never actually seen one. For example, in 1557 there were five black slaves in Trujillo, and three in Cáceres, both smallish Extremaduran cities. Perhaps that explains why the municipal ordinances (1583) of a remote village like Los Santos de Maimona (Badajoz) referred to slaves.[73] We must remember that Extremadura bordered on both Portugal and Andalusia, entry points for most of Castile's black slaves. Furthermore, many wealthy Extremadurans (particularly returning conquistadores and their families) could afford the luxury of slaves. Consequently, an occasional slave could be found in the villages of the area. For example, there was a slave living in Palomas (Badajoz) in 1590, but we are not told his race. In general, however, outside of Andalusia it was unlikely for a Castilian village to have a slave. The two household slaves of the widow Ana López, in the Toledan village of Menasalbas, were not only the only ones in town, they were probably the only ones in the entire district. And slaves were exceedingly rare in the villages of northern Castile. Nevertheless, even here they did occur. In Villa de Pun, for example, a Rioja village of ninety-eight families, a census taken in 1575 showed Captain Gaspar Delgado's household with a slave (of unstated origin) named Rafael, in addition to two non-slave maidservants.[74]

With the passage of time, many slaves gained freedom for themselves or their children through purchase or through manumission by benevolent owners. Freedmen never comprised a large proportion of the population, but in cities like Seville former slaves and their descendants came to be quite visible working as masons, street peddlers, stevedores, and in other low-prestige occupations. And in Palos de la Frontera (Huelva) nearly one-fifth of the children born between 1568 and 1579 were described as black. Palos was a fishing village between Portugal and Seville, thus unusually apt to have slaves enter its territory.[75] The typical Castilian village was rather unlikely to become the abode of slaves or ex-slaves. Yet, inevitably, some freedmen ended up in ordinary rural communities, injecting an exotic element into villages that otherwise might have been remote from the slaveholding world. I have found a few documentary references to these. One is from a lawsuit that reached the Chancillería of Granada in 1568. The suit was between olive grower Pedro Suárez de la Vega and the village of Alcolea (apparently Alcolea del Río, upriver from Seville on the Guadalquivir) over olive trees planted on land that the village government wanted to reserve for pasture. In any case, Suárez was represented at the Chancillería by a certain Francisco Camacho, described in his power of attorney as "a dark-skinned free citizen of the said village of Alcolea," and as "a black man" by the officials in Granada, who were plainly surprised by his color. It seems quite clear that this freedman (or descendant) was of African heritage. Yet, he must have been a person of considerable standing in his community, else he would hardly have been entrusted as legal spokesman before the High Court.[76] Men like Camacho must have been authentic rarities, however, in rural Spain. The other two ex-slaves that I have found were in far more humble situations. One was Catalina González "the swarthy," a widow living in Puente del Arzobispo (Toledo) in 1561. The widow was described as a former slave who was "poor, with no property whatever." And finally, a certain Tomás de Etiopía (literally, "Thomas from Ethiopia"), a free black married man residing in the hospice of Puerto de Santoña (Santander) in 1578. Although not identified as such, surely this black man was a freed slave or a descendant of slaves.[77]

OTHER EUROPEAN NATIONALITIES

It is well known that a numerically modest, but exceedingly important, number of French, Portuguese, Genoese, German, Flemish, and other foreign merchants, shippers, financiers, and professionals came to early modern Spain on business trips, often settling in the country permanently. These foreigners operated principally in the cities. Nevertheless, their presence affected rural areas economically and culturally, because of the continuous interchanges between town and country. But foreign nationals also had an impact on rural Spain in a more direct way. In the first place, despite the *arbitrista* Lope de Deza's assertion (1618) that foreigners in Spain were not food producers but mere consumers, there was a considerable flow of rural workers into the country from its two immediate neighbors: Portugal and France.[78]

Given Portugal's long common border with Spain, it would be surprising if there had been no human migration between the two. And in fact, villages in the Spanish border provinces were highly likely to contain Portuguese immigrants – both temporary and permanent. There were no effective governmental restrictions on border crossings, and during the sixty years (1580–1640) that Portugal was ruled by Spanish kings, it was even easier for Lusitanians to move to Spain. Portuguese immigration into rural areas came at all societal levels. Many Lusitanian youths found jobs in Spain as life-cycle servants (*mozos de soldada*). Castilblanco, a village in the border province of Badajoz, had one of these Portuguese young men in 1586. Other immigrants found similar low-paying jobs: two Portuguese shepherds were working in Cordovilla (Salamanca) in 1629; and in Puente del Arzobispo (in Toledo province at its boundary with Cáceres) a census of 1561 listed Catalina Alvarez, a poor single Portuguese who supported herself by sewing and by teaching embroidery to village girls. Inevitably, the presence of Portuguese immigrants caused some local resentment because of their competition for jobs and land. We have evidence of that in a suit against a Portuguese alleged to have illegally farmed land on the Spanish side of the border near Badajoz.[79]

But it appears that relations with Lusitanian immigrants were usually quite cordial – not surprising, because they were so similar to Spaniards, physically and culturally. In fact, it was not at all rare for Spaniards to take Portuguese spouses. This happened at all social levels, from the royal families of the two countries to the most humble villagers. Thus we should not be surprised that in Villar de la Yegua, a village near the Portuguese border in Salamanca province, at least two prominent families had a recent Lusitanian connection: the widow of a local hidalgo married a Portuguese husband; and the local *corregidor* took a Portuguese wife.[80]

As we would expect, the sixteenth-century economic boom in Andalusia brought by the American trade attracted numerous immigrants from Portugal, and many of these came as rural workers. In fact, in the 1600s we find Portuguese reapers as seasonal migratory workers in Cádiz province, and it seems that this was a practice of long standing. There had certainly been Portuguese cowboys and swineherds in the area in the early 1500s.[81] And in Rute, a relatively inaccessible village in the hills of southern Córdoba province, there was such an influx of Portuguese that by 1591 they represented 3.5 percent of the population.[82]

Portuguese immigrants were not nearly as common in the central and eastern parts of Castile. Nevertheless, they appear with some regularity in early modern censuses even in these areas. For example, a 1576 roster of the citizens of Fernancaballero, in the province of Ciudad Real, included Pedro Fernández, a Portuguese whose wife also may have been from Portugal. Another example of longer-distance immigrants is a Portuguese couple living in Mohedas (Toledo).[83] And in little Avellaneda (Avila), a mountain village with only 118 households, a census of 1578 listed a surprising number of Lusitanian immigrants:

- two orphaned children (presumably of deceased Portuguese immigrants) in the charge of a local priest;
- one Portuguese household head who had been granted local citizenship;
- two Portuguese servants working in local households;
- and a Portuguese who had moved to the village, seemingly with his wife and children, a year earlier.

We can only speculate why a little pocket of Portuguese ended up in this rather unlikely spot. But networks of kin or friendship were surely involved. Perhaps the Portuguese who had become established as a citizen was responsible for bringing the others to Avellaneda.[84]

The importance of rural French immigration into early modern eastern Spain – notably Catalonia, Aragon, and Valencia – is well known, thanks to a number of demographic studies published since 1960.[85] Catalonia in particular received large numbers of immigrants from north of the Pyrenees. It is noteworthy that the overwhelming majority of French immigrants came from the south of France – the most accessible area of Spain's northern neighbor. In fact, the Pyrenees had always been a porous border, permitting the development of a longstanding tradition of transnational migratory exchanges. As Natalie Zemon Davis related in *The Return of Martin Guerre*, national boundaries were no obstacle to early modern villagers seeking escape, adventure, or jobs.[86] Much of the emigration to Spain was spontaneous and individualistic, to be sure. But in various parts of France veritable emigration networks sprang up, based upon kinship and acquaintance, to facilitate the movement of people to target locations in Spain, which came to have concentrations of Gallic immigrations. In many places this system allowed successive generations to move temporarily or permanently to Spain. Once in Spain, the immigrants took urban or rural jobs. In the sixteenth and seventeenth centuries, French immigrant employment tended to be predominantly rural in Catalonia, about evenly rural and urban in Aragon, and overwhelmingly urban in Valencia.[87]

French immigrants to Castile, however, seem to have gone almost totally into urban jobs, with a mere 1 or 2 percent working in agriculture. I have seen hundreds of census rolls of early modern Castilian villages, and I do not recall seeing a single Frenchman on the rolls. Certainly there must have been many villages with French immigrants, particularly along the border; I simply have not encountered any in my censuses. It is not completely clear why French immigrants were so rare in the villages of Castile, at a time when French immigration was of major importance in rural areas of eastern Spain. We know, however, that the various parts of the Iberian peninsula followed different demographic and economic rhythms. Consequently, they had differing manpower needs and differing opportunities for immigrants. The geographical distribution of French workers certainly reflected those realities.[88]

There is, despite my own failure to encounter French immigrants in censuses of rural Castile, evidence that they existed in substantial numbers. The Marquis de Villars, French ambassador to Spain in 1679–81, wrote of hundreds of agricultural workers and shepherds in Navarre, and of thousands of laborers in the two Castiles, Extremadura, Galicia, Asturias, and Andalusia. Villars was prone to exaggeration. But his general impression was confirmed by Père Labat, who wrote at the century's end that there were over 20,000 French workers in Andalusia alone, of whom many had agricultural jobs. It appears that these were life-cycle workers, rather than permanent immigrants, because Labat was informed that most of them returned to France after a few years in Spain. Antoine de Brunel, who visited Spain in 1655, similarly was impressed by the numbers of French immigrant workers, including migrant reapers. And there is evidence of a substantial number of French workers in eighteenth-century Castile.[89] This is a subject that deserves further investigation, using local records. Since the compilers of censuses were usually quick to identify foreigners, it should not prove difficult to count them.

Before leaving the subject of French agricultural workers in Castile, I want to mention the use of prisoners of war. Over fifty years ago Carmelo Viñas y Mey, in his pioneering study, cited a mid-seventeenth-century report from the Council of Castile documenting the use of captured French soldiers to perform various kinds of labor including reaping and other field work – apparently in the Madrid–Guadalajara area. According to this report, the prisoners were treated with generosity by their Castilian captors (in contrast to the abuses that they suffered at the hands of the Aragonese), and were even paid for their work. I have seen no other reference to French captives being pressed into service for agricultural work. It would certainly merit a detailed study.[90]

THE IMPACT ON VILLAGE SOCIETY

The travelers, Moriscos, Gypsies, slaves and ex-slaves, and various Europeans who entered the village territory were a potential destabilizing force to village society. Whether these outsiders were merely passing through, or whether they tarried to patronize local businesses, to work, or to peddle their wares, they exposed the local population to new faces (often with different races and speaking unknown tongues), and perhaps

154 THE VILLAGE AND THE OUTSIDE WORLD

unfamiliar objects and new ways of thinking. The presence of the travelers, or other "alien" visitors, was likely to disrupt local norms and routines. These contacts between villagers and outsiders had the power to transform both parties, in unpredictable ways. At times the contacts were mutually advantageous, and at other times they had negative consequences for one side or the other. Some of the contacts left visible marks; others were so subtle that it is difficult to detect, much less measure them. But the travelers and "aliens" exemplified the highly mobile and dynamic character of early modern Castilian society, and they brought to the rural world a touch of the unexpected, or even of the exotic.

8

ADDITIONAL CONTACTS WITH THE
OUTSIDE WORLD

PAUPERS, VAGABONDS, AND HOSPICES

Moriscos, Gypsies, slaves, and foreigners were groups with high geographical mobility. These were minorities, of course, distinct from the mainstream. But the Castilian population itself included a minority whose existence was equally itinerant, or even more so. These were the country's "vagabonds" (*vagabundos*), who included homeless drifters, the unemployed poor, *pícaros*, and criminals. There had always been vagabonds in Spain, but the seventeenth-century depression dramatically increased their number. Many were rural people looking for a job outside their native village. Naturally, they were attracted to cities, especially the expanding capital, and they often traveled great distances to get there. For example, in 1675 a shelter (*hospital*) in Madrid reported that many of its residents had come from Galicia. Seville, similarly, was inundated by a flood of vagrants – including what Ruth Pike calls "a continuous stream of landless peasants from the countryside." Periodic harvest failures brought even greater numbers of destitute peasants into the city. Municipal officials constantly complained about the hordes of vagrants that swarmed into Seville and other prosperous cities. They found it impossible to estimate their numbers, let alone control them.[1]

Spain was by no means unique in this respect: all of Europe had its roaming destitute poor – people who were driven from home by hunger. These migrants often traveled considerable distances in search of subsistence. As in Spain, they tended to congregate in large cities such as London and Paris, where there were greater opportunities for work and for charity, but they often moved on once their immediate needs were satisfied, or after their welcome had worn thin. The cities found the hordes of vagrant beggars alarming, and sometimes tried to expel them. Nevertheless, the European urban environment was usually more hospitable for homeless migrants than were its villages, where outsiders were more conspicuous, and more likely to be viewed with suspicion or even hostility.[2]

But although vagabonds and beggars were present everywhere in early modern Europe, both domestic and foreign observers agreed that they were more numerous in Spain than in northern countries. Spaniards were famous for their generosity, a quality that encouraged not only native beggars, but also an influx of immigrant charity-seekers from France, Italy, Germany, and Flanders. Like their Spanish counterparts, the foreign beggars tended to congregate in Madrid, leading many commentators to think that they were more numerous than they actually were. Pedro Fernández de Navarrete, for example, wrote in 1626 that "all the scum of Europe" had come to Spain, particularly those who were lame, blind, or had other disabilities.[3]

Since medieval times begging in Spain had been accepted by civil and religious authorities alike, and it had even gained a certain respectability. Some theologians pointed out that begging not only provided relief for the needy, but also gave pious Christians an opportunity to win divine grace through acts of charity. But attitudes toward beggars differed. It was well known that many so-called beggars were actually scam artists, thieves, and criminals; and it was difficult to distinguish between these and the truly deserving poor. A person who became an itinerant beggar was not necessarily penniless. Some took to the road merely because they could earn more by begging than by working at rural jobs. In certain cases, this was because of a physical handicap. Andrés de Cortés, for example, a citizen of the Asturian village of Cazo, had a crippled arm that prevented him from doing heavy farm work. Consequently, he left his village to become a wandering beggar, while his wife remained to care for their fields and animals. Presumably the crippled Cortés was genuinely needy, because the officials of Cazo described him as "poor" despite the fact that he owned a few livestock and perhaps even some land. In any case, Cortés became part of early modern Spain's multitude of physically impaired beggars. The most pitiful of these were the lame and the blind, who obviously had to depend upon charity for their survival. Cervantes and other Golden Age writers gave them a prominent place in their works. These handicapped beggars sometimes received generous handouts from sympathetic citizens. In fact, the success of the handicapped led many unscrupulous able-bodied people to feign disabilities in order to beg. Municipal governments attempted to weed out the undeserving, and to control the giving and receiving of alms through a system of licensing. But the itinerant nature of beggary, exacerbated by the underworld activities of many of its practitioners, defied official regulation. Many places tried to expel vagrants who had come in from other parts of Spain, with the aim of providing relief primarily to local destitutes. But this ran counter to the tradition of Christian charity, and was difficult to execute.[4]

The prosperous years of the sixteenth century witnessed a proliferation of *hospitales* (literally, hospitals) in cities, towns, and villages throughout

Spain. Despite the name, these were usually not medical facilities, but rather hospices (or shelters) created to provide food and lodging for the needy. Institutions of that type had existed in Spain since the early Middle Ages, and by the 1500s were an established feature of urban and rural society.[5] The funding of hospices came from various sources: wealthy individuals such as nobles; the crown; municipal governments; and religious brotherhoods (cofradías and hermandades) along with monasteries and other arms of the church. Some municipalities were eager to subsidize hospices, because that enabled them to exercise a degree of control over vagrancy.[6]

The Relaciones, as well as other early modern Spanish documents, show that nearly every village had its hospital, or hospice. In fact, the larger and more prosperous villages often had more than one. Camarena, for example, a community in the province of Toledo with 408 families, had one hospice (founded by the village government) for traveling poor people and pilgrims, and another (endowed by a local widow) that ministered to needy permanent residents. Getafe, a village of 950 families in Madrid province, also had two hospitales: one, located in an impressive building with white stone pillars and a chapel, was dedicated to caring for the sick of Getafe and other places; the other, in far more modest quarters, offered food and a bed to wandering beggars.[7]

Villages that were small, or not so prosperous, had hospitales that were barely worthy of the name. Bargas, for example, a 300-family village 9 kilometers north of the city of Toledo, had nothing but an ordinary little village house, where they offered sleeping space to poor travelers. Some hospices were endowed with the funds to supply food as well as lodging, but many had to rely on donations, and simply could not afford the expense. As the officials of San Martín de Valdepusa (Toledo) put it, their hospital offered travelers no other hospitality than a bed for the night. The hospice of Menasalbas (also in Toledo province) was also poorly endowed: located in a small house, it had to manage with a miserable annual endowment of a bushel and a half of rye – scarcely enough for essential maintenance.[8] We should not get the idea that hospices in small villages were inevitably ill endowed, however: Alcabón (Toledo), with barely over a hundred families, boasted a venerable facility that had been established so long ago that no one could even remember the names of the founders. Nevertheless, the village scheduled fifteen masses each year (undoubtedly a condition of the donors) for the benefactors' souls. Alcabón's hospice had a paid caretaker who managed the place and washed the linens of its four beds. It was the practice in Alcabón to give lodging and a single meal to the poor and sick who used the hospice, then to escort them to the next town. Burguillos (Toledo) also forced its hospice guests to move on after a single day. And that policy seems to have been widely followed – the hosts' charitable instincts tempered by a suspicion of their vagrant guests, and by financial considerations as well. Unless the recipients of local charity were permanent residents of the village, they would likely be urged to move on as soon as possible. Consequently, between visits by needy travelers, the village hospice often lay vacant.[9]

Many villages, however, permitted longer stays, whether out of genuine charity, or a more generous endowment, or a conviction that a given individual would eventually find a job and become a tax-paying permanent resident. An apparent example of long-term charitable sensitivity to the needs of a local person can be found in Montenegro de Cameros (Soria). This involved a widowed seamstress named Mari García, who in 1584 was living in Montenegro's hospice. The document does not reveal how long the widow had been living there, but it describes her as "poor," and notes that "people give her alms." Similarly, a 1612 census of Los Balbases (Burgos) reported that Pedro Infante and his wife and son were living – apparently on a long-term basis – in the local hospice, while eking out an existence through begging.[10] Not all beneficiaries of the local *hospital* stayed in the local hospice, however. A census of Puente del Arzobispo (Toledo) in 1561 listed two poor widows and one other poor woman living in "little houses" owned by the local *hospital*, which presumably supplied them with low-income housing.[11]

And we should mention that extended stays in village hospices were by no means limited to native-born residents: a census of 1586 revealed that the hospice of Castrillo de las Piedras (León) was still providing lodging for an Asturian woman who had arrived eight days earlier. In 1575 a Portuguese immigrant couple remained in the hospice of Mohedas de la Jara (Toledo) for nearly a month, before passing on. And in 1561 in Puente del Arzobispo (Toledo) a poor unmarried Portuguese woman was living – apparently on a long-term basis – in a house owned by the local *hospital*.[12]

THE RELIGIOUS ESTABLISHMENT

Spain after the expulsion of the Jews and Muslims was supposed to be a homogeneous nation of Christians faithful to the doctrines and religious leadership of Rome. Obviously, Rome was a foreign capital, but Spain had been converted a thousand years earlier, and the Roman Catholic religion had become so thoroughly Hispanized that no one thought of it as an alien influence. Moreover, *rural* Spaniards were considered almost by definition to be "Old Christians," unlikely to have been contaminated by intermarriage with Jews or Moors, or by the various heresies that the Inquisition strove to eliminate. Those were primarily urban problems. Nevertheless, the apparent religious uniformity of early modern rural Spain was an illusion, because in many respects each village had its own religious system. The faith of a given rural community was linked to the outside ecclesiastical world, with its clerical hierarchy and doctrines. But to the people of every Spanish village, their own local traditions had far deeper spiritual significance than any dogmas or directives from Rome, Toledo, or even from their own bishop.[13]

Since most villages had only one church, "parish" and "village" were practically synonymous. Religion was a corporate, or community thing, virtually inseparable from civic responsibility. In fact, there was a jurisdictional overlapping and frequent confusion of "parish" and "village." The parish church was not merely a religious edifice; it was a symbol of social and political solidarity as well. Over the centuries, deep-seated traditions grew up around certain saints, sacred relics and images, holy shrines, pilgrimages, and religious festivals. Each village developed its own devotional practices that differed from those of neighboring communities. And the villagers were fiercely loyal and proud of the distinct character of their own traditions, considering them to be superior to all others.[14] The village laity were active in religious brotherhoods, which took charge of a wide range of local charitable and devotional affairs. And these villagers were so comfortable with their institutions and practices that they often refused to submit to clerical authority when it conflicted with their own traditions and theology.[15]

THE VILLAGE PRIEST

In large measure, the tension between villagers and parish priest (*cura*) reflected the fact that the priest was usually an outsider, with no sentimental attachment to local traditions. When this outsider asserted that certain local religious practices were ignorant superstitions, his parishioners were likely stubbornly to defend their customs against what they regarded as unwarranted interference with their way of life.[16]

Although the documentation that I have seen indicates that most parish priests were from outside the village where they served, they were often from the same district. For example, the parish priest of Torrecilla (apparently Torrecilla de los Angeles, in Cáceres province) in 1586 was Alonso Muñino, a native of Santa Cruz (seemingly Santa Cruz de Paniagua, a scant 10 kilometers to the southeast); and the priest of Mohedas de la Jara (Toledo) in 1575 was Francisco Serrano, a native of El Puente del Arzobispo, a much larger community some 20 kilometers to the north.[17] It seems that the overwhelmingly illiterate environment of small villages in early modern Spain was not fertile ground for producing clergy, unless there was a nearby monastery or privately endowed school. Even before the reforms of the Council of Trent, a young man had to be literate in order to become a priest, and in the first half of the sixteenth century it was often difficult to get schooling in rural areas. So we should not be surprised if the parish priests serving small villages were outsiders, from communities large enough to support a teacher or a school. Nevertheless, Sara Nalle tells us that in the diocese of Cuenca, one-fifth of parish priests were natives of the places they served, and another one-quarter worked within 30 kilometers of their home towns.[18] Furthermore, many villages – especially those with a hundred or more households – had more than one priest. The parish priest was likely to have an assistant (*teniente de cura*) or two. Moreover, wealthy communities often had other priests employed by privately endowed chapels, religious brotherhoods, shrines, or *hospitales*. And these additional clergy were frequently sons of local families, as was Francisco García of Poveda de Obispalía (Cuenca) in 1578. They were supposed to be under the supervision of the parish priest, but it was difficult to discipline these additional priests because some of them lacked a genuine religious calling. And people complained that there were too many of them. Palacios de Goda (Avila), for example, a village of only 128 households in 1597, had no fewer than six priests. And Cubo (apparently in the La Bureba district of Burgos province), with only 60 or 70 households, had four clergymen in 1549.[19]

THE TRIDENTINE REFORMS

The Council of Trent (1545–63) redefined the doctrines of the Roman Catholic Church that had been attacked by Protestant reformers, and adopted important reforms to revitalize Roman Catholicism and to eliminate abuses. Although the doctrines of the church remained essentially unchanged, the Tridentine reforms had a major impact on local religion throughout Roman Christendom. Thanks to Sara Nalle's recent book (1992) about religious reform in the diocese of Cuenca, we have for the first time a systematic study of the reform movement on the local level in Castile.[20]

Nalle demonstrates that major changes were made in Spanish religious life, despite the strong degree of political and cultural autonomy of Castilian municipalities, and despite the powerful sentimental attachment to local traditions. Cuenca's reform bishops were able to recruit a cadre of well-educated parish priests to implement reforms at the village level. A substantial minority (around one-fifth) of these served their own home towns, and another one-quarter served parishes in the same district as their home towns. Furthermore, most of the assistant priests came from the communities where they worked. This made it possible for the reform priests to introduce changes without being attacked as outsiders trying to impose alien customs on their parishioners. Thanks to the Tridentine reforms, the educational level and moral standards of the priesthood improved, and increasingly it became expected that the clergy should have university-level training. The better-educated reform priests were more familiar with church doctrine than their predecessors had been. Hence, they were better able to instruct their parishioners, and they were quite successful in channeling local religious expressions in directions consistent with orthodox Catholic theology.[21]

As a consequence, local religion lost some of its autonomy, but the time-honored local religious customs were never completely extinguished. The Catholic Reformation did not seek to destroy the local side of religion, but merely to correct its errors and excesses. The villagers were not forced to abandon their local saints, but they were encouraged to pay more attention to universal figures like the Virgin and Christ. Even these, of course, were often localized in specific shrine images such as Our Lady of Riansares, or the Christ of Urda, which the local villagers proudly held to be superior to all other Virgins and Christs. But thanks to Trent, there was greater clerical supervision than ever before, and less deviation from European norms.[22]

RELIGIOUS PILGRIMS

For centuries one of the most popular forms of religious expression had been pilgrimages. Spain was dotted by shrines of local and regional importance that were regularly visited by the faithful. Most of the devotees of these local and regional shrines lived within a day's journey. But it was by no means rare for villagers to travel several days to pay homage to their favorite saint.[23] The most important of the Spanish holy places was in Galicia: the monument to Spain's patron saint in Santiago de Compostela, one of the most important pilgrimage sites in Christendom. Since the mid-tenth century hordes of pilgrims had trodden the roads to Santiago, coming from all parts of Europe. Because of its proximity, France provided the bulk of foreign visitors to Santiago de Compostela. The French traveler Antoine de Brunel found their numbers impressive, writing in 1665: "I cannot describe the quantity of French pilgrims coming and going to Santiago." Another contemporary witness, Cristóbal Pérez de Herrera, reported that eight to ten thousand or more foreign pilgrims, mainly French, stayed at the Royal Hospice (Hospital Real) outside Burgos on their way to Santiago every year. According to this witness, Germans and other foreigners were drawn not only by religious sentiments, but also by the ease of obtaining free food and lodging, and even cash subsidies along the way from generous Spanish hosts.[24]

Map 12 shows the major foreign pilgrimage routes to the famous shrine. Villages along these routes – and along other roads connecting with them – were unusually exposed to outside influences, both Spanish and foreign.

As mentioned above, religious brotherhoods and other charitable organizations in Spain established hospitals and shelters for the care of the sick and of those needing lodging. These facilities were frequently located along major roads and bridges for the convenience of travelers. Naturally,

Map 12. Pilgrimage routes to Santiago de Compostela (Coruña)
Adapted from the undated (apparently early seventeenth-century) "Cartes des
chemins de S. Jacques de Compostelle," reproduced in *Galicia and the Holy Year of
Saint James* (Santiago de Compostela: Xunta de Galicia, 1991).

in the minds of charitably minded Christians, their co-religionists traveling to shrines were particularly deserving of help. And since the medieval period, one of the most fashionable benevolent activities was providing lodging and food for religious pilgrims. By the sixteenth century hospices lined the most frequented pilgrimage routes, especially the roads to Santiago de Compostela. The needs of the traveling faithful dictated that many of these facilities be located in relatively out-of-the-way rural areas. In northern Zamora province alone, for example, the brotherhood of Our Lady of the Carballeda erected 35 bridges and 30 hospices for the benefit of pilgrims.[25] In the same part of western Spain, Saint Julian the Pauper's deeds in the service of pilgrims became legendary. Julian was a Leonese who had murdered his parents, for which he was sentenced by the Pope to do penance by dedicating his life to helping pilgrims. Julian's fame spread throughout Europe in the high and late Middle Ages, and inspired the building of numerous shelters for people on pilgrimages.[26]

Inevitably in the Spain of the *pícaro*, the generosity of pious Christians toward pilgrims was abused by unprincipled opportunists. This type of fraudulent activity inspired Philip II's pragmatic of June 1590, which required Castilians and foreigners alike to obtain a license from local and diocesan authorities before wearing pilgrim's habits or going on pilgrimages. It seems that many vagabonds and criminals had been disguising themselves as pilgrims to exploit the charitable instincts of the faithful, to prey on unwary travelers, and to escape suspicion under the cloak of piety.[27]

The pilgrim routes also presented an opportunity for clever people interested in more than salvation. Many enterprising pilgrims carried with them marketable merchandise which they sold for a profit in communities along the way. Thus northern European goods were brought into Spain, and the same pilgrims often left with their baggage full of Spanish products that were in demand in their home countries. This type of commercial activity stimulated the development of marketing networks linking Spain with northern European countries.[28]

ABSENTEE PROPERTY OWNERS

In Spain, as in the rest of early modern Europe, there was a growing investment by city dwellers in rural property. One reason for this was that city dwellers since the days of the Roman Empire had associated social prestige with land ownership. Moreover, urbanites recognized that purchasing agricultural property could enhance their long-term economic security. When the population growth of the sixteenth century brought higher prices for food products, the profit motive as never before became a consideration in buying productive land. The annual returns on one's investment (averaging about 10 percent in the Tierra de Campos, according to Bartolomé Yun Casalilla) were not as high as in trade, but there was far less risk. And as land prices rose, some city dwellers even purchased land as a speculative venture.[29] These bureaucrats, merchants, artisans, and other urban folks who invested in land were seldom interested in taking an active role in agricultural production. They preferred to be absentee landowners, so they could continue their urban life style, while renting their property to villagers who would actually farm it. Village life seemed boring to most city people. Consequently, they tended to visit their estates infrequently and briefly. However, these urban investors tried to buy land near the city where they lived, so they could enjoy fresh agricultural products from their estates, and so they could derive the maximum social prestige from their investment.[30]

By the last quarter of the sixteenth century urban investment in rural property was becoming quite pronounced. It was especially noticeable in Castilian villages near large cities such as Madrid, Toledo, Burgos, and Valladolid. The village of Vicálvaro, for example, became the focus of investment by wealthy citizens of nearby Madrid. That urban investment transformed the economic character of what until the sixteenth century had been a traditional, relatively self-sufficient rural community. As Madrid developed into an important capital, more and more citizens of Vicálvaro sold their produce, and even took jobs in the city. At the same time, prosperous madrileños began purchasing land in the village. Thus, whereas initially Vicálvaro had been a community of small and medium landowners, by 1576 only a third of village families owned any land at all. The new landless, however, were doing quite well in the labor and produce markets of Madrid.[31] An even more extreme example from the same area is Ribas de Jarama. In the 1570s it had a population of twenty-five vecinos – all independent peasant-farmers (labradores). But none of them owned the lands that he tilled, because residents of Madrid had bought up all the village arable lands, converting every one of the local farmers into tenants.[32]

The urbanization of rural landownership was not limited to zones around Spain's largest cities: it also occurred around modest regional market towns like Ciudad Real, Medina de Rioseco (Valladolid), and Plasencia (Cáceres). Thanks to a lawsuit in the 1530s and 1540s, we can see how the process worked in Plasencia: when crop failures occurred, many labradores were obliged to sell or mortgage their lands to obtain money for subsistence. The merchant and administrative oligarchy of Plasencia were quick to exploit the situation, buying rural property at depressed prices during the agricultural crisis. And by the time the crisis was over, a large proportion of the arable lands of Plasencia's villages was in the hands of city dwellers. The lawsuit that tells this story was filed by the villagers when the new urban landowners – although commoners – attempted to claim the tax exemptions traditionally enjoyed by hidalgos. The villagers could not tolerate that, because it would have raised their own tax rates.[33]

The process must have been similar in other parts of Spain. Prosperous merchants, and other urban investors, used part of their capital to acquire rural property. They were aided in this by the fact that the merchant oligarchies dominated the city governments, which enabled them to influence village affairs even before they became landowners there. Once the urban elite became major property owners in a village, they gained increased leverage over village matters. As an ex-farmer who has rented arable land, I know that these absentee landlords would have been able to influence their tenants in subtle or not-so-subtle ways.[34] And absentee landowners would not have to control all, or even most, of the land of a village to exercise a powerful political influence over local politics. For example, a 1553 census showed that five citizens of the city of Burgos owned houses and farm land in the 62-household village of Frandovínez. That meant that absentee landowners probably rented to *at least* five citizens of the place. If these five citizens of Frandovínez had been among the political leaders of the village, their votes could have carried many an election.[35] Of course, at the same time that urban investors were accumulating rural properties, the most prosperous *labradores* took advantage of the same buying opportunities to expand their own holdings at the expense of their less fortunate neighbors. And by the mid-1600s the rich *labradores* owned more land than they had in the sixteenth century. The crown's sale of *villazgos* and of *tierras baldías*, we should add, facilitated the concentration of landownership in the hands of prosperous *labradores* and of absentee proprietors.[36]

The intrusion of urban ownership into the village world was not a sudden phenomenon but a long process that went on for centuries, with contractions and expansions. Urban investment was merely one more link connecting town and country – the village and the world beyond – and binding their economies and societies to a common future.

EPIDEMICS

The swift and devastating spread of contagious diseases is terrifying proof that people and goods moved regularly in and out of communities of all sizes throughout Spain. Various infectious diseases made their way across the peninsula during the early modern period, but the most fearful and calamitous was bubonic plague. Since the medieval Black Death, there had been periodic episodes of plague, and governing authorities were anxious to prevent fresh outbreaks. By the 1500s Spanish ports had adopted the practice established by Italian trading cities of placing any ship suspected of carrying plague under a forty-day quarantine. But all too frequently the plague managed to filter past such barriers, and every two or three years the malady appeared somewhere in Spain, usually limited to a single port city or region. But periodically, at unpredictable intervals, the plague swept through the entire country. It was widespread in 1506–7, then the remainder of the sixteenth century was reasonably plague-free until 1596, when the disease raged into the peninsula and remained in epidemic form until 1602. The 1600s began with the plague, and turned out to be considerably more plague-prone than the previous century: there were widespread epidemics in 1628–31, again in 1648–52, and yet again in 1677–85. The most devastating of these was the great plague of 1596–1602, which wiped out 10 percent of Castile's total population.[37]

This epidemic began in the north in November 1596, entering Spain through the ports of Santander and Castro Urdiales with a load of textiles and passengers aboard two ships arriving from Dunkirk and Calais. Following the established trade routes, by Christmas of 1596 the plague had reached the village of Cogollos, 15 kilometers south of Burgos. Being an important stop on the road to Madrid, Cogollos had business interests to protect, and succeeded in concealing the presence of plague (thus undoubtedly contributing to its transmission) until the end of May. In the meanwhile, the normal traffic of people and goods brought the epidemic ever deeper into Spain: the Basque provinces and Navarre, Old Castile, then across the Guadarrama mountains to Madrid and Toledo, while affecting also Asturias, Galicia (following the pilgrimage routes to Santiago de Compostela) and Portugal, and finally Andalusia. A map drawn by demographic historian Vicente Pérez Moreda shows that few areas of Castile escaped the effects of this plague.[38]

Historians once considered this end-of-century plague to be primarily an epidemic affecting urban areas. And certainly the cities of Castile were hard hit: Burgos, for example, lost around half of its population. But rural areas were also stricken, with varying degrees of severity. Francis Brumont found that villages in the Tierra de Campos suffered rather mild population losses, compared to those in other parts of Castile – perhaps because the inhabitants of that major grain-producing area had better diets than those of other areas. In any case, villages in the center of Spain seem to have had far higher mortality rates during that epidemic.[39]

But Brumont found that an earlier and lesser-known outbreak of plague (1564–8) seems to have brought higher casualties to the villages of the Burgos–Tierra de Campos area. Also arriving from France, this epidemic entered Spain via the overland route to Zaragoza, from which it progressed westward to Logroño, Nájera, and Vitoria, reaching Burgos in March of 1565, and the Tierra de Campos by January of 1566. Plague mortality varied greatly from village to village, but the average population loss was perhaps between 30 and 40 percent.[40]

It seems to have been typical for the plague (or some other epidemic) to follow a period of poor harvests, which caused food shortages that weakened the population's natural resistance to disease. There are local studies bearing this out: for example, Ramón Sánchez González found that the La

Sagra district of Toledo province suffered terrible casualties from the plague in 1507, during a period of crop failures. And that was true also of the great plague of 1596–1602, which prompted the Golden Age novelist Mateo Alemán to pen the famous phrase lamenting the convergence of "the famine ascending from Andalusia, and the plague descending from Castile."[41]

Villagers of the period knew that the plague was contagious, and they tried to protect themselves from infection by keeping strangers out. That was exceedingly difficult, given the high mobility of Spain's population. But villagers took various collective steps to isolate themselves from outside contagion. In 1598, for example, the council of Illescas (Toledo), upon receiving news that the plague had reached Madrid (34 kilometers northward), appointed special guards to stand at the village gates denying access to all outsiders (forasteros). Nevertheless, the plague gained entry, and decimated the local population. After all, complete isolation was virtually impossible except over a very short period. But since there was no other effective way to avoid contagion, village governments continued to seek protection by barring the gates to the outside world. In 1629, with plague again ravaging the province, Añover de Tajo (Toledo) walled off certain of its streets and posted guards along all others leading to the village. This seems to have been effective, and Illescas did the same thing during fresh appearances of plague in 1649–51, and in 1676.[42]

The plagues affected the movement of goods and people in diverse and often contradictory ways. The epidemics caused some traffic to shut down, because of illness or fear of contamination; but at the same time unaffected persons in a plague-ridden village sought to flee, to save themselves. A report from Cameño (Burgos), a village hit by the plague in 1565–6, indicates that local trade and communications halted while the epidemic ran its course. The inhabitants of neighboring villages untouched by the disease avoided going to Cameño, refusing even to buy wine from the place, lest it be contaminated. But everyone who could, fled Cameño: many went to live in huts in the rural countryside, while others abandoned the territory altogether. Some of these refugees from plague-struck Cameño probably joined the ranks of wandering vagabonds and beggars traversing Castile – possibly unwittingly spreading the disease in the process. The refugees often found it hard to find a place of asylum. They tended to seek out charitable institutions in towns and cities, but they were often not welcomed. The city of Toledo, for instance, in 1599 refused to admit villagers seeking refuge there, even when they carried proof that they came from plague-free areas. But the refugees eventually found places that would accept them. And there is reason to believe that in a general sense, the end-of-century epidemics accelerated the existing currents of migration from northern and central Castile to the south.[43]

Historians once attributed to the plague a major share of the blame for the economic difficulties of Spain in the 1600s. After all, the plague disrupted trade, crippled production, and killed huge numbers of people. But today's historians are more cautious in appraising the consequences of the epidemic. Bartolomé Yun Casalilla and Vicente Pérez Moreda, for example, view the plague as merely one of many factors that modified the sixteenth-century system of production. Similarly, Francis Brumont concludes that the seventeenth-century Castilian crisis was brought on not so much by plague mortality as by social and economic changes that had been developing throughout the 1500s, and that suddenly became noticed as the next century began.[44] In any event, the plague was an outside influence that left few villages unscathed, and it unquestionably contributed to changes that profoundly altered the lives of many rural families.

MISCELLANEOUS AGENTS OF OUTSIDE CONTACT

There were countless other ways through which Castile's villages were linked with the outside world. One was the theater. Golden Age Spain is famous for the great dramatic works of such luminaries as Lope de Vega, Tirso de Molina, and Calderón de la Barca. We might be inclined to think that they were performed only in the theaters of Madrid and other large cities. But their distribution was far wider than that: in fact, traveling actors brought Golden Age drama to ordinary villages throughout Spain. The smallest and most humble villages could not support the more elaborate stage productions, but there was some type of theatrical entertainment for almost everyone in the rural world.[45]

Since Castile's villages could seldom afford the playhouses (corrales) that had sprung up in the cities, the itinerant entertainers had to improvise, performing in the courtyard of an inn or private mansion, or in the village square. Agustín de Rojas in 1604 identified several types of traveling actors who brought Golden Age literature to the rural world: (1) The most basic and inexpensive was the bululú, a lone actor who walked from village to village to perform a play by himself, altering his voice for the different parts. This entertainer was content with a minimal compensation for his efforts. (2) The gangarilla was a group of three or four male actors accompanied by a boy who played the female roles. These actors expected to be decently fed in the villages where they performed. The cambaleo was a troupe of four male actors and an actress (usually a singer). They charged what the audience would bear – only food in the poorest communities, and a cash payment in prosperous villages. (3) The farándula were the elite among the theatrical performers found in the rural setting. Usually numbering six or seven men and three women, the farándula traveled on mules or carts, dressed elegantly, dined well, and commanded high fees. They performed only in communities where there was money.[46] Don

Quixote (II, 11) met such a group riding carts on a road in La Mancha. Still in costume, they had performed that morning in one village, and were en route to another village to put on the same play (seemingly Lope's *Las Cortes de la muerte*) in a neighboring village that afternoon.

These itinerant theatrical groups were called *compañías de la legua* (road companies, literally "companies of the league"). Although they provided much-appreciated entertainment for the rural population, the companies fell into official disfavor during the crisis of the 1640s. Some groups had gotten a reputation as a refuge for social misfits and criminals. Moreover, the theater had come under attack by *arbitristas* such as Lope de Deza, who blamed it for enticing rural people away from agriculture. The monarchical government officially disbanded the *compañías de la legua* in 1644, using the war with Portugal as an excuse. But the ban seems to have been ignored outside Madrid, and after 1650 the road companies were officially tolerated again.[47]

In addition to theatrical groups, the villages were visited by various other entertainers, such as musicians, puppet shows, and animal acts. We have little information about such performers except that they seem to have been exceedingly well received by rural audiences. That, in fact, is what excited the ire of moralizers in Madrid: that villagers, who were supposed to attend to the serious business of food production, spent part of their time and money on such frivolous activities.[48]

On a more prosaic note, the village setting was the scene of activity of numerous other outsiders. In addition to those mentioned in previous chapters, representatives of various professions visited the villages of Castile, and sometimes even lived there. Official business, for example, had to be conducted in the presence of a notary (*escribano público*), who would act as a clerk writing out the appropriate documents, and certify the correctness of what was therein. These *escribanos* tended to be outsiders, because literacy was an obvious prerequisite, and many villages lacked the primary training required for the job. Like practitioners of other trades in small communities, the *escribanos* often served several villages, moving from one to another as needed.[49] Towns with dependent villages exercised the right to appoint *escribanos* to serve in their subject communities. These tended to be from the towns, and were certified by town officials as to competency. But *escribanos* imposed upon a village by outside authority were apt to be resented, regardless of how competent or diligent they were. And one of the first things that a village was likely to do upon gaining its juridical independence was to dismiss those officials named by the former master, and to appoint its own. Espinoso del Rey (Toledo) did this in the early 1580s, after gaining its independence from Talavera de la Reina. The action provoked a suit by Talavera, seeking to maintain the privilege of naming Espinoso's *escribano*.[50] But regardless of how they were chosen, the village *escribanos* – like tax collectors, priests, and others with special skills or training – served as important intermediaries linking the village with the outside world.

Postal service was another avenue through which outsiders entered the supposedly "isolated" village world. A diplomatic postal system had been established by Spain's medieval kings, and Ferdinand and Isabella made the first steps toward creating a modern post, patterned after German organization. But the postal system was not fully developed until the reign of Charles V. Initially, it was exclusively for the use of the royal government, but after 1580 the official Postal Service was opened to private use, thus becoming a public service. The task of the Postal Service was to move documents rapidly and safely from one place to another. This was done by couriers on horseback. But the Postal Service's mounts could also be rented by private persons needing rapid transportation. The French traveler Antoine de Brunel did this in 1665. He wrote that Spain's post horses were the finest in the world, but that their saddles were dreadfully uncomfortable, and for that reason almost everyone preferred to rent a mule from a private party.[51]

Beyond official governmental correspondence, the mail was used primarily by wealthy people and by businessmen. We can get an idea of who patronized the Postal Service from the grouping of mail couriers in 1561: the city of Burgos had 14; Valladolid 18; Medina del Campo 9; Segovia 2; and Salamanca 1. The first three were major commercial or governmental centers and lay astride major international routes. By contrast, Segovia and Salamanca were backwaters, but they still must have generated a significant correspondence. In those days it was the recipient, rather than the sender of a letter who paid the postage. And rates were so high that receiving letters on a regular basis was out of reach for ordinary villagers. Nevertheless, the Postal Service from time to time must have brought governmental documents and other important missives to the typical Castilian village. Communications with the outside world were also brought by messengers, hired by private or governmental organizations.[52]

CONCLUSION

---

*T*he two best-known characters in Golden Age Spanish literature are Don Quixote and Lazarillo de Tormes. Both are archetypically mobile individuals: Quixote the eccentric and idealistic knight errant; and Lazarillo the pragmatic wandering vagrant. Both of these characters are stereotypes, with the exaggerated traits that we would expect of the genre. But Quixote and Lazarillo were successful as literary figures not because they were unbelievably exotic, but because they were familiar enough to be credible. Although we should certainly not assert that these two fictional characters were typical of the Castile of the day, their high mobility – their continual encounters with new people in new places – may be taken as symbolic of the high degree of social and geographic mobility of early modern Castile. And we might point out that the country's monarchs set a prominent example of mobility. Spain's Golden Age of world power was ushered in by Ferdinand and Isabella, whose style of governing was exceedingly itinerant. There being no fixed capital, the royal pair were continually on the move, spending a few weeks here and a few weeks there, throughout both Castile and Aragon. And Ferdinand and Isabella's grandson, the Holy Roman Emperor Charles V, was probably the most peripatetic ruler of Europe (if not, indeed, the world). Charles not only had Spain to govern – and visit, but also extensive territories elsewhere in Europe. Not until the reign of Charles' son Philip II (1556–98) did Madrid become the permanent capital, and with that the monarchs of Spain were no longer as mobile as before. But, as we have seen, geographical mobility affected virtually all sectors of society.

No one can dispute that there were large numbers of Castilians with mobile life styles. But to what extent did migration and mobility affect the villagers who made up four-fifths of the population? It is not difficult to assemble anecdotal evidence that early modern Castilian villagers migrated from place to place, temporarily or permanently. A far more difficult task is to calculate how prevalent this was. Is it possible to quantify

Table 6. *Household contacts with the outside world: twelve Castilian villages*

Place (province)	AGS EH Leg.	Year of census	A No. of households	B Households with outside servants	C Households with outside family	D Households with family out-migrated	E Combined B + C + D	F % Households with outside contacts
Estépar (Burgos)	274	1553	58	14	4	6	23	40
Hérmedes de Cerrato (Palencia)	288	1580	41	2	2	8	10	24
Herreruela (Cáceres)	34	1586	80	0	0	14	14	18
Ibrillos (Burgos)	368	1575	29	4	1	6	10	34
La Puerta (Guadalajara)	368	1597	132	1	0	14	15	11
Modino (León)	322	1583	40	12	6	3	16	40
Puebla del Príncipe (Cd. Real)	366	1589	68	4	3	5	12	18
Puerto de Santoña (Santander)	368	1578	118	21	7	16	44	37
Santa Cruz (Toledo)	382	1579	179	2	18	24	43	24

Note: The figures in column E, lines 1, 2, 4, 6, and 9, have been adjusted downward to avoid counting twice those households included in more than one B, C, or D category.

the migratory habits of Golden Age Castilian villagers? The data presented above, relating to life-cycle service and to out-marriage, certainly attest to the fact that geographical mobility was quite ordinary in the sixteenth-century rural world. But ideally we would have a more complete analysis of migrations, including such factors as annual turnover rates; the migrants' age, sex, place of origin, and occupation; the incidence of return migration; the geographical distribution of marriage markets; the geographical distribution of migration; sex- and job-specific mobility; and the generational depth of families in a given location.[1]

Since the problem of sources makes it unlikely that we can ever assemble the data necessary for that kind of complete analysis, we are reduced to manipulating that information that we do have. In Table 6 I have employed data from Simancas fiscal censuses to gauge what proportion of households experienced important personal contacts with the outside world, through: (1) hiring non-native servants; (2) outside origins of family members; or (3) family members living outside the village. Unfortunately, Simancas censuses seldom include this type of information, and since it is listed inconsistently even when present, we cannot compare the proportions for the villages in the table. Generally, when a village shows "0" in a given category (e.g. Herreruela in columns B and C, the reason is not that the place had no households in that category, but rather that the census taker did not think it appropriate to enumerate that type of data. Similarly, I think it highly unlikely that there was only one household in La Puerta with a non-native servant, and the reason for La Puerta's "1" in column B is that the census taker was not really interested in listing servants.

I have seen thousands of fiscal censuses, and have found a couple of hundred with detailed household information.[2] Although I have not yet been able to analyze more than this handful, my distinct impression is that the more information the censuses include, the higher the degree of mobility and household contacts with the outside. In other words, Table 6 probably reveals differences in data collection as much as actual household differences. Nevertheless, the table tells us that a substantial proportion of households in these villages maintained some sort of personal contact with the exterior world. And if my guess is correct, had the census takers enumerated the information, the actual percentage of households with outside contacts (i.e., column F) would have been at least 40 or 50 percent for every village.[3]

Because of disputes over counting and other factors, censuses were often re-done, and the Simancas archive contains many of these recounts. In some cases, they provide detailed information about demographic changes during the period between census dates, and this enables us to learn something about mobility. The village of Almaraz (Zamora),[4] for instance, had census counts in 1533 and again in 1550. The 1533 census listed 70 *vecinos* living in the place. By 1550 only 20 of the original *vecinos* were still alive and living in the village: 36 had died, and 15 had emigrated. There were new additions, however; between 1533 and 1550, 29 new *vecinos* had been recognized: 11 sons of *vecinos* who had established their own households; 4 outsiders who married local girls and settled in Almaraz; 6 other outsiders who migrated to the place (presumably with their families); one abandoned wife of a 1533 *vecino* who now was accorded citizenship; and 7 new *vecinos* of unspecified origin. But Almaraz was clearly in decline, with a mere 45 *vecinos*[5] in 1550. Thirty of the 76 houses in the village were unoccupied, including 19 that were uninhabitable, because they had collapsed. We have another glimpse at in- and out-migration in El Puente del Arzobispo (Toledo), where a census of 1561 included a brief summary of demographic changes in the village since 1538. The register of 1561 included 359 *vecinos*. The census-makers estimated that 38 *vecinos* (presumably with their families) had left the place since 1538, but 56 newcomers had settled in the village, and were granted citizenship.[6]

In her recent study of early modern Spanish municipal government, Helen Nader describes inter-municipal population moves as normal occurrences, writing that "ordinary citizens moved to escape unhealthful or overcrowded towns or to find better land" and "they seem to have moved in massive numbers in the fifteenth century."[7] It is quite clear that geographical mobility continued into the sixteenth century as well. The *Relaciones topográficas* do not really provide satisfactory data for quantitative analysis on this point, but after studying them José Gentil da Silva concluded: "The peasant masses shift from place to place, they move. Furthermore, it is easy to move," and "The villages seem to be the places with the greatest mobility."[8] In the seventeenth century, this mobility continued, perhaps even at an accelerated pace, as we have indicated in previous chapters.

THE IMPACT OF PRE-INDUSTRIAL POPULATION MOBILITY

What was the impact of all of this population movement? Fernand Braudel asserted that migration was an unsettling element in early modern society. In his view, the traditional rural system was upset by a combination of a rising urban market economy, and by the consequent movement of peasants into towns, and of urban craftsmen into rural areas.[9] But the hypothesis that urban contacts stimulated rural change has been rejected by demographic historian David-Sven Reher, who argues that the existence of urban areas actually bolstered traditional structures. The surplus rural population – who were unable to find local marriage partners, land, jobs, or homes – could migrate to towns. This enabled village communities to maintain traditional modes of behavior long after they had lost their economic or demographic utility. Since early modern towns suffered perennially negative natural population growth rates, migration from rural areas contributed to the maintenance of overall demographic stability. Reher found that urban Cuenca complemented the fundamentally rural character of the province. The town, rather than acting as a catalyst for rural change, instead served as a kind of safety valve against change.[10] Ramón Lanza García, in his study of villages in the Liébana district of Santander province, arrives at the same conclusion: the regular population migrations from and to the area did little to alter the stability and traditional mentality of Liébana's rural population. On the contrary, the migrations made it possible for local ways to survive.[11] And certainly, continuity was a hallmark of early modern Spanish rural society. In many respects, the juridical-institutional-technological-demographic characteristics of the late medieval period retained their validity down to the nineteenth, and even into the twentieth century.[12]

Migration in early modern Spain should be regarded as a normal structural characteristic of society. We should avoid explaining migration as a reaction to economic difficulty or other problems, and instead we should think of it as a basic and essential component of the socioeconomic structure. The migratory habits of early modern Castile, far from being a symptom of something wrong, instead should be taken as proof of the adaptability of a dynamic society able to transform itself in changing circumstances by allowing individuals to move from areas where they were not needed to other areas with greater employment opportunities. We should be impressed by how easily people were able to move about, in an age with primitive transportation facilities. David Reher was right to characterize pre-industrial Castile as a "Culture of Mobility."[13]

In any case, it is clear that, despite their reputation for traditionalism and long-lasting stability, early modern villages were not stagnant pools of humanity isolated from the mainstream of Castilian society. Although much work remains to be done to clarify the details and the extent of population movements, there is no doubt that Castilian villagers maintained extensive economic and personal contacts with the outside world. The population of early modern Castilian village communities was surprisingly dynamic, continually in the process of transformation by migration to and from the village.[14] The traditional image of a stable rural community – still held by many historians despite increasing evidence to the contrary – is nothing but a mirage, a myth created by people unacquainted with the facts. It is time to shed this myth once and for all, and to recognize that in Castile – as in the rest of Europe – a high degree of population mobility has been with us for a very long time.[15]

NOTES

INTRODUCTION

1. Bailey (1968: 5–21); Commager (1967).
2. The quotes are from McKay, Hill, and Buckler (1992: 360); and Esler (1992: 229). These may be considered typical treatments of the subject. The most recent text that has crossed my desk is Duiker and Spielvogel (1994), which does nothing to dispel the myth.
3. The quotes are from Hanawalt (1986: 19); and from Huppert (1986: 1). The other allusions are to Fossier (1988: 126) and to Sabean (1984: 12–13).
4. Bouchard (1972). This work was published a quarter century ago. But as Moch mentions (1992: 23) there are still French historians who cling (despite growing evidence to the contrary) to the stereotype of a sedentary pre-industrial rural population. Fresh examples of this are Poussou (1994: 217–18) and Perrenoud (1994: 484).
5. Blum (1982) (quote from p. 10).
6. The reader is left with the image of an unchanging and immobile peasant life in the collection of essays edited by Shanin (1987). Examples from that volume are pieces by Fei Hsiao Tung and by Dobrowolski. The essentially closed nature of peasant society is also portrayed by Delano-Smith (1979: 27–9). Åkerman (1994: 73–4) laments the fact that many Scandinavian scholars persist in the misconception that "the old peasant society" was stable and immobile. The pervasiveness of the myth among historians is noted in recent books by Moch (1992: 1, 31, 36) and Gottlieb (1993: 40). In the fall of 1992, I tested the power of the myth among students at the University of Texas–Pan American by distributing an anonymous questionnaire (designed to conceal what I was really looking for) to a class of forty history majors and minors. The responses showed a virtually unanimous and total acceptance of the myth of immobility.
7. Amelang (1993: 372) correctly observes that the consensus of cutting-edge scholarship has discarded "the worn cliché of early modern Spain (and Castile in particular) as a rigid and immobile society."
8. Karl Marx and Frantz Fanon displayed an almost pathological loathing of the peasantry, which they regarded as a hopelessly anti-revolutionary class that would have to be destroyed. Lenin held the same view, but adopted the expedient of enlisting the peasants as partners in his revolution by promising them land. Later, once the landlords had been eliminated, the peasants were betrayed by being forced into collective and state farms where land ownership

176

and decision-making were solidly in the hands of the central government. The Marxist views concerning the peasantry are summarized by Critchfield (1981: 299–301).

9. I am indebted to Susan Tax Freeman for bringing to my attention the gap between social scientists and historians in understanding the nature of the peasantry, and for directing me to non-stereotypic visions of the rural world. Eric R. Wolf (1966, especially pp. 2–4, 10–13) provided a highly respected and widely accepted definition of the peasantry. But the title of the same author's 1967 article, "Closed Corporate Peasant Communities in Meso-america and Central Java," may have caused some historians to assume that peasant communities were isolated from the outside world – a gross distortion of the anthropologist's actual findings. In any case, historians who persisted in their outmoded ideas had no excuse, because the distinguished medievalist R.H. Hilton provided an up-to-date definition of the peasantry in Chapter 1 of his 1975 book. Hanawalt's more recent study of medieval English peasant families employs (1986: 5, 9) Hilton's definition.

10. The urban myth idea was suggested by the sociologist Wylie (1974: 351–3), and expanded by Lowry (1982: 78–9).

11. We must acknowledge the longevity of rural technology and institutions in rural Spain: this is emphasized by A. García Sanz (1988: 41, 44) and is the thesis of Behar's historico-anthropological study of a Leonese village (1986). But the longevity of tools and customs is not tantamount to immobility, as this book demonstrates.

12. For example, Brandes (1975: 47) pictured a mid-twentieth-century Avila village as a place with a general lack of mobility; and Blázquez (1905: 16) wrote that in La Mancha since the time of the *Relaciones* (mid-1570s) "almost everything rural has remained the same, without experiencing important change" (*casi todo lo rústico queda invariable [sin sufrir] cambio importante*). Even as informed a scholar as Richard Kagan wrote (1974: 180) that the early modern Spanish countryside was "poor, illiterate, backward, and immobile." Folklorist Luis Díaz Viana (1984: 105) asserted: "No resulta nada difícil documentar ... la permanencia de la misma familia durante los cinco últimos siglos en la misma aldea y ese escaso movimiento de la población y su casi nulo contacto – en lo que se refiere a casamientos – con gentes de otras zonas se ha mantenido ... hasta tiempos bien recientes." Attempting to put a nuance on the topic, demographic historian Antonio Eiras Roel (1994: 45–7) recog-nizes that there was substantial mobility in pre-industrial Spain's peripheral provinces, but he repeats the refrain of immobility for the center of the country, while giving statistics that suggest the contrary.

13. Fussell (1972: 100).

14. The quotations ("el campesino sedentario, un labrador apegado a su terruño," and "[el] inmovilismo de la tierra ... , con su escasa o nula evolución") are from Fernández Alvarez (1989: I, 86, 99). The first edition of that work was awarded the Premio Nacional "Historia de España" in 1985, attesting to its acceptance by the country's intellectual community. The popular work is by José Calvo, a respected educator and author of several earlier books on seven-teenth–eighteenth-century Spain. The original of the quoted passage (Calvo 1989: 44): "[Frente a la imagen de movilidad ofrecida por algunos testimo-

nios, la realidad era muy distinta y] el sedentarismo más absoluto la norma." An earlier, and classic view of an immobile Spain is Chaunu (1966). The isolation and unchanging nature of the Spanish peasantry is emphasized by Aranguren (1966: 40).

15. Several recent works have pointed to aspects of flexibility and mobility in early modern Spanish society. But these revisionist works have not yet succeeded in changing the prevailing mistaken notions about a rigid and unchanging early modern Spain. A superb commentary on recent revisionist scholarship along these lines is James Amelang's Review article "Society and Culture in Early Modern Spain" (1993).

16. There is an extensive bibliography of works dealing with European population mobility. An outstanding recent study dealing with a period later than my own is Moch 1992. Works covering earlier centuries include Coleman and Salt (1992: 14, 25–7); Le Roy Ladurie (1987: 11–12); Razi (1980: 79, 117–20); and Watts (1984: 160). The importance of migration and mobility in Spain and in the rest of Europe was made clear by the 75 papers presented at the first European Conference of the International Commission on Historical Demography, "Internal and Medium-Distance Migrations in Europe, 1500–1900," Santiago de Compostela, September 22–25, 1993 (published at the Conference in two volumes of proceedings, and in 1994 as: vol. I: *Les migrations internes et à moyenne distance en Europe, 1500–1900;* and vol. II: *Migraciones internas y medium-distance en la Península Ibérica, 1500–1900,* ed. by Antonio Eiras Roel and Ofelia Rey Castelao. Santiago de Compostela: Xunta de Galicia). Many of the Santiago papers are cited in this book.

17. Ruiz Gómez (1990: 263) has noted a similar void in medieval Spanish historiography. And T. Ruiz (1994: 72, note 23) deplores that Spanish historians have been unable to equal the "vivid reconstruction of rural life in England and France." I might add that Ruiz in his 1994 book has made a substantial contribution toward the humanization of medieval studies. And Brumont (1993b: 322–31) provides brief family histories for the village elite in Golden Age Fuentes de Nava (Palencia). That type of unaccustomed attention to individuals and families should be emulated by other scholars.

18. Amelang (1993: 374) lays no claim to be the first to point out this shortcoming in Spanish historiography. In fact, he cites John Elliott making the same observation in his 1989 *Spain and Its World, 1500–1700* (New Haven, Conn.: Yale University Press 1989, p. 65).

19. I addressed the question of local patriotism in a recent paper (1994c). See also Gómez-Centurión Jiménez (1989b: 29–32); Caro Baroja (1957); Velasco (1981: 85–106); Kamen (1984: 17–19); Brandes (1975: 5); and Behar (1986: especially 184–5, 263, 273–4).

20. Item no. 263 in the collection by Gonzalo Correas (1571–1631), included in *Refranero clásico español* (1966).

21. Pérez-Díaz (1967: 123, 129–30); Watts (1984: 98). Amelang (1993: 372–3) observes that recent monographs recognize "the importance of agency and decision making by individuals within all social ranks."

22. Silva (1967: 21, 27).

23. Ruiz (1994: 33). See also Delano-Smith (1979: 129–35); Caro Baroja (1963: 38); Kenny and Knipmeyer (1983: 10–11, 38); C. Phillips (1979: 43–4);

Zagorin (1982: 78–9); and Braudel (1975: 278).

24. Casado Alonso (1987: 453–510); Weisser (1976: 56–62); García de Cortázar (1988: 224); Valdeón Baruque (1975: 16–17); and A. García Sanz (1977: 173–8).

25. Vassberg (1984: 57–64); Casado Alonso (1987: 538); Represa (1979: 7–17); and the suit *Toro* v. *La Bóveda*, ACHVA, FA (F), 60.

26. Helen Nader (1990: xv–xvi) prefers to reserve the term "village" for dependent municipalities under the control of a larger municipality. Nader employs "town" for rural communities that gained their jurisdictional autonomy (see the section on *villazgos* below, in Chapter 6). It was essential for Nader to make that distinction in her book about the process of attaining jurisdictional autonomy. But for my purposes in this book, the word "village" seems to be the proper one, because "town" suggests a community that is more urban than rural.

27. Marcos de Rejas testified in 1565 in the suit *Rejas* v. *Pedro Zapata*, ACHVA, PC, FA (F), 56. Nader (1990: 31–2) notes the surname practice and cites some examples, but refrains from using them to calculate migration rates. Borrero Fernández (1983: 164–72) employs toponymics to analyze migration, but she does so cautiously.

28. In many cases my instincts tell me that a certain individual is an immigrant, but I regard him as a native unless the document says otherwise. For example, the 1579 census of Santa Cruz (Toledo) lists a *vecino* named Pedro López de Cebolla. He is probably a naturalized immigrant from the nearby village of Cebolla. Another *vecino* of Santa Cruz was Alonso Hernández de Sevilleja, in all likelihood from the village of Sevilleja. I accept both of these individuals as natives of Santa Cruz because Spaniards (in those days as today) frequently used the surnames of *both* parents. Thus "de Cebolla" could have been the surname of the mother of Pedro López.

I THE VILLAGE COMMUNITY

1. Gómez-Centurión Jiménez (1989b: 29–32); Watts (1984: 110–11); Kamen (1984: 17–19); Corral García (1987: 24–5); Altman (1989: 278); Brandes (1975: 5); Pitt-Rivers (1971: 30).

2. There are abundant documentary references in Spain's municipal archives to periodic boundary inspections. And because of disputes and jurisdictional changes, many also entered the central archives. For example, see papers of Juez Juan de Salas' 1588 visit to Torrelobatón (Valladolid) in AGS, EH, 403; and testimony about the years 1536–7 in the suit *Congosto* v. *Ahumada*, ACHVA, PC, FA (F), 3. For lawsuits over municipal boundaries see Kagan (1981: 119, 135–7). The seventeenth-century ordinances of the village of Andiñuela (León) include guidelines (number 26) about boundary markers (transcribed Rubio Pérez 1993: 290).

3. Freeman (1968b: 42–4); Casado Alonso (1990: 286–92).

4. Christian (1981: 154–5); García de Cortázar (1988: 74, 154–6).

5. An example of kinfolk living in adjacent houses may be seen in a 1575 census of Menasalbas (Toledo), AGS, EH, 319. Flandrin (1979: 34–7) found membership in rural neighborhoods in France more powerful than ties of kinship, as

did Brandes (1975: 145) in a twentieth-century village in Avila.

6. Sixteenth- and early seventeenth-century censuses preserved in the Expedientes de Hacienda section of the Archivo General de Simancas show this very clearly. This is also noted by Zagorin (1982: 77–8). And Brandes (1975: 47) found the same to be true in a late twentieth-century village in the province of Avila. See also Delano-Smith (1979: 29).

7. Vassberg (1992: 155–6); Blum (1971: 157, 163–4); Corral García (1987: 24–5); Nader (1990: 27–45).

8. The citation is from *Refranero español* (1968: 42).

9. Nader (1990: 27–45).

10. The importance of community was the subject of the Mesa Redonda Internacional "Modelos de Comunidad Rural en la España Moderna (Siglos XVI–XIX)" held at the Casa de Velázquez, Madrid, April 12–13, 1991. General conclusions for that meeting were published as Vassberg (1992: 152–8). See also Casado Alonso (1987: 535–6; 1990: 286–304); Martín Cea (1991: 443–8); and Watts (1984: 110–11).

11. Behar (1986: 125–85); Casado Alonso (1992: 201–6); Vassberg (1992: 152–4); Freeman (1987: 472–4, 479–80). See also Gilmore (1980: 6–7); Pérez-Díaz (1967: 125–30); Blum (1971: 164); and Watts (1984: 115–16). The situation in the Basque country of the Kingdom of Navarre was quite similar, according to Floristán Imízcoz and Imízcoz Beunza (1993: 32–5, 37).

12. Because of their small population, and physical remoteness, it was difficult for many villages to obtain essential supplies from the outside world, because itinerant vendors did not find it profitable to go there. For example, see documents about Palomas (Badajoz) from 1575 in AGS, EH, 906; and about La Zarza (Cáceres) from 1597 in AGS, EH, 189–59. See also Salomon (1964: 51–73); Watts (1984: 105); Weisser (1976: 73–4); and Corchón García (1963: 198–9).

13. By no means peculiar to Spain, the same sentiments existed in other European rural communities. See Blum (1971: 164–5); and Segalen (1983: 153–4). It is interesting that Brandes (1975: 37–40) found powerful anti-outsider sentiment in late twentieth-century Becedas (Avila province). And Gilmore (1980: 123–7) found that the residents of "Fuenmayor" in the early 1970s ridiculed the people of neighboring towns, calling them "stupid."

14. See fiscal censuses in AGS, EH, 111; and the suit (1565–8) *Rus v. Vecinos de Baeza*, ACHGR, 3–426–3. The spelling of the cited word from Rus was "estrañas."

15. Nader (1990: 27–45); Behar (1986: 129–43); Suárez Alvarez (1982: 139); García de Valdeavellano (1968: 543); Corral García (1978: 203–4); Zabalza Seguín (1994b: 177–206).

16. García de Valdeavellano (1968: 547–50); Corral García (1978: 210–12); Casado Alonso (1990: 295–8).

17. In 1539 the village council of Torbaneja (seemingly in Burgos province) denied an application for citizenship by a priest named Juan de Rozas, saying "no tiene necesidad de más clerigo en el dho lugar, ny han de recibir en él persona por vecino que por razon de ser clerigo sea esento y goze de los propios y no aproveche al dho concejho en las cargas dél." From the suit *Juan de Rozas v. Torbaneja*, ACHVA, PC, FA (F), 30. According to the 1546

Ordinances of Cuéllar, hidalgos and secular clergy were counted as *vecinos*, but members of religious orders were not, except in special cases (Corral García 1978: 207–8, 210). See also Vassberg (1984: 139); Salomon (1964: 230–1); and transcriptions of village ordinances in Rubio Pérez (1993: 257, 331, 338). And for the typology of poverty, see Carasa Soto (1988b).

18. See, for example, Probanza del concejo de Fuente Obejuna (1531), ACHGR, 3-512-3 (bis).

19. In Cantabrian villages, for instance, *vecino* status was limited to "casado o viudo, con casa y hacienda propia." Widows and "solteros no emancipados" were not considered *vecinos*, and could not participate in the concejo abierto, according to Rodríguez Fernández (1986: 31). See also Alvar Ezquerra (1988: 884–91); Zabalza Seguín (1994b: 177–206); O'Callaghan (1975: 270); García de Valdeavellano (1968: 543); Corral García (1978: 203–4, 207–8); Espejo Lara (1985: 22). According to Lanza García (1988: 127) *vecino* status in the Liébana area was limited to adult males with some cultivated land, even if it was only a small rented or share-cropped parcel. A census where people were counted variously as a whole *vecino*, 1/2 *vecino*, or not at all, may be found in papers relating to Horcajo de las Torres (1558), AGS, EH, 292.

20. Reports from Villar de la Yegua (1634), AGS, EH, 245; Nader (1990: 28–34); Behar and Frye (1988: 16–17); Suárez Alvarez (1982: 139); Alvar Ezquerra (1988: 889–91). One may compare village citizenship in early modern Germany in Sabean (1984: 12–13).

21. A 1554 census of Coín (Málaga) included a number of non-citizen residents (*estantes*). It was explained that "[se] llamam estantes porque diz [sic] que no tienen bienes rayzes en [Coín] ny en su dezmería y es gente que se va e viene quando quyeren e les paresce." AGS, EH, 269. See also García de Valdevellano (1968: 543); and Corral García (1978: 203–4).

22. Corral García (1978: 205–7); Suárez Alvarez (1982: 139, 142).

23. Examples may be found in Rojas Gabriel (1987: 204); Corral García (1978: 207); Suárez Alvarez (1982: 140–2). The census for Viloria de Rioja is in AGS, EH 368–7.

24. See the suit *Juan de Rozas v. Torbaneja*, ACHVA, PC, FA (F), 30; Corral García (1578: 208); Rodríguez Fernández (1986: 34–8, 57–8, 62); and Suárez Alvarez (1982: 143–4). Note also no. 86 of the 1621 Ordenanzas of Castrotierra, transcribed in Rubio Pérez (1984: 269).

25. For Paredes de Nava, see Martín Cea (1991: 440–1). See also Corral García (1978: 208).

26. Ordenanzas del Lugar de Castrotierra (1621), no. 68, transcribed in Rubio Pérez (1984: 265).

27. The anti-outsider sentiment in the European context is mentioned by Genicot (1990: 54). And Pitt-Rivers (1971: 8–11, 26–8) and Freeman (1970: 23, 112–13, 120–4) discuss suspicion and hostility toward outsiders in twentieth-century Spanish villages.

28. See the suit *Salvaleón v. Francisco Durán y el Alcalde Mayor del Estado de Feria* (1585–7), ACHGR, 3-269-3. For the use of lawsuits by peasants in confrontations with their lords, see Kagan (1981: 11, 13, 100–3).

29. See the suits *Alonso de Tordesillas v. Villaconejos* (1543–50), ACHVA, PC, FA (F), 34; and *Rus v. Vecinos de Baeza* (1565–8), ACHGR, 3-426-3. See also Nader

(1990: 163–4); Franco Silva (1974: 24–30); Kagan (1981: 135–7). For the *derrota de mieses* see Vassberg (1984: 13–18).

30. Kamen (1984: 17–18); Arco y Garay (1941: 883–4); *Quixote*, II, 27. Polish villagers displayed a similar antagonism toward outsiders, according to Dobrowolski (1987: 274).

31. See the suit *El Burgo v. Villamunyo* (1545), ACHVA, PC, FA (F), 14. Martín Cea (1991: 264–6) observes that conflict between neighboring villages was commonplace.

32. Testimony of Cristóbal de Porras, a *vecino* of Zamora, in AGS, EH, 360. My English version is rather roughly translated. In the Spanish original, the people of Casaseca:

> salieron con lanças e ballestas e hondas, e a campana repicada para efecto de los herir e matar, de manera q. no quedó mochacho de 14 años arriba, ni mugeres en el dho lugar q. no salieron con asadores e varales e piedras a ayuda e faboreçer al concejo del dho lugar de Casaseca, ansí los fueron siguiendo hasta encerrarlos en sus casas del dho lugar del Vayllo, y aun allí quisieron hundir la casa de Villarreal a pedradas q. sobre el tejado cayan, e ... quando yban en su seguimiento, uvieron de matar a Jn. de Villa Lobos, secretario del consistorio de la çibdad de Çamora e a un alcalde de Çamora q. salió a apaciguar el ruido.

The relation concludes with this marvelous understatement: "por las susodhas raçones es de creer q. tienen demasiada pasión."

33. See documents for Cumbres de Medio (*sic*) in AGS, EH, 269.

34. See testimony from Codesal in the suit *Codesal v. Anta de Tera*, ACHVA, PC, FA (F), 59:

> a son de campana tañida y a manera de alboroto, armados de diversas harmas ofensivas e defensivas, fueron a los dhos términos ... y ... prendaron y llevaron ... mas de 50 vacas y otros ganados, dándolos e maltratándolos, los llevaron al dho lugar de Anta, e ... pusieron las lanças a los pechos a los pastores que los guardavan, e les dieron de lançadas e palos, y a los dhos ganados e pastores hizieron otros muchos malos tratamientos.

35. Díaz Viana (1984: 94–7).

36. Christian (1981: 118–19); Salomon (1985: 565–6); Pitt-Rivers (1971: 11–12).

37. For Los Santos de Maimona see Guerra (1952: 520–1); for Escuredo, see no. 16 of the ordinances transcribed in Rubio Pérez (1993: 303). On municipal protectionism see also A. García Sanz (1977: 194–5); Huetz de Lemps (1967: 175); Salmerón (1777: 94–5); and Rodríguez Arzua (1963: 393–4).

38. Rubio Pérez (1984: 168); Martín Cea (1991: 162–4); and the suit *El Bachiller Alonso Ruiz Quevedo y consortes v. Yeste*, ACHGR, 512-2156-21.

2 MARKET CONTACTS WITH THE OUTSIDE WORLD

1. John Lynch (1984: I, 114) remarks that "the traditional opinion that Spaniards had little aptitude for commerce needs to be modified," yet he goes on to write that "large-scale commercial operations could hardly be expected in a country insufficiently urbanised and among a people lacking the traditions of business enterprise." The general Spanish commercial networks are

analyzed by Ringrose (1983: 164, 278–9); Yun Casalilla (1994c); Domínguez Ortiz (1974: 93–8); and Phillips and Phillips (1977). Regional markets are covered in Yun Casalilla (1987: 183–6); Marcos Martín (1985: 71–4); and Bennassar (1967: 91–119). For an up-to-date analysis of the medieval foundations of long-distance Castilian trade, see T. Ruiz (1994: 196–227). The last concludes (p. 227) that late medieval Castile had "a sophisticated system of interdependence and exchanges vital to the economic survival of the realm and closely related to its rural economy."

2. The traditional peasant attitude toward self-sufficiency, money, and the market is described by Douglass (1975: 93; and 1976: 46–7); Watts (1984: 153); and Delano-Smith (1979: 82). See also Weisser (1976: 73–4). Yun Casalilla (1994a) places the Castilian situation in the European and world-wide perspective.

3. Helen Nader (1990) regularly uses "farmer" rather than "peasant." Personally, I wrestled with the question in a previous work (1984: 141–3), and finally opted to sidestep the problem by employing the Spanish *labrador*, which I defined as "an independent peasant-farmer." I still have not found a completely satisfactory solution to the dilemma.

4. Yun Casalilla (1987: 142–50).

5. See a report from Morales in AGS, EH, 360. Comparable peasant marketing in medieval England is described in Bennett (1987: 52–7).

6. See a report (1588) from the Adelantamiento de León in AGS, EH, 209. It was not that Friday was a forbidden day in Old Castile, because Paredes de Nava (in the Tierra de Campos) held its market on Fridays, according to a document from 1581 in AGS, EH, 209.

7. Rubio Pérez (1984: 165–8); Vassberg (1984: 184–7). Martínez Sopena (1993: 200–3) gives some medieval antecedents for this practice.

8. Brumont (1993b: 156–61); Salomon (1964: 115–21, 340–1). A recent coffee-table book (González Díez 1993) depicts the importance of fairs in Castile-León from the medieval period to the present.

9. Freeman (1979b: 104–5). Indeed, the longevity of this is depicted in González Díez (1993).

10. AGS, EH, 906.

11. Vassberg (1984: 186–7); Martín Cea (1991: 133–6); Cabo Alonso (1955: 94–5). The Trigueros information is from a 1587 document in AGS, EH, 189-21; and the Casasola quote is from AGS, EH, 329:

> Este dho lugar está a 8 leguas de la villa de Balladolid a donde oy feria franca cada año, y 7 leguas de Medina de Rioseco a do ay 2 ferias francas cada año y algunos mercados y a 13 leguas de la çiudad de Çamora donde asimismo ay 2 ferias francas, y a 3 leguas de la çiudad de Toro donde ay ferias y mercados francos, en las quales dhas çiudades y villas y ferias y mercados francos dellas los vs. deste dho lugar an acostumbrado y acostumbran vender ordinariamente su trigo, çebada, ganados y casi todos los mas vienes muebles que venden.

12. In a list of the citizens of Montánchez (Cáceres) who marketed things during the first third of 1590, only 5 in 105 were women (AGS, EH, 130-8-ii). Brandes found (1975: 50) that it was the men of twentieth-century Becendas who marketed agricultural surpluses. But in nineteenth-century rural France,

it was the women who took chickens, butter, cheese, and cream to nearby markets. The fairs, however, held only two or three times a year for marketing animals or grain, were normally all-male affairs (Segalen 1983: 150–4).

13. See Vassberg (1994b); Rábade Obradó (1988: 126–7).
14. Silva (1967: 33–5); Marcos Martín (1994b: 220–8); A. García Sanz (1977: 36); Anonymous (BN 1607: folios 64, 79v–80); Relación de Palomas (1575), AGS, EH, 906; Relación de Navalvillar de Pela (1597), AGS, EH, 189-76; Quirós (1965: 227); Martín Galindo (1961: 176–7).
15. Yun Casalilla (1987: 186–95) provides a clear analysis of the Castilian system of fairs. Information about *corredores* in the villages of the Count of Alba may be found in testimony from 1588 regarding the Adelantamiento de León, in AGS, EH, 209.
16. See the suit *La Cd. de Segovia* v. *sus lugares*, ACHVA, PC, FA (F), 2; and Pérez-Crespo (1969: 462–5); A. García Sanz (1977: 58); Bosque Maurel (1971: 68–9, 80–1); Cabo Alonso (1955: 94–5); Huetz de Lemps (1967: 288–98); Medina (1549: cxl); Weisser (1976: 56–62); Casado Alonso (1987: 453–510); Yun Casalilla (1987: 142–50, 183–218); "Leganés," *Relaciones (Madrid)*, 338–49; González (1958: 135–43); and Anonymous (1607: 103).
17. Chevalier (1983: 277–9); Pereiro (1987: 19–20).
18. See documents about Morales de Toro in AGS, EH, 329; and Huetz de Lemps (1959: 113–23).
19. This was in 1498, and the local official was the Comendador of San Juan. See Ladero Quesada (1985: 216, especially note 18).
20. Ringrose (1983), in which an overview may be found in pp. 1–16 and 312–16. My quote is from p. 15.
21. Ringrose (1983: 22–3, 312–16).
22. Ringrose (1983: 144–5, 194–202, 253–77, 281–94); Hiltpold (1989); Brumont (1988).
23. See a report from Montenegro in AGS, EH, 130-13-i. Goubert (1986: 146–7) reports that peddlers had a similar role in early modern French villages.
24. I confess that my translation is rather loose, in the interest of smooth reading. The original goes

> porque en este lugar no ay quien haga xabon y muchos se proven de Trugillo y si algun forastero viene a vender es por estar horro el carbon viene siete y ocho leguas y si alguna vez viene a venderse es por estar horro que si no en esta villa avria gran falta dello el hierro y azero y madera de arados en seys anos viene una vez mas ahorrase por convenyr a las labranças y quando alguna madera viene es algunos timones de la villa de Garciaz questa seys leguas deste pueblo y los mercaderos de comer ahorranse porque si no ... no hay quien lo sirva. AGS, EH, 189-72

25. Espejo Lara (1985: 52, note 73; 89–90).
26. Salomon (1964: 249–50); Weisser (1971: 228); C. Phillips (1979: 60–1); *Actas*: XIII, 136–7; XX, 413–20; XXI, 317–18.
27. The document for Higuera de Martos is in AGS, EH, 67. The itinerant Portuguese vendors (called *caniculeros*, possibly because they spent so much time in the streets during the hottest part of the year) are described in Pereiro (1987: 20–1). Brumont (1993b: 157, n. 59) found two Portuguese merchants frequenting local fairs in northern Castile in 1603.

28. Relación de corregidores (undated, but said to date from the last years of the reign of Philip II), Biblioteca Nacional (Madrid), MSS, 9,372 = Cc.42, pp. 32–3; Vincent (1970: 232–6); Domínguez Ortiz (1963: 212); Le Flem (1965: 223–4).

29. Martín Galindo (1961: 193–4); Lanza García (1988: 57); Ortega Valcárcel (1966: 104–5); Burkholder (1990: 71–4). Professor Laureano Rubio Pérez commented persuasively on the "bourgeois" mentality of the *maragatos* at the Congreso Internacional: La Burguesía Española en la Edad Moderna, held in Madrid, December 16–18, 1991. The last scholar's most recent book (1995) expands upon the topic of the *maragatos*.

30. Ringrose (1970a: 66, 70–7); Puñal Fernández (1993: 125–32).

31. Behar (1986: 30).

32. The quotation, from the suit *Peñafiel* v. *Quintanillalla*, ACHVA, PC, FA (F), 59, was "vienen a ella todos o los mas dias especialmente los jueves de cada semana a los mercados que se hazen en la dha villa e a conprar e aprobeerse de sus vastimentos e cosas neszesarias." See also Weisser (1971: 225–6); and *Quixote* II, 19.

33. Report from Morales de Toro (1569), AGS, EH, 329. The story, by Carlos García from the year 1619, is included in Chevalier (1983: 277–9). Change came slowly to Spain's mountain villages: Brandes (1975: 50) reported that the typical village women from Becedas (Avila) around 1970 made an annual trip to Béjar – always on a Thursday (which was market day) – to buy needles, thread, cloth, and other necessities not available in the village. Brandes found this yearly trip to have become a fixed institution, considered essential to the maintenance of the household. It is possible that the institution dated from the early modern period.

34. González (1958: 134). The Burgos information is from Brumont (1993b: 151–4).

35. The seasonal nature of Castilian transport is described by Ringrose (1970a: 49–50, 54–7).

36. Report from Penilla (*sic*) de los Barruecos, AGS, EH, 142-10; Ortega Valcárcel (1966: 104–5); Lanza García (1988: 57); Huetz de Lemps (1959: 121); Ringrose (1970a: 51–4). Part-time carting in England is mentioned in Hanawalt (1986: 131–2).

37. Ringrose (1970a: 56–7) insists upon the essential nature of these inter-regional transfers of rural products. For the importance of part-time trans-porting for villagers in the Burgos area, see Brumont (1993b: 154–6).

38. Martín Galindo (1961: 193–4); Ortega Valcárcel (1966: 104–5); Ringrose (1970a: 60–1); Rubio Pérez (1995: 203–50).

39. Ringrose (1969: 46–50); Tudela (1963); Gil Abad (1983: 43).

40. Lanza García (1988: 57); Tudela (1963: 349–94); Ringrose (1970a: 65–7). It is a commonplace among historians that the high cost of transportation with carts was a serious deterrent to long-distance hauling. But Hiltpold (1989: 88–90) found this not to have been the case in the Burgos area in the 1590s, when grain was often transported from sources over 100 kilometers away.

41. Item no. 1345 in the collection by Gonzalo Correas (1571–1631), included in *Refranero clásico español* (1966).

42. See a report from Garrafe del Torío, AGS, EH, 187. See also Tudela (1963: 355); Ringrose (1969: 47); Peris Barrio (1983: 175–6); Gil Abad (1983: 43); Domínguez Ortiz (1974: 95–6).

43. Molénat (1971: 117–20); Pérez-Bustamante (1981: 163–5).

44. Rubio Pérez (1993: 255, 373) transcribes seventeenth-century ordinances from villages in León province that prescribe communal participation in road repair and in similar public works. And according to Ruiz (1994: 61) the traditional communal work obligations still survive in Castilian and Leonese villages today.

45. Molénat (1971: 117–28); Pérez-Bustamante (1981: 164–71). See also Monturiol González (1993).

46. Pérez-Bustamante (1981: 164–78); Molénat (1971: 137–41, 155–60); Bennassar (1967: 87). Hanawalt (1986: 26) indicates that the roads of late medieval England were also frequently in poor repair.

47. See the suit *Olivares v. Xpoval Nuñez y consortes*, ACHVA, PC, FA (F), 24; and a report from Leza (1561) in AGS, EH, 904.

48. See the suits *La Cd. de Segovia v. Sus lugares*, ACHVA, PC, FA (F), 2; and *Sesmeros de la Tierra de Almazán v. Almazán*, ACHVA, PC, FA (F), 89.

49. See the suit *La Hermandad de Montes Doca v. Velorado*, ACHVA, PC, FA (F), 20.

50. The quote is from Segura Graíño (1993: 46). On the condition of Spanish roads see García Tapia (1989: 49–53); Ringrose (1970a: vi, 43, 45–6); Martín Cea (1991: 448–50).

51. C. Phillips (1987), A. García Sanz (1989), and Yun Casalilla (1990 and 1994c) give perceptive analyses of the rural depression. The recent (1994) volume edited by Thompson and Yun Casalilla makes available the latest revisionist thinking about the seventeenth-century Castilian crisis. We must not forget that there were areas of Spain that went through this period relatively unscathed. Nader (1990: 202–3) observes that in the Alcarria district spanning the Guadalajara and Cuenca provinces "even in the depths of the seventeenth-century depression, farm families maintained a level of consumption at least comparable to what they had enjoyed in the palmier days of the sixteenth century."

52. A. García Sanz (1977: 59). This was in the province of Segovia, but Weisser (1971: 64–72) described a similar situation in the Montes of Toledo. Yun Casalilla (1989 and 1994a: 131–2) stressed the general negative consequences for rural Castile–León of the contraction of urban populations. See also Llopis Agelán (1994).

53. An outline of Spain's sixteenth- and seventeenth-century economic difficulties may be found in Yun Casalilla (1987: 269–505); and Vassberg (1984: 184–229). See also the sources cited above, note 51; and for fiscal fraud and corruption, Yun Casalilla (1994d).

54. See Yun Casalilla (1987: 151–218). Marcos Martín (1994b: 224–9) relates the role of debt in the downfall of the fairs of Medina del Campo; and Diago Hernando (1993: 125–8) addresses the question of peasant indebtedness in early sixteenth-century Soria.

55. Yun Casalilla (1987: 269–306, 398–408); Vassberg (1984: 184–229); Brumont (1993b: 259–79); Llopis Agelán (1994).

56. Writing about the Netherlands in the sixteenth century, Jan de Vries

concluded (1974: 113) that "the restructuring of the economy engendered an enormous movement of people into the centers of new activity." And we might apply this principle to seventeenth-century Spain. But according to Sune Åkerman (1994: 77) most migration, historically, *"is not triggered off as a simple reaction to economic conditions or change of such conditions"* (emphasis in original). Åkerman writes from a Swedish perspective, but argues that the principle is valid for other countries as well. And indeed, it appears to be compatible with what we know about migration in early modern Spain.

57. Marcos Martín (1994a: 219–36; and 1994b: 237–8); Ringrose (1983: 34–58, 254–8).

3 MANUFACTURING AND ARTISANAL CONTACTS WITH THE OUTSIDE WORLD

1. Report from Santa Cruz del Valle (1567), AGS, EH, 382.
2. Report from Cazo (*sic*) in AGS, EH, 48; Martín Galindo (1961: 193–4). See also a 1597 report from Pinilla de los Barruecos (Burgos) in AGS, EH, 142-10. Braudel (1982: 255–6, 307) noted that craft industry throughout Europe tended to develop among the poorest peasantry: mountain dwellers, for example, who needed to find activities to compensate for the inadequacy of their agriculture.
3. Ordenanzas de la Corta (1529) de Puebla de Montalbán, AGS, EH, 400; Lanza García (1988: 57–9, 127).
4. Pretel Marín (1989: 70, especially note 52).
5. Delano-Smith (1979: 83).
6. Fortea Pérez (1994); Silva (1967: 145–6); García de Cortázar (1988: 222–3); the Alameda report (1562–6), in AGS, EH, 209; and the Leza report (1561) in AGS, EH, 904. The original of the last reads: "Hazen alguno paño grosero de colores y pardo, lo qual hazen para ellos se alimentar y vestir ... y algunos trabajan ... en cardar e ylar lana por sus jornales para vecinos de la ciudad de Logroño e de Nalda y Viguera, e que si no lo hiziesen padescerían necesidad de anbre."
7. Fortea Pérez (1994: 137–44); A. García Sanz (1977: 208–9, 215); Chevalier ed. (1983: 401–2); Yun Casalilla (1987: 207–8); Brumont (1993b: 131–42).
8. The Getafe quote is from Salomon 1964: 99: "y de lo que mas se hace en este pueblo es xerga y costales para cosa de albardería ... y en lo que toca a xerga y costales no se labra tanto en ningun lugar del reino de Toledo." See also a Libro de Tazmía from Monteagudo (1580) in AGS, EH, 130-5-1, and the Alameda report (1562–6), in AGS, EH, 209.
9. AGS, EH, 130-13-ii.
10. Espejo Lara (1985: 81–3). The quote from the Villavaquerín witness is in the suit *Castrillo Texeriego v. Olivares*, ACHVA, PC, FA (F), 3. Brumont (1985: 59) mentions a weaver in a Rioja village who similarly styled himself a *labrador*. And Burkholder (1990: 228–9) indicates the continued low prestige of weaving among late eighteenth-century villagers in the Sierra de Gredos.
11. The information about Garrafe is from AGS, EH, 187. For an interesting comparison, see the linen production in twentieth-century Basque villages described by Douglass (1975: 90–1).

12. Delano-Smith (1979: 83–4); Garzón Pareja (1972: 32–97, 105–47, 243–70); Fortea Pérez (1994: 137–9, 144–7).
13. Vassberg (1984: 177–8); Delano-Smith (1979: 84–5).
14. Garzón Pareja (1972: 105–6); Garrad (1956: 73–104); Villegas Molina (1972: 247–9); Domínguez Ortiz (1963: 120).
15. For Tudela, see a report in AGS, EH, 189-81. See also T. Ruiz (1983: 424); Contreras Jiménez (1988: 102–4); and Rábade Obradó (1988: 125–6). Hanawalt (1986: 132, 146, 158) found that women were predominant in baking in medieval English villages, and Bennett (1987: 56–7, 190–1) found women in medieval England taking an ever greater role in baking. For comparison with the role of women in Germany, see Ozment (1983: 13).
16. Pérez-Crespo (1969: 462–5); Medina (1549: cxl); the suit *Alberca* v. *Las Majadas*, ACHVA, PC, FA (F), 35; *Actas*, VI: 861–2.
17. Vassberg (1984: 128–34).
18. Brumont (1993b: 114–17); Yun Casalilla (1987: 132, 142–4). Huetz de Lemps, of course (1967), is the pioneer and essential work about the wines of Old Castile during this period.
19. Bennassar (1967: 69–70, 309–11); Ringrose (1983: 197–202).
20. These contracts, called *complant* agreements, typically left the peasant cultivator with ownership of half of the vineyard. See G[arcía] de Valdeavellano (1968: 250, 257); Huetz (1967: 588–603).
21. The importance of charcoal making for the poor is stressed in a 1575 report from Andújar (Jaén), in AGS, EH, 220. See also Bravo Lozano (1993); Vassberg (1984: 36–40, 53–4); Arco y Garay (1941: 872–3); Espejo Lara (1985: 86); and the suit *Toro* v. *La Bóveda*, ACHVA, PC, FA (F), 1. See also López-Salazar Pérez (1986: 32); and Ortega Valcárcel (1969: 140).
22. A list of woodcutting tools may be found in the suit (1550) *Peñafiel* v. *Quintanilla*, ACHVA, PC, FA (F), 59. The quoted verses are from Ac. IX, 558a, cited in Arco y Garay (1941: 872):

> Yo me sustento,
> gran señor, y a mi familia,
> que mujer y hijos tengo,
> en vender cargas de leña
> con un cansado jumento.

23. See a report from Garrafe in AGS, EH, 187.
24. See the suit (1545–62) *Burgos* v. *Concejos de Juarros*, ACHVA, PC, FA (F), 23; and Salomon (1964: 101).
25. See the suit *San Sebastián de los Reyes* v. *Alcobendas*, ACHVA, PC, FA (F), 81; Silva (1967: 63); and Alvar Ezquerra (1990a: 208–15).
26. Examples of *monte*-protection ordinances may be found for Castro del Río (1564) in AGS, EH, 252; Arjona (1537), AGS, EH, 223; and for Trujillo (1499) in AM, Executorias Trujillo, December16, 1521. Some examples of suits over firewood cutting are *Peñafiel* v. *Quintanilla de Abajo*, ACHVA, PC, FA (F), 59; and *Toro* v. *La Bóveda*, ACHVA, PC, FA (F), 1; and *Campillo de Altobuey* v. *Paracuellos*, ACHGR, 504-838-1. See also Alvar Ezquerra (1990a: 208–15).

27. See a Libro de Tazmía from Monteagudo (1580) in AGS, EH, 130-5-i; Anon. (1607: folio 43); Estella (1989); Lanza García (1988: 57); Salomon (1964: 101); Merino Alvarez (1915: 364); Represa (1979: 15–16); and the suit *Soria* v. *Francisco de Vinuesa*, ACHVA, PC, FA (F), 44. Gil Abad (1983) supplies detailed information about Soria's carter-woodsmen.

28. Nader (1977; and 1979: 114). Atienza Hernández (1994: 264) reports that the duke of Osuna, in ways not entirely lawful, imposed monopolies on bakeries, oil presses, tanneries, and other activities within his jurisdiction.

29. Silva (1967: 31–2); Rodríguez Galdo (1976: 137–8); Franco Silva (1974: 73–5). Yun Casalilla (1987: 200–9) estimates that barely 10 percent of the *vecinos* of small villages in the Tierra de Campos were in service and artisanal professions. But Brumont (1992: 138–40) found some villages in the province of Burgos where 25 percent or more of the *vecinos* were artisans. Goubert (1986: 143–4) found similar peasant "semi-artisans" in pre-industrial French villages. And Braudel (1982: 255) observed that European peasants every-where responded to unfavorable agricultural conditions by "plying a hundred extra trades: crafts, the wine-making 'industry' as it should be termed, [and] haulage." Brumont (1984: 137–42) turned up an unusual type of peasant industry: two villages in the Bureba area (Burgos province) that were centers of salt production.

30. Brumont (1992: 120–1).

31. Espejo Lara (1985: 62, 85).

32. Delano-Smith (1979: 82); Salomon (1964: 97–102); Lanza García (1988: 86).

33. The Cazalegas report is in AGS, EH, 218.

34. The quote is from Salomon (1964: 102): "Lo que se hace en este pueblo mejor que en otra parte ninguna de la tierra donde vivimos, es barrenas para carreteros y otros oficios porque acontecen venir de cuarenta y cincuenta leguas por ellas de mano de un oficial que se dize Muñoz, y casi tiene la misma fama de azadones ... "

35. See testimony (1550) in the suit *Congosto* v. *Ahumada*, ACHVA, PC, FA (F), 3; and a report from Villanubla in AGS, EH, 429. See also Espejo Lara (1985: 55–6).

36. Brumont (1993b: 126–7) gives the Ampudia information; that about Pineda is from a report in AGS, EH, 142-11.

37. The censuses of Morales de Toro are in AGS, EH 329 and AGS, EH 360. See also Jiménez de Gregorio (1971: 111), Brumont (1992: 139) found a docu-mentary reference to a pair of blacksmiths of Santibáñez Zarzaguda (Burgos) who made plowshares and other tools for local peasant-farmers, and for those of other places – that is to say, they were itinerant artisans. These peasants, by the way, supplied the iron for the smiths to work. Braudel concluded that the artisans of early modern Europe were essentially rootless men ready to emigrate in search of better economic conditions. He called them (1982: 307) "the most mobile sector of the population."

38. Brumont (1992: 141) tells us that the peasants of Santibáñez Zarzaguda (Burgos) paid their blacksmiths not in cash, but in grain. According to Sánchez González (1993: 164–5) grain was used as payment also in the villages of La Jara (Toledo). The same author mentions the smith–farrier

linkage. López-Salazar Pérez (1986: 204) found that Luciana (Ciudad Real), a village with only 80 households, adopted an ordinance providing for a smith to be offered a minimum salary paid from an assessment on draft animals. The ordinances of Los Santos de Maimona (Badajoz) included a similar provision (Guerra 1952: 532), adding that the smith would be expected to charge moderate fees in exchange for the basic salary guarantee.

39. See a census of Peñaflor (1664) in AGS, EH, 356. The document indicates that both Merloque and his wife were paid a salary by the village government.

40. See Espejo Lara (1985: 51); and testimony (1540) by Francisco Hernández Sylestero in the suit *Alberca* v. *Las Majadas*, ACHVA, PC, FA (F), 35.

41. See a report from Garrafe in AGS, EH, 187.

42. The Castrillo census, made by the *corregidor* of the city of León, is in AGS, EH, 251.

43. See a report from Garrafe in AGS, EH, 187. Another example of a peasant-carpenter with a flexible attitude was Francisco Sánchez, a citizen of Torrecilla de los Angeles (Cáceres). A census of 1586 identified Sánchez as a carpenter, but indicated that he was then running the village butcher shop. He had a flock of thirty goats to supply his shop, and also planted enough grain to harvest 10 *fanegas*. But the census described him as "poor." Supporting a wife and four children evidently was a strain even for one so resourceful as he.

44. *Quixote* I, 2 and I, 21; Brumont (1992: 141); Rojo Vega (1993: 23–6, 34–5). Behar (1986: 221) found that the village of Santa María del Monte (León) in the nineteenth century hired castrators to make periodic visits to operate on all animals of cloven hoof of the place. In payment, the castrators received an *azumbre* (slightly over 2 liters) of wine for every visit, supplemented by two carts of firewood per year after 1873.

45. Rojo Vega (1993: 20–6). We are dealing here with ordinary village doctors. But the famous surgeons of the time also led highly migratory careers. In fact, Rojo Vega (1993: 28) writes that "the most characteristic thing about the great surgeons of the sixteenth century is their constant mobility" (*lo más característico de los grandes cirujanos del XVI es su permanente movilidad*).

46. The Spanish original, cited by Rojo Vega (1993: 21) was: "e ir a los dichos lugares y ver los enfermos todas las veces que fuere llamado y verá las orinas de todos ellos sin llevar cosa alguna."

47. Rojo Vega (1993: 41–4).

4 IN-MIGRATION AND OUT-MIGRATION

1. The *arbitrista* Martín González de Cellorigo (1991 [1600]: 37) deplored the moving of so many Spanish villages to unhealthy sites. On the subject of disappearing villages (*despoblados*) see, for example: Terrasse (1968: 154); A. García Sanz (1977: 34–5); López-Salazar Pérez (1986: 62–4); Jiménez de Gregorio (1971: 98–9); Cabo Alonso (1955: 92–3); and Merino Alvarcz (1915: 314–16).

2. The La Mina census is in AGS, EH, 321.

3. The fate of Villalaín is the subject of the lawsuit *El Lugar de Espinoso* v. *La Villa de Aguilar*, ACHVA, PC, FA (F), 46. For the deserted villages of the Tierra de

Campos, see Yun Casalilla (1987: 56–60, especially the map on p. 57). See also Borrero Fernández (1983: 172–85), for a penetrating analysis of the disappearance of villages in an area near Seville. The phenomenon in other parts of Spain receives the attention of Nader (1990: 47, 51, 158, 164), and of Diago Hernando (1991). Disappearing villages in England are mentioned by Hanawalt (1986: 24–5) and in Europe in general by F. and J. Gies (1990: 200–1).

4. See censuses of Santa Cruz in AGS, EH, 382.
5. Sáenz Lorite (1974: 336–8); Bosque Maurel (1971: 81–2; and 1973: 487–95).
6. Higueras Arnal (1961: 143).
7. The process is described in García de Cortázar (1988: 163–7, 210, 241–2). See also Brumont (1993b: 199–202). And for an overview of migratory harvest labor in northern Europe, 1650–1750, see Moch (1992: 40–3).
8. Vassberg (1984: 143–4); Brumont (1993b: 199–202); García de Cortázar (1988: 163–6); Martín Cea (1986: 101–2); Domínguez Ortiz (1971: 151). For information about labor contracting, see C. Phillips (1979: 39, 151 fn. 17).
9. The jornaleros were profoundly displeased by these local ordinances, and protested to the Archbishopric of Toledo, which suspended them. That action gave rise to a suit (1568) in which the two villages attempted to reassert their right to impose such economic controls. In this case, the outcome is not clear, but the fifteenth and sixteenth centuries generally saw increasing power for local governments. See Martín Cea (1986: 101–2); and the suit Iznatoraf y Villanueva del Arzobispo v. El Arzobispo de Toledo, ACHGR, 321-4328-18.
10. The quotation is from Domínguez Ortiz (1994: 362), citing Andrés Florindo's Adición al libro de Ecija y sus grandezas. In the original: "Es gente casi sin número los que vienen de Castilla, La Mancha y Extremadura."
11. The report from Palomas is in AGS, EH, 906. Fernández Duro (1882–3: II, 553); Herrera Puga (1971: 431–5).
12. Doyle (1978: 114) deals with migrant mountaineers in Europe in general; Poitrineau (1994) with France; Belfanti and Romani (1994) with Italy; and Lanza García (1991: 383–92, and 1988: 56) with Castile.
13. The census of Hornillos is in AGS, EH, 116. Brumont (1985: 33–4) gives examples of inhabitants of other Rioja villages who spent their winters in Valencia and in other parts of Spain.
14. C. Phillips (1979: 39, 151 fn. 17); Blázquez (1905: 25); Brumont (1984: 142); Rábade Obradó (1988: 123); a 1561 report from Leza de Río (Logroño) in AGS, EH, 904; and Martín Cea (1986: 101–2).
15. Sánchez González (1993: 176).
16. AGS, EH, 219-13. On the unruliness of migrant workers, see also an account of a reapers' strike in Córdoba in 1595 in de la Torre (1931: 103–4).
17. For the French, see Alcouffe (1966: 179); and Salas Ausens (1988: 34–5, 38–9); for the Portuguese, see a 1575 report from Escacena del Campo (Huelva), AGS, EH, 272; and a 1578 report from La Abellaneda (Avila), AGS, EH, 209. As an example of Lusitanian immigrants, a 1575 census of Montearagón (Toledo) included a servant named P[edro?], a Portuguese who had entered the household of Alonso de Andrada (himself a recent arrival

from Talavera de la Reina) only two weeks before. See AGS, EH, 323.

18. The bibliography of the Mesta is large, and this is not the place to repeat it. An impressive recent work, by outstanding scholars and including up-to-date bibliographies, is Gonzalo Anes and Angel García Sanz (eds.), *Mesta, trashumancia y vida pastoril* (Valladolid, 1994). The reader will also find it fruitful to consult sources listed in A. García Sanz (1989: 184); and López-Salazar Pérez (1987: especially notes on pp. 2–6). And for the privileges of the Mesta, see A. García Sanz (1994b).

19. See a report in AGS, EH, 130-13-i; and A. García Sanz (1977: 65–7). A fascinating glimpse of transhumant herding in Spain is Manuel del Río's *Vida pastoril*, originally published in 1828. Born in 1757, del Río was a Sorian shepherd and medium property owner who wrote from personal experience of the problems encountered by migratory shepherds. Though his book is from the 1800s, the practices described were in place four centuries earlier. A reprint, with an introduction by José Luis Gozálvez Escobar, was published in 1978. I learned of it thanks to Susan Tax Freeman, who found it in Spain and was kind enough to send me a copy.

20. See the suit *Mesta v. Antonio Collacos* (1556), ACHVA, PC, FA (F), 2; and Nieto Soria (1988: 309).

21. See a report in AGS, EH, 321. Medieval Castilian poetry depicts the continuous mobility of shepherds (and shepherdesses) accompanying their flocks in search for green pastures, according to Nieto Soria (1988: 309). The example from Montaragón is from a census in AGS, EH, 323. Zabalza Seguín (1994b: 209–15) shows that shepherds in contemporary Navarre were also highly mobile, frequently changing jobs and addresses.

22. Rucquoi (1981) describes the various attractions that a city offered to rural people in fifteenth-century Spain, as do Gelabert (1994: 188); and Freeman (1976) for later periods. For Europe in general, see Moch (1992: 13, 44–5); Seccombe (1992: 196); and Watts (1984: 75). The quote is from Braudel (1981: 489–90).

23. Reher (1990: 263–71, 275, 297, 300). The Puente del Arzobispo example is from a census in AGS, EH, 367; that from Ibrillos from AGS, EH, 368-7.

24. Moch (1992: especially pp. 22–3); Reher (1990: 249–50, 297–8, 302–3); Gelabert (1994: 188–205).

25. Lanza García (1988: 60–7, 163–4). The 1561 census of El Puente del Arzobispo (cited above, note 23) lists four emigrants who had gone to Andalusia: one identified as a *bodegonero* and another as a *tavernero*. The 1590 census of Palomares (León) includes two women "from Andalusia" who are probably examples of the same type of return migration. See AGS, EH, 354. The relationship between property rights and geographical mobility is an intriguing topic, and would warrant further investigation. Coleman and Salt (1992: 25) conclude that individual property rights helped produce the surprising mobility of the early modern English rural population. This is confirmed by Macfarlane (1984: 347–9). Moch (1992: 37–9) agrees that throughout Europe people with no landholdings were more likely to move (alone, or with their families) than peasants with land. And de Vries (1974: 112–13) found that population mobility was pervasive among the rural population of the Netherlands in the 1500s.

26. Weisser (1976: 124) noted the dearth of sixteenth-century Castilian marriage and funeral registers, as does López-Salazar Pérez (1986: 63–4). The latter observes (n. 14, pp. 106–7): "Despite the advances of historical demography in the last years, migratory movements are still little understood. We can say that this topic constitutes one of the most important gaps in our understanding of social and economic life in the sixteenth and seventeenth centuries." In the original: "Pese al avance de la demografía histórica española en los últimos años, los movimientos migratorios son todavía poco conocidos. Podemos decir que este tema constituye una de las lagunas más importantes para el conomimiento de la vida social y económica de los siglos XVI y XVII." Since this was written, a number of important works have been published (as my bibiography attests) to fill in these gaps. But far more can be done, despite the inadequacies of parish records.

27. Ruiz Gómez (1990: 255–6). Åkerman (1994: 73–4, 85–6), writing about the Swedish model but applying it to other European countries as well, emphasizes the high mobility of rural populations. Moreover, Åkerman insists that rural migrants based their decisions to migrate upon a flow of reliable information about opportunities in different places.

28. Borrero Fernández (1983: 164–72); Suárez Alvarez (1982: 142–3).

29. Torres Sánchez (1991: 140–50); Rey Castelao (1994: 96–8); Marcos Martín (1994a: 230–1); Gelabert (1994: 198–201); Atienza Hernández (1994: 268–70); Nadal (1988: 45–6). See also Chacón Jiménez (1986: 188–25), who indicates that seventeenth-century immigration into Murcia came principally from the provinces of Albacete and Valencia, followed by Alicante and Cuenca, but with other Castilian provinces also prominently represented. And note Marcos Martín (1985: 585–95) for mid- and late seventeenth-century immigration into Palencia.

30. Reher (1990); Lázaro Ruiz et al. (1988, especially pp. 22–37, 45–8).

31. Kagan (1974: 179–82).

32. Deza ([1618] 1991: 52). The cited passage in the original: Quitan muchos mozos robustos a la Agricultura las universidades de leyes donde son muchos los que acuden, y siendo sus padres labradores, ellos se crían allí afeminadamente, riéndose de las comidas y trajes de sus casas, pareciéndoles a ellos que han medrado en salir de aquella virtuosa rusticidad que da de comer a todos.

33. For Ibrillos, AGS, EH, 368-7; for Puebla del Príncipe, AGS, EH, 366; and for Los Balbases, AGS, EH, 228. The reference to the student from Fuentes de Nava is from Drumont (1993a: 369).

34. The reference to Juan de Herrán is from Brumont (1993a: 369); the Cuenca information from Nalle (1992: 102).

35. The Salas example is cited in Rojo Vega (1993: 20–1).

36. Brumont (1993b: 197–8); Nalle (1992: 84, 91–6); Kagan (1974: 23–6, 186–8).

37. Sánchez González (1993: 168–9); Rojo Vega (1993: 23–6); Kagan (1974: 23–6). The village schools were for boys, because rural people of the day did not normally think that girls needed to be literate. Members of the rural elite, however, often saw to it that their daughters learned to read and write. Brumont (1993b: 348–9) concluded that the girls must have received instruction at home. But perhaps not: a 1561 census of El Puente del Arzobispo

(Toledo), a village of around 350 families, lists a widow named Ysabel de Horgaz as a teacher for girls (*maestra de enseñar niñas*). Such a person might have used her home as a classroom. Unfortunately, the document is mute on that point. See the list of widows in the census in AGS, EH, 367.

38. Dillard (1984: 204–6); Weisser (1976: 77). I have not made a study of crime and punishment in early modern Castile, but testimony from the northern part of the kingdom indicates that a woman was flogged and exiled for theft in the 1530s, and that around the same time a man had his ears cut off as punishment for having stolen a bell from a chapel. See the suit (1544) *Villaporquera v. Andrés Carreño*, ACHVA, PC, FA (F), 17. Subsequent to the book cited above, Weisser published *Crime and Punishment in Early Modern Europe* (Atlantic Highlands, N.J.: Humanities Press, 1979), which places the topic in a broader context.

39. See censuses of Miranda in AGS, EH, 321.

40. The census of Puente del Arzobispo is in AGS, EH, 367.

41. For Villar de la Yegua, see censuses in AGS, EH, 245; for Valverde, see the suit (1552–3) *Bachiller Romo, Antonio Peinado, & Luis de Matos v. Francisco de Oviedo, alguacil mayor de Badajoz*, ACHGR, 3-936-8.

42. Dillard (1984: 144–7) gives the medieval antecedents of migration as a consequence of irregular or illegal marriages.

43. Yun Casalilla (1980: 303–4), for example, writes of peasants fleeing the Córdoba region to avoid debt imprisonment during the crisis of 1506–8.

44. The Los Balbases census is in AGS, EH, 228. Another person who fled to avoid paying his debts was Juan Gómez, who left a wife and two daughters in Villar de la Yegua (Salamanca) in the early 1630s, according to censuses in AGS, EH, 150.

45. The Negueruela reference is from a report in AGS, EH, 150. I have not succeeded in locating Negueruela on a map, which suggests that it did indeed become depopulated – not surprising, because it had only five families in 1586, plus a non-taxpaying priest who was monopolizing the resources of the area. Abandoned wives are commonplace in sixteenth-century censuses, but there are some examples in the 1561 census of El Puente del Arzobispo (Toledo), in AGS, EH, 367.

46. *Actas*, xv (Cortes de Madrid, 1592–8): 540, 748–65. The *arbitrista* Lope de Deza ([1618] 1991: 45–7) cites the emigration of *labradores* to the colonies as the first cause for the decadence of Spanish agriculture. Salazar Rincón (1986: 192–3) cites other contemporary writers. See Marcos Martín (1994a: 212–13, 228–9) for a recent appraisal. Sánchez Belén (1989: 280–4) devotes a perceptive section to the lure of America. Altman, of course (1989), is essential on this point.

47. See Altman (1991: 32–3); Jacobs (1991); Nadal (1988: 39–54); Sanz Sampelayo (1988: 181–91); and Le Flem (1967: 255). Angel García Sanz concludes (1991: xxxi–xxxiii) that while we cannot deny the influence of emigration to the Indies, it had less demographic impact on rural communities than migration to urban centers within Spain. That assessment is undoubtedly true, but we must remember that internal migration had a pervasive impact on the rural world.

48. Borrero Fernández (1983: 171–2).

49. AGS, EH 368.
50. Lanza García (1988: 60–7); Jacobs (1991: 75–9). The census of Morales is in AGS, EH, 329.
51. Altman (1989: 193–4, 204, 277, 282–3); Vassberg (1978: 51); and Le Flem (1967: 257–8). Altman (1989: 247–74) devotes an entire chapter to the return to Spain of emigrants to America. The quote is from Altman (1991: 53).
52. For the interconnectedness of Spain and Spanish America, see Altman's concluding chapter (1989: 275–84).

5 FAMILY RELATIONS WITH THE OUTSIDE WORLD

1. Early modern life-cycle service is discussed at length in Kussmaul (1981); and is mentioned in Gottlieb (1993: 158–63); Moch (1992: 13, 32–5, 137–8); Coleman and Salt (1992: 14); Herlihy (1985: 153); Kertzer and Brettell (1987: 102); Mitterauer and Sieder (1982: 41, 98–9); Watts (1984: 52–5, 74–6); Seccombe (1992: 197); and Åkerman (1994: 76–7). Macfarlane (1986: 83) incorrectly calls sending children away from home as servants a "peculiar English tradition." The continuation of life-cycle service into the twentieth century may be found in Brettell (1986: 39, 93–4); and Douglass (1976: 54–60).
2. Other sources for European life-cycle service include Kitch (1992: 65–6); Howkins (1992: 87–96); Kertzer (1984: 5, 40, 112–13); Hilton (1975: 30–5, 51–3); Horn (1980: 248–51; 1987: 76–7, 126–7, 163). Segalen (1987: 216) asserts that it was unusual for French peasants, except for poor families, to place their children elsewhere as servants, but information in Moch (1992: 32–5) suggests that Segalen may be mistaken.
3. Cervantes, *Quixote* II, 9.
4. For Espinosa, see AGS, EH, 267. Servants in pre-industrial England were also highly mobile (Kitch 1992: 65–6), as they were throughout Europe (Gottlieb 1993: 6–12, 27, 40, 43). Zabalza Seguín (1994b: 209–15) documents the mobility of young servants in early modern Navarre.
5. For Souto de Vigo, which had 64 households, see AGS, EH, 99-30; and for Fuentepinilla, which had 75 households, AGS, EH, 42.
6. The census for Fuentepinilla is in AGS, EH, 42; that for Ibrillos in AGS, EH, 368-7.
7. See a census in AGS, EH, 209.
8. The Castrillo example is from a 1586 census in AGS, EH, 251; and that from Viloria (Villoria in the document) is from a census in AGS, EH, 368-7. For the status of widows, see Vassberg 1994b.
9. For the Morales information, see a 1569 census in AGS, EH, 360; for La Mina (not found on the map, but identified in the document as being in the jurisdiction of Talavera de la Reina), censuses of 1575 and 1578 in AGS, EH, 321. See also Lanza García (1988: 136–8); Mitterauer and Sieder (1982: 98–9); and Kertzer and Brettell (1987: 102). García Herrero (1988: 284) found documentary reference to poor parents placing their children in service to cover pressing financial needs.
10. The census for Montearagón is in AGS, EH, 323. See also Lanza García (1988:

136, 170). Similar situations in early modern France are described in Flandrin (1979: 43–5).

11. The Estépar data are from a census in AGS, EH, 274; those for Miranda in AGS, EH, 321; and those for Santoña in AGS, EH, 368. On the relationship between property ownership and pushing children into service, see Wall (1984: 454–9).

12. See a 1553 census of Frandovínez in AGS, EH, 274. In the original, the text read "porque los dhos sus hijos la syrben."

13. See a census of Viloria (Villoria in the document) in AGS, EH, 368-7.

14. For the Cubillo census, see AGS, EH, 269. The census for Miranda is in AGS, EH, 321. Saavedra (1992: 163) found that many Galician households maintained more servants than they really needed, to provide economic aid to poor relations. Surely this practice existed also in the Castilian heartland. Moch (1992: 17–18) mentions relatives as servants elsewhere in Europe.

15. See a census of Espinosa in AGS, EH, 273. The original reads: "las mozas estan fuera deste lugar, que andan a servir con sus curadores".

16. The census of Viloria (Villoria in the document) is in AGS, EH, 368-7. A 1576 census of Fernancaballero (Ciudad Real) mentions children aged seven and eight (the offspring of Antón López's wife from a previous marriage) who were in other villages a soldada, is in AGS, EH, 320. And García Herrero (1988: 277) found documentary evidence of a girl entering service in Zaragoza before the age of seven! For other evidence about the age of beginning service, see the testimony of witnesses in the following suits in ACHVA, PC, FA (F): Alberca v. Las Majadas (1542), Leg. 35; Rejas v. Pedro Zapata (1565), Leg. 56; Congosto v. Ahumada (1545), Leg. 3; Castrillo Texeriego v. Olivares (1549), Leg. 3; Toro v. La Bóveda (1542), Legs. 1 and 60; and Cea v. Valderaduey (1545), Leg. 63. It is interesting that girls in late nineteenth-century Portugal also began life-cycle service as young as eight (Brettell 1986: 93–4), and in late nineteenth-century Italy as early as ten (Kertzer 1984: 40). And some children in late eighteenth- and early nineteenth-century rural England began working at even earlier ages (Horn 1980: 248–9).

17. See censuses in AGS, EH, 320 and 268.

18. The Abelgas census is in AGS, EH, 209; that of Jubín in AGS, EH, 299. See also the lawsuits listed in note 16, above.

19. For the Cortes information, see Martín Cea (1986: 88, 100–1); and Rábade Obradó (1988). The relationship between wealth and household size was examined in Vassberg (1991).

20. The census for Escazena (apparently Escacena del Campo, Huelva province) is in AGS, EH, 272; and that for Santa Cruz (Toledo) in AHS, EH, 382. Other examples of apprentices may be found in a 1569 census of Morales de Toro, AGS, EH, 360; and in García Herrero (1988: 277–8). A highly unusual type of life-cycle servant/student was a boy living in Felipe del Aro's household in Santoña (Santander) in 1578. The lad was English, and was there "to learn the language." See a census in AGS, EH, 368. Apprenticeship in the European context is discussed by Moch (1992: 159–67).

21. See Rojo Alboreca (1988: 176); Rábade Obradó (1988); Pérez de Tudela y Velasco (1988); Reher (1990: 269–70, 296); and García Herrero (1988). Zabalza Seguín (1994b: 211–12) notes the relationship between inheritance

and mobility.

22. See a census compiled in 1586 for Garrafe in AGS, EH, 187. The Zaragoza information is from García Herrero (1988).

23. Camos is cited in Salomon (1985: 643–4).

24. For abuses of female servants, see Contreras Jiménez (1988: 107). The normal (cordial) relationship between master and servant is described in Rojo Alboreca (1988: 175–6). The Santoña household is from a census in AGS, EH, 368. For comparison, see a charge of abuse in late medieval England reported by Hilton (1975: 51–2).

25. See Rábade Obradó (1988: 122–3, 131–2); Contreras Jiménez (1988: 106–7); and Guerra (1952: 527).

26. For Zaragoza, see García Herrero (1988: 276–7). The Miranda census is in AGS, EH, 321. By way of comparison, see the description of life-cycle contracts in early modern England in Watts (1984: 52–5); and in late medieval England in Hilton (1975: 51–2). Weisser (1976: 83) found that unwritten work agreements were the norm in early modern villagers in the Montes de Toledo. The agreement could be secured on the basis of a hand-shake, or some other sign of mutual trust.

27. Reher (1990: 296).

28. Rojo Alboreca (1988: 176–7).

29. See a 1580 census of Poveda de Obispalía in AGS, EH, 360; a 1590 census of Palomas (called Palomares in the document), AGS, EH, 354; and a 1630 census of Villanubla in AGS, EH, 429. See also García Herrero (1988); Watts (1984: 54–5, 76); and Mitterauer and Sieder (1982: 41). The hidalgo servant is in a census in AGS, EH, 34.

30. See Seccombe (1992: 197–8); Mitterauer and Sieder (1982: 41); and Coleman and Salt (1992: 14).

31. Hilton (1975: 27–8, 34–5) observes that a similar difficulty exists in the use of English poll tax records.

32. The Monleón census is in AGS, EH, 323.

33. For Zarza see AGS, EH, 189–74.

34. This was in 1528. See ACHVA, PC, FA (F), 33. García Herrero (1988: 276) called life-cycle service for rural girls from the Zaragoza area "un compor-tamiento harto habitual."

35. In the mid-eighteenth-century Liébana district (Santander) only 10.57 percent of households had servants, but among households headed by a "don" it was 62.27 percent, according to Lanza García (1988: 137–8). See also Vassberg (1983b). In early modern rural England, one farmer in four had one or two life-cycle servants living in his household. It should be obvious that these farmers included not only the wealthiest members of the community, but also individuals with a middling standard of living. See Watts (1984: 52–5); Coleman and Salt (1992: 14); and compare also with Hilton (1975: 51–3).

36. For Escacena, see a census in AGS, EH, 272.

37. García Herrero (1988: 276–7).

38. From testimony given in 1565 in the suit *Rejas* v. *Pedro Zapata*, ACHVA, PC, FA (F), 56.

39. See the lawsuit *Congosto* v. *Ahumada* (1545), ACHVA, PC, FA (F), Leg. 3.

40. See a census in AGS, EH, 368-7. In this census, nearly all household servants are called *criados*, but it seems quite certain that they were *mozos de soldada*.

41. Jacques Dupâquier, while presiding over the session "Europa" of the 1st European Conference of the International Commission on Historical Demography, "Internal and Medium-Distance Migrations in Europe, 1500–1900" (Santiago de Compostela, September 24, 1993) remarked upon *la hypermobilité des domestiques*. This could certainly be seen in papers presented at that conference by Dupâquier himself, and by Fauve-Chamoux, Åkerman, and by me. It is also addressed by Moch (1992: 56–7, 135, 140–5) and by Gottlieb (1993: 6–12, 27, 40, 43).

42. In-marriage was about 84 percent in rural early modern England, according to Coleman and Salt (1992: 25–7); and Flandrin (1979: 34) found it typically over 70 percent in seventeenth- and eighteenth-century French villages. Late medieval English villages seem to have had an in-marriage rate of 66–74 percent, according to Bennett (1987: 97) and Hanawalt (1986: 200–1).

43. Kamen (1984: 17–18). On literary depictions of youthful antagonism toward outsiders, see Arco y Garay (1941: 883–4). For bachelor societies in twentieth-century Spanish villages, see Brandes (1975: 133–5); and Freeman (1970: 51–60). Compare with bachelor groups in early modern France in Flandrin (1979: 47). According to Gottlieb (1993: 57), popular opinion throughout Europe was on the side of marrying within the community.

44. Lanza García (1988: 53–6); Bourin and Durand (1984: 143). The information about Alfonso the Wise is from Casey (1989: 71); and the proverb was repeated orally by Professor Laureano M. Rubio Pérez at the Congreso Internacional: La Burguesía Española en la Edad Moderna, Madrid, December 16–18, 1991. On popular resistance to out-marriage, see also Díaz Viana (1984: 105).

45. Herlihy (1985: 135–6); and (Hanawalt 1986: 81). But see also Flandrin (1979: 47–8). The Abelgas census is in AGS, EH, 209.

46. Lanza García (1988: 53–6, 159–60). In Extremadura, similarly, there was a higher degree of in-marriage among hidalgos than in the general population, according to Rodríguez Cancho (1994: 334), as there was among the elite of sixteenth-century Fuentes de Nava (Palencia) according to Brumont (1993b: 333).

47. Lanza García (1991: 381–3); Floristán Imízcoz (1982: 146–50); Rubio Pérez (1987: 125–8). Sánchez-Montes González, however, found (1989: 128–46) only a 16 percent rate of out-marriages recorded in seventeenth-century Granada.

48. For Llerena, see Rodríguez Cancho (1994: 334–5); for Rute, García Jiménez (1987: 68–70, 331–3).

49. On the question of parish records underestimating geographical mobility, see Coleman and Salt (1992: 25–7); Moch (1992: 36); Nader (1990: 31–2); and Razi (1980: 120–4).

50. Reher (1990: 267, 271).

51. Bennassar (1967: 425); B. García Sanz (1989: 336); Rodríguez Cancho (1994: 334–6).

52. My next project (which will require several years of intensive work) will be the computer analysis of these census data, with the aim of producing a book-

length study about rural households in sixteenth- and seventeenth-century Castile.

53. Flandrin (1979: 34) found that early modern French villages had proportions of in-marriages varying from 31 percent to 93 percent, a range similar to that in Italian villages, according to Delille (1994: 345).

54. Gottlieb (1993: 158–9); Moch (1992: 32–6); Macfarlane (1986: 86, 90–4).

55. Those proportions come from my analysis of a handful of sixteenth-century censuses in AGS, EH, and are from my paper "The Structure of the Rural Family in Sixteenth Century Castile," at the annual meeting of the Society for Spanish and Portuguese Historical Studies (Austin, Texas, 1987). As I indicated above (note 52), my next project is greatly to expand my sample, to answer this and many other questions about early modern rural households.

56. Ramón Lanza García (1988: 124–5, 138, 163–4) develops the relationship between family economy and family structure and size. See also Zabalza Seguín (1994b: 211–12).

57. A 1626 census of Centenera (Guadalajara), for example, listed Juan de Martín Sánchez in the household of his widowed sister Catalina. Juan was from Alcalá de Henares, and had come to Centenera because Catalina was ill. See AGS, EH, 262. By way of contrast, complex households in England are analyzed by Macfarlane (1986: 95–102).

58. See a census of Monteagudo in AGS, EH, 323; and a 1654 census of Santa Cruz in AGS, EH, 382. The original of the quote from the last: "a la cual tiene [habrá 8 meses] sirviendo en la Cd. de Avila."

59. In the European context, Åkerman (1994) emphasizes the importance of the flow of information for rural people making decisions about migration. Reher (1990: 270, 275–9, 302–3) makes the case for pre-industrial Cuencan villagers. See also Moch (1992: 180).

60. Pedro Martínez, for example, had been a resident of Centenera (Guadalajara). But when his wife died, he returned to Lupiana, the village of his birth, according to a 1626 census in AGS, EH, 262. And Mari Ximénez, who had married Juan Vázquez from Espinoso, returned to her home town of Santa Cruz (Toledo), when her husband died, according to a 1579 census in AGS, EH, 382.

6 RELATIONS WITH THE STATE

1. The Pedro de Alcocer quote (*tres lobas rabiosas*, in the original) is from Sánchez González (1991: 517), who also provides a detailed account (1991: 545–50) of the destruction that the Comuneros Revolt brought to villages in Toledo's La Sagra district.

2. Thompson (1976: 103) calls it "the largest armed force in Christendom," estimating that Philip II at times had over 100,000 military men in his pay. Although oriental potentates of the day were probably able to muster larger hosts, it is unlikely that they matched the overall fighting abilities of the Spanish military at its peak.

3. Vassberg (1984: 219–26). See also B. García Sanz (1989: 235–88); (Brumont 1984: 191–4; and 1993b: 315–18).

4. The military's right to lodging, meals, and supplies are spelled out in Castillo de

Bobadilla (1608, II: 484–5); and in Salomon (1964: 236–8). The best English-language source for the details of the military's impact on Spain is Thompson (1976), in which the effects of billeting are described on pp. 109–16.

5. Cervantes' exemplary novel *El licenciado Vidriera* (first published in 1613) mentions billeting; as does Captain Alonso de Contreras in Chapter IX of his memoirs covering the period 1597–1630. See p. 102 in the cited (1965) edition.

6. For the attitude of early modern French peasants toward soldiers, see Goubert (1986: 181–2, 210–13).

7. Domínguez Ortiz (1960: 333–6).

8. *Política de corregidores*, Chapter I, book VI. Quoted in Viñas y Mey (1941: 177, note 31).

9. See the Consejo de Guerra's instructions to an artillery captain, dated in El Pardo, January 16, 1572, in a suit involving the town of Briones, in ACHVA, PC, FA (F), Leg. 24; and Vassberg (1984: 225–6).

10. Thompson (1976: 113). See also Watts (1984: 24–5).

11. The unfairness of hidalgo exemptions was bitterly resented by non-hidalgos who were forced to quarter troops, and led to numerous lawsuits. See, for instance, the suit *Briones v. Los hijosdalgo della* (1571–4), ACHVA, PC, FA (F), 24.

12. *Relaciones (Madrid)*: p. 268.

13. The maximum rations are stipulated in the Consejo de Guerra's instructions to an artillery captain, dated in El Pardo, January 16, 1572, in a suit involving the town of Briones, in ACHVA, PC, FA (F), 24.

14. See a report in AGS, EH, 219-13. In the original text: "soldados, que pasan muchos por el dho lugar ... les hurtan y comen los carneros y gallinas, y aun intentan y acometen ha hazer otras cosas peores." The "worse things" (*cosas peores*) were suggested later in the same document, which reported "that a soldier had told [a friend of his], in front of many other people, that if he didn't give him some chickens and kill them for him to eat, he would rape his wife" ("que un soldado le abia dicho [a un amigo suyo] delante de otros muchos, que sy no le davan gallinas e se las mataban para comer, que le forçaria la muger)". Alonso de Contreras related the lengths to which a soldier would go to get what he considered a substantial meal. Quartered with a Morisco family in Hornachos (Badajoz), one of Captain Contreras' soldiers was dissatisfied with the supper of syrup (*arrope*) and figs offered by his hosts. Convinced that they were hiding some chickens from him, the soldier thoroughly searched the house, and discovered a hidden subterranean cache of contraband weapons. See Chapter VII (pp. 81–2 in the 1965 edition that I used).

15. *Política de corregidores*, Chapter I, book VI. Quoted in Viñas y Mey (1941: 177, note 31). The original text reads: "No hay género de maldad que ignoren y no intenten: cada uno de éstos parece caudillo de amotinadores y capitán de ladrones. No dejan huerta ni jardín que no talen, ni vituallas que no tomen, deshonestidad que no intenten, ni insolencias que no cometan, sin que haya justicia que les castigue, miedo ni vergüenza que los enfrene." Additional reports of crimes by soldiers are cited in Kamen (1980: 170–1).

16. Vassberg (1984: 226–7); López-Salazar Pérez (1986: 88).

17. A contemporary account of bribing soldiers to go away may be found in Ocampo, *Sucesos*, BN, MSS 9.937, folios 64–5. Bribery is also mentioned, along with ransom demands by the military, in the Consejo de Guerra's instructions to an artillery captain, dated in El Pardo, January 16, 1572, in a suit involving the town of Briones, in ACHVA, PC, FA (F), 24. The examples of Illescas and Villaseca are cited by Sánchez González (1991: 555–6).

18. The report of the *corregidor*, from the late 1500s, is in BN, MSS 9.372–Cc. 42. The same document mentioned the destructive effects of quartering and provisioning – often unpaid – in Burgos, Antequera, Lorca, Loja, and Alhama. In the same vein, see a 1569 complaint to the monarch by villagers from Borox (Toledo), cited in Sánchez González (1991: 555).

19. Quoted in Gutiérrez Nieto (1989: 70). The original Spanish text reads:

> Viene la compañía a su pueblo, danle un soldado [a un campesino típico]. Lo que tenía para comer él y todos sus hijos y casa un mes, lo come el soldado solo en ocho días. El labrador, receloso del huésped, sale a su labor salido el sol, dejando a su gente levantada. Llega a uncir las mulas a las ocho, desunce a la tarde a las cuatro, por llegar de día a su casa. Ha perdido cuatro horas de su hacienda [sobre el horario normal ...], que son el tercio del día ... por [causa del] huésped.

20. *El alcalde de Zalamea*, probably written in the early 1640s, is available in countless Spanish editions and translations. I used the one edited by Jose María Ruano de la Haza, Madrid: Colección Austral, Espasa-Calpe, 1988. The topic of military–villager relations in Golden Age drama is given excellent treatment in Salomon (1985: 747–60).

21. The incident in Puertollano is reported in López-Salazar Pérez (1986: 88). The edict (*bando*) of Philip II, originally reported by Marcelino Menéndez y Pelayo, is cited in Salomon (1985: 754).

22. Reported in Salomon (1985: 747–50); and in Thompson (1976: 115–16).

23. My translation is rather loose. The original text reads: "porque todas o las mas cosas de la guerra traen consigo aspereza, riguridad y desconveniencia."

24. Castillo de Bobadilla (1608: II, 484–5); and López-Salazar Pérez (1986: 88–90).

25. See the suit *Briones v. Los hijosdalgo della* (1571–4), ACHVA, PC, FA (F), 24; and a report about Villanueva de Andújar in AGS, EH, 429.

26. The Navarre incident and the Lope de Soria quote are from Thompson (1976: 114).

27. Freeman (1970: 25) reported that type of pragmatic realism in the nineteenth- and twentieth-century hamlet of Valdemora, in the Sierra Ministra of Old Castile.

28. The report of the *corregidor*, from the late 1500s, is in BN, MSS 9.372–Cc. 42; and the information about Bobadilla is from the suit *Alonso de Port y sus menores v. Bobadilla del Camino* (1567), ACHVA, PC, FA (F), 29.

29. "El Agineta. Decreto por la cual se les dio espera por la mitad de lo que deven para S. Mig[uel] de 1584 ... hasta S. Miguel de 1585," AGS, Contadurías Generales, 362. Another village with financial problems exacerbated by billeting was Belorado (Burgos), which in 1577 obtained the approval of the Chancillería of Valladolid for a special tax assessment of 600 *ducados*. See the suit *Vecinos particulares de Velorado [sic] v. La justicia della*, ACHVA, PC, FA (F), 19.

30. Reported in Domínguez Ortiz (1960: 336).
31. Thompson (1976: 113–14); Vassberg (1984: 226); Gutiérrez Nieto (1989: 69–70); B. García Sanz (1989: 263); Watts (1984: 24–5).
32. *Relaciones (Madrid)*: pp. 290–1.
33. Altman (1989: 95).
34. The hypothesis is not mine; it was advanced by López-Salazar Pérez (1986: 86).
35. That is the estimate of Thompson (1976: 103); also accepted by Marcos Martín (1994a: 213). Thompson (1976: 103–45) gives a detailed description of the recruitment process.
36. Parker (1972: 40, especially note 1) makes the observation that his documentary evidence suggests that most recruiting was done in Castilian towns, rather than villages. This flies in the face of Golden Age literary tradition and of numerous first-hand reports, which portray the bulk of Spanish soldiers as country boys. In the end, Parker allows that recruiting captains, although based in towns, might have recruited rural men directly or indirectly. A study of local records would surely clarify this issue.
37. In the original: "¡Que galán y alentado!/Envidia tengo al traje de soldado"; and "Es linda vida."
38. See the autobiographical account (covering the period 1597–1630) *Vida del Capitán Alonso de Contreras*, ed. Manuel Criado del Val. Madrid: Taurus, 1965.
39. This was in 1610–17, and Juan got more adventure than he had counted on, because he was captured by Moslem pirates, enslaved, and forced to become a pirate himself before escaping to Spanish territory. See B. and L. Bennassar (1989: 29–31).
40. Salomon (1985: 755, note 141).
41. The Venetian ambassador is quoted in Defourneaux (1970: 206); and Gutiérrez de los Ríos in Salomon (1985: 749).
42. Sánchez Belén (1989: 300–4).
43. In the original text: "A la guerra me lleva/mi necesidad;/si tuviera dineros,/no fuera en verdad."
44. Throughout most of the 1500s, the ordinary Spanish soldier's basic salary remained at 3 *escudos* per month. The lack of movement in military pay, in the face of general price inflation, has led many scholars to conclude that unfavorable pay was a deterrent to enlistment. But Parker (1972: 158–9) has calculated that military pay actually increased in real terms during this period, because the *escudo* rose steadily in value, and because soldiers received various bonuses and supplements. The main disadvantage of military pay, according to Parker, was not that it was inadequate, but that it was disbursed with distressing irregularity. Indeed, in 1573 a Spanish commander complained (quoted in Parker 1972: 159–60) that his troops did not even know the meaning of pay (*No saben que cosa es paga*). This was an exaggeration, because soldiers were invariably given ten days' pay upon enlistment – it was subsequent payments that were delayed. See also Sánchez Belén (1989: 294); Altman (1989: 94).
45. See the Consejo de Guerra's instructions to an artillery captain, dated in El Pardo, January 16, 1572, in a suit involving the town of Briones, in ACHVA, PC, FA (F), 24. See also Thompson (1976: 112–13); and Parker (1972: 37).

46. Thompson (1976: 104–5); Sánchez Belén (1989: 300–4); Defourneaux (1970: 206–7).
47. Thompson (1976: 103–45) analyzes the Spanish government's efforts to deal with the military manpower shortage. When the centralized system (using royally appointed recruiting captains) failed, the government turned to private (or contract) recruitment. But the results were disappointing. Finally, it attempted to establish a militia, administered by the towns. Initially it was hoped that voluntary enrollments would produce the necessary number of troops, but in the end it was necessary to resort to compulsion. And in reality, the militia was nothing but a form of conscription supervised by local authorities. Service in the militia had widespread opposition on the local level. There was resentment over the compulsive nature of the militia, and over inequities and favoritism in the selection process. Furthermore, the municipalities who were supposed to be administering the system were often unwilling to put it into effect, both on grounds of principle and because of the high costs that they would have to pass on to their citizens.
48. Resistance to conscription was the subject of an illuminating recent paper by MacKay (1994), whose forthcoming Ph.D. dissertation (University of California, Berkeley) will deal more fully with the subject. For interesting details about draft evasion in La Sagra villages, see Sánchez González (1991: 551–2).
49. Sánchez Belén (1989: 294–300). On the drafting of Portuguese, see Sánchez Pérez (1987: 145–50). The Council of Castile report is cited in Viñas y Mey (1941: 207); and the report of Galicia's draft dodgers is cited in Kamen (1980: 173). Goubert (1986: 212–13) indicates that troop levies were equally unpopular in rural France.
50. López-Salazar Pérez (1986: 87). See also Parker (1972: 36, Figure 5).
51. The Peguerinos census is in AGS, EH, 273.
52. AGS, EH, 329. Valdepeñas (Ciudad Real) in the years before 1582 had lost eight men: one sentenced to the galleys, another gone to the Indies; two in Italy (very likely in the army); two others explicitly in the wars; and two that had simply "left the town." Of these, probably at least five were directly involved in the Spanish military. See Thompson (1968: 261).
53. The Villarrobledo information is from López-Salazar Pérez (1986: 87, 675); the direct quote comes from p. 87 of the same source. In the original: "Los labradores y pastores se han dejado y dejan las labores y ganados en los campos solos y no hay gente que los cuide, ni sirve, y se teme una muy grande ruina no poniendo remedio." For the number of troops levied in La Sagra villages, see Sánchez González (1991: 551).
54. Redondo Alcaide (1992: 173).
55. Altman (1989: 95).
56. AGS, EH, 368. Unfortunately, the census gives no indication of the economic wellbeing of the soldier's family. But it lists no children in the household at the time.
57. AGS, EH, 381.
58. See a census in AGS, EH, 228. Unfortunately, the document gave no family or economic data for María Cides. Her village had 273 households.

59. See a census of Peguerinos in AGS, EH, 273. The Villaseca information is from Sánchez González (1991: 554).
60. For the Castilian system of laws see Kagan (1981: 22–32).
61. Kagan (1981: 32–42).
62. Kagan (1981: 34–6).
63. Nader (1990: xv–xvi) prefers to use "village" for dependent municipalities, and "town" for all villages that gained their autonomy. I think that she was right to make this distinction in a book about the process of moving from *aldea* to *villa* status. But in this book I prefer to stick with "village" for all rural communities of modest size. To me, the word "town" suggests a community that is more urban than rural, thus is potentially misleading.
64. Vassberg (1984: 165–6); Nader (1990: 130–1).
65. Weisser (1976: 102–5).
66. For the Talavera requirements see a report from Castilblanco (1555), AGS, EH, 251; for the Medina attempt, see the suit (which it prompted) *La Seva v. Medina del Campo* (1600–3), ACHVA, PC, FA (F), 59.
67. Puñal Fernández (1993: 129). The Castilblanco information is from a 1554 report in AGS, EH, 251. Travelers in sixteenth- and seventeenth-century Spain could only manage between 4 and 6 leagues per day, on the average, according to García Tapia (1989: 52).
68. Nader's work (1990), the only systematic study of the Spanish Habsburg rulers' sale of *villazgos*, is essential for understanding how Castile's early modern communities operated. Nowhere else is there so lucid and complete a description of local government, of the rights and obligations of citizenship, of the juridical system, or of the intricate relationships between citizen, local government, seignorial lord, and crown. Moreover, Nader's book makes for fascinating reading, thanks to numerous vignettes of rural life in early modern Castile.
69. Nader (1990: 207–9).
70. Asenjo González (1986: 496–7).
71. Sometimes the census was simply taken from the testimony of village officials, but more often it was carried out through a house-to-house survey, in either case duly witnessed and notarized. The procedure of census taking is detailed in AGS, EH, 366 for a count made by royal *juez* Licenciado Enríquez in Puebla del Príncipe (Ciudad Real) in 1589; and in AGS, EH, 382 for a count made by royal *juez* Francisco Juárez Delgadillo in 1579.
72. Nader (1990: 105–12) describes the rituals during one week in 1575 that transformed Carrión de los Ajos (Seville) from a village of the Order of Calatrava to a royal village, and finally to a seignorial village of the Céspedes family.
73. Papers relating to the *villazgo* of Sienes may be found in AGS, EH, 393.
74. See the suits *Peñafiel v. Quintanilla* (1551–6), ACHVA, FA (F), 59; and *Trujillo v. las villas y lugares de su tierra* (1552–1631), ACHGR, 3-958-1. Other similar suits are noted in Vassberg (1984: 239, note 9).
75. Soria y Vera (1633: 42–3); Vassberg (1984: 168–9); Nader (1990: 208). For *villazgo*-generated emigration, see López-Salazar Pérez (1986: 90–9).
76. A. García Sanz (1980: 120–2). The quote from Caxa de Leruela is from A. García Sanz (1980: 121–2). In the original: "La exención de los pueblos no es

otra cosa, que novación de la costumbre antigua, para abusar de la jurisdic-
ción, y de la administración de justicia, y de que se haga entre compadres, y
someter los pobres a los ricos, disipar los propios del común, dar rienda a la
insolencia."

77. The quote (una actividad casi cotidiana) is from Martín Cea (1986: 53). On the
length of boundary disputes see also Kagan (1981: 119). Citizen protests
against costly court battles are recorded in the suits Hernando Alonso y
consortes v. Cubo (1549–87), ACHVA, PC, FA (F), 64; and Lugares de la Tierra
de Béjar v. La villa de Béjar (1586), ACHVA, PC, FA (F), 42. Village representatives to the outside world are mentioned by Espejo Lara (1985: 122) and by
Franco Silva (1974: 79).

78. Vassberg (1984: 92–111); López-Salazar Pérez (1987: 101, 131); Nader
(1990: 9).

79. Kagan (1981: 13–14, 46, 87–9, 104, 106–7, 225, 230, and [quote from]
136).

80. Guilarte (1987); Atienza Hernández (1994); Colás Latorre (1993); B. García
Sanz (1989: 17–79).

81. Yun Casalilla (1994b: 281–5, 297); Atienza Hernández (1994: 250–2,
260–6); Actas (Cortes of 1576), v: 19–20. The quote in the original: "por el
grave daño que los súbditos de vuestra Magestad reciben en ser entregados
por vasallos de los particulares."

82. Vassberg (1984: 96–9); Nader (1990: 2); Sánchez Belén (1989: 282–3);
Gelabert (1994: 198–201); Atienza Hernández (1994: 268–70).

83. The Chancillerías of Granada and Valladolid are full of cases brought against
seignorial lords. For example, the citizens of Antoñana in the 1580s took their
lord to court to resist his traditional privilege of reviewing the actions of
outgoing village council officials: see Antoñana v. Juan de Mendoza, ACHVA, PC,
FA (F), 26. See also Kagan (1981: 11, 137–8); López-Salazar Pérez (1986:
99–101).

84. See the suit Pedro Barba v. Castrillo de Falle (1527–45), ACHVA, PC, FA (F), 17.
The Audiencia's sentence was mostly in favor of the village, but it confirmed
the lord's right to one week's free housing in the village once a year.

85. Tax collection is described by Brumont (1984: 191–2); Nader (1990:
193–203, 208–9); and by Salomon (1964: 228–31). The Expedientes de
Hacienda (EH) section of the Archivo General de Simancas (AGS) is a rich
source of documents about the mechanics of tax collection on the village
level. I am planning an eventual article on village councils' various ways of
assessing royal taxes on local citizens.

86. Yun Casalilla (1987: 90–6, 100–8, 228–44; 1994b: 281–5; 1994d: 51–2;
1995: 175–81); Casado Alonso (1987: 541–2); Nader (1990: 195–6).

87. Nader (1990: 193–4). About the tithe, see Vassberg (1984: 220–1). The
quote about Garrafe ("que siempre son personas de León, y de fuera del dho
lugar") is in AGS, EH, 187. Additional information about contacts from tax
collecting may be found in the suit La Hermandad de Montes Doca v. La Villa de
Velorado, ACHVA, PC, FA (F), 20.

88. Yun Casalilla (1990: 555–7); Vassberg (1984: 221–5); Brumont (1984:
191–8, 312–15); Nader (1990: 194–6, 200–1).

89. Yun Casalilla (1990: 555–7); Brumont (1984: 191–8, 312–15). C. Phillips

(1987: 545) agrees that "taxes canot be blamed for halting sixteenth-century growth." B. García Sanz, however (1989: 271–2, 283–8), calculated that royal taxes paid by the peasants of the Tierra de Curiel and the Tierra de Peñafiel (Valladolid) rose from 4.04 percent in 1578 to 12.85 percent in 1646, while the seignorial tributes during that period went from 8.9 percent to 9.5 percent. That confirms the rising rates of royal taxation, and also reaffirms the inequities of the tax system, from one place to another in Castile.

90. Vassberg (1975: 634–5).
91. The sale of the *tierras baldías* is the subject of Vassberg (1975 and 1983a); and Alvar Ezquerra (1990b). For similar royal actions elsewhere in Europe, see Gordon (1982). The sale of public offices receives the attention of Cuartas Rivero (1982 and 1984), but she does not specifically mention villages, and in any case is more interested in fiscal yields to the Treasury than in the impact on local government. López-Salazar Pérez (1986: 95–6) mentions briefly how the sale of offices affected La Mancha villages. On this topic, see also Yun Casalilla (1994d: 51, 57).
92. Vassberg (1975 and 1983a). The *arbitrista* Lope de Deza ([1618] 1991: 68–9) railed about the *jueces de comisión* who came to Castilian villages extracting money from rural people, who often allowed themselves to be unjustly exploited because they did not understand their legal rights.
93. López-Salazar Pérez (1986: 165–82); Alvar Ezquerra (1990b: 90, 129). Both scholars call for further research to determine the impact of the sales. López-Salazar Pérez, in fact (1986: 174), observes that the topic would merit a separate study.
94. Yun Casalilla (1987: 285–306). The quote (p. 291) in the original: "[la venta] fue un hecho decisivo en la historia de la comarca ... [because of the] repercusiones que tuvo en las haciendas municipales y economías particulares de los terracampinos." Yun Casalilla mentioned emigration as a consequence of the sales in his 1989 paper at St. Louis.
95. A. García Sanz (1980: 117–19, 124–7).
96. A. García Sanz (1980: 124–7).

7 CONTACTS WITH TRAVELERS AND "ALIENS"

1. See a report about Cumbres de Enmedio in AGS, EH, 269.
2. Brumont (1984: 164–5; 1993b: 148). See also Segura Graíño (1993: 47).
3. For Castrillo, which had only fifteen *vecinos*, see an *alcabala* report in AGS, EH, 65; for Villarrodrigo, see a census in AGS, EH, 200; and for Villalbal (which I was unable to locate on a map), a report in AGS, EH, 64–87. The information about Carril is from the 1634 ordinances of the place, transcribed in Rubio Pérez (1993: 258–60).
4. Molénat (1971: 136–9); Maravall (1979: 108–11); Puñal Fernández (1993: 133–6).
5. The information about Monleón is from a census in AGS, EH, 323. See also Nieto Soria (1988: 313–15). Segura Graíño suggests (1993: 47) that the inns of the province of Madrid were especially designed, according to specifications laid down by the municipal government. I have been unable to verify this for other parts of Castile, because the only municipal regulations that I have seen

involved prices and standard measures.

6. The information about Fuentepinilla is from a census in AGS, EH, 42; and that about Tórtola from a census in AGS, EH, 189-6-1. See also Huppert (1986: 4); and Brumont (1984: 165–6).

7. See the suit *Herrín* v. *Yban [sic] de Escobar*, ACHVA, PC, FA (F), Leg. 5; and a census of Puente del Arzobispo in AGS, EH, 367; and Maravall (1979: 108–11). The widow Juana Martínez was identified as a *bodegonera*. Brumont (1993b: 148) tells of the widow of an innkeeper (both Basques, incidentally) in Villodrigo (Burgos) who continued running the establishment after her husband's death. For women innkeepers in medieval times, see Carlé (1988: 70).

8. See a 1561 census of Puente del Arzobispo in AGS, EH, 367; and an *alcabala* report for Morales de Toro in AGS, EH, 360.

9. For the inn in Monleón, see a 1558 census in AGS, EH, 323. Similarly, Burkholder (1990: 72, note 13) indicates that eighteenth-century inns in the Sierra de Gredos were domestic enterprises offering the most spartan accommodations for their infrequent guests.

10. Defourneaux (1970: 15–16); Alvar Ezquerra (1989b: 123–4). Although municipal officials regularly inspected the local inns (as indicated by Puñal Fernández 1993: 136), their primary concern seems to have been prices and measurements, rather than comfort for guests. Seventeenth-century foreign travelers such as Barthélemy Joly (1603–4), Antoine de Brunel (1665), and François Bertaut (1659) described the wretched conditions in Spanish inns (*Viajes* II: 86–7, 405, 554, 556, 570, 594).

11. See a 1555 report in AGS, EH, 269. In the language of the original document: "muchas rebullas y quystiones, ansi entre los v⁰ˢ del dho lugar como entre los foresteros, y muertos, sin que aya abido justicia ni punicion." Cruz (1989: 148) mentions the thieving innkeeper in the 1527 picaresque novel *La lozana andaluza*.

12. Defourneaux (1970: 15–16); Alvar Ezquerra (1989b: 123–5).

13. Typical requirements for inns may be found in a 1580 report from Castilblanco in AGS, EH, 218; and in a 1583 official inspection of the inn of Sienes (Guadalajara), in AGS, EH, 393. An innkeeper of Montánchez was fined 600 *maravedís* in 1574 for failing to have a sign (*tablilla*) identifying his place of business, according to a list of sentences of the *alcaide* in AGS, EH, 323. The Frenchman Barthélemy Joly, who traveled in Spain in 1603–4, described the signs required in Spanish inns (*Viajes* II: 86–7).

14. Franco Silva (1974: 76–7).

15. The Spanish attitude toward reselling is demonstrated in *Actas* (1579–82), VI: Capítulo LXX, pp. 862–3. See also Rábade Obradó (1988: 126–7); Pérez Gallego (1992: 55–6).

16. See a 1595 census in AGS, EH, 189-6-1.

17. Chevalier (1982: 107–12).

18. See the autobiographical account (covering the period 1597–1630) *Vida del Capitán Alonso de Contreras*, ed. Manuel Criado del Val. Madrid: Taurus, 1965, Chapter X (p. 108 in the cited edition).

19. Alvar Ezquerra (1989b: 124–5).

20. Ringrose (1970a: 77–8).

21. Casado Alonso, however, found (1992: 207, note 14) that taverns in late medieval Burgos villages were usually in a municipally owned building, which the local council rented to the person holding the wine concession, on an annual basis.

22. Early modern Spain had no universal standards of measurement. Consequently, each village could establish its own standards. These usually corresponded to the measures of the nearest important town or city, but the metrological system of Spain was exceedingly complex. In Sienes (Guadalajara), the standard measures for wine were the half-*arroba* – about 8 liters; the *azumbre* – roughly 2 liters; the *cuartillo* – a quarter of an *azumbre*, and measures equal to the amount of wine that 1 or 2 *maravedís* would purchase. See an official inspection of the tavern in January 1583, AGS, EH, 393. By way of contrast, the wine measures in Usagre (Badajoz) were the *quartezna*, *media quartezna*, and *dinarada*, according to Contreras Jímenez (1988: 106). In fifteenth-century Paredes de Nava (Palencia) the local measures were inspected by an *apreçiador de las cubas e carrales*, often a carpenter who was charged with manufacturing the council's measuring standards (Martín Cea 1991: 211).

23. Examples of local regulations may be found in an official inspection of the tavern of Sienes (Guadalajara) on January 17, 1583, AGS, EH, 393; in documents relating to the tavern of Morales de Toro in 1564–5, in AGS, EH, 360; in documents from 1562 concerning the tavern of Alameda, in AGS, EH, 209; and in documents relating to the *alcabalas* of Magán (Toledo) in 1564–74, in AGS, EH, 185.

24. Documents (1570–95) about the tavern of Montenegro may be found in AGS, EH, 130-i and 130-ii. Similarly, the tavern keeper of Morales de Toro was required to bring in wine "de la Cd. de Toro o de San Román o donde fuese bueno," according to documents relating to the tavern of Morales de Toro in 1564, in AGS, EH, 360. Censuses from the period that include information about livestock ownership often specify that the tavern keeper used his animals for wine carrying. Thus, the operator of the tavern of Monleón (Salamanca) had *una bestia en q. va por el dho vino*, according to a 1558 document in AGS, EH, 323.

25. See documents relating to the tavern of Morales de Toro in 1566–8, in AGS, EH, 360. Incidentally, these documents report that *besides* the tavern sales, 178 of the 250 households in Morales de Toro had sold white and red wine from their own production.

26. See a census of Los Barrios (de Villadiego), AGS, EH, 198.

27. See a document about the tavern of Montenegro, in AGS, EH, 130-ii.

28. Castellanos paid at least 30 *reales* per year, and Castrillo paid 1/2 *carga* of wheat and 1/2 *carga* of barley. For Garrafe, see a 1586 *alcabala* report, in AGS, EH, 187; for Castellanos, see a similar report (from 1597) in AGS, EH, 74-13; and for Castrillo, a report from 1579 in AGS, EH, 65. I have not located Castellanos on a map, but according to the document it was within the trading zone of Ponferrada.

29. In mid-twentieth-century Becedas (Avila) there was an interesting survival of the service and profit motives seen in Golden Age tavern operation. The management of the bar in Becedas was rotated annually by auction, much as

the right to run a tavern was decided by auction, in places where there was an economic incentive. See Brandes (1975: 33).

30. See documents relating to Monleón in AGS, EH, 323.
31. See an official inspection of Sienes in AGS, EH, 393; and documents about Barrundia in AGS, EH, 56-29. I have seen many other references to women taverners. For medieval women tavern keepers, see Contreras Jiménez (1988: 106), and Carlé (1988: 70); and for the García story, see Chevalier (1983: 299). I could cite dozens of places with outsiders as taverners. One was Castrillo de Rucios (Burgos) in 1579, according to a document in AGS, EH, 65. Another was Bogajo (Salamanca) in 1570, according to a document in AGS, EH, 434-1.
32. See a census in AGS, EH, 222, where Bravo is identified as the *tavernero*, with no indication that he had another source of income; and an *alcabala* report for Calera in AGS, EH, 177-69.
33. The Abelgas census may be found in AGS, EH, 209.
34. Maravall (1979: 108–11).
35. Chevalier (1982: 113–18; 1983: 298–9).
36. My personal research has been primarily in Spain's central archives, and I have limited experience in municipal archives, but I am certain that a study of the fines levied by local officials would indicate whether tavern keepers of Spanish villages watered their wine. In the Simancas archive (EH, 323) I found a list of fines imposed by the *alcaide* of the fortress of Montánchez in 1574. There was no hint of "baptizing" wine, but there were numerous examples of the use of fraudulent measures. None of these dishonest measurers, however, was identified as a taverner. On the other hand, Casado Alonso (1992: 207, note 14) found that taverners in the villages around late medieval Burgos were regularly fined for watering their wines, and that these fines were a dependable source of revenue for minor municipal expenditures.
37. The bibliography of the Spanish Moriscos is extensive, and I will only briefly summarize it here. The general outlines of the story, along with bibliographies of the most important specialized studies, may be found in Lovett (1986) and in Kamen (1983). In Spanish the essential works are Vincent and Domínguez Ortiz (1978) and Vincent (1987), which should be supplemented by Sanz Ayán (1989b) and Sánchez Rubio et al. (1994: 747–71).
38. Nalle (1992: 120–1, 127–9, 133); Thompson (1968: 263).
39. Nevertheless, the resettled Granada Moriscos must have had an impact on the communities where they were sent, because the Cortes of 1573 heard complaints that they were depressing wages for Christian workers (*Actas,* VI; 364). For differences between Morisco and Castilian agriculture, see Bosque Maurel (1971: 126–30; 1973: 497); and Vassberg (1984: 176–83).
40. Le Flem (1965); Domínguez Ortiz (1963).
41. "Relación de lo que an informado los corregidores ... " BN, MSS 9.372 (transcribed as Appendix I of Viñas y Mey 1941: 215–26). Le Flem (1967: 256–7), after studying Morisco censuses in Plasencia in the late 1500s, was struck by the marked population changes, suggesting high mobility of Morisco families. Subsequent research proved this to be true, as indicated by Vincent (1987: 215–37), and by Sánchez Rubio et al. (1994: 759–61). Salazar Rincón (1986: 205–8) gives examples of literary works attesting to the Morisco

210 NOTES TO pp. 140–146

affinity for peddling and transport.

42. Le Flem (1965: 226–9); Domínguez Ortiz (1974: 182–4).
43. Lovett (1986: 272–6); Kamen (1983: 219–22); Haliczer (1989: 55–7).
44. Reglá (1974); Lovett (1986: 272–6); Kamen (1983: 219–22); Ringrose (1969: 51). Bernard Vincent indicates (1981: 604–8; 1987: 229–30; and 1990: 508–10) that a minority of Moriscos were able to remain in Spain despite the official expulsion, because their Christian neighbors and employers certified that they possessed essential special skills, or otherwise collaborated in their permanent residence.
45. Prejudice against the Moriscos is discussed in Haliczer (1989: 55–7); and in Hutchinson (1992: 184–8). For the fate of the Moriscos in Extremadura, see Sánchez Rubio et al. (1994).
46. AGS, EH, 74. In the original text, "todos pobres, gue no hacen trato ni grangeria mas de sus trabajos."
47. AGS, EH, 34.
48. The report of the *corregidor* of Ciudad Real is quoted in López-Salazar Pérez (1986: 66). For the mixed marriages, and other indications of acculturation and accommodation in Extremadura, see Sánchez Rubio et al. (1994: 759–63); for Almería, see Vincent (1990: 498–510).
49. Freeman (1989a: 2–4) gives an anthropologist's view of the Gypsies as a marginated group, while Hutchinson (1992: 180–2) examines literary representations.
50. Sanz Ayán (1989b: 134–5); Domínguez Ortiz (1974: 181); Maravall (1979: 78–9); Cardaillac (1983: 13, 18); Leblon (1985: 163–219).
51. The original text: "Parece que los gitanos y gitanas nacieron en el mundo para ser ladrones; nacen de padres ladrones, críanse con ladrones, estudian para ladrones, y, finalmente, salen con ser ladrones corrientes y molientes a todo ruedo; y la gana de hurtar y el hurtar son en ellos como accidentes inseparables que no se quitan sino con la muerte." Cited in Arco y Garay (1952: 247).
52. Leblon (1985: 121–2); Domínguez Ortiz (1974: 181–2); and Cardaillac (1983: 11, 13, 18).
53. The quotation in the original: "Harto peligro traen la fe en las obras, pues viven una vida desalmada, intentan sólo maldades y consiste la perfección de su vida en descuidar más su alma. Sus engaños, o son pactos del demonio, o embustes para robar ... Bien los llamé vasallos del demonio porque no es otra cosa un aduar de gitanos que un exército de Satanás," from Sanz Ayán (1989b: 135). The other citations are mentioned in Maravall, (1979: 78–9); and Sanz Ayán (1989b: 134–5).
54. Sanz Ayán (1989b: 135, 370 note 19).
55. Leblon (1985: 163–228) cites Inquisition cases against Gypsies in Palomares de Huete, Barchín del Hoyo, Requena, Toboso, Huete, Requena, Maqueda, San Clemente, Santa María del Campo, Rus, and Villarejo del Espartal (with dates from 1539 to 1639).
56. García Jiménez (1987: 289).
57. For example, in 1561 the local government of Higuera de Martos (Jaén) exempted Gypsies from the *alcabala* sales tax, to encourage them to come in with their goods. See a report in AGS, EH, 67.

58. Leblon (1985: 110–25).
59. AGS, EH, 329. In the original text:

a poco que comenzó a servir en el dho oficio los v⁰ˢ ... comenzaron a tomar con él odio
y enemystad e a no resgar el pescado e azeyte de su tienda porque fue notorio que
hechava orines de cavallo en el pescado seçial y que con el azeite de comer echava
azeyte de linaja, y que hazía otras cosas malas ... y aún los jornaleros dezían que se
llevavan pan sólo y no pescado de su tienda, y porque no quería fiar ninguna
mercadería a ningún v⁰ del pueblo, y que se le tiene por mal Xpiano por lo susocho y
porque no yba a la yglia syno tarde y de domyngo en domyngo, y por persançión quel
cura déste lugar le hazía dello, y porque era hombre de mala quenta ... y por lo susodho
y por otras muchas cosas el q⁰ deste lugar le avorresció, y tuvo por bueno que no acavase
de servir el dho vastecimy⁰, y se fue ... donde no a podido ser preso pa le castigar, y
qués fama en este lugar ... quel susocho a bido compañía de Xitanos, y por
sobrenombre se llama Al⁰ Maldonado Xitano.

60. Cardaillac (1983: 18).
61. W. Phillips (1985) gives an excellent survey about medieval and early modern
slavery. For a penetrating analysis of European attitudes toward slavery, see
Eltis (1993); and for Golden Age Spanish attitudes see Domínguez Ortiz
(1952: 406–18).
62. Eltis (1993: 1407–10); Thompson (1968: 244–6).
63. Thompson (1968: 264–5).
64. Bennassar (1979: 105–6); Domínguez Ortiz (1952; 1974: 178–9).
65. W. Phillips (1985: 154–61); Pike (1972: 170–5); Bennassar (1979: 105–6);
Domínguez Ortiz (1952: 372–3; 1974: 178–9).
66. I am grateful to Bernard Vincent for making available to me the written
version of his address on Iberian slavery at the 25th annual meeting of the
Society for Spanish and Portuguese Historical Studies, Chicago, April 7–10,
1994. This paper provides a tantalizing preview of a forthcoming book on the
subject, written by Vincent in collaboration with Alessandro Stella, which will
fill an obvious void in Spanish historiography. The last fifty years of scholarship on the topic is the subject of a recent bibliographical essay by Lobo
Cabrera (1990). Stella's recent (1992) *Annales* article sheds new light on the
use of slaves in Golden Age Andalusia.
67. See the written text (Vincent 1994b) cited in the previous note.
68. The Gracián quote is from Domínguez Ortiz (1952: 378). See also Domínguez
Ortiz (1974: 179–80; 1994: 363–4); and Pike (1972: 177–80). Another good
source for slavery in early modern Spain is Bennassar (1979: 105–17). And
slavery in late sixteenth-century La Laguna (Canary Islands) is the subject of
an important article by Marcos Martín (1992 [1980]). To make up for the
country's demographic losses from plagues in the last decade of the sixteenth
century, some Spanish intellectuals called for the increased importation of
slave workers. A good example is Gonzalez de Cellorigo's *Memorial de la política
necesaria y útil restauración a la república de España*, published in 1600. See pp.
65–9 in the Pérez de Ayala edition.
69. Stella (1992: 55).
70. Kamen (1980: 286–8).
71. Domínguez Ortiz in an early work (1952: 387) ventured that slave labor
played no role in rural production, a situation that he explained by the abun-

dance of low-cost free labor. But more recently Vincent (1994b) correctly observes that many "domestic" slaves were in fact used to care for crops or animals. Unquestionably there *were* slaves who specialized in agriculture and herding, but they may have been too few in number to be of great economic significance. In the rural world, villages near the slave markets of Seville were more likely than most to have a slave or two. For instance, a 1631 census of Espartinas listed domestic slaves (without disclosing their origin) in two households; and a 1629 census of Bormujos listed a *mulata* slave, in a household with four other (free) servants. See documents in AGS, EH 272 and 237, respectively. The Málaga census information is from Vincent (1987: 252–3).

72. See the suit *Luis Alvarez* v. *Vélez Málaga* (1553), ACHGR, 511-2157-2. The Caballar census is in AGS, EH, 66, fol. 1.

73. For slaves in Trujillo and Cáceres, see Le Flem 1967: 257–8. See Ordinances nos. 47, 92, 93, and 97 of Los Santos de Maimona, in the transcription by Guerra (1952). Similarly, Domínguez Ortiz (1952: 382) found slavery mentioned in the ordinances of Baena (Córdoba) and Jerez de los Caballeros (Badajoz) – both relatively small and out-of-the-way municipalities, as well as Burguillos, a village off the beaten path north of Seville. I regret that I have been unable to consult Fernando Cortes Cortes, *Esclavos en la Extremadura meridional, siglo XVII* (Badajoz 1987), cited in Vincent's 1994 SSPHS paper (1994b).

74. The information about Palomas (called "Palomares" in the document) is in AGS, EH, 354. The slave in Palomas, incidentally, was married to a certain María Estévan, apparently a free resident of the place. Menasalbas, according to the census of 1575, had around 400 households. The document did not identify the race or origin of the slaves – a mother and her daughter. See AGS, EH, 319. The census of Villa de Pun, taken by a royally appointed official, is in AGS, EH, 368.

75. Domínguez Ortiz (1952: 385–97); Pike (1972: 182–92). W. Phillips (1985: 163) gives the Palos statistics, unfortunately without specifying whether the parents of these black children were slave or free.

76. See the suit *Pedro Suárez de la Vega* v. *Alcolea* (1568), ACHGA, 3-559-12 bis.

77. For Puente del Arzobispo, see a census in AGS, EH, 367; for Puerto de Santoña (called "Puerto de Santoria" in the document), see a census in AGS, EH, 368.

78. See p. 47 in the García Sanz edition of Deza. Domínguez Ortiz's statement (1974: 177) that "in Castile the foreign colony was totally urban" is an unfortunate error, perhaps derived from sources like Deza. Certainly, the most *visible* foreign presence in Castile was urban, but there were large numbers of foreigners (mainly French and Portuguese) in rural areas as well. But although in remote areas, they were not necessarily engaged in agricultural pursuits. Nevertheless, their presence would have been observed by villagers. For example, Stella (1992: 39) found that 150 Germans worked in the Sierra Morena as technicians in the silver mines of Guadalcanal (Seville). There must be many similar examples of foreign specialists working in different parts of Castile. Surely there would have been a certain amount of interaction between neighboring villagers and these foreigners. Unfortunately, I was unable to consult J.M. Bello León's *Extranjeros en Castilla (1474–1501). Nota y documentos para el estudio de su presencia en el reino a fines del siglo XV* (Tenerife, 1994), which promises to be highly useful.

79. For Castilblanco, see a census in AGS, EH, 74-14-iii; for Cordovilla, which had fifty-one households at the time (one including a Portuguese widow working as a domestic), see a census in AGS, EH, 268. The suit is *Bachiller Romo, Antonio Peinado, & Luis de Matos v. Francisco de Oviedo, Alguacil Mayor de Badajoz* (1552–3), ACHGR, 3-936-8. Altman (1989: 193) writes that there were numerous Portuguese immigrants and transients in early modern Cáceres; and Sánchez Pérez (1987: 148) notes that the authorities in that area decided to subject them to the military draft in the 1640s, despite the fact that Portugal was an enemy nation at the time. Pereiro (1987: 20–1) found that there were so many itinerant Portuguese street vendors in the city of Málaga in the mid-1500s that local merchants repeatedly complained about their competition.

80. For Villar de la Yegua (called "Caraveo" in the document), see censuses of 1631 and 1634 in AGS, EH, 245.

81. Pérez Cebada (1994: 860–1).

82. García Jiménez (1987: 288).

83. For Fernancaballero, see a census in AGS, EH, 320; for Mohedas, a census in AGS, EH, 322-1. The Portuguese couple in Mohedas, incidentally, after spending about a month in the village hospice, died of unstated causes.

84. The Avellaneda information is from a census in AGS, EH, 209.

85. For French immigration into Spain, see the bibliographical citations in Amalric (1994).

86. Davis (1983: especially pp. 6, 21–6, 125).

87. Amalric (1994: 413–21); Salas Ausens (1988: 34–5, 38–9).

88. Amalric (1994: 419–21); Salas Ausens (1988: 39–42).

89. Villars and Labat are both quoted in Kamen (1980: 184–5); and Brunel is cited in Moch (1992: 29). See also Alcouffe (1966: 179), who mentions agricultural workers in La Mancha; Domínguez Ortiz (1960: 339) for seventeenth-century French immigrants following various professions in Castile; and Moch (1992: 83–8) who relates information about the eighteenth century.

90. Viñas y Mey (1941: 207).

8 ADDITIONAL CONTACTS WITH THE OUTSIDE WORLD

1. Martz (1983: 3–6, 31); Kamen (1980: 173); Pike (1972: 17–18, 192–4).

2. Moch (1992: 47–8); Eltis (1993: 1411–12).

3. The Fernández de Navarrete citation is from Kamen (1983: 251).

4. Castilian attitudes, laws, and institutions concerning beggars, the poor, and poor relief are covered by Martz (1983: 7–91); Flynn (1985, especially pp. 336, 348); Pérez (1983); and by Carasa Soto (1994: 382–98). See also Kamen (1980: 276–80); Pike (1972: 194–6); Bennassar (1979: 136–8); and Arco y Garay (1952: 233–9). The Cazo information is from a 1586 census in AGS, EH, 48.

5. For the medieval antecedents of Spain's *hospitales*, see López Alonso (1986: 407–74); Carlé (1988: 136–45); and Casado Alonso (1990: 291–2).

6. Pedro Carasa Soto (1988a) devotes an entire book to the subject of hospices and other relief agencies in the province of Burgos. Although his work is dedi-

cated principally to the eighteenth and nineteenth centuries, it includes some historical background of both urban and rural *hospitales*. See also Carasa Soto (1994).

7. For the hospices of Camarena, Getafe, and of other villages that responded to the questionnaires, see responses 54 and 39 of the *Relaciones*. The response from Camarena indicated that the hospice for local residents usually had four or five elderly women living there. And the medical *hospital* of Getafe was reported to care for as many as thirty sick persons.

8. Bargas, San Martín, and Menasalbas are all listed in the *Relaciones*. The hospice of the last is also mentioned in a 1575 document in AGS, EH, 319. At the time, the Menasalbas hospice was occupied by a poor couple, from outside the village.

9. The information about Alcabón and Burguillos is from the *Relaciones*. A house-to-house census (see AGS, EH, 366) of Puebla del Príncipe (Ciudad Real) in 1598 found the local *hospital* uninhabited. In some villages the hospice provided employment and lodging for local people. For example, in 1664 Francisco Rodríguez and his wife were living in the shelter of Peñaflor de Hornija (Valladolid). The village officials explained that they had allowed them to stay in the house out of charity, in exchange for managing the place. See a census in AGS, EH, 356. The city of Toledo's hospices, similarly, had a policy of denying long-term relief, according to Martz (1983: 13–28, 77, 123, 148–50). And Trujillo and Cáceres did much the same (Altman 1989: 101).

10. The census of Montenegro is in AGS, EH, 130-13; that of Los Balbases in AGS, EH, 228.

11. The census of Puente del Arzobispo is in AGS, EH, 367.

12. For Castrillo, see a census in AGS, EH, 251; for Mohedas, a census in AGS, EH, 322-1. The Portuguese couple, incidentally, "passed on" not merely to the next village, but actually *died* in the hospice, of unstated causes. The census of Puente del Arzobispo is in AGS, EH, 367.

13. Christian (1981, especially pp. 20–1, 161–2, 166–7).

14. Christian (1981: 20–1); Casado Alonso (1990: 286–8); García de Cortázar (1988: 90–5).

15. Christian (1981: 70–1, 141–2, 166–7). Critchfield (1981: 343–4) included in a list of universal characteristics of village society a skepticism towards organized religion, and a suspicion of outside clergy.

16. Christian (1981: 166–7); Nalle (1992: 80–1).

17. For Torrecilla, see a census in AGS, EH, 188-7-ii; for Mohedas, a census in AGS, EH, 322-1.

18. Nalle (1992: 84–7, 102); Kagan (1974: 23–7).

19. See a census of Poveda in AGS, EH, 360; Nalle (1992: 81–2); and a census of Palacios de Goda in AGS, EH, 43-1-xii. For Cubo, see testimony (1549) in the suit *Hernando Alonso v. Cubo*, ACHVA, PC, FA (F), 64.

20. For Catalonia, Kamen's even more recent book (1993) studies religious life in Mediona, a village in the Penedes district. Kamen's work sets the Catalan reforms within the general Spanish framework.

21. Nalle (1992, especially pp. 71–210); Christian (1981: 166–80).

22. Christian (1981: 175–80); Nalle (1992: 208–10).

23. Muñoz Fernández (1993) provides an illuminating study of pilgrimages to

shrines in the province of Madrid during the fifteenth and sixteenth centuries; while Graña Cid (1993) studies the geographical mobility of late medieval mendicant orders in Madrid province.

24. For the medieval antecedents of the Santiago traffic see T. Ruiz (1994: 220–3) and Martínez Sopena (1993). The Brunel quote is from *Viajes de extranjeros* II: 409. In the Spanish version: "No os sabré decir la cantidad de peregrinos franceses que iban o que venían de Santiago de Galicia." The Pérez de Herrera statement is cited in Domínguez Ortiz (1960: 340).

25. Flynn (1985: 339–40).

26. Flynn (1985: 343).

27. Martz (1983: 77).

28. Ruiz (1994: 220–3); Martínez Sopena (1993: 199–211).

29. The phenomenon of urban investment in rural property has received the attention of numerous scholars. See, for example: Delano-Smith (1979: 136–7); Braudel (1975: 424–5); Gómez Mendoza (1967); Yun Casalilla (1987: 248–59); Casado Alonso (1990: 280); García de Cortázar (1988: 202–5); T. Ruiz (1994: 152–69); Brumont (1993b: 288–9); Diago Hernando (1993: 124–5); Weisser (1976: 44–5); Asenjo González (1986: 493–4); and Bennassar (1967: 322–5).

30. Domínguez Ortiz (1974: 164–5); Nader (1979: 118, 225, note 23); T. Ruiz (1994: 152); Brumont (1993a: 367). Casado Alonso (1990: 282) wrote that he had *never* seen evidence of urban (or noble or ecclesiastical, for that matter) large landowners directly exploiting the soil in the province of Burgos. They invariably preferred to let their property to villagers in rental or other similar agreements.

31. Pérez-Crespo (1969: 462–5).

32. Terrasse (1968: 152). We should not necessarily deplore the fact that the farmers of Ribas de Jarama were not landowners. In an earlier work (Vassberg 1984: 211–18) I concluded that in many respects it was better to rent, rather than to own, agricultural land. More recently T. Ruiz (1994: 156–61) provides evidence that late medieval Castilian peasants often sold their land to obtain cash to pay debts, while remaining on the same land as tenants.

33. For Plasencia, see the suit *Plasencia v. los lugares de su Tierra* (1531–49), ACHVA, PC, FA (F), 64. See also Yun Casalilla (1987: 248–59); C. Phillips (1979: 65–75); Ruiz (1994: 156–61).

34. I speak from personal experience, as well as observation and reading: my father was a farmer who always rented land, to supplement that which he owned; and during the five years that I farmed on my own, I was in a similar situation. See also Casado Alonso (1990: 280).

35. The Frandovínez census is in AGS, EH, 274.

36. Brumont (1993a: 366); A. García Sanz (1980: 117–27).

37. Earlier estimates of plague losses were much higher. Elliott, for example (1963: 294) ventured that the plague probably wiped out the 15 percent population growth of the sixteenth century. The classic study of the plague during this period is Bennassar (1969), a model of historical scholarship. For the recurring plague outbreaks in Spain, see his p. 10. Pérez Moreda (1994: 35–6) provides a more recent appraisal of the effects of the plague in Castile.

38. Brumont (1988: 217–20) supplies details about the entry of the 1596 plague,

including a map showing its spread from the coast to Cogollos. See also Pérez Moreda (1994: 35–6); Bennassar (1969: 20); and Brumont (1993b: 230–2).

39. Bennassar (1969: 79–80); Brumont (1993b: 233–4); Pérez Moreda (1994: 35–47).

40. Brumont (1993b: 242–6). Brumont cites some exceedingly high mortality rates (up to 87 percent for Nidáguila), but rightly expresses skepticism over the population figures supplied by local authorities.

41. Sánchez González (1993: 105–9). The Alemán quote, from the picaresque novel *Guzmán de Alfarache* (1599), cited Sánchez González p. 109, in the original: "el hambre que sube de Andalucía con el mal que desciende de Castilla." On the relationship between plague and famine, see Pérez Moreda (1994: 36, note 15).

42. Sánchez González (1993: 109–17; 1991: 533–45).

43. The Cameño information is in AGS, EH, 69-13. (In the document, the name is "Carmeno." I took it to be Cameño because I could find no closer alternative in the La Bureba district, where the village was located.) The Toledo policy is from Sánchez González (1991: 534). On the plague as a promoter of migration, see Pérez Moreda (1994: 56–9).

44. Yun Casalilla (1990: 562); Pérez Moreda (1994: 56–8); Brumont (1993b: 234, 246).

45. Sanz Ayán (1989a: 196–201).

46. The Rojas categories are cited by Salazar Rincón (1986: 176–8).

47. McKendrick (1989: 186–7, 205–7); Deza ([1618] 1991: 51).

48. Cervantes in *Don Quixote* (II, 25–7) tells of a traveling marionette show going from village to village, and in *El Coloquio de los perros* describes a successful animal act. Lope de Deza ([1618] 1991: 51) was indignant that peasants were attracted to musical and theatrical performances.

49. The *escribano* used for an investigation in Castañar de Ibor (Cáceres) in 1597 was from nearby Garvín, according to a document in AGS, EH, 177. And Brumont (1992: 141) indicates that the *escribano* of Estépar (Burgos) also served more than one village.

50. See documents about Espinoso in AGS, EH, 843.

51. The early modern Spanish Postal Service is described in Domínguez Ortiz (1974: 98–9); and its medieval antecedents in Uriol Salcedo (1993: 40–1) and in Cuadra García (1993: 206–7). For Brunel's experience with postal mounts, see *Viajes de extranjeros* (II: 491–2).

52. Bennassar (1967: 90) gives the statistics about postmen; Domínguez Ortiz (1974: 98–9) writes about rates; and Cuadra García (1993: 205–15) about messengers.

CONCLUSION

1. I am basing this list upon Reher (1990: 248).

2. My next project is the computerization and statistical analysis of data for about 200 villages, from fiscal censuses in the EH section of the Simancas archive. It is a long-term project that will require several years, and is intended ultimately to produce a book entitled "The Rural Family in Habsburg Castile: Structures, Social Stratification, and Economic Function." I expect that this

projected book will provide additional supporting evidence for rural Castilian population mobility.

3. In addition to the tabulated sixteenth-century censuses, I have analyzed data from three early seventeenth-century censuses. They are Aravaca (Madrid), Centenera (Guadalajara), and Marzales (Valladolid). Their column F proportions were, respectively: 18, 22, and 31. See censuses in AGS, EH, 222, 262, and 316.

4. I have not located Almaraz on the map, to my satisfaction. The Simancas documents place it in the Partido de Toro – hence in the province of Zamora. Current maps show a village named Almaraz de Duero in that province, but it lies on the other side of the city of Zamora, and I am not certain that it is the Almaraz of the census. In any case, the documents are in AGS, EH, 186.

5. If the figures do not exactly add up to 45, that is probably because of (1) clerical errors in the document; or (2) the common practice of counting some persons (e.g. widows, hidalgos, or property-owning orphans) as 1/2 *vecino*.

6. AGS, EH, 367.

7. Nader (1990: 31).

8. Silva (1967: 21–2). In the original: "La masa campesina se remueve, se traslada. Además, trasladarse es cómodo" and "Los lugares, más pequeños, aparecen como los de mayor movilidad."

9. Braudel (1982: 257–8).

10. Reher (1990: 279, 300).

11. Lanza García (1988: 56). The same was true of the rest of Europe, to be sure. Jacques Dupâquier, during the Round Table discussion of the 1st European Conference of the International Commission on Historical Demography, "Internal and Medium-Distance Migrations in Europe, 1500–1900" (Santiago de Compostela, September 25, 1993), remarked that a certain mobility was necessary to maintain the "sedentary" population of Europe during the *ancien régime*.

12. A. García Sanz (1988: 41, 44) and Behar (1986: *passim*) have emphasized the longevity of rural technology and institutions, as did the earlier scholar Blázquez (1905: 16–17).

13. That is the title of Reher's Chapter 8 (1990: 299–304).

14. Spanish sociologist Pérez-Díaz recognized this over a quarter century ago (1967: 123), writing that "Rural communities such as those of Castile cannot be considered as closed, integrated, and stable. In fact they have submitted *throughout their history* to a continuous process of change as a result of external pressures as well as internal tensions" (emphasis mine).

15. The importance of migration and mobility in Spain and in the rest of Europe was made clear by the 75 papers presented at the 1st European Conference of the International Commission on Historical Demography, "Internal and Medium-Distance Migrations in Europe, 1500–1900," Santiago de Compostela, September 22–25, 1993 (circulated at the Conference in two volumes of *Actas*), and published subsequently as vol. I: *Les migrations internes et à moyenne distance en Europe, 1500–1900*; and vol. II: *Migraciones internas y medium-distance en la Península Ibérica, 1500–1900*, ed. by Antonio Eiras Roel and Ofelia Rey Castelao (Santiago de Compostela: Xunta de Galicia, 1994).

   Concerning the alleged isolation of Spain, it is noteworthy that even during

the period when Philip II attempted to protect the country from the heretical
ideas of northern Europe, and despite unfavorable political relations with the
English, the Dutch, and others, Spain continued to have contacts with the rest
of Europe. Kamen (1993: 387) concludes that despite Philip's efforts to erect
a sort of *cordon sanitaire*, Spain maintained "uninterrupted and active
contacts" with the rest of Europe.

BIBLIOGRAPHY

UNPUBLISHED ARCHIVAL SOURCES

Archivo General de Simancas (AGS)
  Diverse types of unpublished documents, most notably censuses (*padrones de vecindad*) and other reports in the Expedientes de Hacienda (EH) Section.
Archivo de la Chancillería de Valladolid (ACHVA)
  Lawsuits on a variety of topics relating to Castile north of the Tagus River.
Archivo de la Chancillería de Granada (ACHGR)
  Lawsuits on a variety of topics relating to Castile south of the Tagus River.
Biblioteca National (BN) (in Madrid)
  Anonymous 1607 document *Floresta española*, MSS 5.989.
  Ocampo, Florián de. "Noticias de varios sucesos acaecidos desde el año 1521 hasta el 1549," MSS 9.937, folios 64–5.
  "Relacion de lo que an informado los corregidores de castilla la bieja y nueva, la mancha, estremadura y andalucia cerca del Remedio que tendra para la conserbación de la labranza y crianza," MSS 9.372. Undated, but said to be from the reign of Philip II.

PUBLISHED CONTEMPORARY SOURCES

Actas de las Cortes de Castilla. 1869–1918. 45 vols. Madrid: Imprenta Nacional, *et al*.
Calderón de la Barca, Pedro. *El alcalde de Zalamea*. Written probably in the early 1640s. Available in countless editions and translations. I used the one edited by José María Ruano de la Haza, Madrid: Colección Austral, Espasa-Calpe, 1985
Castillo de Bobadilla, Jerónimo. 1608. *Política para corregidores y señores de vasallos en tiempo de paz y de guerra*, 2 vols. Medina del Campo: Christóval Lasso y Francisco García. First published 1597.
Cervantes Saavedra, Miguel de. *El ingenioso hidalgo Don Quixote de la Mancha* (Part I first published in 1605, and Part II in 1615, available in countless editions and translations).
  Novelas ejemplares (First published in 1615, available in countless editions and translations).
Chevalier, Maxime. (ed.) 1983. *Cuentos folklóricos en la España del Siglo de Oro*. Barcelona: Editorial Crítica.
Contreras, Alonso de. 1965 (Memoirs of the period 1597–1630). *Vida del Capitán*

Alonso de Contreras, ed. by Manuel Criado del Val. Madrid: Taurus.

Deza, Lope de. 1991 [1618]. *Gobierno político de agricultura (1618)*, ed. by Angel García Sanz. Madrid: Instituto de Estudios Fiscales.

Don Quixote de la Mancha, see Cervantes Saavedra, Miguel de

González de Cellorigo, Martín. 1991 [1600]. *Memorial de la política necesaria y útil restauración a la república de España y estados de ella y del desempeño universal de estos reinos (1600)*, ed. by José L. Pérez de Ayala. Madrid: Instituto de Estudios Fiscales.

Guerra, Arcadio. (ed.) 1952. "Ordenanzas municipales de Felipe II a Los Santos de Maimona," *Revista de estudios extremeños*, 8: 495–534.

Medina, Pedro de. 1549. *Libro de Grandezas y cosas memorables de España*, 2nd edn. Seville: Domenico de Robertis.

Refranero clásico español y otros dichos populares, 2nd (1966) edn, by Felipe C.R. Maldonado. Madrid: Taurus.

Refranero español. Colección de ocho mil refranes populares, ordenados, concordados y explicados, precedida del «Libro de los proverbios morales» de Alonso de Barros, 7th (1968) edn, by José Bergua. Madrid: Ediciones Ibéricas.

Relaciones histórico-geográfico-estadísticas de los pueblos de España hecho por iniciativa de Felipe II: Provincia de Madrid; Reino de Toledo; Ciudad Real, ed. by Carmelo Viñas y Mey and Ramón Paz. Madrid: Consejo Superior de Investigaciones Científicas, 1949–71.

Soria y Vera, Melchor. 1633. *Tratado de la Iustificación y conveniencia de la tassa de el pan, y de la dispensación que en ella haze su magestad con todos los que siembran.* Toledo: Juan Ruiz de Pereda.

Viajes de extranjeros por España y Portugal: Tomo II, siglo XVII, trans. and ed. by J. García Mercadal. Madrid: Aguilar, 1959.

CITED SECONDARY WORKS

Åkerman, Sune. 1994. "Time of the Great Mobility. The Case of Northern Europe," pp. 73–99 in vol. I of *Les migrations internes et à moyenne distance en Europe, 1500–1900* (Papers of I Conferencia Europea de la Comisión Internacional de Demografía Histórica, Santiago de Compostela, 22–25 September 1993), ed. by Antonio Eiras Roel and Ofelia Rey Castelao. Santiago de Compostela: Xunta de Galicia, Consellería de Educación e Ordenación Universitaria.

Alcouffe, Daniel. 1966. "Contribution à la connaissance des émigrés français de Madrid au XVIIᵉ siècle," *Mélanges de la Casa de Velázquez*, 2: 179–99.

Altman, Ida. 1989. *Emigrants and Society: Extremadura and America in the Sixteenth Century*. Berkeley: University of California Press.

    1991. "A New World in the Old: Local Society and Spanish Emigration to the Indies," pp. 30–58 in *"To Make America" European Emigration in the Early Modern Period*, ed. by Ida Altman and James Horn. Berkeley: University of California Press.

Alvar Ezquerra, Alfredo. 1988. "Control social, cuestionarios, riqueza y pobreza en el último cuarto del siglo XVI; algunas noticias referidas al mundo rural madrileño," *Hispania. Revista española de historia*, 48: 875–907.

    1989a. "Las ciudades españolas," pp. 71–90 in *La vida cotidiana en la España de Velázquez*, ed. by José N. Alcalá-Zamora. Madrid: Ediciones Temas de Hoy.

1989b. "Viajes, posadas, caminos y viajeros," pp. 109–26 in *La vida cotidiana en la España de Velázquez*, ed. by José N. Alcalá-Zamora. Madrid: Ediciones Temas de Hoy.

1990a. "Una aproximación a la geohistoria de Madrid: su geografía, toponimia y protección ecológica inmediatamente después de 1561," *Anales del Instituto de Estudios Madrileños*, 29: 195–215.

1990b. *Hacienda real y mundo campesino con Felipe II: las perpetuaciones de tierras baldías en Madrid*. Madrid: Conserjería de Agricultura y Cooperación de la Comunidad de Madrid.

Amalric, Jean-Pierre. 1994. "Les migrations françaises en Espagne à l'époque moderne (XVIe–XVIIIe siècles)," pp. 413–30 in vol. I of *Les migrations internes et à moyenne distance en Europe, 1500–1900* (Papers of I Conferencia Europea de la Comisión Internacional de Demografía Histórica, Santiago de Compostela, 22–25 September 1993), ed. by Antonio Eiras Roel and Ofelia Rey Castelao. Santiago de Compostela: Xunta de Galicia, Consellería de Educación e Ordenación Universitaria.

Amelang, James. 1993. "Society and Culture in Early Modern Spain," *Journal of Modern History*, 65: 357–74.

Anes, Gonzalo and Angel García Sanz (eds.). 1994. *Mesta, trashumancia y vida pastoril*. Valladolid: Sociedad V Centenario del Tratado de Tordesillas.

Aranguren, José Luis L. 1966. *Moral y sociedad: introducción a la moral social española del siglo XIX*, 2nd edn. Madrid: Editorial Cuadernos Para el Diálogo.

Arco y Garay, Ricardo del. 1941. *La sociedad española en las obras de Lope de Vega*. Madrid: Real Academia Española.

1952. "La ínfima levadura social en las obras de Cervantes," pp. 209–90 in *Estudios de historia social de España*, vol. II, ed. by Carmelo Viñas y Mey. Madrid: Consejo Superior de Investigaciones Científicas.

Asenjo González, María. 1986. *Segovia. La ciudad y su Tierra a fines del Medievo*. Segovia: Diputación Provincial [?].

Atienza Hernández, Ignacio. 1994. "'Refeudalisation' in Castile during the Seventeenth Century: A Cliché?" pp. 249–76 in *The Castilian Crisis of the Seventeenth Century: New Perspectives on the Economic and Social History of Seventeenth-Century Spain*, ed. by I.A.A. Thompson and Bartolomé Yun Casalilla. Cambridge: Cambridge University Press.

Bailey, Thomas A. 1968. "The Mythmakers of American History," *Journal of American History*, 40: 5–21.

Behar, Ruth. 1986. *Santa María del Monte: The Presence of the Past in a Spanish Village*. Princeton: Princeton University Press.

Behar, Ruth and David Frye. 1988. "Property, Progeny, and Emotion: Family History in a Leonese Village," *Journal of Family History*, 13: 13–32.

Belfanti, Marco Carlo; and Marzio A. Romani. 1994. "Sur la route: les migrations montagnardes vers la Plaine du Pô (XVIIe–XVIIe siècles)," pp. 609–15 in vol. I of *Les migrations internes et à moyenne distance en Europe, 1500–1900* (Papers of I Conferencia Europea de la Comisión Internacional de Demografía Histórica, Santiago de Compostela, 22–25 September 1993), ed. by Antonio Eiras Roel and Ofelia Rey Castelao. Santiago de Compostela: Xunta de Galicia, Consellería de Educación e Ordenación Universitaria.

Bennassar, Bartolomé. 1967. *Valladolid au siècle d'or: une ville de Castille et sa campagne au XVIe siècle*. Paris: Mouton.

1969. *Recherches sur les grandes épidemies dans le nord de l'Espagne à la fin du XVIe siècle*. Paris: SEVPEN.

1979. *The Spanish Character: Attitudes and Mentalities from the Sixteenth to the Nineteenth Century*, trans. Benjamin Keen. Berkeley: University of California Press.

Bennassar, Bartolomé and Lucile Bennassar. 1989. *Los cristianos de Alá: la fascinante aventura de los renegados*, trans. José Luis Gil Aristu. Madrid: Editorial Nerea.

Bennett, Judith M. 1987. *Women in the Medieval English Countryside: Gender and Household in Brigstock before the Plague*. Oxford: Oxford University Press.

Berkner, Lutz K. 1972. "The Stem Family and the Development Cycle of the Peasant Household: An Eighteenth-Century Austrian Example," *American Historical Review*, 77: 398–418.

Birriel Salcedo, Margarita María. 1989. *La Tierra de Almuñécar en tiempo de Felipe II: expulsión de moriscos y repoblación*. Granada: University of Granada.

Blázquez, Antonio. 1905. *La Mancha en tiempo de Cervantes: conferencia leída el día 3 de mayo de 1905 en la velada que la Real Sociedad Geográfica dedicó a conmemorar la publicación del Quijote de la Mancha*. Madrid: Imprenta de Artillería.

Blum, Jerome. 1971. "The European Village as Community: Origins and Functions," *Agricultural History*, 45: 157–78.

1982. "The Village and the Family," pp. 9–24 in *Our Forgotten Past: Seven Centuries of Life on the Land*, ed. by Jerome Blum. London: Thames and Hudson.

Borrero Fernández, Mercedes. 1983. *El mundo rural sevillano en el siglo XV: Aljarafe y Ribera*. Seville: Diputación Provincial.

Bosque Maurel, Joaquín. 1971. *Granada, la tierra y sus hombres*. Granada: Organización Sindical, Consejo Económico Sindical Provincial.

1973. "Latifundio y minifundio en Andalucía oriental," *Estudios geográficos*, 34: 487–95.

Bouchard, Gérard. 1972. *Le village immobile: Sennely-en-Sologne au XVIIIe siècle*. Paris: Plon.

Bourin, Monique and Robert Durand. 1984. *Vivre au village au moyen âge: les solidarités paysannes du 11e au 13e siècles*. Paris: Messidor, Temps Actuels.

Brandes, Stanley H. 1975. *Migration, Kinship, and Community: Tradition and Transition in a Spanish Village*. New York: Academic Press.

Braudel, Fernand. 1975. *The Mediterranean and the Mediterranean World in the Age of Philip II*, 2 vols., trans. Siân Reynolds. New York: Harper and Row.

1981. *The Structures of Everyday Life*: vol. I of *Civilization and Capitalism, Fifteenth–Eighteenth Century*, trans. and rev. by Siân Reynolds. New York: Harper and Row.

1982. *The Wheels of Commerce*: vol. II of *Civilization and Capitalism, Fifteenth–Eighteenth Century*, trans. Siân Reynolds. New York: Harper and Row.

Bravo Lozano, Jesús. 1993. *Montes para Madrid: el abastecimiento de carbón vegetal a la villa y corte entre los siglos XVII y XVIII*. Madrid: Caja de Madrid.

Brenner, Robert. 1985a. "Agrarian Class Structure and Economic Development in Pre-Industrial Europe," pp. 10–63 in *The Brenner Debate: Agrarian Class Structure and Economic Development in Pre-Industrial Europe*, ed. by T.H. Aston and C.H.E. Philpin. Cambridge: Cambridge University Press.

1985b. "The Agrarian Roots of European Capitalism," pp. 213–328 in *The Brenner Debate: Agrarian Class Structure and Economic Development in Pre-Industrial Europe*, ed. by T.H. Aston and C.H.E. Philpin. Cambridge: Cambridge University Press.

Brettell, Caroline B. 1986. *Men Who Migrate, Women Who Wait: Population and History in a Portuguese Parish*. Princeton: Princeton University Press.

Brumont, Francis. 1984. *Campo y campesinos de Castilla la Vieja en tiempos de Felipe II*, trans. Juan Manuel Figueroa Pérez. Madrid: Siglo Veintiuno.

1985. "La Rioja en el siglo XVI," *Segundo coloquio sobre historia de La Rioja*, II, pp. 11–69. Logroño: Colegio Universitario de La Rioja.

1988. "Le pain et la peste: épidémie et subsistances en Vielle-Castille à la fin du XVIe siècle," *Annales de démographie historique*, pp. 207–20.

1992. "Economía, actividades industriales y artesanales, agricultura y ganadería," pp. 95–145 in *Historia de Burgos*, vol. III, no. 2. Burgos: Caja de Ahorros Municipal.

1993a. "Société rurale et production agricole (XVIe–XVIIe s.)," pp. 357–71 in *Señorío y feudalismo en la Península Ibérica, SS. XII–XIX*. Zaragoza: Institución "Fernando el Católico".

1993b. *Paysans de Vieille-Castille aux XVIe et XVIIe siècles*. Madrid: Casa de Velázquez.

Burkholder, Suzanne Hiles. 1990. "From Wool to Wine: Demographic and Economic Change in the Sierra de Gredos, 1750–1887." Unpublished Ph.D. dissertation, University of California, San Diego.

Cabo Alonso, Angel. 1955. "La Armuña y su evolución económica," *Estudios geográficos*, 16: 73–136, 367–427.

Calvo, José. 1989. *Así vivían en el Siglo de Oro*. Madrid: Anaya.

Carasa Soto, Pedro. 1988a. *Crisis del Antiguo Régimen y acción social en Castilla*. Valladolid: Junta de Castilla y León.

1988b. "Cambios en la tipología del pauperismo en la crisis del Antiguo Régimen," *Investigaciones históricas*, 7: 133–50.

1994. "Las clases populares urbanas y el mundo de la pobreza en Castilla," paper presented at (and published in proceedings of) Congreso Internacional de Historia: El Tratado de Tordesillas y su Época.

Cardaillac, Louis. 1977. *Morisques et chrétiens: un affrontement polémique (1492–1640)*. Paris: Klincksieck.

1983. "Vision simplificatrice des groupes marginaux par le groupe dominant dans l'Espagne des XVIe et XVIIe siècles," pp. 11–22 in *Les problèmes de l'exclusion en Espagne (XVIe–XVIIe siècles). Idéologie et discours. Colloque International (Sorbonne, 13, 14 et 15 mai 1982)*, ed. by Augustin Redondo. Paris: Publications de la Sorbonne.

Carlé, María del Carmen. 1988. *La sociedad hispano medieval. Grupos periféricos: las mujeres y los pobres*. Buenos Aires: Editorial Gedisa.

Caro Baroja, Julio. 1957. "El sociocentrismo de los pueblos españoles," pp. 263–92 in *Razas, pueblos, linajes*. Madrid: Revista de Occidente.

1963. "The City and the Country: Reflexions on Some Ancient Commonplaces," pp. 27–40 in *Mediterranean Countrymen: Essays in the Social Anthropology of the Mediterranean*, ed. by Julian Pitt-Rivers. Paris: Mouton.

Casado Alonso, Hilario. 1987. *Señores, mercaderes y campesinos: la comarca de Burgos a fines de la Edad Media*. Valladolid: Junta de Castilla y León.

1990. "Solidaridades campesinas en Burgos a fines de la Edad Media," pp. 279–304 in *Relaciones de poder, de la producción y parentesco en la Edad Media y Moderna. Aproximación a su estudio*, ed. by Reyna Pastor. Madrid: Consejo Superior de Investigaciones Científicas.

1992. "Le banquet de l'assemblée communale rurale en Vieille Castille," pp. 201–8 in *La sociabilité à table: commensalité et convivialité à travers les ages. Actes du Colloque de Rouen, 14–17 novembre 1990*. Rouen: Publications de l'Université de Rouen.

Casey, James. 1989. *The History of the Family*. Oxford: Basil Blackwell.

Castellote, Eulalia. 1979–80. "Carbón y carboneros en la provincia de Guadalajara," *Revista de dialectología y tradiciones populares*, 35: 187–208.

Chacón Jiménez, Francisco. 1986. *Los murcianos del siglo XVII: evolución, familia y trabajo: demografía y estructura socio-profesional en la ciudad y huerta de Murcia durante el siglo XVII*. Murcia: Biblioteca Básica.

Chaunu, Pierre. 1966. "La société espagnole au 17e siècle: sur un refus collectif de mobilité," *Bulletin hispanique*, 68: 104–15.

Chevalier, Maxime. 1982. *Tipos cómicos y folklore (siglos XVI–XVII)*. Madrid: EDI-6, S.A.

(ed.). 1983. (*See* list of published contemporary sources).

Christian, William A., Jr. 1981. *Local Religion in Sixteenth-Century Spain*. Princeton: Princeton University Press.

1989 [1972]. *Person and God in a Spanish Valley*, revised edn. Princeton: Princeton University Press.

Colás Latorre, Gregorio. 1993. "La historiografía sobre el señorío tardofeudal," pp. 51–105 in *Señorío y feudalismo en la Península Ibérica, SS XII–XIX*. Zaragoza: Institución "Fernando el Católico" de la Diputación de Zaragoza.

Coleman, David and John Salt. 1992. *The British Population: Patterns, Trends, and Processes*. Oxford: Oxford University Press.

Commager, Henry Steele. 1967. *The Search for a Usable Past and Other Essays in Historiography*. New York: Alfred A. Knopf.

Contreras Jiménez, María Eugenia. 1988. "La mujer trabajadora en los fueros castellano-leoneses," pp. 99–112 in *El trabajo de las mujeres en la Edad Media hispana*, ed. by Angela Muñoz Fernández and Cristina Segura Graíño. Madrid: Asociación Cultural Al-Mudayna.

Corchón García, Justo. 1963. *El Campo de Arañuelo (estudio geográfico de una comarca extremeña)*. Madrid: Dirección General de Enseñanza Media.

Coronas Vida, Luis Javier. 1994. *La economía agraria de las tierras de Jaén (1500–1650)*. Granada: Universidad de Granada.

Corral García, Esteban. 1978. *Las comunidades castellanas y la villa y tierra antigua de Cuéllar (S. XIII–XVI)*. Salamanca: Diputación de Segovia (sic).

1987. *El escribano de concejo en la Corona de Castilla (siglos XI al XVII)*. Burgos: Ayuntamiento de Burgos.

Criado de Val, Manuel. 1993. "Los caminos de Madrid en la Cosmografía de Hernando Colón," pp. 335–46 in *Caminos y caminantes por las tierras del Madrid medieval*, ed. by Cristina Segura Graíño. Madrid: Asociación Al-Mudayna.

Critchfield, Richard. 1981. *Villages*. Garden City, N.Y.: Anchor Press-Doubleday.

Croot, Patricia and David Parker. 1985. "Agrarian Class Structure and the Development of Capitalism: France and England Compared," pp. 79–90 in *The Brenner Debate: Agrarian Class Structure and Economic Development in Pre-Industrial Europe*, ed. by T.H. Aston and C.H.E. Philpin. Cambridge: Cambridge University Press.

Cruz, Anne J. 1989. "Sexual Enclosure, Textual Escape: The *Pícara* as Prostitute in the Spanish Female Picaresque Novel," pp. 135–59 in *Seeking the Woman in Late Medieval and Renaissance Writings: Essays in Feminist Contextual Criticism*, ed. by Sheila Fisher and Janet E. Halley. Knoxville: University of Tennessee Press.

Cuadra García, Cristina. 1993. "Los mensajeros de la Villa a fines de la Edad Media," pp. 205–15 in *Caminos y caminantes por las tierras del Madrid medieval*, ed. by Cristina Segura Graíño. Madrid: Asociación Al-Mudayna.

Cuartos Rivero, Margarita. 1982. "La venta de oficios públicos en el siglo XVI," pp. 225–60 in *Actas del IV Symposium de Historia de la Administración (Alcalá de Henares, diciembre de 1982)*. Madrid: Colección Estudios de Historia de la Administración.

1984. "La venta de oficios públicos en Castilla-León en el siglo XVI," *Hispania. Revista española de historia*, 44: 495–516.

Davis, Natalie Zemon. 1975. *Society and Culture in Early Modern France*. Stanford: Stanford University Press.

1983. *The Return of Martin Guerre*. Cambridge, Mass.: Harvard University Press.

Defourneaux, Marcelin. 1970. *Daily Life in Spain in the Golden Age*, trans. Newton Branch. London: George Allen and Unwin.

Delano-Smith, Catherine. 1979. *Western Mediterranean Europe: A Historical Geography of Italy, Spain and Southern France since the Neolithic*. New York: Academic Press.

Delille, Gérard. 1994. "Migrations internes et mobilité sociale dans le royaume de Naples (XVe–XIXe siècles)," pp. 343–56 in vol. I of *Les migrations internes et à moyenne distance en Europe, 1500–1900* (Papers of I Conferencia Europea de la Comisión Internacional de Demografía Histórica, Santiago de Compostela, 22–25 September 1993), ed. by Antonio Eiras Roel and Ofelia Rey Castelao. Santiago de Compostela: Xunta de Galicia, Consellería de Educación e Ordenación Universitaria.

Diago Hernando, Máximo. 1991. "Los términos despoblados en las comunidades de villa y tierra del sistema ibérico castellano a finales de la Edad Media," *Hispania. Revista española de historia*, 51: 467–515.

1993. *Soria en la Baja Edad Media: espacio rural y economía agraria*. Madrid: Editorial Complutense.

Diaz, May N. 1967. "Introduction: Economic Relations in Peasant Society," pp. 50–6 in *Peasant Society: A Reader*, ed. by Jack M. Potter, May N. Diaz, and George M. Foster. Boston: Little, Brown, and Company.

Díaz Viana, Luis. 1984. *Rito y tradición oral en Castilla y León*. Valladolid: Ambito.

Diccionario de historia de España. 1968–9. 2nd edn, rev. and enl. in 3 vols. ed. by Germán Bleiberg. Madrid: Revista de Occidente.

Dillard, Heath. 1984. *Daughters of the Reconquest: Women in Castilian Town Society, 1100–1300*. Cambridge: Cambridge University Press.

Dobrowolski, Kazimierz. 1987. "Peasant Traditional Culture," pp. 261–77 in

Peasants and Peasant Societies, ed. by Teodor Shanin, 2nd edn. Oxford: Basil Blackwell.

Domínguez Ortiz, Antonio. 1952. "La esclavitud en Castilla durante la Edad Moderna," pp. 367–428 in *Estudios de historia social de España*, II (1952), ed. by Carmelo Viñas y Mey. Madrid: Consejo Superior de Investigaciones Científicas.

——— 1960. "Los extranjeros en la vida española durante el siglo XVII," pp. 291–426 in *Estudios de historia social de España*, IV (1960), vol. II, ed. by Carmelo Viñas y Mey. Madrid: Consejo Superior de Investigaciones Científicas.

——— 1963. "Los moriscos granadinos antes de su definitiva expulsión," *Miscelanea de estudios árabes y hebráicos*, 12–13: 113–28.

——— 1971. *The Golden Age of Spain*, trans. James Casey. New York: Basic Books.

——— 1974. *El Antiguo Régimen: los Reyes Católicos y los Austrias*, 2nd edn. Madrid: Alianza Editorial.

——— 1994. "La inmigración de corto y medio radio en la Andalucía moderna: modalidades y comportamientos," pp. 357–79 in vol. II of *Migraciones internas y medium-distance en la Península Ibérica, 1500–1900* (Papers of I Conferencia Europea de la Comisión Internacional de Demografía Histórica, Santiago de Compostela, 22–25 September 1993), ed. by Antonio Eiras Roel and Ofelia Rey Castelao. Santiago de Compostela: Xunta de Galicia, Consellería de Educación e Ordenación Universitaria.

Domínguez Ortiz, Antonio and Bernard Vincent. 1978. *Historia de los moriscos: vida y tragedia de una minoría*. Madrid: Revista de Occidente.

Douglass, William A. 1975. *Echalar and Murelaga: Opportunity and Rural Exodus in Two Spanish Basque Villages*. London: C. Hurst and Co.

——— 1976. "Serving Girls and Sheepherders: Emigration and Continuity in a Spanish Basque Village," pp. 45–61 in *The Changing Faces of Rural Spain*, ed. by Joseph B. Aceves and William A. Douglass. Cambridge, Mass.: Schenkman.

Doyle, William. 1978. *The Old European Order, 1600–1800*. Oxford: Oxford University Press.

Dubert, Isidro. 1992. *Historia de la familia en Galicia durante la época moderna, 1550–1830 (estructura, modelos hereditarios y conflictividad)*. La Coruña: Ediciós do Castro.

Duiker, William J. and Jackson J. Spielvogel. 1994. *World History*. St. Paul, Minn.: West Publishing Company.

Dupâquier, Jacques. 1994. "Mobilité géographique et mobilité sociale," pp. 3–25 in vol. I of *Les migrations internes et à moyenne distance en Europe, 1500–1900* (Papers of I Conferencia Europea de la Comisión Internacional de Demografía Histórica, Santiago de Compostela, 22–25 September 1993), ed. by Antonio Eiras Roel and Ofelia Rey Castelao. Santiago de Compostela: Xunta de Galicia, Consellería de Educación e Ordenación Universitaria.

Durrenberger, E. Paul. 1984. "Introduction," pp. 1–25 in *Chayanov, Peasants, and Economic Anthropology*, ed. by E. Paul Durrenberger. New York: Academic Press.

Eiras Roel, Antonio. 1994. "Migraciones internas y medium-distance en España en la Edad Moderna," pp. 37–83 in vol. II of *Migraciones internas y medium-distance en la Península Ibérica, 1500–1900* (Papers of I Conferencia Europea de la Comisión Internacional de Demografía Histórica, Santiago de

Compostela, 22–25 September 1993), ed. by Antonio Eiras Roel and Ofelia Rey Castelao. Santiago de Compostela: Xunta de Galicia, Consellería de Educación e Ordenación Universitaria.

Elliott, John H. 1963. *Imperial Spain, 1469–1716*. New York: New American Library.

Eltis, David. 1993. "Europeans and the Rise and Fall of African Slavery in the Americas: An Interpretation," *American Historical Review*, 98: 1399–1423.

Esler, Anthony. 1992. *The Human Venture: A World History from Prehistory to the Present*, 2nd edn. Englewood Cliffs, N.J.: Prentice Hall.

Espejo Lara, Juan Luis. 1985. *Una comunidad agraria en el siglo XVI: Mijas*. Málaga: Diputación Provincial.

Estella, Margarita. 1989. "El comercio de la madera en Madrid (primera mitad del siglo XVI)," *Revista de dialectología y tradiciones populares*, 44: 295–306.

Fallers, L.A. 1967. "Are African Cultivators to be Called 'Peasants'?" pp. 35–41 in *Peasant Society: A Reader*, ed. by Jack M. Potter, May N. Diaz, and George M. Foster. Boston: Little, Brown, and Company.

Fauve-Chamoux, Antoinette. 1994. "Female Mobility and Urban Population in Preindustrial France (1500–1900)," pp. 47–71 in vol. I of *Les migrations internes et à moyenne distance en Europe, 1500–1900* (Papers of I Conferencia Europea de la Comisión Internacional de Demografía Histórica, Santiago de Compostela, 22–25 September 1993), ed. by Antonio Eiras Roel and Ofelia Rey Castelao. Santiago de Compostela: Xunta de Galicia, Consellería de Educación e Ordenación Universitaria.

Fei Hsiao Tung. 1987. "Peasantry as a Way of Living," pp. 57–9 in *Peasants and Peasant Societies*, ed. by Teodor Shanin, 2nd edn. Oxford: Basil Blackwell.

Fernández Alvarez, Manuel. 1989. *La sociedad española en el Siglo de Oro*, 2 vols., 2nd rev. edn. Madrid: Editorial Gredos.

Fernández Duro, Cesáreo. 1882–3. *Memorias históricas de la Ciudad de Zamora*, 4 vols. Madrid: Sucesores de Rivadeneyra.

Flandrin, Jean-Louis. 1979. *Families in Former Times: Kinship, Household, and Sexuality*. trans. Richard Southern. Cambridge: Cambridge University Press.

Flinn, Michael W. 1981. *The European Demographic System, 1500–1820*. Baltimore: Johns Hopkins University Press.

Floristán Imízcoz, Alfredo. 1982. *La Merindad de Estella en la Edad Moderna: los hombres y la tierra*. Pamplona: Diputación Foral de Navarra.

Floristán Imízcoz, Alfredo and José María Imízcoz Beunza. 1993. "La sociedad navarra en la Edad Moderna. Nuevos análisis. Nuevas perspectivas," *Príncipe de Viana*, 54, no. 15: 11–48.

Flynn, Maureen M. 1985. "Charitable Ritual in Late Medieval and Early Modern Spain," *Sixteenth Century Journal*, 16: 335–48.

——— 1989. *Sacred Charity: Confraternities and Social Welfare in Spain, 1400–1700*. Ithaca, N.Y.: Cornell University Press.

Fortea Pérez, José Ignacio. 1994. "The Textile Industry in the Economy of Cordoba at the End of the Seventeenth and the Start of the Eighteenth Centuries: A Frustrated Recovery," pp. 136–68 in *The Castilian Crisis of the Seventeenth Century: New Perspectives on the Economic and Social History of Seventeenth-Century Spain*, ed. by I.A.A. Thompson and Bartolomé Yun Casalilla. Cambridge: Cambridge University Press.

Fossier, Robert. 1988. *Peasant Life in the Medieval West*, trans. Juliet Vale. Oxford: Basil Blackwell.

Foster, George M. 1967. "Introduction: What Is a Peasant?" pp. 2–14 in *Peasant Society: A Reader*, ed. by Jack M. Potter, May N. Diaz, and George M. Foster. Boston: Little, Brown, and Company.

Franco Silva, Alfonso. 1974. *El concejo de Alcalá de Guadaira a finales de la Edad Media (1426–1533)*. Seville: Diputación Provincial.

Freeman, Susan Tax. 1968a. "Corporate Village Organisation in the Sierra Ministra: An Iberian Structural Type," *Man*, 3: 477–84.

1968b. "Religious Aspects of the Social Organization of a Castilian Village," *American Anthropologist*, 70: 34–49.

1970. *Neighbors: The Social Contract in a Castilian Hamlet*. Chicago: University of Chicago Press.

1976. "Dos caminos a Madrid: españoles dentro y fuera de dos ámbitos rurales," pp. 63–86 in *Anales de moral social y económica: expresiones actuales de la cultura del pueblo*. Madrid: Centro de Estudios Sociales del Valle de los Caídos.

1979a. "The 'Municipios' of Northern Spain: A View from the Fountain," pp. 161–93 in *Currents in Anthropology: Essays in Honor of Sol Tax*, ed. by Robert Hinshaw. Paris: Mouton.

1979b. *The Pasiegos: Spaniards in No Man's Land*. Chicago: University of Chicago Press.

1987. "Egalitarian Structures in Iberian Social Systems: The Contexts of Turn-Taking in Town and Country," *American Ethnologist*, 14: 470–90.

1989a. "A Cultural Approach to Marginality in Spain," pp. 1–9 in *Marginated Groups in Spanish and Portuguese History. Proceedings of the Seventeenth Annual Meeting of the Society for Spanish and Portuguese Historical Studies, University of Minnesota, Minneapolis, April, 1986*, ed. by Wiliam D. Phillips, Jr. and Carla Rahn Phillips. Minneapolis: Society for Spanish and Portuguese Historical Studies.

1989b. "Identity in Iberia: Some Remarks," pp. 197–204 in *Iberian Identity: Essays on the Nature of Identity in Portugal and Spain*, ed. by Richard Herr and John H.R. Polt. Berkeley: Institute of International Studies, University of California.

Fussell, George Edwin. 1972. *The Classical Tradition in West European Farming*. Newton Abbot: David and Charles.

García de Cortázar, José Angel. 1988. *La sociedad rural en la España medieval*. Madrid: Siglo Veintiuno Editores.

G[arcía] de Valdeavellano, Luis. 1968. *Curso de historia de las instituciones españolas, de los orígenes al final de la Edad Media*. Madrid: Revista de Occidente.

García Herrero, María del Carmen. 1988. "Mozas sirvientas en Zaragoza durante el siglo XV," pp. 275–85 in *El trabajo de las mujeres en la Edad Media hispana*, ed. by Angela Muñoz Fernández and Cristina Segura Graíño. Madrid: Asociación Cultural Al-Mudayna.

García Jiménez, Bartolomé. 1987. *Demografía rural andaluza: Rute en el Antiguo Régimen*. Córdoba: Diputación Provincial.

García Sanz, Angel. 1977. *Desarrollo y crisis del Antiguo Régimen en Castilla la Vieja: economía y sociedad en tierras de Segovia de 1500 a 1814*. Madrid: Akal.

1980. "Bienes y derechos comunales y el proceso de su privatización en Castilla durante los siglos XVI y XVII: el caso de Tierras de Segovia," *Hispania. Revista española de historia*, 40: 95–127.

1988. "Agricultura y Ganadería," *Enciclopedia de historia de España*, 1: *Economía. Sociedad*, ed. by Miguel Artola. Madrid: Alianza.

1989. "El sector agrario durante el siglo XVII: depresión y reajustes," pp. 161–235 in *Historia de España Menéndez Pidal*, ed. by José María Jover Zamora, vol. XXIII: *La crisis del siglo XVII: La población. La economía. La sociedad*. Madrid: Espasa-Calpe.

1991. "Estudio preliminar," pp. ix–xliv of Lope de Deza's *Gobierno político de agricultura (1618)*, ed. by Angel García Sanz. Madrid: Instituto de Estudios Fiscales.

1994a. "Competitivos en lanas, pero no en paños: lana para la exportación y lana para los telares nacionales en la España del Antiguo Régimen," *Revista de historia económica*, 12: 397–434.

1994b. "Los privilegios de la Mesta: contexto histórico y económico de su concesión y de su abolición, 1273–1836 (una necesaria revisión de la obra de Julius Klein)," pp. 17–31 in the facsimile edition *Quaderno de leyes y privilegios del honrado concejo de la mesta*. Valladolid: Lex Nova.

García Sanz, Angel and Gonzalo Anes. (eds.) 1994. *Mesta, trashumancia y vida pastoril*. Valladolid: Sociedad V Centenario del Tratado de Tordesillas.

García Sanz, Benjamín. 1989. *Los campesinos en la sociedad rural tradicional: marco institucional, producción, presión fiscal y población (Tierra de Curiel y Tierra de Peñafiel, siglos XVI–XVIII)*. Valladolid: Diputación Provincial.

García Tapia, Nicolás. 1989. *Técnica y poder en Castilla durante los siglos XVI y XVII*. Valladolid: Junta de Castilla y León.

Garrad, K. 1956. "La industria sedera granadina en el siglo XVI y su conexión con el levantamiento de las Alpujarras (1568–1571)," *Miscelánea de estudios árabes y hebraicos*, 5: 73–104.

Garzón Pareja, Manuel. 1972. *La industria sedera en España; el arte de la seda de Granada*. Granada: Gráficas del Sur.

Gelabert, Juan E. 1994. "Urbanisation and Deurbanisation in Castile, 1500–1800," pp. 182–205 in *The Castilian Crisis of the Seventeenth Century: New Perspectives on the Economic and Social History of Seventeenth-Century Spain*, ed. by I.A.A. Thompson and Bartolomé Yun Casalilla. Cambridge: Cambridge University Press.

Genicot, Léopold. 1990. *Rural Communities in the Medieval West*. Baltimore: Johns Hopkins University Press.

Gerbet, Marie Claude. 1989. *La nobleza en la Corona de Castilla: sus estructuras sociales en Extremadura (1454–1516)*, trans. María Concepción Quintanilla Raso. Cáceres: Institución Cultural "El Brocense" (Diputación Provincial).

Gies, Frances and Joseph Gies. 1987. *Marriage and the Family in the Middle Ages*. New York: Harper and Row.

1990. *Life in a Medieval Village*. New York: Harper and Row.

Gil Abad, Pedro. 1983. *Junta y Hermandad de la Cabaña Real de Carreteros, Burgos-Soria*. Burgos: Diputación Provincial.

Gilmore, David D. 1980. *The People of the Plain: Class and Community in Lower Andalusia*. New York: Columbia University Press.

Gómez-Centurión Jiménez, Carlos. 1989a. "La iglesia y la religiosidad," pp. 255–78 in *La vida cotidiana en la España de Velázquez*, ed. by José N. Alcalá-Zamora. Madrid: Ediciones Temas de Hoy.

1989b. "Los horizontes geográficos de los españoles," pp. 29–41 in *La vida cotidiana en la España de Velázquez*, ed. by José N. Alcalá-Zamora. Madrid: Ediciones Temas de Hoy.

Gómez Mendoza, Josefina. 1967. "Las ventas de baldíos y comunales en el siglo XVI: estudio de su proceso en Guadajajara," *Estudios geográficos*, 28: 499–559.

González, Nazario. 1958. *Burgos, la ciudad marginal de Castilla: estudio de geografía urbana*. Burgos: Imprenta de Aldecoa.

González Castaño, Juan. 1992. *Una villa del Reino de Murcia en la Edad Moderna (Mula, 1500–1648)*. Murcia: Real Academia Alfonso X El Sabio.

González Díez, Emiliano. 1993. *De feria en feria por Castilla y León*. Valladolid: Junta de Castilla y León, Conserjería de Agricultura y Ganadería.

Gordon, Michael D. 1982. "Royal Power and Fundamental Law in Western Europe, 1350–1650: The Crown Lands," pp. 255–70 in *Diritto e potere nella storia europea. Atti del quarto Congresso internazionale della Società Italiana di Storia del Diritto, in onore di Bruno Paradisi*. Florence: Leo S. Olschki Editore.

Gottlieb, Beatrice. 1993. *The Family in the Western World from the Black Death to the Industrial Age*. Oxford: Oxford University Press.

Goubert, Pierre. 1986. *The French Peasantry in the Seventeenth Century*, trans. Ian Patterson. Cambridge: Cambridge University Press (original French version published 1982).

Graña Cid, María del Mar. 1993. "Frailes, predicación y caminos en Madrid. Un modelo para estudiar la itinerancia mendicante en la Edad Media," pp. 281–321 in *Caminos y caminantes por las tierras del Madrid medieval*, ed. by Cristina Segura Graíño. Madrid: Asociación Al-Mudayna.

Guerra 1952. (*See* list of published contemporary sources).

Guilarte, Alfonso María. 1987. *El régimen señorial en el siglo XVI*, 2nd edn. Valladolid: University of Valladolid.

Gutiérrez Nieto, Juan Ignacio. 1989. "El campesinado," pp. 43–70 in *La vida cotidiana en la España de Velázquez*, ed. by José N. Alcalá-Zamora. Madrid: Ediciones Temas de Hoy.

Haliczer, Stephen. 1989. "The Outsiders: Spanish History as a History of Missed Opportunities," pp. 53–60 in *Marginated Groups in Spanish and Portuguese History. Proceedings of the Seventeenth Annual Meeting of the Society for Spanish and Portuguese Historical Studies, University of Minnesota, Minneapolis, April, 1986*, ed. by William D. Phillips, Jr. and Carla Rahn Phillips. Minneapolis: Society for Spanish and Portuguese Historical Studies.

Hanawalt, Barbara A. 1986. *The Ties that Bound: Peasant Families in Medieval England*. Oxford: Oxford University Press.

Herlihy, David. 1985. *Medieval Households*. Cambridge, Mass.: Harvard University Press.

Herrera Puga, Pedro. 1971. *Sociedad y delincuencia en el Siglo de Oro: aspectos de la vida sevillana en los siglos XVI y XVII*. Granada: University of Granada.

Herrero, Miguel. 1977. *Oficios populares en la sociedad de Lope de Vega*. Madrid: Editorial Castalia.

Higueras Arnal, Antonio. 1961. *El Alto Guadalquivir: estudio geográfico*. Zaragoza:

Departamento de Geografía Aplicada del Instituto Juan Sebastián Elcano.

Hilton, R.H. 1975. *The English Peasantry in the Later Middle Ages.* Oxford: Clarendon Press.

Hiltpold, Paul. 1989. "The Price, Production, and Transportation of Grain in Early Modern Castile," *Agricultural History,* 63: 73–91.

Horn, Pamela. 1980. *The Rural World, 1780–1850: Social Change in the English Countryside.* London: Hutchinson.

1987. *Life and Labour in Rural England, 1760–1850.* Basingstoke: Macmillan Education.

Howkins, Alun. 1992. "The English Farm Labourer in the Nineteenth Century: Farm, Family and Community," pp. 85–104 in *The English Rural Community: Image and Analysis,* ed. by Brian Short. Cambridge: Cambridge University Press.

Huetz de Lemps, Alain. 1959. "El viñedo de la 'Tierra de Medina' en los siglos XVII y XVIII," trans. Jesús García Fernández. *Estudios geográficos,* 20: 111–25 [First published as "Le vignoble de la 'Tierra de Medina' aux XVIIᵉ et XVIIIᵉ siècles," *Annales, Economies, Sociétés, Civilisations,* 3: 403–17].

1967. *Vignobles et vins du Nord-Ouest de l'Espagne,* 2 vols. Bordeaux: University of Bordeaux Press.

Huppert, George. 1986. *After the Black Death: A Social History of Early Modern Europe.* Bloomington: Indiana University Press.

Hutchinson, Steven. 1992. *Cervantine Journeys.* Madison: University of Wisconsin Press.

Jacobs, Auke Pieter. 1991. "Legal and Illegal Emigration from Seville, 1550–1650," pp. 59–84 in *"To Make America": European Emigration in the Early Modern Period,* ed. by Ida Altman and James Horn. Berkeley: University of California Press.

Jacobsen, Grethe. 1988. "Female Migration and the Late Medieval Town," pp. 43–55 in *Migration in der Feudalgesellschaft,* ed. by Gerhard Jaritz and Albert Müller. Frankfurt: Campus Verlag.

Jiménez de Gregorio, Fernando. 1971. "La población en el Señorío de Valdepusa (Toledo)," *Estudios geográficos,* 32: 75–112.

Kagan, Richard L. 1974. *Students and Society in Early Modern Spain.* Baltimore: Johns Hopkins University Press.

1981. *Lawsuits and Litigants in Castile, 1500–1700.* Chapel Hill: University of North Carolina Press.

(ed.) 1989. *Spanish Cities of the Golden Age: The Views of Anton van den Wyngaerde.* Berkeley: University of California Press.

Kamen, Henry. 1980. *Spain in the Later Seventeenth Century, 1665–1700.* London: Longman.

1983. *Spain 1469–1714: A Society of Conflict.* London: Longman.

1984. *European Society, 1500–1700.* London: Hutchinson.

1993. *The Phoenix and the Flame: Catalonia and the Counter Reformation.* New Haven, Conn.: Yale University Press.

Kenny, Michael and Mary C. Knipmeyer. 1983. "Urban Research in Spain: Retrospect and Prospect," pp. 25–52 in *Urban Life in Mediterranean Europe: An Anthropological Perspective,* ed. by Michael Kenny and David I. Kertzer. Urbana: University of Illinois Press.

Kertzer, David I. 1984. *Family Life in Central Italy, 1880–1910: Sharecropping, Wage Labor, and Coresidence*. New Brunswick: Rutgers University Press.

Kertzer, David I. and Caroline Brettell. 1987. "Advances in Italian and Iberian Family History," *Journal of Family History*, 12: 87–120.

Kitch, Malcolm. 1992. "Population Movement and Migration in Pre-industrial Rural England," pp. 62–84 in *The English Rural Community: Image and Analysis*, ed. by Brian Short. Cambridge: Cambridge University Press.

Klima, Arnost. 1985. "Agrarian Class Structure and Economic Development in Pre-Industrial Bohemia," pp. 192–212 in *The Brenner Debate: Agrarian Class Structure and Economic Development in Pre-Industrial Europe*, ed. by T.H. Aston and C.H.E. Philpin. Cambridge: Cambridge University Press.

Kussmaul, Ann. 1981. *Servants in Husbandry in Early Modern England*. Cambridge: Cambridge University Press.

Ladero Quesada, Miguel-Angel. 1985. "La alimentación en la España medieval. Estado de las investigaciones," *Hispania. Revista española de historia*, 45: 211–19.

Lanza García, Ramón. 1988. *Población y familia campesina en el Antiguo Régimen: Liébana, siglos XVI–XIX*. Santander: Universidad de Cantabria, Ediciones de Librería Estudio.

    1991. *La población y el crecimiento económico de Cantabria en el Antiguo Régimen*. Madrid: Universidad Autónoma.

    1992. *Camargo en el siglo XVIII: la economía rural de Cantabria en el Antiguo Régimen*. Camargo: Asamblea Regional de Cantabria.

Laslett, Peter. 1971. *The World We Have Lost: England Before the Industrial Age*, 2nd edn. New York: Charles Scribner's Sons.

Lázaro Ruíz, Mercedes, Pedro A. Gurria García, and Alonso R. Ortega Berrugete. 1988. "La emigración vasca a La Rioja durante la Edad Moderna: los libros de parroquiamos de la ciudad de Logroño," *Ernaora. Revista de historia de Euskal Herria*, S: 7–50

Leblon, Bernard. 1985. *Les gitans d'Espagne: le prix de la difference*. Paris: Presses Universitaires de France.

Le Flem, Jean-Paul. 1965. "Les Morisques du nord-ouest de l'Espagne en 1594 d'après un recensement de l'Inquisition de Valladolid," *Mélanges de la Casa de Velázquez*, I: 223–43.

    1967. "Cáceres, Plasencia y Trujillo en la segunda mitad del siglo XVI," *Cuadernos de historia de España* (Buenos Aires), 248–99.

    1982. "Los aspectos económicos de la España moderna," pp. 11–133 in *La frustración de un imperio (1476–1714)*, vol. v of *Historia de España*, ed. by Manuel Tuñón de Lara. Barcelona: Labor.

Le Roy Ladurie, Emmanuel. 1987. *The French Peasantry, 1450–1660*, trans. Alan Sheridan. Aldershot, Hants: Scolar Press.

Llopis Agelán, Enrique. 1994. "Castilian Agriculture in the Seventeenth Century: Depression or 'Readjustment and Adaptation'?" pp. 77–100 in *The Castilian Crisis of the Seventeenth Century: New Perspectives on the Economic and Social History of Seventeenth-Century Spain*, ed. by I.A.A. Thompson and Bartolomé Yun Casalilla. Cambridge: Cambridge University Press.

Lobo Cabrera, Manuel. 1990. "La esclavitud en España en la Edad Moderna: su investigación en los últimos cincuenta años," *Hispania. Revista española de historia*, 50: 1091–1104.

López Alonso, Carmen. 1986. *La pobreza en la España medieval: estudio histórico-social*. Madrid: Centro de Publicaciones, Ministerio de Trabajo y Seguridad Social.

López de la Plaza, Gloria. 1993. "De la tierra a la villa. Desplazamientos de corto alcance vinculados a la función administrativa de Madrid: las vecindades," pp. 165–72 in *Caminos y caminantes por las tierras del Madrid medieval*, ed. by Cristina Segura Graíño. Madrid: Asociación Al-Mudayna.

López-Salazar Pérez, Jerónimo. 1986. *Estructuras agrarias y sociedad rural en La Mancha (SS. XVI–XVII)*. Ciudad Real: Instituto de Estudios Manchegos.

1987. *Mesta, pastos y conflictos en el Campo de Calatrava durante el siglo XVI*. Madrid: Consejo Superior de Investigaciones Científicas.

Lovett, A.W. 1986. *Early Habsburg Spain, 1517–1598*. Oxford: Oxford University Press.

Lowry, Shirley Park. 1982. *Familiar Mysteries: The Truth in Myth*. Oxford: Oxford University Press.

Luis López, Carmelo. 1987. *La comunidad de villa y tierra de Piedrahita en el tránsito de la Edad Media a la Moderna*. Avila: Institución "Gran Duque de Alba" (Diputación Provincial).

Lynch, John. 1984. *Empire and Absolutism, 1516–1598*: vol. I of *Spain under the Habsburgs*, 2 vols., 2nd edn. New York: New York University Press.

Macfarlane, Alan. 1984. "The Myth of the Peasantry; Family and Economy in a Northern Parish," pp. 333–49 in *Land, Kinship and Life-cycle*, ed. by Richard M. Smith. Cambridge: Cambridge University Press.

1986. *Marriage and Love in England: Modes of Reproduction, 1300–1840*. Oxford: Basil Blackwell.

McKay, John P., Bennett D. Hill, and John Buckler. 1992. *A History of World Societies*, 3rd edn. Boston: Houghton Mifflin.

MacKay, Ruth. 1994. "Luck of the Draw: Resistance to Conscription during the Reign of Philip IV." Paper presented at the 25th Annual Meeting of the Society for Spanish and Portuguese Historical Studies, Chicago, April 7–10.

McKendrick, Melveena. 1989. *Theatre in Spain, 1490–1700*. Cambridge: Cambridge University Press.

Magagna, Victor V. 1991. *Communities of Grain: Rural Rebellion in Comparative Perspective*. Ithaca: Cornell University Press.

Manning, Roger B. 1986. "Rural Societies in Early Modern Europe," *The Sixteenth Century Journal*, 17: 352–60.

Maravall, José Antonio. 1979. *Poder, honor y élites en el siglo XVII*. Madrid: Siglo Veintiuno.

Marcos Martín, Alberto. 1985. *Economía, sociedad, pobreza en Castilla: Palencia, 1500–1814*, 2 vols. Palencia: Diputación Provincial.

1992. "La esclavitud en la ciudad de La Laguna durante la segunda mitad del siglo XVI a través de los registros parroquiales," pp. 11–42 in *De esclavos a señores: estudios de historia moderna*. Valladolid: University of Valladolid [First published in *Investigaciones históricas*, 2 (1980): 5–35].

1994a. "Movimientos migratorios y tendencias demográficas en Castilla la Vieja y León a lo largo de la época moderna," pp. 209–45 in vol. II of *Migraciones internas y medium-distance en la Península Ibérica, 1500–1900* (Papers of I

Conferencia Europea de la Comisión Internacional de Demografía Histórica, Santiago de Compostela, 22–25 September 1993), ed. by Antonio Eiras Roel and Ofelia Rey Castelao. Santiago de Compostela: Xunta de Galicia, Consellería de Educación e Ordenación Universitaria.

1994b. "Medina del Campo, 1500–1800: An Historical Account of Its Decline," pp. 220–48 in *The Castilian Crisis of the Seventeenth Century: New Perspectives on the Economic and Social History of Seventeenth-Century Spain*, ed. by I.A.A. Thompson and Bartolomé Yun Casalilla. Cambridge: Cambridge University Press.

Marín Barriguete, Fermín. 1994. "Bibliografía general," pp. 241–9 in *Mesta, trashumancia y vida pastoril*, ed. Gonzalo Anes and Angel García Sanz. Valladolid: Sociedad V Centenario del Tratado de Tordesillas.

Martín Cea, Juan Carlos. 1986. *El campesinado castellano de la Cuenca del Duero: aproximaciones a su estudio durante los siglos XIII al XV*. Valladolid: Junta de Castilla y León, Consejería de Educación y Cultura.

1991. *El mundo rural castellano a fines de la Edad Media: el ejemplo de Paredes de Nava en el siglo XV*. Valladolid: Junta de Castilla y León.

Martín Galindo, José Luis. 1961. "Arcaísmo y modernidad en la explotación agraria de Valdeburón (León)," *Estudios geográficos*, 22: 167–222.

Martínez Sopena, Pascual. 1993. "El Camino de Santiago y la articulación del espacio en Tierra de Campos y León," paper presented at (and published in proceedings of) XX Semana de Estudios Medievales (Estella, 1993).

Martz, Linda. 1983. *Poverty and Welfare in Habsburg Spain: The Example of Toledo*. Cambridge: Cambridge University Press.

Mendras, Henri. 1976. *Sociétés paysannes: éléments pour une théorie de la paysannerie*. Paris: Armand Colin.

Merino Alvarez, Abelardo. 1915. *Geografía histórica del territorio de la actual Provincia de Murcia desde la Reconquista por D. Jaime I de Aragón hasta la época presente*. Madrid: Imprenta del Partonato de Huérfanos de Intendencia e Intervención Militares.

Mitterauer, Michael and Reinhard Sieder. 1982. *The European Family: Patriarchy to Partnership from the Middle Ages to the Present*, trans. Karla Oosterveen and Manfred Hörzinger. Chicago: University of Chicago Press.

Moch, Leslie Page 1992. *Moving Europeans: Migration in Western Europe since 1650*. Bloomington: Indiana University Press.

Molénat, Jean-Pierre. 1971. "Chemins et ponts du nord de La Castille au temps des Rois Catholiques," *Mélanges de la Casa de Velázquez*, 7: 115–62.

Molina Molina, Angel-Luis. 1987. *La vida cotidiana en la Murcia bajomedieval*. Murcia: Academia Alfonso X El Sabio [Comunidad Autónoma de la Región de Murcia].

Monturiol González, Angeles. 1993. "Vías de comunicación y hacienda local en Madrid en el último tercio del siglo XV," pp. 141–64 in *Caminos y caminantes por las tierras del Madrid medieval*, ed. by Cristina Segura Graíño. Madrid: Asociación Al-Mudayna.

Muñoz Fernández, Angela. 1993. "Santuarios locales y circulación devocional en la Tierra y Arciprestazgo Madrileños (SS. XV y XVI)," pp. 255–80 in *Caminos y caminantes por las tierras del Madrid medieval*, ed. by Cristina Segura Graíño. Madrid: Asociación Al-Mudayna.

Nadal, Jordi. 1988. "La población española durante los siglos XVI, XVII y XVIII. Un balance a escala regional," pp. 39–54 in *Demografía histórica en España*, ed. by Vicente Pérez Moreda and David-Sven Reher. Madrid: Ediciones El Arquero.

Nadal Oller, Jordi (ed.). 1991. *La evolución demográfica bajo los Austrias*. Alicante: Instituto de Cultura Juan Gil Albert [Diputación de Alicante].

Nader, Helen. 1977. "Noble Income in Sixteenth-Century Castile: The Case of the Marquises of Mondéjar, 1480–1580," *Economic History Review*, 2nd ser., 30: 412–28.

    1979. *The Mendoza Family in the Spanish Renaissance, 1350 to 1550*. New Brunswick, N.J.: Rutgers University Press.

    1990. *Liberty in Absolutist Spain: The Habsburg Sale of Towns, 1516–1700*. Baltimore: Johns Hopkins University Press.

Nalle, Sara T. 1992. *God in La Mancha: Religious Reform and the People of Cuenca, 1500–1650*. Baltimore: Johns Hopkins University Press.

Nieto Soria, José Manuel. 1988. "Aspectos de la vida cotidiana de las pastoras a través de la poesía medieval castellana," pp. 303–19 in *El trabajo de las mujeres en la Edad Media hispana*, ed. by Angela Muñoz Fernández and Cristina Segura Graíño. Madrid: Asociación Cultural Al-Mudayna.

O'Callaghan, Joseph. 1975. *A History of Medieval Spain*. Ithaca: Cornell University Press.

Ojeda Nieto, José. 1989. *Alaejos, un pueblo de Castilla la Vieja en la España del siglo XVI (enmarque espacial y cénit socio-económico de una villa señorial tras los acontecimientos de la Guerra de las Comunidades)*. Valladolid: Diputación Provincial.

Oliveira, António. 1994. "Migrações internas e de média distância em Portugal de 1500 a 1900," pp. 1–36 in vol. II of *Migraciones internas y medium-distance en la Península Ibérica, 1500–1900* (Papers of I Conferencia Europea de la Comisión Internacional de Demografía Histórica, Santiago de Compostela, 22–25 September 1993), ed. by Antonio Eiras Roel and Ofelia Rey Castelao. Santiago de Compostela: Xunta de Galicia, Consellería de Educación e Ordenación Universitaria.

Ortega Valcárcel, José. 1966. *La Bureba; estudio geográfico*. Valladolid: Universidad de Valladolid.

    1969. "La evolución del paisaje agrario del Valle de Mena (Burgos)," *Estudios geográficos*, 30: 107–64.

Ozment, Steven. 1983. *When Fathers Ruled: Family Life in Reformation Europe*. Cambridge, Mass.: Harvard University Press.

Parker, Geoffroy. 1972. *The Army of Flanders and the Spanish Road, 1567–1659; The Logistics of Spanish Victory and Defeat in the Low Countries' Wars*. Cambridge: Cambridge University Press.

Pereiro, Presentación. 1987. *Vida cotidiana y élite local: Málaga a mediados del Siglo de Oro*. Málaga: Diputación Provincial.

Pérez, Joseph. 1983. "A propos de l'exclusion des mendiants: bienfaisance et esprit bourgeois au XVIᵉ siècle," pp. 161–6 in *Les problèmes de l'exclusion en Espagne (XVIᵉ–XVIIᵉ siècles). Idéologie et discours*, ed. by Augustin Redondo. Paris: Publications de la Sorbonne.

Pérez-Bustamante, Rogelio. 1981. "El marco jurídico para la construcción y reparación de caminos. Castilla, siglos XIV y XV," pp. 163–78 in *Les communications dans la Péninsule Ibérique au Moyen-Age (Actes du Colloque de Pau,*

28–29 mars 1980). Paris: Maison des Pays Ibériques, Editions du Centre National de la Recherche Scientifique.

Pérez Cebada, Juan Diego. 1994. "La emigración portuguesa a Jerez (SS. XVI–XVII)," pp. 859–72 in vol. II of *Migraciones internas y medium-distance en la Península Ibérica, 1500–1900* (Papers of I Conferencia Europea de la Comisión Internacional de Demografía Histórica, Santiago de Compostela, 22–25 September 1993), ed. by Antonio Eiras Roel and Ofelia Rey Castelao. Santiago de Compostela: Xunta de Galicia, Consellería de Educación e Ordenación Universitaria.

Pérez-Crespo, María Teresa. 1969. "Vicálvaro: contribución al conocimiento de los contornos de Madrid," *Estudios geográficos,* 30: 455–87.

Pérez-Díaz, Victor. 1967. "Process of Change in Rural Castilian Communities," pp. 123–41 in *The Changing Faces of Rural Spain,* ed. by Joseph B. Aceves and William A. Douglass. Cambridge, Mass.: Schenkman.

Pérez Gallego, Manuel. 1992. *Antequera a fines del siglo XV.* Málaga: Editorial Algazara.

Pérez Moreda, Vicente. 1994. "The Plague in Castile at the End of the Sixteenth Century and Its Consequences," pp. 32–59 in *The Castilian Crisis of the Seventeenth Century: New Perspectives on the Economic and Social History of Seventeenth-Century Spain,* ed. by I.A.A. Thompson and Bartolomé Yun Casalilla. Cambridge: Cambridge University Press.

Pérez de Tudela y Velasco, María Isabel. 1988. "El trabajo de la mujer castellano-leonesa durante la Alta Edad Media," pp. 141–61 in *El trabajo de las mujeres en la Edad Media hispana,* ed. by Angela Muñoz Fernández and Cristina Segura Graíño. Madrid: Asociación Cultural Al-Mudayna.

Peris Barrio, Alejandro. 1983. "Arriería y carretería en la provincia de Madrid durante la segunda mitad del siglo XVIII," *Revista de dialectología y tradiciones populares,* 38: 175–206.

Perrenoud, Alfred. 1994. "L'incidence de la migration sur la dynamique et les comportements démografiques," pp. 483–506 in vol. I of *Les migrations internes et à moyenne distance en Europe, 1500–1900* (Papers of I Conferencia Europea de la Comisión Internacional de Demografía Histórica, Santiago de Compostela, 22–25 September 1993), ed. by Antonio Eiras Roel and Ofelia Rey Castelao. Santiago de Compostela: Xunta de Galicia, Consellería de Educación e Ordenación Universitaria.

Phillips, Carla Rahn. 1979. *Ciudad Real, 1500–1750: Growth, Crisis and Readjustment in the Spanish Economy.* Cambridge, Mass.: Harvard University Press.

1987. "Time and Duration: A Model for the Economy of Early Modern Spain," *American Historical Review,* 92: 531–62.

Phillips, Carla Rahn and William D. Phillips. 1977. "Spanish Wool and Dutch Rebels: The Middelburg Incident of 1574," *American Historical Review,* 82: 312–30.

Phillips, William D., Jr. 1985. *Slavery from Roman Times to the Early Transatlantic Trade.* Minneapolis: University of Minnesota Press.

Pike, Ruth. 1972. *Aristocrats and Traders: Sevillian Society in the Sixteenth Century.* Ithaca: Cornell University Press.

Pitt-Rivers, Julian A. 1971. *The People of the Sierra,* 2nd edn. Chicago: University of

Chicago Press (first publ. 1954).

Poitrineau, Abel. 1994. "Déplacements professionelles. Les migrations des montagnards," pp. 431–41 in vol. I of *Les migrations internes et à moyenne distance en Europe, 1500–1900* (Papers of I Conferencia Europea de la Comisión Internacional de Demografía Histórica, Santiago de Compostela, 22–25 September 1993), ed. by Antonio Eiras Roel and Ofelia Rey Castelao. Santiago de Compostela: Xunta de Galicia, Consellería de Educación e Ordenación Universitaria.

Poussou, Jean-Pierre. 1994. "Les migrations internes et à moyenne distance en France à l'époque moderne et au XIXᵉ siècle," pp. 205–24 in vol. I of *Les migrations internes et à moyenne distance en Europe, 1500–1900* (Papers of I Conferencia Europea de la Comisión Internacional de Demografía Histórica, Santiago de Compostela, 22–25 September 1993), ed. by Antonio Eiras Roel and Ofelia Rey Castelao. Santiago de Compostela: Xunta de Galicia, Consellería de Educación e Ordenación Universitaria.

Pretel Marín, Aurelio. 1989. *La "Comunidad y República" de Chinchilla (1488–1520). Evolución de un modelo de organización de la oposición popular al poder patricio.* Albacete: Instituto de Estudios Albacetenses.

Puñal Fernández, Tomás. 1993. "El Camino Real de Toledo y las relaciones comerciales del concejo de Madrid," pp 125–39 in *Caminos y caminantes por las tierras del Madrid medieval*, ed. by Cristina Segura Graíño. Madrid: Asociación Al-Mudayna.

Quirós, Francisco. 1965. "Sobre geografía agraria del Campo de Calatrava y Valle de Alcudia," *Estudios geográficos*, 26: 207–30.

Rábade Obradó, María del Pilar. 1988. "La mujer trabajadora en los ordenamientos de Cortes, 1258–1505," pp. 113–40 in *El trabajo de las mujeres en la Edad Media hispana*, ed. by Angela Muñoz Fernández and Cristina Segura Graíño. Madrid: Asociación Cultural Al-Mudayna.

Razi, Zvi. 1980. *Life, Marriage and Death in a Medieval Parish: Economy, Society and Demography in Halesowen, 1200–1400.* Cambridge: Cambridge University Press.

Redfield, Robert. 1967. "The Social Organization of Tradition," pp. 25–34 in *Peasant Society: A Reader*, ed. by Jack M. Potter, May N. Diaz, and George M. Foster. Boston: Little, Brown, and Company.

Redondo Alcaide, María Isabel. 1992. *Villarejo de Salvanés: una historia viva. Pasado y presente de un municipio de la provincia de Madrid.* Villarejo de Salvanés: Cuétara.

Reglà, Joan. 1974. *Estudios sobre los moriscos*, 3rd edn. Barcelona: Editorial Ariel.

Reher, David-Sven. 1990. *Town and Country in Pre-Industrial Spain: Cuenca, 1550–1870.* Cambridge: Cambridge University Press.

Represa, Amando. 1979. "Las comunidades de villa y tierra castellanas: Soria," *Celtiberia* (Soria: Centro de Estudios Sorianos), 57: 7–17.

Rey Castelao, Ofelia. 1994. "Movimientos migratorios en Galicia, siglos XVI–XIX," pp. 85–130 in vol. II of *Migraciones internas y medium-distance en la Península Ibérica, 1500–1900* (Papers of I Conferencia Europea de la Comisión Internacional de Demografía Histórica, Santiago de Compostela, 22–25 September 1993), ed. by Antonio Eiras Roel and Ofelia Rey Castelao. Santiago de Compostela: Xunta de Galicia, Consellería de Educación e Ordenación Universitaria.

Ringrose, David R. 1969. "The Government and the Carters in Spain, 1476–1700," *Economic History Review*, 22: 45–57.

1970a. *Transportation and Economic Stagnation in Spain, 1750–1850*. Durham, N.C.: Duke University Press.

1970b. "Carting in the Hispanic World: An Example of Divergent Development," *Hispanic American Historical Review*, 50: 30–51.

1983. *Madrid and the Spanish Economy, 1560–1850*. Berkeley: University of California Press.

Rodríguez Arzua, Joaquín. 1963. "Geografía urbana de Ciudad Rodrigo," *Estudios geográficos*, 24: 369–435.

Rodríguez Cancho, Miguel. 1994. "Migraciones internas en la Extremadura moderna," pp. 321–55 in vol. II of *Migraciones internas y medium-distance en la Península Ibérica, 1500–1900* (Papers of I Conferencia Europea de la Comisión Internacional de Demografía Histórica, Santiago de Compostela, 22–25 September 1993), ed. by Antonio Eiras Roel and Ofelia Rey Castelao. Santiago de Compostela: Xunta de Galicia, Consellería de Educación e Ordenación Universitaria.

Rodríguez Fernández, Agustín. 1986. *Alcaldes y regidores: administración territorial y gobierno municipal en Cantabria durante la Edad Moderna*. Santander: Institución Cultural de Cantabria, y Ediciones de Librería Estvdio.

Rodríguez Galdo, María Xosé. 1976. *Señores y campesinos en Galicia. Siglos XIV–XVI*. Santiago de Compostela: Editorial Pico Sacro.

Rodríguez Grajera, Alfonso. 1990. *La Alta Extremadura en el siglo XVII. Evolución demográfica y estructura agraria*. Cáceres: Universidad de Extremadura.

Rodríguez Pascual, Francisco. 1986. "Reglamento o estatuos de la Sociedad de Mozos de la villa de Camporredondo, titulada 'Amor y Fraternidad,'" *Revista de dialectología y tradiciones populares*, 41: 255–66.

Rojas Gabriel, Manuel. 1987. *Olvera en la Baja Edad Media (siglos XIV–XV)*. Cádiz: Diputación Provincial.

Rojo Alboreca, Paloma. 1988. "El trabajo femenino en Extremadura durante la Baja Edad Media a través de la documentación testamentaria," pp. 163–78 in *El trabajo de las mujeres en la Edad Media hispana*, ed. by Angela Muñoz Fernández and Cristina Segura Graíño. Madrid: Asociación Cultural Al-Mudayna.

Rojo Vega, Anastasio. 1993. *Enfermos y sanadores en la Castilla del siglo XVI*. Valladolid: University of Valladolid.

Rubio Pérez, Laureano M. 1984. *El Señorío Leonés de los Bazán: aproximación a su realidad socio-económica (1450–1650)*. La Bañeza: Instituto Comarcal de Estudios Bañezanos.

1987. *La Bañeza y su Tierra, 1650–1850: un modelo de sociedad rural leonesa (los hombres, los recursos y los comportamientos sociales)*. León: University of León.

1993. *El sistema político concejil en la provincia de León*. León: University of León.

1995. *La burguesía maragata: dimensión social, comercio y capital en la Corona de Castilla durante la Edad Moderna*. León: University of León.

Rucquoi, Adeline. 1981. "Valladolid: pole d'immigration au XVe siècle," pp. 179–89 in *Les communications dans la Péninsule Ibérique au Moyen-Age (Actes du Colloque de Pau, 28–29 mars 1980)*. Paris: Maison des Pays Ibériques, Editions du Centre National de la Recherche Scientifique.

Ruiz, Teófilo F. 1983. "Notas para el estudio de la mujer en el área del Burgos medieval," pp. 419–28 in vol. I of *Edad Media* of *El pasado histórico de Castilla y León*. Burgos: Junta de Castilla y León.

1994. *Crisis and Continuity: Land and Town in Late Medieval Castile*. Philadelphia: University of Pennsylvania Press.

Ruiz Gómez, Francisco. 1990. "El parentesco y las relaciones sociales en las aldeas castellanas medievales," pp. 263–77 in *Relaciones de poder, de la producción y parentesco en la Edad Media y Moderna. Aproximación a su estudio*, ed. by Reyna Pastor. Madrid: Consejo Superior de Investigaciones Científicas.

Saavedra, Pegerto. 1992. *A vida cotiá en Galicia de 1550 a 1850*. Santiago de Compostela: Servicio de Publicacións da Universidade de Santiago de Compostela.

Sabean, David W. 1984. *Power in the Blood: Popular Culture and Village Discourse in Early Modern Germany*. Cambridge: Cambridge University Press.

Sáenz Lorite, Manuel. 1974. "El Valle del Andarax y Campo de Níjar: estudio geográfico," Unpublished Ph.D. thesis, University of Granada.

Salas Ausens, José Antonio. 1988. "Movimientos migratorios en la España de la Edad Moderna," *Boletín de la Asociación de Demografía Histórica*, 6: 29–53.

Salazar Rincón, Javier. 1986. *El mundo social del "Quijote."* Madrid: Editorial Gredos.

Salmerón, Fray Pasqual. 1777. *La antigua Carteia, o Carcesa, hoy Cieza, villa del Reyno de Murcia*. Madrid: Joachín Ibarra.

Salomon, Noël. 1964. *La campagne de Nouvelle Castille à la fin du XVIe siècle d'après les "Relaciones topográficas"*. Paris: SEVPEN (Spanish version published as *La vida rural castellana en tiempos de Felipe II*, trans. Francesc Espinet Burunat. Barcelona: Editorial Ariel, 1982).

1985. *Lo villano en el teatro del Siglo de Oro*, trad. Beatriz Chenot. Madrid: Editorial Castalia (first published as *Recherches sur le thème paysan dans la "comedia" au temps de Lope de Vega*. Bordeaux: Feret et Fils, 1965).

Sánchez Belén, Juan Antonio. 1989. "Colonos y militares: dos alternativas de promoción social," pp. 279–304 in *La vida cotidiana en la España de Velázquez*, ed. by José N. Alcalá-Zamora. Madrid: Ediciones Temas de Hoy.

Sánchez González, Ramón. 1991. "Hambres, pestes y guerras. Elementos de desequilibrio demográfico en la comarca de La Sagra durante la época moderna," *Hispania. Revista española de historia*, 51: 517–58.

1993. *La población de La Sagra en la época de los Austrias*. Los Yébenes, Toledo: Editorial FEP.

Sánchez-Montes González, Francisco. 1989. *La población granadina del siglo XVII*. Granada: University of Granada.

Sánchez Pérez, Antonio José. 1987. *Poder municipal y oligarquía: el concejo cacereño en el siglo XVII*. Cáceres: Institución Cultural "El Brocense" [Diputación Provincial].

Sánchez Rubio, Rocio, Mª Angeles Hernández Bermejo, and Isabel Testón Núñez. 1994. "Huir del miedo: los movimientos migratorios de una minoría religiosa (los moriscos extremeños 1570–1610)," pp. 747–71 in vol. II of *Migraciones internas y medium-distance en la Península Ibérica, 1500–1900* (Papers of I Conferencia Europea de la Comisión Internacional de Demografía Histórica, Santiago de Compostela, 22–25 September 1993), ed. by Antonio Eiras Roel and Ofelia Rey Castelao. Santiago de Compostela: Xunta de Galicia,

Consellería de Educación e Ordenación Universitaria.

Santamaría Arnáiz, Matilde. 1989. "La alimentación," pp. 305–36 in *La vida cotidiana en la España de Velázquez*, ed. by José N. Alcalá-Zamora. Madrid: Ediciones Temas de Hoy.

Sanz Ayán, Carmen. 1989a. "Fiestas, diversiones, juegos y espectáculos," pp. 195–215 in *La vida cotidiana en la España de Velázquez*, ed. by José N. Alcalá-Zamora. Madrid: Ediciones Temas de Hoy.

1989b. "Minorías y marginados," pp. 127–47 in *La vida cotidiana en la España de Velázquez*, ed. by José N. Alcalá-Zamora. Madrid: Ediciones Temas de Hoy.

Sanz Sampelayo, Juan F. 1988. "La demografía histórica en Andalucía," pp. 181–91 in *Demografía histórica en España*, ed. by Vicente Pérez Moreda and David-Sven Reher. Madrid: Ediciones El Arquero.

Seccombe, Wally. 1992. *A Millennium of Family Change: Feudalism to Capitalism in Northwestern Europe*. London: Verso.

Segalen, Martine. 1983. *Love and Power in the Peasant Family: Rural France in the Nineteenth Century*, trans. Sarah Matthews. Oxford: Basil Blackwell.

1987. "Life-Course Pattern and Peasant Culture in France: A Critical Assessment," *Journal of Family History*, 12: 213–24.

Segura Graíño, Cristina. 1993. "Los caminos y Madrid," pp. 43–51 in *Caminos y caminantes por las tierras del Madrid medieval*, ed. by Cristina Segura Graíño. Madrid: Asociación Al-Mudayna.

Shanin, Teodor (ed.). 1987. *Peasants and Peasant Societies*, 2nd edn. Oxford: Basil Blackwell.

Silva, José Gentil da. 1967. *Desarrollo económico, subsistencia y decadencia en España.* trans. Valentina Fernández Vargas. Madrid: Ciencia Nueva.

Stavenhagen, Rodolfo. 1975. *Social Classes in Agrarian Societies*, trans. Judy Adler Hellman. Garden City, New York: Anchor Press/Doubleday.

Stella, Alessandro. 1992. "L'esclavage en Andalousie à l'époque moderne," *Annales, Economies, Sociétés, Civilisations*, 47: 35–64.

Suárez Alvarez, María Jesús. 1982. *La villa de Talavera y su tierra en la Edad Media (1369–1504)*. Oviedo: Universidad de Oviedo & Diputación Provincial de Toledo.

Terrasse, Michel. 1968. "La région de Madrid d'après les "Relaciones topográficas" (peuplement, voies de communication)," *Mélanges de la Casa de Velázquez*, 4: 143–72.

Thompson, I.A.A. 1968. "A Map of Crime in Sixteenth-Century Spain," *Economic History Review*, 21: 244–67.

1976. *War and Government in Habsburg Spain 1560–1620*. London: University of London, The Athlone Press, 1976.

Thompson, I.A.A. and Bartolomé Yun Casalilla (eds.). 1994. *The Castilian Crisis of the Seventeenth Century: New Perspectives on the Economic and Social History of Seventeenth-Century Spain*. Cambridge: Cambridge University Press.

Torre, José de la. 1931. "De otros tiempos: cómo se solucionaba una huelga de campesinos en el siglo XVI," *Boletín de la Academia de Ciencias, Bellas Letras y Nobles Artes de Córdoba*, 10: 103–4.

Torres Sánchez, Rafael. 1991. "Decadencia demográfica castellana y migración. La emigración hacia la periferia levantina en el tránsito al siglo XVII," pp. 135–51 in *Evolución demográfica bajo los Austrias (Actas del II Congreso de la*

Asociación de Demografía Histórica. Alicante, abril de 1990. Volumen III), ed. by Jordi Nadal Oller. Alicante: Instituto de Cultura Juan Gil Albert.

Tudela, José. 1963. "La cabaña real de carreteros," pp. 349–94 in vol. 1 of *Homenaje a don Ramón Carande*. Madrid: Sociedad de Estudios y Publicaciones.

Uriol Salcedo, José Ignacio. 1993. "Los caminos en Madrid en la Edad Media," pp. 33–51 in *Caminos y caminantes por las tierras del Madrid medieval*, ed. by Cristina Segura Graíño. Madrid: Asociación Al-Mudayna.

Valdeón Baruque, Julio. 1975. *Los conflictos sociales en el Reino de Castilla en los siglos XIV y XV*. Madrid: Siglo Veintiuno.

Vassberg, David E. 1975. "The Sale of *Tierras Baldías* in Sixteenth-Century Castile," *Journal of Modern History*, 47: 629–54.

1978. "Concerning Pigs, the Pizarros, and the Agro-Pastoral Background of the Conquerors of Peru," *Latin American Research Review*, 13: 47–61.

1983a. *La venta de tierras baldías: el dominio público y la corona en Castilla durante el siglo XVI*, trans. David Pradales Ciprés, Julio Gómez Santa Cruz, Gilbert Heartfield, and Gloria Garza-Swan. Madrid: Servicio de Publicaciones, Ministerio de Agricultura.

1983b. "Juveniles in the Rural Work Force of Sixteenth-Century Castile," *The Journal of Peasant Studies*, 11: 62–75.

1984. *Land and Society in Golden Age Castile*. Cambridge: Cambridge University Press.

1991. "Composición de la familia de la burguesía rural en Castilla durante el siglo XVI," paper delivered at the Congreso Internacional: La Burguesía Española en la Edad Moderna, Madrid, 16–18 December.

1992. "La comunidad rural en España y en el resto de Europa," *Mélanges de la Casa de Velázquez*, 28: 151–66.

1994a. "Life-Cycle Service as a Form of Age-Specific Migration in the sixteenth and seventeenth Centuries: Rural Castile as a Case Study," pp. 385–402 in vol. 1 of *Les migrations internes et à moyenne distance en Europe, 1500–1900* (Papers of I Conferencia Europea de la Comisión Internacional de Demografía Histórica, Santiago de Compostela, 22–25 September 1993), ed. by Antonio Eiras Roel and Ofelia Rey Castelao. Santiago de Compostela: Xunta de Galicia, Consellería de Educación e Ordenación Universitaria.

1994b. "The Status of Widows in Sixteenth-Century Rural Castile," pp. 180–95 in *Poor Women and Children in the European Past*, ed. by John Henderson and Richard Wall. London: Routledge.

1994c. "Sociocentrism and Xenophobia in Golden-Age Castilian Villages," paper delivered at the 25th Annual Meeting of the Society for Spanish and Portuguese Historical Studies, Chicago, April 7–10.

Velasco, Honorio. 1981. "Textos sociocéntricos: Los mensajes de identificación y diferenciación entre comunidades rurales," *Revista de dialectología y tradiciones populares*, 36: 85–106.

Villegas Molina, Francisco. 1972. *El Valle de Lecrín: estudio geográfico*. Granada: Consejo Superior de Investigaciones Científicas.

Vincent, Bernard. 1970. "L'expulsion des Morisques du royaume de Grenade et leur répartition en Castille (1570–1571)," *Mélanges de la Casa de Velázquez*, 6: 211–46.

1981. "Los moriscos del Reino de Granada después de 1570," *Nueva revista de filología hispánica*, 30: 594–608.

1987. *Minorías y marginados en la España del siglo XVI*. Granada: Diputación Provincial.

1990. "50.000 moriscos almerienses," pp. 489–514 in *Almería entre culturas, siglos XIII al XVI. Coloquio de Historia*. Almería: Instituto de Estudios Almerienses.

1994a. "Les émigrations morisques," pp. 403–11 in vol. 1 of *Les migrations internes et à moyenne distance en Europe, 1500–1900* (Papers of I Conferencia Europea de la Comisión Internacional de Demografía Histórica, Santiago de Compostela, 22–25 September 1993), ed. by Antonio Eiras Roel and Ofelia Rey Castelao. Santiago de Compostela: Xunta de Galicia, Consellería de Educación e Ordenación Universitaria.

1994b. "La esclavitud en España y Portugal del siglo XV al XIX," paper read at the Twenty-Fifth Annual Meeting of the Society for Spanish and Portuguese Historical Studies, Chicago, April 7–10.

Vincent, Bernard and Antonio Domínguez Ortiz. 1978. *Historia de los moriscos: vida y tragedia de una minoría*. Madrid: Revista de Occidente.

Viñas y Mey, Carmelo. 1941. *El problema de la tierra en la España de los siglos XVI–XVII*. Madrid: Consejo Superior de Investigaciones Científicas.

Vries, Jan de. 1974. *The Dutch Rural Economy in the Golden Age, 1500–1700*. New Haven: Yale University Press.

Wall, Richard. 1984. "Real Property, Marriage and Children: The Evidence from Four Pre-industrial Communities," pp. 443–79 in *Land, Kinship and Life-Cycle*, ed. by Richard M. Smith. Cambridge: Cambridge University Press.

Ward, Barbara E. 1967. "Cash or Credit Crops: An Examination of Some Implications of Peasant Commercial Production with Special Reference to the Multiplicity of Traders and Middlemen," pp. 135–51 in *Peasant Society: A Reader*, ed. by Jack M. Potter, May N. Diaz, and George M. Foster. Boston: Little, Brown, and Company.

Watts, Sheldon J. 1984. *A Social History of Western Europe, 1450–1720: Tensions and Solidarities among Rural People*. London: Hutchinson University Library.

Weisser, Michael R. 1971. "Les marchands de Tolède dans l'économie castillane, 1565–1635," trans. Joëlle Mathieu, *Mélanges de la Casa de Velázquez*, 7: 223–36.

1976. *The Peasants of the Montes: The Roots of Rural Rebellion in Spain*. Chicago: University of Chicago Press.

Wolf, Eric R. 1966. *Peasants*. Englewood Cliffs, N.J.: Prentice-Hall.

1967. "Closed Corporate Peasant Communities in Mesoamerica and Central Java," pp. 230–46 in *Peasant Society: A Reader*, ed. by Jack M. Potter, May N. Diaz, and George M. Foster. Boston: Little, Brown, and Company.

Wylie, Laurence. 1974. *Village in the Vaucluse*, 3rd edn. Cambridge, Mass.: Harvard University Press.

Yun Casalilla, Bartolomé. 1980. *Crisis de subsistencias y conflictividad social en Córdoba a principios del siglo XVI*. Córdoba: Diputación Provincial.

1987. *Sobre la transición al capitalismo en Castilla: economía y sociedad en Tierra de Campos (1500–1830)*. Valladolid: Junta de Castilla y León.

1989. "Estado, estructuras sociales y cambio económico entre 1550 y 1630 en Castilla la Vieja y León," paper read at the Annual Meeting of the Society for

Spanish and Portuguese Historical Studies, St. Louis, Missouri.

1990. "Estado y estructuras sociales en Castilla: reflexiones para el estudio de la 'Crisis del siglo XVII' en el Valle del Duero (1550–1630)," *Revista de historia económica*, 8: 549–74.

1994a. "Economic Cycles and Structural Changes," pp. 113–45 in *Handbook of European History, 1400–1600: Late Middle Ages, Renaissance and Reformation*, vol. I: *Structures and Assertions*, ed. by Thomas A. Brady, Jr., Heiko A. Oberman, and James D. Tracy. Leiden: E.J. Brill.

1994b. "The Castilian Aristocracy in the Seventeenth Century: Crisis, Refeudalisation, or Political Offensive?" pp. 277–300 in *The Castilian Crisis of the Seventeenth Century: New Perspectives on the Economic and Social History of Seventeenth-Century Spain*, ed. by I.A.A. Thompson and Bartolomé Yun Casalilla. Cambridge: Cambridge University Press.

1994c. "Spain and the Seventeenth-Century Crisis in Europe: Some Final Considerations," pp. 301–21 in *The Castilian Crisis of the Seventeenth Century: New Perspectives on the Economic and Social History of Seventeenth-Century Spain*, ed. by I.A.A. Thompson and Bartolomé Yun Casalilla. Cambridge: Cambridge University Press.

1994d. "Corrupción, fraude, eficacia hacendística y economía en la España del siglo XVII," pp. 47–60 in *El fraude fiscal en la historia de España*. Madrid: Instituto de Estudios Fiscales.

1995[?]. "Seigneurial Economies in Sixteenth and Seventeenth Century Spain. Economic Rationality or Political and Social Management?" pp. 173–82 in *Entrepreneurship and the Transformation of the Economy (Tenth–Twentieth Centuries): Essays in Honour of Herman Van der Wee*, ed. by Paul Klep and Eddy Van Cauwenberghe. Leuven: Leuven University Press.

Yun Casalilla, Bartolomé and I.A.A. Thompson (eds.). 1994. *The Castilian Crisis of the Seventeenth Century: New Perspectives on the Economic and Social History of Seventeenth-Century Spain*. Cambridge: Cambridge University Press.

Zabalza Seguín, Ana. 1993. "En torno a la sociedad navarra del Antiguo Régimen (matizaciones en el caso de la merindad de Sangüesa)," *Príncipe de Viana*, 54, no. 15: 273–9.

1994a. "Migración y estructura familiar en el Pirineo navarro (XVI–XVIII). Sobre la correlación entre troncalidad y migración," pp. 679–88 in vol. II of *Migraciones internas y medium-distance en la Península Ibérica, 1500–1900* (Papers of I Conferencia Europea de la Comisión Internacional de Demografía Histórica, Santiago de Compostela, 22–25 September 1993), ed. by Antonio Eiras Roel and Ofelia Rey Castelao. Santiago de Compostela: Xunta de Galicia, Consellería de Educación e Ordenación Universitaria.

1994b. *Aldeas y campesinos en la Navarra prepirenaica (1550–1817)*. Pamplona: Gobierno de Navarra, Departamento de Educación y Cultura.

Zagorin, Perez. 1982. *Rebels and Rulers, 1500–1660*, vol. I: *Society, States, and Early Modern Revolution: Agrarian and Urban Rebellions*. Cambridge: Cambridge University Press.

INDEX

246

INDEX

Christian, William A., Jr., 12, 23
Church (parish), 12, 98–100, 159
Church bells, 12, 22
Church policies, 82, 98, 133, 156
Cides, María, 115
Ciempozuelos (Madrid), 19
Cities, 6–7, 30, 36–7
Citizenship (acquiring), 7, 14–18, 62, 152, 173–4, 181 n. 17, 182 n. 19
Ciudad Real, 142, 164
Clergy, 15, 79–80, 106, 159–61 (see also Church, Priests, Religion)
Codesal (Zamora), 22
Cogollos (Burgos), 166
Coín (Málaga), 181 n. 21
Colás Latorre, Gregorio, 121
Colonization, 15–17, 68–70 (see also Reconquest)
Commons, 7, 13, 17, 19–20, 48, 61, 116, 119, 121, 125–8
Communal woodlands, 48, 55–7, 60, 119
Communal work projects, 43
Comuneros Revolt, 41, 104
Concejos (see Village government)
Congosto (Zamora), 61
Conquistadores, 3, 13, 83–5, 149
Contreras, Captain Alonso de, 111, 134, 200 nn. 5 & 14
Córdoba, 52, 191 n. 16
Cordovilla (Salamanca), 89, 90, 94, 151
Corregidores, 35, 42–4, 107, 116, 118, 138, 142, 151
Cortes, 29, 54, 71, 83, 90, 92, 108, 121, 123, 144, 209 n. 39
Cortés, Andrés de, 156
Council of Trent, 80, 160–1 (see also Clergy, Church, Priests, Religion)
Courts of law (see Justice system)
Covaleda (Soria), 23
Craftsmen and artisans (see Manufacturing)
Credit sales, 35
Crespo, Juan, 110–11
Crops, yields, and commercialization, 25–31, 46–7, 54–5, 58–60
Cubo (Burgos), 160
Cuéllar (Segovia), 17, 181 n. 17
Cuenca, province of, 6, 41, 57
Cuenca, 74–6, 90, 92, 100, 144, 174–5
Cuenca (diocese of), 160
Cumbres Bajas (Huelva), 22
Cumbres de Enmedio (Huelva), 22, 129, 133
Curiel-Peñafiel area (Valladolid), 100

Daimiel (Ciudad Real), 29
Davis, Natalie Z., 152
Day-laborers (see Jornaleros)
Debts, 46, 51, 82, 109, 119, 126–8

Deforestation (see Commons, Communal woodlands)
Del Río, Manuel, 192 n. 19
Delgado, Captain Gaspar, 149
Delgado, Juan, 88
Demographic decline, 46–7, 67–8
Dentists, 65
Dependent villages, 20, 116–19 (see also Jurisdiction)
Depression (see Economic crises)
Derrota de mieses, 19
Deza, Lope de, 78, 151, 169, 194 n. 46, 216 n. 48
Díaz, Agustín, 103
Díaz Camargo, Pedro, 82
Díaz Viana, Luis, 177 n. 12
Doctors (see Physicians)
Domínguez, Sebastián, 71
Domínguez Ortiz, Antonio, 148
Don Quixote, 13, 20, 36, 80, 86, 91, 147, 169, 171
Don Quixote, 64, 91, 107, 111, 133, 134, 142, 216, n. 48
Donhierro (Segovia), 94
Donkeys (see Mules and donkeys)
Drama (see Theater)
Dueñas (Palencia), 28
Dupâquier, Jacques, 198 n. 41, 217 n. 11

Economic crises, 33, 45–7, 77, 78, 126–8, 155, 165–8, 174–5
Education, 78–80 (see also Literacy, Schools, Universities)
Eiras Roel, Antonio, 177 n. 12
El Cubillo de Uceda (Guadalajara), 89
Elites, 7, 15, 36, 78–9, 119
Emigration, 76–7, 80–5, 102–3, 110, 113, 119, 122, 128, 167, 192 n. 25
Encabezamientos (see Taxes)
Entertainers, 169 (see also Theater)
Epidemics (see Plagues)
Escacena del Campo (Huelva), 90, 94, 191 n. 17
Escorial (Madrid), 41
Escuredo (León), 23
Espartinas (Seville), 212 n. 71
Esparto grass and weavers, 60
Espinosa de la Ribera (León), 86, 89, 90, 94
Espinoso del Rey (Toledo), 169, 199 n. 60
Estavillo (Alava), 131
Estella (Navarra), 98, 101
Estépar (Burgos), 88, 102, 172, 216 n. 49
Estévan, María, 212 n. 74
Etiopía, Tomás de, 150
Exile, 80–3
Extremadura, 30, 51, 70–1, 83, 85, 92, 100, 149

also Households, Soldiers)
Wolf, Eric, 177 n. 9
Women, 28–9, 53, 71, 72, 92, 131, 136,
  151 (see also Households, Wives,
  Widows)
Wood, woodcutting, and woodworking,
  48–9, 55–7 (see also Communal
  woodlands)
Wool, 50, 52

Xenophobia, 14, 18–20 (see also
  Protectionism, Solidarity)
Ximénez, Catalina, 81, 92
Ximénez, Mari, 199 n. 60

Ybarguena, Father Domingo de, 87
Yeste (Albacete), 24
Youths, 20
Yun Casalilla, Bartolomé, 26, 46, 50, 54,
  68, 121, 124, 128, 163–4, 168, 194 n.
  43

Zaballos, Juan de, 89
Zafra (Badajoz), 28
Zamora, 22, 28, 70–1
Zaragoza, 91, 94
Zarza, La (Cáceres), 93, 180 n. 12
Zuñeda (Burgos), 129